Merry Christmas 1974
from the
YPS of St. Paul

The Shepherd under Christ

The Shepherd under Christ

A Textbook
for Pastoral Theology

Armin W. Schuetze
Irwin J. Habeck

"And when the chief Shepherd shall appear, ye shall receive a crown of glory that fadeth not away"

(1 Pe 5:4)

Northwestern Publishing House
Milwaukee, Wisconsin

Library of Congress Catalog Card Number: 74-81794
Northwestern Publishing House
3624 W. North Ave., Milwaukee, Wis. 53208
Published 1974
Printed in the United States of America

CONTENTS

PREFACE

When Professor John Schaller in 1913 published his *Pastorale Praxis*, he realized that his presentation departed in certain respects from that of the revered teachers of the seventeenth century. Because these teachers were properly recognized as reliable in the study of dogmatics, they were almost uncritically followed also in their presentations of pastoral ethics. It was at first not noticed that the relationship of the church to the state in seventeenth-century Europe necessarily affected their presentation of the duties and rights of a pastor, so that as a result a certain legalistic tone permeated their pastoral ethics.

Professor Schaller, recognizing this, set about to apply the basic scriptural truths and principles to the new circumstances in America. Free from any pressures on the part of the state, the ministry could now be carried out in an evangelical manner that was difficult for the fathers of the seventeenth century to attain. In his *Pastorale Praxis* a handbook that breathed an evangelical spirit became available for instructing the Wisconsin Synod clergy at its seminary.

Schaller's volume served the church well for a number of decades. However, as the use of German declined, so did the usefulness of *Pastorale Praxis*. It was only natural that Fritz's *Pastoral Theology*, a reworking into English of Walther's *Pastoraltheologie*, found ready acceptance among the Wisconsin Synod students when it appeared in 1932. When this went out of print, it found a less worthy successor in *The Pastor at Work*, a 1960 Concordia Publishing House production that continued in print for about a decade.

The need for an English successor to Schaller's *Pastorale Praxis* was felt for some time, but all the more so when Fritz's *Pastoral Theology* no longer was available. The suggestion was made to translate Schaller's handbook. However, although the scriptural principles did not change in the sixty years since 1913, their application would have to take into account the changing circumstances in the world into which God has placed His church and in which the pastor carries out his ministry. A mere translation could hardly do this. The result was that the undersigned, both responsible for teaching Pastoral Theology at Wisconsin Lutheran Seminary, Mequon, Wisconsin, were asked to prepare a textbook for Pastoral Theology, using Schaller's *Pastorale Praxis* as a basis.

Like Schaller, every member of the Wisconsin Lutheran Seminary faculty is committed to the Holy Scriptures as the inspired Word of God and thus the only source of Christian doctrine and the only infallible guide for the church's practice. We make no apologies for letting this commitment become evident on every page of this book. The faculty was also concerned that the biblically evangelical spirit so evident in Schaller's volume might not be lost. We leave it to others to judge how well the present volume succeeds in this.

Another major concern for us was that these chapters might address themselves to circumstances as they are in the average congregation of the Wisconsin Evangelical Lutheran Synod at the present time. Professors are often thought of as living in an ivory tower. They do not serve a congregation, the place where the action is, where the pastor daily ministers to God's people. For this reason a series of twelve meetings was arranged for consultation purposes. This enabled us to draw on the wisdom and experience of many different people (pastors, teachers, professors, executives, and laymen) in preparing those chapters where such consultation was most needed and would be most helpful. The list of those to whom we owe a deep debt of gratitude is too long to include here. Nevertheless, we want to add our public thanks to that already expressed privately to those who so willingly and ably participated in the consultations.

Copies of the first draft of each chapter were distributed to all members of the Seminary faculty for comments and suggestions. We wish to thank these colleagues of ours for giving of their time in the midst of often crowded schedules to read these pages and record their helpful comments.

Special thanks are due the people who assisted most in preparing the manuscript for the printer. Mrs. T. Ganyo, secretary to the faculty, with her usual skill typed the first draft and the final copy. Pastor Harold Wicke, the editor in chief of Northwestern Publishing House, gave the manuscript a careful reading and contributed perceptive suggestions on style and content.

Not to be forgotten is the generous grant made by the Aid Association for Lutherans, Appleton, Wisconsin, toward this project. It was this support that made the consultations referred to above financially feasible. A major portion of the grant subsidized the publication costs. This is reflected in a lower price per copy than would otherwise have been possible. We thank the Association for this support.

A few comments on externals are in order. We chose not to add a lengthy bibliography to each chapter. In its place a brief, annotated list of books "For Additional Reading" has been included with many of the chapters. It was felt this would serve the student better than a long list of titles, many of which might remain to a great extent meaningless without some added guide to their content. The reader may also note that a simple form of abbreviations (omitting also the usual periods) has been adopted for the books of the Bible and some few other frequently used abbreviations.

The absence of an index is not an oversight. After giving considerable thought to the matter, we decided against an index so that this volume might not be used simply as a quick reference book in which to find a ready solution to specific problems. Rather than directing the reader to a single sentence or paragraph for a brief discussion of some problem we prefer to have longer sections studied so that specific problems are seen in their broader context. Using a textbook like this for a shortcut to problem solving could easily lead to a legalistic application of single statements taken out of context. We believe the table of contents will prove adequate for finding the chapter and section that concerns itself with a desired topic.

And so we send this book on its way with the prayer that the Lord would bless its use in the preparation of men for the parish ministry. We dare to hope that it may also serve pastors who are already in the field as a handbook to which they will find it profitable to refer for guidance, stimulation, and perhaps correction in their ministry. The preparation of this volume has proved to be a rich source of blessing for the authors. We pray that the Lord may use it to bless many students and pastors and, through them, many sheep in the flocks which they are permitted to shepherd.

Armin W. Schuetze
Irwin J. Habeck

INTRODUCTION

Some of the courses covered at the Seminary serve the purpose of providing the student with a fund of knowledge upon which he will be drawing again and again as he performs the duties of the office for which he is being prepared (Isagogics, Textual Criticism, Hermeneutics, Exegesis, Symbolics, Systematic Theology, Church History, Church Music). Others are intended to provide him with the skills which he will need in order to perform specific duties connected with his office (Homiletics, Christian Education, Liturgics). The course in Pastoral Theology is intended to give him a broad perspective of the pastor and his work.

Merely learning what is taught in these courses in itself will not make a good pastor of the student. The Lord must do that. "Our sufficiency is of God; who also hath made us able ministers of the new testament" (2 Cor 3:5,6). Luther's axiom points up the means which He uses: *Oratio, meditatio, tentatio faciunt theologum.* When the pastor is overwhelmed by the greatness of the responsibility which has been entrusted to him, when he is painfully aware of his own inadequacy, when he faces baffling problems, he needs to remember that not only does he have the privilege of casting his concerns and cares upon the Lord (1 Pe 5:7), but also that all of the resources of the wisdom and power of his heavenly Father are placed at his disposal in the promise that his prayer will be heard and answered. Great men of God like St. Paul and Luther were made what they were partly through their intense use of prayer and the Lord's answer to their prayer.

The meditation which Luther had in mind was primarily meditation upon the Word of God. The Spirit working through the Word as the pastor reads it devotionally will shape and develop him. Paul reminded Timothy that the Scriptures would equip him in an ever increasing measure to do the good works which his position would give him the opportunity to perform (2 Tm 3:14-17). The pastor who applies himself to meditation may look forward to the time when he may humbly say with the Psalmist: "I have more understanding than all my teachers: for thy testimonies are my meditation" (Ps 119:99).

While prayer and meditation require initiative on the part of the pastor, testing is something which the Lord brings upon him, something in which the pastor is passive. The fact that he in a special way has been set apart for the Lord's service does not exempt him from testing through trouble. "Whom the Lord loveth he chasteneth, and scourgeth every son whom he receiveth" (He 12:6). St. Paul grew strong in the inner man through trial: "Most gladly therefore will I rather glory in my infirmities, that the power of Christ may rest upon me" (2 Cor 12:9). Luther attributed his spiritual growth in part to the severe tests which he had to endure, and proposed himself as an example of what every faithful pastor will have to expect: "As long as the Word of God is taught by you, the devil will come upon you and make a real doctor of you and by his temptations teach you to search the Scriptures and to love them. For I myself must give unto papists much credit because they, by means of the devil's furious attacks, have so harassed me and pounced upon me and made me afraid, that is, they have made a pretty good theologian of me, which otherwise I never would have been" (quoted in Fritz, *Pastoral Theology*, p 9). How the Lord through testing develops pastors for increased usefulness is indicated by the apostle's words: "Blessed be God, even the Father of our Lord Jesus Christ, the Father of mercies, and the God of all comfort; who comforteth us in all our tribulation, that we may be able to comfort them which are in any trouble, by the comfort wherewith we ourselves are comforted of God" (2 Cor 1:3,4).

What has been said above does not eliminate the need for a course in Pastoral Theology. It too is a means which the Lord uses in preparing men to serve as pastors. Seminary students need to learn what is involved in being a pastor: the qualifications which are required, the many-sided work which is to be done, the problems which may be faced.

In the study of Pastoral Theology it will be necessary to distinguish between the principles which are set forth in the Word of God, on the one hand, and the manner in which these principles are applied in the contemporary life of our congregations, on the other. The principles are timeless, sacred to all who as true disciples of our Lord want to continue in His Word (Jn 8:31,32). The manner in which these principles are applied, however, may change with the times. Not all of the practical suggestions which Luther made can be applied today, but the Word of God which guided him has not changed. The duty of Christians to confess their faith is set forth in the Word of God. The application of this principle to the organized evangelism program of a congregation is of recent origin. If the distinction between principles which are timeless and their application which is flexible is not observed, there is danger, on the one hand, that the principles of God's Word may be abandoned with the plea that times change and, on the other hand, that the manner in which a principle is applied in a given case may be considered binding for all time with resultant rigid legalism. It is our hope that the student, and subsequently the pastor, will become so thoroughly imbued with the Word that he will react intuitively in many situations, sensing at once what is true or proper. Naturally he dare not expect people to accept his reaction because he felt that it was right. Rather, he will need to probe, to discover, what specific revelation in the Word of God made him react as he did and point others to that Word for their guidance.

Reference will be made to cases of casuistry. This term is applied to situations in which it is not immediately clear what course of action ought to be taken, or in which even conscientious pastors do not always come up with the same solution. To admit that there are such cases may seem to deny the perspicuity of Scripture, but it does not. The principles laid down in Scripture are clear. But when cases of the nature referred to arise, it is because the situation is complicated. Some facets seem to indicate that one of the divine principles ought to be applied, other facets seem to call for the application of another scriptural principle. Our human limitations make it difficult for us to ferret out all aspects of the matter and to evaluate what we do know so unerringly that we know which aspect is predominant. Any pastor who has had to deal in divorce cases could cite abundant examples. While cases of casuistry will be referred to for the purpose of supplying guidance, no attempt will be made to offer definitive solutions, both because cases vary infinitely and because pat solutions can easily be abused in a legalistic manner. Scriptural principles will, it is hoped, be set forth clearly and examples of how they have been applied in the life of the church cited in the hope that students as future pastors will learn to minister with evangelical concern in the varied situations which will confront them. In short, no attempt will be made in our study to compile a set of rules of canon law.

At Wisconsin Lutheran Seminary, we aim to give our students the well rounded theological education which they as parish pastors will need, and therefore also a course in Pastoral Theology which endeavors to cover all facets of the pastor and his work. If one of our graduates is subsequently led into an area of service which makes specialized expertise desirable, we are confident that his background of theological training and practical experience in the parish ministry will enable him to be discriminating as he acquires additional and specialized training. To draw a comparison from the field of medicine, this course is intended to be an aid in the training of general practitioners and not of specialists.

1

The Shepherd

"If a man desire the
office of a bishop"

(1 Tm 3:1)

I. HIS CHARACTER

"This is a true saying, if a man desire the office of a bishop, he desireth a good work" (1 Tm 3:1). With these words the apostle indicates that those who are pastors ought to be in the ministry because they have desired it. Moral coercion on the part of parents, relatives, pastors, or teachers to prod a youth into entering the ministry is therefore to be frowned upon. Encouragement on their part to create and stimulate a desire for the office is a different matter.

The apostle furthermore implies that the desire for the office of a bishop will spring out of a living faith in the Savior and a desire to serve Him. Financial security, prestige, opportunity for cultural pursuits, and least of all the prospect of leading a comparatively easy life ought never be allowed to tip the scales in favor of entering the ministry. A pastor who is not dedicated and convinced of the sacredness of his office may indeed still do some good, for the efficacy of the means of grace does not depend upon the person who administers them. On the other hand, the dictum is still true: "You can't fool all of the people all of the time." People will sense the lack of conviction on the part of the pastor and be offended in the scriptural sense of the term, either by being

1

shocked, grieved, and disturbed in their own simple faith, or by being tempted to follow the example of the pastor who still has the form of godliness but denies the power thereof (2 Tm 3:5). It is written: "Unto the wicked God saith, What hast thou to do to declare my statutes, or that thou shouldest take my covenant in thy mouth?" (Ps 50:16).

The soil out of which a desire for the bishop's office springs is indicated in the words of the apostle: "Unto me, who am less than the least of all saints, is this grace given, that I should preach among the Gentiles the unsearchable riches of Christ" (Eph 3:8). This passage speaks of a deep realization of personal sinfulness and sinning, a deep appreciation for grace which reached down to save the sinner from guilt and doom and worked in him the miracle of faith. It speaks of the awareness that to be entrusted with the ministry is added grace, a totally undeserved privilege. It speaks of the vision of what this ministry can do as it leads others who need grace to realize their need, to accept forgiveness and salvation, and to go on to an abundant enjoyment of all that the Savior has to offer. These factors, which combine to create the desire for the bishop's office, may not be fully clear in the mind of a boy who wants to be a pastor, nor even in the mind of a student who enrolls at the seminary, but they ought to have crystallized in the heart of the man who asks to be presented to the church as a candidate for the holy ministry. The pastor ought to be a humble believer in his Savior Jesus, and his desire to serve as pastor ought to be a fruit of that faith. Cf. John 21:15-17; 2 Corinthians 5:14.

Nor will this be the only fruit of that faith. In common with all Christians the pastor is encouraged not to be conformed to this world, but to be transformed by the renewing of his mind that he may prove what is that good, and acceptable, and perfect will of God, and, knowing it, to do it as an expression of his gratitude for the mercies of God which have been bestowed upon him (Ro 12:1, 2). Though he too will have to admit with the apostle that he has by no means attained perfection (Php 3:12), he dare not settle for the level of sanctification which has been attained by the average member of his congregation. For to him the Lord's injunction is given: "Be thou an example of the believers" (1 Tm 4:12). He is in the public eye, both as far as his own people and as far as the community in general are concerned. Lapses which might pass unnoticed in the case of his members can easily undermine the effectiveness of his ministry if they occur in his case. On the other hand, evidence of his sincerity and dedication to his Lord will command the respect both of his people and of the community in general. It is for this reason that the Lord has listed the qualifications which a pastor ought to possess.

It has been observed that the qualifications which are required in pastors, especially in 1 Timothy 3:1-7 and Titus 1:6-9, in general do not go beyond what might be expected of every Christian. The exceptions are the requirements that he be "apt to teach" (1 Tm 3:2; cf. also 2 Tm 2:2 and Tt 1:9) and that he maintain good discipline in his own home (1 Tm 3:4, 5; Tt 1:6). But in a pastor these qualities ought all to be present to a marked degree and consistently. We shall consider first the positive and then the negative qualities. Unless otherwise indicated, they are mentioned in 1 Timothy 3:1-7 and Titus 1:6-9.

While the Lord through the apostle is speaking of qualifications which must be possessed by those who have already been entrusted with the public ministry, what is said occurs in a context which refers also to aspirants for the office (1 Tm 3:1). Whether a grave moral lapse in his past record must disqualify a man from being eligible to become a theological student or a candidate for the holy ministry must be determined by those who have been entrusted with the responsibility of enrolling students and recommending men to the church as candidates for the ministry. On the one hand, it will be their concern not to admit to the sacred office one who, because of his reputation which he damaged by his sin, would be an offense and bring blame upon the ministry (2 Cor 6:3) and cause men to mock the gospel. On the other hand, they will remember that the Lord did call a Saul and reinstate a penitent Peter. Not precedent, however, but what the Lord says must be the starting point in determining what should be done in a given case.

Positive Qualifications

Blameless does not mean without sin, for then no man would be fit for the pastor's office, but it does mean that no charge of a grave moral offense can be sustained against him. This is shown by the amplification: "He must have a good report of them which are without; lest he fall into reproach and the snare of the devil" (1 Tm 3:7). A grave lapse undermines the effectiveness of a man's ministry both as far as the pastoral care of his own people and his

3

efforts to win the outsider are concerned. Furthermore, he is exposed to especially severe temptations of the devil, either to cover up by lying, or to relax principles in doctrine and practice in order to curry favor and to maintain his position, or to sink into despair. At the same time sanctified common sense is necessary in applying this qualification in specific cases, for it is relative and not absolute. A man who receives a ticket for overtime parking and pays a fine technically is no longer blameless, but one would hardly say that he has disqualified himself for the ministry. A single instance of drunkenness may place obstacles in the way of a man's continuing in the ministry where he has been serving, but if he repents, it need not absolutely disqualify him from serving in an area far removed from the scene of his offense. On the other hand, any seeming concession in a given instance dare not be allowed to open the door for laxity in applying the qualifications which the Lord demands of pastors. A precedent dare never be the starting point in determining what is proper in a given case, but rather what the Lord Himself says.

Sober describes a man who is well balanced in his judgment, his emotions, and his impulses; the opposite of the fanatic, the enthusiast, the man who acts before he thinks. *Vigilant* stresses this quality especially insofar as it does not allow a man to be carried away by outside influences and refuses to let thinking which has been shaped by the Word of God become beclouded. Thus the apostle after describing the trend of things in times to come tells Timothy: "Watch thou in all things" (2 Tm 4:5). But there are misleading influences arising also from within, and these are to be met by the quality of being *temperate*. This involves spiritual strength exerted toward within, curbing the lusts, the appetites, the passions. Since the sexual impulse is particularly strong and the temptations for a pastor are many, Paul specifically admonishes Timothy and all other pastors as well to behave "with all purity" (1 Tm 5:2); "flee youthful lusts" (2 Tm 2:22).

Of good behavior covers the wide range of orderliness and propriety, ruling out slovenliness, habitual tardiness, discourtesy, and all else of which one might say that it is not proper for an ambassador of Christ.

Since the service that a pastor renders is bound to involve him with all kinds of people, the Lord also requires those qualifications which have to do with his attitude toward others. Since the second table of the law does govern our relations and attitude toward our fellow men, the pastor is to be *just*, conforming to this divine standard. Specifically he is told not to be provocative or abrasive, but rather *patient*, displaying *meekness* (2 Tm 2:25). Since our Lord Jesus ascribes meekness to Himself (Mt 11:29) and still when the situation demanded it could be firm and sharp, it is evident that patience and meekness are not to be confused with weakness or the willingness to yield a principle for the sake of avoiding trouble. Since both his doctrine and practice will on occasion call forth opposition and abuse, the pastor is to *endure afflictions* (2 Tm 4:5) without seeking to take revenge or to crush an opponent.

The pastor is to be *a lover of good men*, a term which in the original (Tt 1:8) is broad enough to include all that is good. In mistaken zeal he might feel that he dare not acknowledge favorably even on the secular level any person who is heterodox, non-Christian, or anti-Christian, or anything which such individuals or groups of such individuals do lest he undermine his own confessional position. But to refuse to see anything good even on the purely human plane outside of one's own confession (for example, the dedication of the Roman Catholic nursing sisters) will serve to antagonize rather than to win confidence. It is only when people draw unwarranted conclusions, for example, that religious fellowship with such people is proper or that they will surely go to heaven, that a careful distinction must be made.

The pastor is to be *given to hospitality*. While conditions have changed considerably since the days when Christians were often forced to flee and looked upon the home of the bishop in the city to which they fled as a refuge, warm hospitality ought still to grace the parsonage. Members ought not to be left standing at the door but made to feel welcome to enter. The kind of hospitality which quickly helps strangers feel that they are no longer strangers ought also to be manifested by the pastor when he is at church or at church functions. While the greeting of visitors who attend the services in his church is not to be his exclusive privilege, he ought to be a good example in this respect. If he has the honest concern that no one ought to feel unnoticed or unwelcome, he will be quick to make arrangements to have others in the congregation function when the size of the congregation makes it impossible for him to see and speak to all visitors. — It might be added that even though he knows that his brethren are under a like injunction in this respect as he, this fact does not justify him

5

in making the home of a brother pastor a convenient stopping place when he is on a trip.

The pastor's relation to his Lord is covered by the requirement that he be *holy*. The opening paragraphs of this chapter with their reference to the personal faith of the pastor, the faith by which he is justified, and the fruit of that faith in the desire to serve his Lord have already amplified this point.

Negative Qualifications

We shall therefore proceed to consider the negative qualifications. It is noteworthy that not only do the terms *not covetous, not given to filthy lucre* appear in the two basic lists of qualifications, but that also after warning against the evils which result from the love of money the apostle expressly tells Timothy (and all pastors): "But thou, O man of God, flee these things" (1 Tm 6:11). Peter is just as emphatic when he tells elders to take the oversight of the flock of God "not for filthy lucre" (1 Pe 5:2). When men who have been entrusted with the ministry lament because their salary scale is lower than that of other professional men, they reveal that they are not free from covetousness. A pastor indeed owes it to his people to train them to observe what the Lord says to them: "Let the one who is taught the word share all good things with him who teaches" (Ga 6:6 - NASB).

But beyond that he will do well to let them take the initiative in salary matters and special gifts for services rendered lest he give the impression that he is serving mammon. He has the promises of the Lord to assure him that his needs will be supplied. Still, because the old Adam looks for security in material possessions, the pastor will have to combat covetousness until his dying day. Church history is not devoid of examples of pastors who have succumbed to the extent of becoming guilty of shady business dealings, embezzlement, fraud, and other gross sins to obtain what had indeed become filthy lucre. Another danger which must be avoided in this area is financial irresponsibility, running up bills and being unable or unwilling to pay them. That this is a moral fault is evident from the words: "The wicked borroweth, and payeth not again" (Ps 37:21).

While the requirement that the pastor be *not given to wine* does not exclude the moderate use of alcoholic beverages on his part, it does exclude from the ministry the alcoholic who must have his drinks regularly, and certainly the drunkard. In this area too it is necessary that the pastor does not set his standards by the customs of the age, but by the Word of his Lord.

Closely related are *not a brawler, not soon angry,* and *no striker.* A pastor who is a gamecock and likes to meddle in strife is not reflecting the spirit of his Savior (cf Lk 9:55, 56). While the very fact that the Lord has created individuals, some of whom are more mercurial in their temperament than others, means that for some it will take more of an effort to control their tempers than for others, the effort must be made. "The wrath of man worketh not the righteousness of God" (Jas 1:20). The man who loses his temper has lost his cause. To fall so far short that one actually is ready to come to blows makes a man a horrible example, not the good example that a pastor ought to be.

Then there is the requirement not to be *self-willed,* a qualification which may not lightly be ignored. Since the pastor has the right and duty to expect obedience when he speaks the Word of God, he is always exposed to the temptation to expect that whenever he expresses a wish it must be fulfilled. But when it comes to purely temporal affairs in the life of the church, his opinion is only one of many and deserves to be scrutinized on the basis of its merits just as well as the opinion of any other member. Even though he may be convinced that the majority is making a foolish decision, he will be careful to abide by the decision of the majority just as other members are expected to do. Time may even reveal that the majority was right after all.

The Pastor's Wife

In the two chief passages concerning the qualifications of a pastor it is taken for granted that in general he will be a married man, the husband of one wife. This rules out not only bigamy, but also premarital and extramarital relations, but not remarriage in the event of a wife's death. To the general requirement of purity we have already referred. It is significant that no qualifications or regulations are set up for the pastor's wife. This indicates that essentially she is a private person and not directly involved in the public ministry of her husband. It is for that reason that we have been averse to instituting special courses for the wives or prospective wives of seminary students lest they receive the impression that they will be incumbents of a special office. We consider it the duty of their husbands or prospective husbands to acquaint them with the uniqueness of a pastor's position. It will need to be

7

a pastor's continuing concern to counteract the idea that by virtue of her marriage to him his wife has a position of leadership. Her calling lies in the area of being wife, homemaker, and mother. In these respects she is to set a good example, all the more so since the parsonage is in the public eye. This indicates that the pastor or future pastor ought to exercise great care in the selection of his wife. His choice ought to be deliberate and not motivated by lust or other base or trivial considerations. Dr. Walther's suggestions concerning the qualities which ought to be possessed by a pastor's wife, presented here in a slightly modified form, are still worthy of consideration: 1. a sincere Christian; 2. a convinced Lutheran (and today we might add: conservative and confessional); 3. suited to be a pastor's wife, possessing qualifications which correspond to those demanded of pastors; 4. coming from a good family, since in a sense a man with his wife marries her entire family; 5. a good housekeeper and manager since the pastor ought to be able to live within his income; 6. fairly well educated, but no erudite snob; 7. not a member of the congregation which the pastor is serving, because this could lead to problems and difficulties.

Of a good pastor's wife it can be said with double emphasis: "Her price is far above rubies" (Pr 31:10), while a frivolous, slovenly, imperious wife can be as a millstone about his neck. A pastor's wife ought to be aware of what the Lord has to say about the wife's relation to her husband (Eph 5:22-24, 33; 1 Pe 3:1-6) and be willing to assume that place. A henpecked pastor-husband loses in stature among his people. On the other hand, a pastor ought not to go to extremes in asserting his headship over his wife. There are domestic areas in which she has more competence than he and in which he wisely ought not to interfere. Nor ought he to resent well-meant criticism from her who loves him and is deeply interested in his success. She may be the only one to whom he can turn for criticism about mannerisms which might be creeping into his sermon delivery or about deficiencies in clarity or vocabulary in the sermon itself. She may have a finer feeling for the social graces than he and be of help to him in acquiring them to replace manners which years of living in a dormitory may have allowed to deteriorate.

A generation ago the question whether it is advisable for a pastor's wife to seek outside employment would hardly have been raised — it just was not being done. Today it is. At least in some geographical areas few members of a congregation would look askance at a pastor's wife if she has an outside job which is worthy of her station. The following arguments are advanced in favor of the practice: her acquired skills, say as nurse, teacher, or secretary, can be put to continued use; she can help to augment her husband's income during the period when the education of the children imposes a strain upon the family budget; outside employment helps to fill a void and reduce emotional stress when the children have become independent. But there are still weighty considerations against the arrangement. 1. A factor which has led to the disruption of many homes and marriages is the working wife. Subconsciously at least a husband may resent the implication that he is not able to support his family, and when the wife actually is able to earn more than her husband, the irritation is all the more severe. Pastors too are human and not immune to these adverse reactions. But a parsonage ought to be an example of Christian marriage at its best. 2. While it is true in general that a woman's place is in the home, there are added reasons why the pastor's wife is needed in the home. She is often the unpaid and unsung secretary who answers the phone and the doorbell when her husband is away from home on official duties or for needed relaxation. While she has no special call from the congregation, she as a helpmate does want to help her husband when and where she can. She will share his concern for his people, and assume the role which has been mentioned as a part of life in a parsonage. 3. A pastor's wife is expected to participate in those activities of a congregation which involve the female members, such as Bible study groups, ladies' societies, or choirs. In this respect too the parsonage is to set a good example. But if she has an outside job, she is either at work when the organizations meet, or too busy with her household tasks, or too tired to participate wholeheartedly. 4. The impression can easily be given that it is not because of financial stringency, but in order to satisfy her expensive tastes that the pastor's wife is working. 5. Especially if there still are younger children at home, the pastor's wife ought to be at home with them. To expect her husband to be the babysitter is to usurp time which ought to be devoted to his prior responsibilities. Since his responsibilities often take him away from home, much of the day-by-day training of the children devolves upon her.

The fact that she must be without her husband's company much of the time is one which a prospective pastor's wife ought to face and a situation to which a pastor's wife ought to be able to adjust. During the day and often well into the evening the pastor is either studying or making calls or attending meetings. Often too he is frustrated because he cannot seem to find time to do all that his official duties require and consequently is not in a mood to listen to household problems or attend to a man's household chores. As a result his wife will have to learn to keep herself busy or entertained without his company. Since a busy pastor's family is often deprived of his company, he ought to make it a practice regularly to set aside some time for his wife and family.

The Pastor's Family

The Lord emphasizes the importance of a good Christian training for the children in the parsonage when He says that the pastor must be "one that ruleth well his own house, having his children in subjection with all gravity; for if a man know not how to rule his own house, how shall he take care of the church of God?" (1 Tm 3:4, 5.) And again: "having faithful children not accused of riot or unruly" (Tt 1:6). An aid in the training of children will be regular family devotions, a matter in which the parsonage ought also to set a good example.

While Christian living is first of all a matter between the believer and his Lord, the Lord does tell him to be concerned about the impression which others receive of him, "the Jews, . . . the Gentiles, . . . the church of God" (1 Cor 10:32); "in the sight of men" (2 Cor 8:21); "them that are without" (1 Th 4:12). This concern ought to be especially strong on the part of those who live in a parsonage, even to the extent of restricting the use of their Christian liberty more than others might find it necessary to do, e.g., in matters like attending movies and plays, cardplaying, or the use of alcohol or tobacco. A pastor, as well as his family, ought to avoid giving the impression of a desire for a comfortable life at all costs; of laziness; of luxurious tastes; of being a slave to fashion; of immoderation in eating and drinking; of selfishness or stinginess; of being hard to get along with; of being unreliable or untruthful; of pride; of jealousy; of hardness; of inability to keep a secret or of listening to gossip; of playing favorites; or of murmuring under the cross.

Summary: The fundamental requisite in the character of a pastor is that he believe in Jesus as his personal Savior. It is from this faith that the desire will arise for the privilege of being permitted to serve his Lord in the public ministry. The Lord has revealed which special qualities of character he is to possess and cultivate, and conversely which faults he ought to avoid. While there are no similar specific directives for a pastor's wife, by implication in Scripture and observation of life in the church qualities are suggested which she ought to cultivate in order to fill her role as her pastor-husband's helpmate. Scripture stresses the importance of good discipline in the training of a pastor's children. In general, life and attitudes in the parsonage ought to be of such a nature that they command respect and set a good example.

II. HIS ÁPTITUDE TO TEACH

The Lord sets up no physical standards which those who are entrusted with the New Testament ministry must meet (Lv 21:17-23 is part of the Old Testament ceremonial law). Since, however, marked deformities or handicaps in a pastor may make it difficult for people to accept him and may hinder him in carrying on his work, pastors may make tactful use of this knowledge in determining whom they will encourage to prepare for the ministry. On the other hand, perfect health is not required, witness Paul's reference to Timothy's "often infirmities" (1 Tm 5:23). But good stewardship in the light of the Fifth Commandment does require a careful husbanding of what physical resources a pastor does have. His ought to be a well-balanced diet. He ought to get what for him is an adequate amount of sleep. Since not all people require the same amount of sleep, he will have to determine what his needs are and meet them. On the one hand, he is not to be a sluggard and, on the other, he will have to realize that if the number of working hours in a given day is so great that his alertness and cheerfulness are impeded on the next, he needs to reevaluate his priorities. Since normally the pastor's day is filled with a variety of activities, it should be possible for him to put in more hours of efficient work than, for example, a man who repeats the same process on an assembly line hour after hour. Nevertheless, he will require time for relaxation and exercise. Hobbies will be helpful if they are kept under control. He will profit by striving to arrange his schedule in such a manner that it does permit him under normal conditions to take one day a week off. Nor should he fail to realize that a vacation every year will help him to return to his work with an improved perspective and renewed mental and physical vigor.

11

While Scripture does not have anything specific to say about the physical endowment of a pastor, it does require mental endowment and training. Scripture states that he must be: "apt to teach" (1 Tm 3:2); "able by sound doctrine both to exhort, and to convince the gainsayers" (Tt 1:9); "a workman that needeth not to be ashamed, rightly dividing the word of truth" (2 Tm 2:15); "able to teach others" (2 Tm 2:2). This involves the ability to learn, to remember, to use the imagination, to evaluate, to think logically, to present clearly. It also involves being able to communicate by commanding respect, maintaining discipline, speaking distinctly enough to be understood and loudly enough to be heard, and in general to fill the role of a leader. These gifts need to be cultivated and exercised through academic training and channeled by means of a thorough theoretical and practical theological training. The lack of the aptitude to teach disqualifies a man for the office of pastor, the loss of it likewise. That it is present is ascertained during the course of theological training or by colloquy. Laying a sound foundation for the aptitude to teach is necessary because the pastor is to be "not a novice, lest being lifted up with pride he fall into the condemnation of the devil" (1 Tm 3:6). The pastor must be prepared to assume the responsibilities which his relative independence brings with it. To a great extent he is his own "boss." He determines his daily schedule, decides what is to be done next, and judges when he may take time for relaxation. But independence involves responsibility. He must decide what ought to be said or done in the vast variety of situations which confront him. His sermons will have to be his own work. All of this requires an aptitude to teach which has been cultivated by thorough training.

Summary: Scripture does not list any specific physical requirements for those who are entrusted with the public ministry. Still a pastor will on the one hand wisely conserve his physical resources, and on the other hand employ them fully in his work. The requirement that he be apt to teach presupposes that he does possess a rather high degree of mental endowment which has been cultivated and directed by a thorough academic and theological training.

III. HIS FAITHFULNESS

Of all the qualities that the Lord seeks in His pastors none ranks higher than faithfulness. "It is required in stewards, that a man be found faithful" (1 Cor 4:2). Those whom Timothy was to train to teach others were to be "faithful men" (2 Tm 2:2). Faithfulness is a comforting term, for it indicates that the Lord does not expect any one pastor to match another in ability or accomplishments, but rather to do only what he has been made able to do. On the other hand, it is a term which covers a broad area, as we shall see.

Faithfulness implies wholehearted devotion to the Lord Jesus, for the pastor will consider himself the Lord's slave (2 Tm 2:24), bound to obey His will in free and grateful love. His ministry, which he is to fill to the brim (2 Tm 4:5), is not an office coupled with high privileges and prerogatives, but a service, first of all to his Lord, and then to the Lord's people. Looking at it in that light, he will fall in line with the exhortation which the Lord through Peter addresses to elders: "Feed the flock of God which is among you, taking the oversight thereof, not by constraint, but willingly; not for filthy lucre, but of a ready mind; neither as being lords over God's heritage, but being examples to the flock" (1 Pe 5:2, 3). One of the chief tests of faithfulness to the Lord is faithfulness to His Word: "If a man love me, he will keep my words" (Jn 14:23). This keeping of His words involves first of all a devotional use of His words as opposed to the professional use. The pastor will want to have his Lord speak to him to nourish and strengthen his own faith, to comfort him, and to guide him in doing what his Lord wants him to do. Then the professional use of the Word to feed and guide his flock and to reach out to those who do not know their Savior will never be formal or cold, but will flow out of conviction and be warm with appreciation and loving concern. Faithfulness to the Lord and His Word involves total adherence to the pure doctrine of that Word, both in declaring "all the counsel of God" (Ac 20:27) and in carefully shunning any and every corruption of this doctrine by denial, compromise, or the addition of human speculation. His Lord tells him: "Take heed unto thyself, and unto the doctrine; continue in them" (2 Tm 4:16).

The pastor who is faithful to his Lord will also be faithful in making the maximum use of what the Lord has entrusted to him. He will not be sparing of his physical energies, but be willing to work as long and as hard as he is able. In the same spirit of faithful stewardship he will, however, also take the long-range view and not undermine his health or his strength, but seek to conserve them for the normal span of years. While on the one hand he will be willing to assume additional responsibilities both in the work of his congregation and in that of the church-at-large, there may be times when he may and must in good conscience decline to assume additional responsibilities or ask to be relieved of some which he had assumed, when it becomes evident to him that his time and energies are being overtaxed.

He will likewise look upon his time as a trust from his Lord for him to manage wisely in his Lord's service. His life, and that means his time, will be dedicated to his ministry. We have already indicated that investing time in rest and relaxation in no wise conflicts with this ideal. But all other matters must remain secondary. The pastor has no time to become entangled with the affairs of this life (2 Tm 2:4) by holding down a job on the side or by becoming involved in investments the management of which consumes much time, nor dare he let his hobbies lead him to neglect his work. If his own time is precious to him, the time of others will be too, and punctuality will be his rule.

Faithful stewardship also involves the intensive use of his mental abilities. The sermon ought to receive the top spot on his weekly list of priorities. Only his best should be good enough when it comes to preaching. His preaching will therefore be preceded by thorough study of the text in the original and a logical ordering of his thoughts. While in the first years of his ministry he will write out his sermons in full, if his gifts permit him to proceed to preaching from only an outline, he would not be guilty of relaxing his standards but would still be striving to do his best. In other areas which involve the presentation of the Word, teaching, devotions in organization meetings, calls on the sick and shut-ins, he will likewise proceed from writing out in detail what he intends to say to cultivating the ability to present fluently the thoughts which he has organized either only in his mind or in brief notes. But never will he depend upon the inspiration of the moment or become slipshod. In his use of liturgical forms he will make sure that he is thoroughly acquainted with them and will read them with full concentration and proper emphasis and not matter-of-factly.

Another facet of faithfulness is being alert for opportunities to perform the work of the gospel ministry and to make the most of them. This may involve leads to mission prospects, or an opening for a well-meant word of instruction or admonition, or an opportunity for giving information and encouragement concerning Christian education. If opportunities for doing good works are set before all believers, we may be sure that opportunities for doing his special kind of good works will be set before the pastor too. Pastors too are the Lord's workmanship, "created in Christ Jesus unto good works, which God hath before ordained that we should walk in them" (Eph 2:10). That making the most of opportunities set before us is part of faithfulness is indicated negatively in the parables of the talents and of the pounds (Mt 25:14-30; Lk 19:11-27), where the unprofitable servants are faulted because they failed to make even minimal use of the options which were open before them. Positively the Lord through His apostle attaches to the command: "Preach the word," the exhortation: "Be instant in season, out of season" (2 Tm 4:2). The "out of season" covers opportunities which might seem to hold little promise, for we never know when the Lord's hour may have come for some individual, as the experience of many a pastor will testify. Pastors will emulate the sense of urgency and eagerness which their Savior displayed: "I must work the works of him that sent me, while it is day; the night cometh, when no man can work" (Jn 9:4). When he is considering a call which he has received to another field, the pastor in a special way will have to evaluate the opportunities which are placed before him.

Referring again to the parables of the talents and of the pounds, we realize that faithfulness involves not only keeping what has been entrusted, but also adding to it. There is the significant word "profiting" in 1 Timothy 4:15, a word which implies progress and growth. The Lord Jesus indicates that in his studying the pastor will constantly find not something different, indeed, but always deeper insights and new applications: "Every scribe which is instructed unto the kingdom of heaven is like unto a man that is a householder, which bringeth forth out of his treasure things new and old" (Mt 13:52). In short, faithfulness implies continuing study.

It ought to be self-evident that a pastor will first of all do the studying which his official routine requires. If he were to pursue diligently some particular area of theology to such an extent that he would cut short the time which ought to be devoted to preparation for his official duties or the performance of them, he would, to say the least, be deficient in faithfulness. The situation would be even worse if an inordinate amount of his time were to be de-

15

voted to subjects like law, architecture, or history. When it comes to the studying which his work requires, two extremes will have to be avoided. The one is that he restricts his studying to the barest minimum which he thinks is needed to "get by." The result of this course would be that what he presents remains superficial and his people get nothing more than milk and are deprived of the "meat" (1 Cor 3:2) which is required for their growth in knowledge. The other extreme is that he devotes so much time to studying, to reading all that he can lay his hands on in preparing his sermons, his catecheses, his presentations to organizations, and to polishing and repolishing what he has prepared that he finds little or no time for contact with people in either pastoral care or missionary outreach. Here he must strive to find a golden mean, employing as an axiom the words which our Lord spoke in a different context: "These ought ye to have done, and not to leave the other undone" (Mt 23:23).

But with wise stewardship of his time, a pastor in most situations will be able to find time for continuing study not immediately required by his daily official duties. This will require self-discipline, for it is easy to consume far too much time reading newspapers, periodicals, novels, and mail, and listening to radio and watching TV. He will therefore arrange his schedule in such a way that time is allotted for study, and then adhere to it if at all possible.

What shall he study? First and foremost the Bible, not as a tool of his trade, but as the Lord's message of mercy to him. His professional training has provided him with the ability to read the Scriptures in the original, and this ability he ought to retain and cultivate. Every man will develop his own method. One suggestion is to start by reading the original, out loud, if possible, to cultivate a feeling for the language. The next step would be to make sure that the vocabulary and grammar are understood. Then comes meditation: "What is my Lord here telling me?" Writing one's own translation may follow as a training in exactness. Finally there will come the consulting of at least two commentaries for the purpose of corroborating one's independent findings and if need be of revising them if the arguments favoring a different interpretation seem to be more weighty than those which one can advance in support of one's own. Our strength as individual pastors lies in living in the Word. To the extent that a church body is made up of men who thus live in the Word to that extent

16

will it retain its Christ-centeredness, its evangelical spirit, and its power, and remain strong against the inroads of error.

A pastor who is Lutheran by conviction will not be content with drawing upon the knowledge of Lutheran doctrine which he has acquired during the course of his theological training, but will review and enlarge that knowledge by continued study. As he grows in experience, he will be impressed anew by the depth of insight and the penetration of Scripture which are revealed in the Lutheran confessions. No less will that be the case when he reads Luther. A full-scale acquaintance with the writings of the conservative Lutheran dogmaticians of the 16th and 17th centuries may be more than the average pastor will be able to attain, but he ought to strive to become familiar with the writings of the two outstanding American Lutheran dogmaticians, Adolf Hoenecke and Francis Pieper. What Solomon observed is still very much true: "Of making many books there is no end" (Ec 12:12), and among these many books are also such which purport to treat of doctrine, but cover the whole spectrum from near orthodoxy to rankest heresy. While a pastor needs to know what is going on in the theological world, he dare not immerse himself so deeply in heterodox writings that he comes under the influence of the authors and veers from his theological bearings. He dare not imagine that his theological training places him above being included in the Lord's warning: "Beware of false prophets, which come to you in sheep's clothing. . . . Do men gather grapes of thorns or figs of thistles?" (Mt 7:17,16.)

Since "there is no new thing under the sun" (Ec 1:9), the pastor will discover that his knowledge of church history enables him to understand people and evaluate trends. This is reason enough for him to want to review and enlarge his knowledge of church history. As he grows in experience, he may find less and less need to read literature which treats of the practical side of the ministry, preaching, teaching, pastoral and mission work. Still he may profit by studying a good book concerning one of these areas to check whether there might not be a better way of doing his work. He will find a variety of articles covering all theological fields in the professional journal edited by the Wisconsin Lutheran Seminary faculty, the *Wisconsin Lutheran Quarterly*. While not giving top priority by any means to reading newspapers, secular periodicals, and an occasional new book, he will still want to read them

17

to keep abreast of developments and to understand what his people are facing.

As far as the method of study is concerned, each pastor will be his own man. Some are efficient at filing, others may consider it a waste of their time. The main matter is to absorb, to retain, and to know where to find. One way in which a pastor can be helped to continue studying is to become a member of a study group made up of a half dozen or so neighboring pastors. While social features may be combined with such gatherings, they ought not to be allowed to dominate. Nor should they be allowed to degenerate into occasions for mere small talk or synodical gossip or develop into a cell promoting synodical politics. Rather, there ought to be a program covering several of the theological branches or concentrating upon exegesis. In so small a group each man will be held to serve as leader rather frequently, and the smallness of the group will encourage all present to join in the discussion.

Attendance at regular pastoral conferences is considered obligatory — and it is wholesome. Chronic absenteeism is a danger signal and calls for the demonstration of fraternal concern. While all conference essays are not equal in quality, their general effect will be to promote theological knowledge, provided that there is a good range of topics. No pastor ought to shrink from accepting a conference assignment because of misdirected humility, or laziness, or even the feeling that he is too busy with other work. Far from resenting constructive criticism the pastor ought to welcome it as an aid to professional growth.

Summary: The faithfulness required of a pastor covers many areas. There is first of all faithfulness to the Lord, His Word, and His people. There is faithfulness in the stewardship of physical resources. There is faithfulness in the management of time. There is faithfulness in striving to do the best work of which he is capable. There is faithfulness in being alert for opportunities to serve. There is faithfulness in striving to retain and to add to his store of knowledge by means of private and joint study.

IV. HIS PUBLIC RELATIONS

Even in his appearance and manners a pastor will be guided by the principle: "Giving no offense in any thing, that the ministry

18

be not blamed" (2 Cor 6:3). First impressions are important. A pastor who is not concerned about the impression which his appearance or manners might make upon others may be erecting a barrier which will lead the unchurched to reject his ministrations offhand, and among his own people arouse prejudices which it will be difficult to overcome. Even those people who themselves are coarse or uncouth do not as a rule expect a pastor to sink to their level. This does not mean, however, that a pastor is to be affected, artificial, or unctuous. He is to be genuine, a man of God all the way through.

The age when a pastor was restricted to wearing clerical black is past. That does not mean, however, that the pendulum needs to swing all the way to the opposite extreme. Extremes in fashion can be interpreted as an evidence of immaturity, instability, or shallowness. In general, a pastor is well advised if he leans toward the conservative in dress and in hair styling. Neatness in combing, shaving, care of his clothes, his nails, and his shoes is also an aid to commanding respect. The same can be said about his car, his premises, and the interior of his home.

His manners too ought to be such as befit a Christian gentleman. While he will be careful not to judge people by their knowledge and practice of the accepted rules of etiquette, he will train himself to follow them since where they are good they apply either the Golden Rule or common-sense principles.

While the preceding paragraphs had in mind the pastor as he moves among the people toward whom his ministry or his outreach are directed, the advice given in them is of wider application and covers what might be termed the entire field of public relations. His work will bring the pastor into frequent contact with hospital personnel, funeral directors, other clergy, merchants, and the public press. In all of these and other contacts he will show friendliness, cooperativeness, and courtesy as befits a Christian gentleman. Even when contending for principle he will remain gentle while being firm. He will not demand special favors. He will not demand respect, but rather command it.

Truly, being a pastor is a many-sided assignment — but a blessed privilege withal.

Summary: While externals do not rank in importance with the matters which have been discussed in the foregoing portions of this chapter, a pastor's appearance and manners ought to be of such a quality that they do not call forth an unfavorable reaction to his person and habits and thus divert attention from what he has to say and do.

2

The Shepherd's Call

"Except they be sent"
(Ro 10:15)

I. THE NEED FOR A CALL

The Public Ministry

God has given the gospel to all Christians, individually and collectively. Jesus entrusted to each Christian and to groups of Christians gathered about the gospel the right to bind or loose, to forgive or retain sins, by declaring or withholding His gospel (Mt 18:18; Jn 20:21-23). Every Christian as a member of the royal priesthood has been called to proclaim the Lord's praises (1 Pe 2:9). He is called to function as a witness and servant of His Lord, as a light to the world (Mt 5:16). He has this call as a member of the universal priesthood of all believers. This is the ministry that Christ has enjoined on His New Testament church and that has been committed to every Christian (Mt 28:18-20; Mk 16:15).

The Lord has also established the *public ministry* in His church. This ministry does not set up a priestly caste apart from the laity, for, as noted above, all Christians are priests of God. The difference lies in the word *public*. The public ministry is a service performed in the church, in behalf of fellow Christians, in their name. Like the public official in a state who functions in the name of his fellow citizens that have elected him, so the minister has an office in which he carries out responsibilities that have

21

been entrusted to him by fellow Christians. These responsibilities are not essentially different from those Christ committed to every Christian. The minister too is to serve in the gospel as did Paul and Timothy (Ph 2:19-23); to labor in the Word and doctrine (1 Tm 5:17); to speak the Word of God (He 13:17). But the minister does this in the church, in behalf of the church, and as a representative of the church.

The pastoral office is one form of this public ministry of the gospel, no doubt the most comprehensive one. Others that come to mind are, e.g., those of the teacher, the professor, the executive secretary, the missionary-at-large, and the president of a synod. Since Scripture does not make the external forms of the ministry a matter of divine mandate, these can change and have changed over the centuries. Even the pastoral office in its external aspects has changed from time to time without doing injury to its essential responsibility — the administration of the means of grace. A study of the pastoral office as it is practiced under God in the church today is the particular concern of pastoral theology.

The Special Call to Public Service

While every Christian has the call to proclaim Christ to the world, for the public ministry, and this includes the pastoral office, a specific call is necessary. Within the church every Christian, being a priest of God, possesses the ministry in equal measure. Good order, therefore, requires that no one function publicly, that is, in behalf of the assembly of Christians, unless these Christians themselves by means of a call have commissioned him to do so (1 Cor 14:40; Ro 10:15; 1 Pe 4:15).

Accordingly our Confessions assert: "Our churches teach that nobody should preach publicly in the church or administer the sacraments unless he is regularly called" (A.C., XIV). Luther states emphatically, "I dare not preach without a call," going even so far as to say, "I must not go to Leipzig or to Magdeburg for the purpose of preaching there, for I have neither call nor office to take me to those places. Yes, even if I heard that nothing but heresy was rampant in the pulpit at Leipzig, I would have to let it go on."[1] By saying this, Luther is not approving of the false preaching. He goes on to say: "A preacher must be sure that he is teaching and preaching God's Word and that he is not dealing in

1. *Luther's Works* (Philadelphia-St. Louis, 1955-   ), XXIII, 227.

doctrines of man or of the devil."[2] He recognized that the pope and bishops also had a call, but they did not have God's Word and hence were abusing their call. To have a call without God's Word is not enough. To have God's Word without a call is not enough. "Both of these points must go together,"[3] he writes. However, he does not view the requirement for a call in absolute terms. In case of great necessity, whoever wishes may begin to preach the Word, "for it is one thing to exercise a right publicly, another to use it in time of emergency. Publicly one may not exercise a right without consent of the whole body or of the church. In time of emergency each may use it as he deems best."[4]

The Call Comes Through the Church

Since Jesus' ascension the church no longer looks to the Lord to provide its public servants by an immediate call as was done with the prophets and apostles. According to 1 Timothy 3:1, a so-called inner call can be understood only as referring to the heart-felt desire and willingness to prepare for the ministry and to place oneself at the disposal of the church. Scripture does not hold out the promise to the church that the Lord will give it public servants through some kind of immediate inner call or through a direct assignment from Him. The Lord calls His public servants through the medium of His church, the assembly of Christians. (Cf Ac 6; Tt 1:5.)

Such a call through the church is, however, no less divine than if it came directly from the Lord. It is God who is working through the congregation and recognizes the validity of the congregation's action. (Mt 18:19f; Eph 4:11f; 1 Cor 12:28). According to Acts 20:28, the elders of Ephesus are told that it is the Holy Ghost who made them overseers with the responsibility to feed the flock of God with His Word. Their call, a mediate call, was nonetheless divine.

Summary: The pastoral office is the most comprehensive form of the ministry of the New Testament that Christ committed to His believers on earth. Since the pastoral office is a public ministry, i.e., performed in the name of the church, no one is to minister

2. L. W., XXIII, 227.
3. L. W., XXIII, 227.
4. L. W., XL, 34.

publicly in the church unless he has been called to this service by the church.

II. THE CHURCH THAT CALLS

A true call (*vocatio rata*) comes into existence when it is extended by those who have the right to call. To call is to commission. Only those can commission another to administer the means of grace for them who themselves possess these means, namely, the believers or saints, who are the church of God. (Apology, VII, VIII, 8-10). Unbelievers who may be associated outwardly with a Christian congregation are not true members of Christ's body, the church. They have no right to call. Similarly, the government, secular institutions, and public schools do not have the right to call chaplains or pastors to administer the means of grace. Christians holding public office can issue valid calls only through the church of which they are a part. They have no calling rights by virtue of their public or governmental office. It is the Christian church, the saints of God, which alone has the right to call.

The Visible Body

The church on earth, however, can function only through a tangible, visible group. Hence the process of calling is carried out by a body of confessing Christians (e.g., a congregation or synod) in whose midst the presence of the church is recognized by the presence of the means of grace (the marks of the church). According to God's promise true believers will be found there (Is 55:11), even if these should happen to be only the baptized children (Ga 3:26f). Human limitations prevent such a group from excluding the hypocrites. These will, therefore, participate in the calling process, but the call in fact proceeds alone from the true Christians involved. It is for them and in their name that the visible congregation acts. Hence a call issued by a congregation which confesses itself to God's holy Word is true and valid before God. All of this is summed up in our Confessions when they state: "Where the true church is, therefore, the right of electing and ordaining ministers must of necessity also be" (*Treatise on the Power and Primacy of the Pope*, 67).

In this connection one must carefully distinguish between the local Christian congregation and the congregation as a legal corporation. The former comes into existence through the bond of a common Christian faith and consists in its essential nature only of the believers who are gathered about the means of grace; the latter is a creation of the state and consists of those who according to the law of the state and following the regulations of the accepted constitution have been received into the corporate body. As a corporation the congregation possesses no spiritual prerogatives, but it has become a legal entity under the state's law, granting it certain legal privileges such as owning property and signing contracts. It is not the legal corporation that engages the pastor, but it is the congregation of believers that calls him. The pastor's relationship to the congregation is therefore not one that involves a contract arrived at by mutual agreement, but one that is established through a divine call, God through the congregation committing the ministry to him. While it may be the same voting members who form the corporation and who function in the calling process, the church that calls consists in fact of all Christians, men, women, and children, in the congregation, the voters acting in their name.

The Representative Calling Group

It will always be only a part of the congregation that actually functions in the calling process. The natural limitations that are part of childhood and the requirements of the Fourth Commandment place this responsibility on those who have reached maturity. 1 Corinthians 14:34f and 1 Timothy 2:12 lead to the further limitation of the calling group to the men of the congregation (the entire question of suffrage is discussed on p 314f). Generally it is the voters' assembly, thus only a representative group of the entire congregation, that does the calling.

Since it is always only a representative group that is active in calling, a call remains valid even if the church should commit this duty to an even smaller group. For a synod, a designated board may function. A congregation may ask the church council to function in its name. However, this smaller calling group must always recognize that it acts by request and authority of the entire congregation or synod and not through any inherent rights. It must keep the welfare of the entire congregation foremost as it acts. The congregation must take care lest delegating to a small group the responsibility of selecting the person and sending the call causes the entire calling process to deteriorate so that it does not receive the consideration it deserves. To issue a divine call in the

Lord's name is a solemn responsibility that must not be taken lightly.

Unanimity of the Calling Church

For a pastor to have a valid call to serve the whole congregation, unanimity on the part of the whole congregation in issuing the call is necessary. If a segment of the congregation refuses to unite with the rest in extending a call, the congregation is in fact divided so that the call that is issued commits to the pastor-elect the office only in the name of a portion of the congregation. Unanimity can be assumed when no well-substantiated objection is raised. In the congregation's call meeting, objections that would prevent unanimity are best raised at the time when the slate of candidates is accepted. It will be well for a congregation at such a time to remove any name against which an objection, even one that may not be too well substantiated, is raised, lest problems of unanimity later arise and lest a pastor be faced with an opposition party from the outset of his ministry. When all have agreed on the names of the candidates, the validity of the call as coming from the whole congregation is not disturbed by the division of votes in balloting. Customarily the person receiving the majority of ballots is by a subsequent resolution declared to be the unanimous choice of the whole congregation.

Even if the written call does not specifically assert the validity and unanimity of the congregation's choice, the pastor will in good conscience assume its validity unless cogent reasons raise doubts. Should a pastor in good faith accept a call, only to dis-

Summary: The church that calls is in reality the congregation of believers. The actual calling, however, is carried out by a visible association of Christians and in practice is performed by a representative group functioning in the name of the whole congregation of believers. A call thus issued is a valid call (*vocatio rata*).

III. LEGITIMATE CALLING PRACTICES

The Choice of the Person

God has determined the qualifications for the public ministry. (Cf 1 Tm 3:1-7; Tt 1:7-9; 2 Tm 2:2; see pp 3-7). Although no pastor will possess these qualifications perfectly, and although all qualifications are not necessary in the same degree, a congregation should not presume to disregard them. Particularly important are those that relate directly to the pastoral office: a sound confessional stand, "holding fast the faithful word as he hath been taught" (Tt 1:9), and the ability to preach and teach, "apt to teach" (1 Tm 3:2), "who shall be able to teach others also" (2 Tm 2:2). A congregation will always remember that the choice of the person called will need to take into account the qualifications God sets forth for the public ministry.

Pastors who are members of the same synod as the calling congregation can be assumed to share the congregation's confessional stand. If this is not the case, the confessional position of the congregation or of the pastor needs clarification before such a person can be considered by that congregation. Before any person not in confessional fellowship with the congregation can be considered as a candidate for the public ministry in its midst, the soundness of his confessional position and his qualifications for the public ministry must be established. Although a congregation could do this for itself, it will in Christian liberty recognize the distinct advantages of using the services of the larger body, the synod, which in the case of the WELS provides for a colloquy committee to function according to provisions agreed upon in the constitution.

The qualifications of students of theology are attested to by the faculty entrusted with their education. Since the candidates have been trained by the church at large, the Synod has agreed that calls should be extended to them through an assignment committee. For a congregation to circumvent this procedure by calling a student directly would be a breach of love and good order.

A congregation will experience the advantages of its membership in the Synod when it needs to choose a new pastor. The elected officials of the Synod can keep themselves informed of the doctrinal and practical qualifications of men far better than any one congregation. Hence the Synod constitution provides that the district presidents are to assist congregations in calling. They are to suggest candidates to the congregation as well as to approve such as the congregation may propose. The pastor who is leaving a congregation does not have the responsibility of providing a successor. Should a congregation ask him to suggest names, it will be advisable for him to do this only through the district president. If the congregation meets to call his successor while the former pastor is still serving, it is generally advisable for him to leave the meeting while the congregation does the calling.

The autonomy of a congregation in the choice of the person called must be maintained. On the other hand, a congregation will appreciate the orderly procedures that have been set up to assist it in this weighty responsibility.

Concern for the Church-at-Large

In following good calling practices, a congregation will show due concern for the church-at-large, its sister congregations. Even the very appearance of disregard for the needs and problems of others should be avoided. The calling congregation may be encouraged as a gesture of fraternal concern to address a letter to the sister congregation whose pastor is being called. If according to the best Christian judgment the church might suffer great harm if a particular worker were called away (e.g., in a mission field; in a young, inexperienced congregation; in the case of unresolved problems of doctrine or practice), concern for the church-at-large ought to lead a congregation to refrain from extending a call to someone whom it would otherwise consider well qualified to fill its own needs. Similarly, lack of consideration is shown if a congregation should tempt a pastor to accept a call for external reasons. For a congregation to ignore the calling procedures agreed upon in the synodical body of which it is a member is against good order and may be indicative of a parochial attitude that shows little interest in maintaining a brotherly relationship with its sister congregations.

Not a Contract

To issue a call in the manner of a secular contract is a practice that cannot be considered legitimate in view of all that Scripture teaches about a call into the public ministry. In a contract two parties mutually agree on its terms to the satisfaction of both. In a call it is God who confers the ministry on the individual, the church acting as His instrument (Eph 4:11; Ac 20:28; 1 Cor 12:28). Hence the terms of a call should not become the object of negotiation between a pastor and the congregation.

In a contract the two parties agree on its duration. Since a call comes from the Lord, He determines the time during which it should be in effect. Where there is a permanent need for pastoral service, the church should issue a permanent call. Arbitrarily to extend a temporary call, renewable at its expiration, corresponds to issuing a contract for a limited time with provisions for renewal. Such a practice is contrary to the nature of the pastoral office, which calls for an enduring relationship (1 Pe 5:1-4). Such a practice tempts the pastor to become a servant of men instead of ruling with the Word of God (1 Tm 5:17; 1 Th 5:12f; He 13:7). The pastor may become more concerned about pleasing men and retaining his office and livelihood than about faithful application of the Word of God, whatever the consequences may be. This can lead to a deterioration of the congregation's spiritual life and of the discipline in its midst.

A permanent call cannot, however, obligate a pastor to remain at a particular congregation for the duration of his life. To issue a permanent call is to place the duration of a man's service to the congregation in the Lord's hands, permitting Him to indicate in some manner when a call should be terminated.

Naturally, where the church's needs are only of a temporary nature or in its sanctified judgment can best be met on a temporary basis (e.g., vacancy pastors, service to military personnel, elective offices), a call with time limitations is proper. Similarly a person's availability may be limited by other God-given responsibilities (e.g., students available for a year's vicarship, limited by the responsibility of completing their ministerial training program). In these cases it is still the Lord who in some manner indicates to the church the time limitations of the call.

Good Order

The congregation should conscientiously carry out its calling procedure according to the provisions of its constitution. Whatever the constitution says about the manner of announcing meetings, setting up a list of candidates, and method of voting should not be circumvented, lest someone raise questions about the congregation's actions. In any case, it is advisable to vote by ballot so that each voter can most fully express his true desires.

The Lord Seeks Out the Man

Since in a call it is the Lord who through His church seeks out a man for a particular office, the office should seek the man and not the man the office. A pastor will not take steps to secure a call to a particular position in the church. It must be considered an objectionable practice for a pastor to let a congregation know that he is available, to offer himself as a candidate to a congregation, or to use acquaintances, friends, or relatives in a congregation to suggest his name and influence the voting in his favor. While the calling process and the financial returns of the ministry will hardly lead to the use of actual financial bribery, the above practices nevertheless are akin to simony (Ac 8:18-21).

Any form of actively seeking the office or the preaching of trial sermons is contrary to the nature of a call and degrading to the sacred office by making it a matter of competition. This readily degenerates into an effort on the part of the pastor to "sell himself" to the congregation.

It is indeed proper for a man to "desire the office of a bishop" (1 Tm 3:1); a man may place himself at the Lord's disposal by saying, "Here am I; send me" (Is 6:8). It is proper for men to make themselves available for the training that qualifies them as candidates for the public ministry (2 Tm 2:2). This, however, is something quite different from efforts to secure a particular position.

There are times when a pastor feels the "need for a change." It may be that problems have arisen that make his ministry difficult. It may be that he has created problems through poor judgment and practice which he believes could best be solved through accepting a call to another congregation. It may be that personal or family health problems arise that can be solved only in a different area or climate. Let the pastor first take this to the Lord in prayer. He may also discuss this with a pastor friend, the visiting elder of the conference, or the district president. However, simply to request another call of the district president could give the appearance of unfaithfulness to his present call, if it is not that in fact.

Luther has some pertinent words: "Here we should carefully see to it that there is no evil design, that no one in any way obtrudes himself as a preacher, either to get a livelihood (*ums Bauchs willen*) or to gain honor. For this is dangerous, nor will it ever turn out well. If you are learned and understand God's Word well and think that you would present it to others faithfully and profitably, then wait. If God wants it, He will have no trouble finding you. My friend, do not let your ability burst your belly. God has not forgotten you. If you are to preach His Word, He will no doubt call on you to do so at His own time. Do not determine the time limit or the place for Him."[5] "You should not doubt that if the Lord wants you, He will seek you out, and even send an angel from heaven to get hold of you."[6]

A call that has been received in an improper way may still be valid. A pastor who has accepted such a call and comes to the recognition of the impropriety connected with it need not resign, if there are no other reasons that demand it. Let him repent of what was done and serve with all the greater faithfulness.

Summary: For calling to proceed in a proper manner (*vocatio legitima*), neither the congregation nor the pastor should do anything that does not fully harmonize with all that Scripture says about the call into the public ministry. The congregation will keep in mind what qualifications Scripture establishes in the choice of the person, will show concern for the church-at-large, and will avoid whatever does not take into account that it is the Lord who calls and not man who places himself into the ministry.

IV. TRANSMITTING THE CALL
The Diploma of Vocation

A call can be issued and accepted orally. This does not affect the validity of a call. Nevertheless, transmitting the call by means of a written diploma of vocation provides irrefutable witness to the validity of the call and is evidence of the congregation's requirements and promises.

The diploma of vocation will charge the pastor to carry out his ministry in accordance with the inspired Word of God and the Lutheran Confessions. It will enjoin on him preaching, pastoral and educational functions, and require a life that accords with his high office. Since a pastor's office is broad in scope, the document may speak in general terms. If a particular area of responsibility is to be stressed or a particular function is to be his exclusive responsibility, the congregation will specify this in the call.

The diploma of vocation will also state the congregation's promises to its called servant. The members assure the recipient of the call that they will respect him as pastor. They promise that

5. *Luthers Saemmtliche Schriften* (St. Louis, 1880-1910), XI, 1911. Trans. in Plass, *What Luther Says* (St. Louis: Concordia, 1959), II, No. 1950.
6. St. L. IV, 628.

they will make use of the means of grace he is called to administer and will support him with their prayers. The call states how the congregation expects to provide for his material needs.

Generally the signatures of the president and of the secretary of the congregation provide two witnesses to the validity of the written document.

Both the pastor and the congregation should recognize that the call requires the pastor to devote his full time and energy to the ministerial work. Hence a congregation should provide for a salary and possible fringe benefits (housing, utilities, travel expense, medical insurance, etc.) that fully meet his and his family's needs. Scripture states the congregation's duties clearly in 1 Corinthians 9:6-14, where the Lord directs "those who proclaim the gospel to get their living from the gospel" (NASB). Similarly Galatians 6:6, "And let the one who is taught the word share all good things with him who teaches" (NASB). (Cf also 1 Tm 5:17f.) Our Savior's word that "the laborer is worthy of his hire" (Lk 10:7) was applied to His disciples as He sent them out as His messengers. Nevertheless, this is not a salary or wages in the ordinary sense, for neither the pastor nor congregation will think of his labor in terms of purchased hourly service resting simply on a financial agreement. The pastor gives himself totally to his ministry; the members of the congregation gratefully acknowledge his labors by sharing with him their material goods.

Good order calls for financial matters to be settled at the time the call is extended. The synodical representative who assists the congregation in calling generally finds this a good time to discuss with the congregation its financial responsibilities to its called servants. A congregation will do well to make it possible for its pastor to live according to the average living standard maintained by the members he must serve.

The pastor too will not forget that he has been called as a full-time servant of the congregation. While this allows the time necessary to meet his family responsibilities and to maintain good health (including a specified time for vacation), the pastor is unfaithful to his call if he seeks outside gainful imployment. Should a congregation not be able to arrange for adequate support in spite of every effort, outside means of support should be sought by the pastor only with the full permission and understanding of the congregation. Because of changing needs and al-

32

tered economic conditions, the pastor may find it necessary at times to inform the congregation of his needs and to instruct the people as to their responsibilities. Let him do this with great care lest he appear to have succumbed to the covetousness against which St. Paul warns Timothy (1 Tm 6:9,10). Let the pastor remember that "godliness with contentment is great gain" (v 6). "Having food and raiment let us be therewith content" (v 8). To help avoid difficult situations, a congregation will do well to review salaries annually, possibly through a committee or the church council. Since the diploma of vocation is not a contract, the financial promises are not a legal arrangement with the called worker and in that sense unchangeable. Salaries may be adjusted in either direction according to circumstances. In all of this a congregation will recognize its moral responsibility under God toward those whom He has sent to preach the gospel. The pastor on his part will emulate the spirit of Paul, "I have learned, in whatsoever state I am, therewith to be content. I know both how to be abased and I know how to abound: everywhere and in all things I am instructed both to be full and to be hungry, both to abound and to suffer need" (Ph 4:11,12).

Perquisites, generally not designated in the diploma of vocation as a part of the pastor's salary, are special gifts given to a pastor in gratitude for certain official services involving individuals (baptism, confirmation, marriage, burial). Since his call requires the pastor to perform these acts, perquisites should not become required fees nor should a pastor consider them his just due and feel disappointment if they are not given. If, however, an individual wishes to express his gratitude in some tangible form, the gift may be accepted gratefully as expressing appreciation for the gospel. As a rule it is inadvisable to accept gifts for sick calls and private communions, lest more frequent visits and the encouragement to more frequent communion appear to be financially motivated. To avoid this suspicion when there are those who insist on making a gift, the pastor may inform the donor that his gift will be placed into the congregational treasury or into some charitable fund. Also the practice of permitting a funeral director to include the pastor's "fee" on his statement of funeral costs to the family is better avoided. By and large, a congregation will do well to provide an adequate salary for its pastor and carefully avoid any suspicion that perquisites are required fees for services rendered.

The Covering Letter

The diploma of vocation is generally accompanied by a covering letter. While the former is an official, somewhat impersonal document (printed forms are most often used), stated in general terms, the covering letter is a personal communication that contains information that cannot be included in the diploma of vocation but may be helpful to the pastor-elect in making a decision on the call. This may include information about the congregation, its size, its special needs as, for example, an anticipated building program, its financial stewardship, the mission possibilities of the area, the community in which the congregation is located. It may inform the recipient of the reasons why the congregation believes it needs his particular services and extend encouragement toward acceptance of the call. It may also include pertinent information about housing and living conditions.

The congregation at its call meeting may want to designate the one who is to write the covering letter. It will need to be someone who is familiar with what should be included in the letter. This may be the vacancy pastor, the district president, the visiting elder. Circumstances may arise when it is advisable to have someone from the congregation, its president, council, or a committee, collaborate in writing the covering letter.

Since the diploma of vocation with its covering letter is an important document, it is customarily sent by registered or certified mail. When for some reason a longer time may elapse between the meeting and the sending of the call, it might be well to inform the called person by telephone that a call and a letter are on the way.

Summary: While a call that has been orally transmitted is valid, it is good practice to issue a written diploma of vocation stating what the congregation expects of its pastor and what it promises to do for him. A covering letter will give added information helpful in giving consideration to the call.

V. ACCEPTING OR DECLINING A CALL

Receipt of a call should be acknowledged by return mail, so that the calling congregation knows that the call has reached its destination. This is common courtesy, but it also shows the high regard the pastor has for a divine call and appreciation for the confidence which the congregation has placed in him by extending the call. The pastor will assure the congregation that the call will receive prayerful consideration in the fear of God. Should the time necessary to arrive at a decision be unusually long (more than the two or three weeks that are normally needed), the pastor should not fail to inform the calling congregation to that effect.

The pastor will do well immediately to inform the congregation he is serving of the call he has received. If he is serving in a mission, the mission board too should receive this information. A note to the district president will help keep him informed.

Every valid call that a Christian congregation extends is a divine call in the sense that the congregation has acted on the basis of a right God has given to it. It can properly be designated a divine call and should in every case receive the kind of treatment that its relationship to God deserves. Whether a particular call is divine also in the sense that it demands acceptance can be established only by a consideration of facts which the calling congregation cannot know or at least not fully evaluate. God has not promised the church direct illumination in the choice of the person. Hence not every call, even though it can in the above sense be called divine, requires acceptance. The Lord may use a vacancy and declined calls in a congregation for salutary training and instruction.

A call is extended to the pastor. It is he who will need to become certain that he must accept or decline a call. The decision will ultimately have to be made by him. He will earnestly pray God to guide him in his deliberation and to lead him to a decision that accords with the Lord's will. Only in the rarest of cases is it advisable for a pastor to make a decision entirely on his own, lest he fail to weigh all sides of the question and act out of selfish motives. Hence he will consult with fellow pastors (neighboring pastors, the visiting elder, the district president). He will consult with his present congregation (and mission board according to circumstances) before arriving at a final decision. Should a congregation pass a resolution relative to the pastor's call, it should be clear that this is in the nature of advice which the pastor will weigh in reaching a decision. However, to disregard a congregation's vote favoring his acceptance of a call to another field may make his future ministry in that congregation difficult. If he arrives at the conviction that the Lord wants him to accept the call, he will ask for a peaceful release from the call under which he is serving.

Should a congregation refuse this and the pastor retain his conviction that he must accept the call, resignation will free him for such acceptance. Such circumstances will be rare; the general course is to follow the way of a peaceful release.

Prayerful, objective consideration of a number of factors involved can help lead the pastor to the certainty he needs for a decision. The question he needs to answer is under which of the two calls the Lord wants him to serve, the one he presently has or the new one that he has received. He will compare the two fields as to size, importance, type of area in which the congregation is located, mission prospects, special problems or programs, etc. It may be that one or the other field is exposed to perils that require his services right at that time. Or it may be that the pastor is convinced that a change would be good for him and for his congregation, not because of any trouble, but because his congregation will benefit by the different gifts of another and he himself will grow by his experience in a new field. Then too, the pastor may possess certain gifts or experience that are particularly needed in the one field and not fully used in the other. The pastor's health may make it impossible for him to serve in one or the other field, or may indicate acceptance of a call that is less demanding. The pastor's God-given responsibilities as head of a family, for example, the health of his wife or a child, may call for attention in the decision. In this, great care must be practiced lest fleshly considerations inject themselves into the decision. Paul warns against those leaders in the church "whose God is their belly . . . who mind earthly things" (Ph 3:19). He calls on Timothy "to endure all things for the elect's sake" (2 Tm 2:10-12), to flee covetousness and the temptations and snares associated with it (1 Tm 6:6-12). The pastor is to take oversight of the flock of God "not for filthy lucre" (1 Pe 5:2). It is sinful to accept or decline a call for reasons dictated by the flesh, e.g., a higher salary, greater prestige, flight from problems, proximity to friends and relatives, opportunities for graduate study or pleasant recreation. The ministry calls for selflessness.

In considering the demands of each field and in looking at his own qualifications, the pastor may be overwhelmed by a feeling of unworthiness and by his own lack of the special gifts the ministry requires, particularly in positions of greater responsibility. Unless they are based on objectively evident realities and not mere human feelings, they should not be the basis for a decision.

Moses felt incapable of leading Israel after forty years in desert seclusion (Ex 4:10-16); Jeremiah's first response to the Lord's call was, "I cannot speak: for I am a child" (Jr 1:4-8); and Paul asked the question, "Who is sufficient for these things?" (2 Cor 2:16.) The Lord not only calls for service, but He also gives the needed gifts. This may not always be evident at the time the call is decided, particularly not to the pastor himself. Latent gifts may blossom forth under the new demands and develop through experience as the pastor faithfully devotes himself to his greater responsibilities under the blessing of the Lord. The pastor, particularly in weighing his gifts and qualifications, will do well to consult with experienced men in the ministry who, he is confident, will give him objective, frank opinions.

An added consideration enters in when the call involves a change in the type of service required. Without doubt, pastoral service in a congregation will be the most satisfying for the majority of men who have been trained for this ministry. This results from the intimate relationship between the shepherd and his flock. To be God's servant in applying the power of the Word of God to people in the midst of life's joys and sorrows, to see this power in action and the comfort and joy it brings, even in the face of death, is a privilege peculiar to the pastorate in a congregation. Nevertheless, a call into the more restricted field of teaching, to a position as an executive secretary, or to be a chaplain in an institution or to men in the armed forces is equally a call into the ministry of the Word and may be equally rewarding to those whom the Lord has given the necessary gifts for this specialized ministry. Nevertheless, such a call cannot simply be decided on the basis of personal preference. The question that needs to be weighed as objectively as possible is where with his particular gifts the recipient of the call can serve most advantageously in the Lord's kingdom.

If a pastor comes to the conviction that he should decline a call, he will immediately write a letter to the calling congregation to that effect, returning the diploma of vocation sent to him. In many cases it may be sufficient to state that prayerful consideration has led him to the conviction to remain at his present congregation. It is not necessary, and sometimes inadvisable, to detail the reasons that led to the decision. Particularly should one avoid giving reasons that may in the future raise questions in the minds of the people. If a pastor for valid reasons accepts another call six months after declining a previous one for the stated reason that he did not consider his work at the present congregation finished, the people will wonder about the sincerity of the reason, since they do not know all the circumstances involved in each call. It is well to state reasons only if it is quite important for the calling congregation to know them, if it is done tactfully, and if the reasons can be given in such a way that they will not be misunderstood.

If the decision is to accept the call, a letter of acceptance is immediately sent to the calling congregation, generally through the vacancy pastor. A personal letter will mention a date and other suggestions for the installation. Inquiries can be made about the moving arrangements. Since the calling congregation customarily pays the moving costs, arrangements for moving should be made in accordance with whatever agreement is reached with that congregation.

The pastor should also immediately inform his district president of the acceptance of the call so that the latter may know of the resulting vacancy and arrange for a vacancy pastor and for a meeting with the congregation to call a replacement. The president of the district in which his new field of labor is located should also be informed immediately and arrangements made with him for the installation. According to the WELS constitution the district president must authorize the installation. If the pastor is moving from one district to another, he must apply for a transfer of his synodical membership to the new district. Whoever has not formerly been a pastor member of the Synod will at this time need to apply for membership with the district president. Every pastor serving in the Synod becomes a pastor member with voting rights by becoming a member of a particular district of the Synod.

The pastor concludes his ministry in a congregation with the farewell service. For the sermon it is often possible and advisable to use the regular text for the Sunday from the pericope series in use at the time. The farewell sermon will reveal whether the pastor has truly done "the work of an evangelist" (2 Tm 4:5). This is hardly the time to chastise a congregation for sins against the pastor, imagined or real. While it would be strange to make no reference to the conclusion of his ministry among them, there is no need to dwell on this in an emotional manner throughout the sermon. Let the last impression of the pastor be that of one who richly nourished them with the gospel as he proclaimed the full truth of Holy Scripture.

Upon leaving a congregation, a pastor should remember that another becomes the called minister of that congregation. He must therefore studiously avoid becoming a "busybody in other men's matters" (1 Pe 4:15). He no longer has a call to advise the congregation or to minister to any of its members. Social visits with its members, spending a vacation among its people, continued correspondence with friends in its midst can give the suspicion of interference if it does not actually lead thereto. Due recognition must be given to the fact that one call has terminated, and another has replaced it.

Although the situation for the ministerial candidate receiving his first call is somewhat different, what is pertinent in the foregoing applies also to him. According to constitutional agreement in the WELS, Seminary graduates receive their first calls through an assignment committee. Since they have responded to the church's needs by saying, "Here am I, send me," and the question of choosing between several calls is not involved, their acceptance of the assigned call is properly taken for granted. If there is a reason why a candidate cannot serve in a foreign field or in a particular climate or area, this information may be given to the assignment committee. For a congregation contrary to the agreed procedure to call a student directly or for a student to accept such a direct call violates good order. It places a strain on the brotherly love that should exist within the church and its congregations.

In all that has been said about deciding a call, it is always taken for granted that the calling church is orthodox, confessing itself to the inspired Scripture as the only norm of faith and life and to the Lutheran Confessions as a true exposition of Scripture doctrine. No pastor may accept a call that commits him to preach or practice in violation of Scripture. However, a call to a congregation whose confessional position is still unclear on some points but that wishes to be instructed fully from Holy Scripture may in good conscience be accepted. It is also to be noted that externals, matters of organization and ceremonies, are adiaphora and not a part of the confession. Nevertheless, Article X of the Formula of Concord recognizes that circumstances can arise under which even church ceremonies may involve the church's confession.

Summary: Since the call is addressed to the pastor, the decision to accept or decline is his personal responsibility. He will approach such a decision prayerfully, calling upon God to give him certainty in his decision. He will seek the advice of his congregation and other pastors, seek the welfare of Christ's church in his decision, and in every way endeavor to follow the orderly procedures that have been agreed upon in the constitution of his church body.

VI. LEAVING THE MINISTRY
A. Resignation

Unless there are valid reasons to the contrary, the pastor's call is issued as one that is permanent. This, however, is not to be understood in the sense that a pastor must for the duration of his life remain in the congregation he is serving or that he must under all circumstances continue serving until death releases him from the ministerial office. Nevertheless, a faithful pastor will not let thoughts of resignation find a ready haven in his heart. To consider resigning from his call for reasons dictated by his flesh (e.g., because he wants to be free of its difficult tasks, because he desires a life of ease, or because he wishes to enter into a vocation that brings increased financial returns), the pastor will recognize as a temptation to unfaithfulness. It is the Lord who through the congregation has called the pastor. Any desire to be rid of his office must reckon not only with the congregation, but with the Lord Himself. And the Lord says, "No man, having put his hand to the plow, and looking back, is fit for the kingdom of God" (Lk 9:62).

That thoughts of resignation will arise in the pastor's mind is not surprising. This is not unusual especially during the early years in the ministry. He may honestly have doubts about his qualifications as he experiences the difficulties of the ministry. But the faithful pastor will recognize that he, too, is subject to temptation and will prayerfully seek the strength of the Holy Spirit to fight the good fight of faith. When thoughts of resignation arise, he will consult with fellow pastors in whose judgment he has confidence to help him distinguish between temptations and valid considerations.

In reality, resignation from the ministry always consists in resignation from a particular call. The pastoral ministry does not exist as an abstract entity apart from a concrete position. Since the call to a particular position places the pastor into the ministry, resignation from that call takes him out of the ministry. Whoever resigns from the ministry as a matter of choice or necessity for reasons other than age and permanently takes other employment should not be asked to preach or perform other pastoral acts lest the impression be given that he retains his pastoral status.

It is of course possible to resign from a specific call in order to accept a call to another field of service. Generally, however, freedom to accept another call is secured through receiving a release from the previous call (cf p 35f). Only in rare cases will the pastor need to proceed via resignation.

Most frequently, therefore, to resign from the ministry refers to a resignation from a specific office with the understanding that one is no longer available for another call. Since the pastor knows that the Lord requires faithfulness in the stewards of His mysteries (1 Cor 4:2), the pastor recognizes that faithfulness will cause him to persevere until the Lord, who called him, gives clear evidence that points to a termination of his ministry. Such evidence may be of various kinds.

Illness

Because of illness a pastor may no longer be able to carry out his ministerial functions as they properly deserve to be carried out. When such illness results in only temporary disability, pastoral assistance for the duration of the illness will prevent a hasty, unnecessary resignation. If, however, the disability is of greater length and doubts remain about an eventual recovery, a conscientious pastor will guard against seeking, or even accepting, a congregation's offer for a prolonged leave of absence, especially if pastoral service can be provided only partially. He will guard against any course that could be injurious to the congregation. While the congregation wishes to act with loving consideration for the pastor, the latter will have the welfare of the congregation at heart and may be in a better position to judge when the congregation is suffering for lack of pastoral service than the members themselves. Similarly a pastor may find himself compelled to resign because the illness of a member of his family unmistakably demands a change that cannot be solved by accepting another call. God has placed these family responsibilities on the pastor, and as such they are not to be ignored. To preserve a good conscience in making decisions of this kind competent medical advice as well as consultation with brother pastors will be invaluable.

41

Debility Caused by Advancing Age

Under God's providence the course of man's life on this earth includes a greater or lesser decline of physical and mental powers with advancing age. Since this usually develops gradually, it can easily escape one's notice. A pastor will do well to examine himself and not fail to acknowledge the waning of his strength when that is taking place. He will need to answer the question whether his declining strength results in injury to the Lord's church. The solution may be a reduction of his responsibilities or removal to a less demanding ministry so that his gifts and experience might still be used according to capacity. On the other hand, this may be evidence from the Lord that resignation is in order. This does not rule out serving the Lord in retirement to the extent proffered opportunities and his strength permit. The pastor should avoid placing the congregation into the very difficult position of being forced to ask for his resignation after years of faithful service because he fails to recognize the injury his failing strength is inflicting on the congregation.

Loss of the Congregation's Confidence

Resignation may be indicated when the pastor recognizes that tactless or legalistic actions have resulted in losing the confidence of many in the congregation. This may be evidence that he does not possess the kind of personal characteristics, the type of personality required in one who must in the ministry work closely with and for many different kinds of people. Since a pastor will not be the most objective judge of his own person and actions, he will hardly act on the basis of his own judgment alone.

However, in these cases the question also must be carefully examined whether the opposition is directed not so much against the pastor's person and manner of proceeding, as against the truth that he has faithfully taught and applied. Resignation must not be a yielding to those "who will not endure sound doctrine" so that they may find the kind of teachers that will satisfy their "itching ears" (2 Tm 4:2-5). Jesus speaks of the opposition those He sends forth will meet in a world where they go as sheep among wolves. Although they will incur the hatred of men, they are to endure to the end (Mt 10:16,22). Resignation should not be an attempt on the part of the pastor to escape the cross such opposition lays upon him.

42

Investigation by impartial, competent Christians, e.g., by the visiting elder or the district president, will help discover whether evil men are troubling the church or whether tactless or legalistic action has evoked resentment. Should the latter be the case, resignation can hardly be avoided without injury to the church.

Change in Doctrinal Position

By accepting a call, the pastor makes a solemn promise that he will teach and preach the full truth of Holy Scripture in accordance with the confessional position of the congregation. Should a change occur in his inner convictions so that he no longer shares with them the truth he once confessed, honesty requires resignation from the call he can no longer carry out according to its original requirements. Since there must be unity of confession between the pastor and the congregation he serves, persistent departure from the former true confession on the part of either is cause for termination of the call. The sanctity of the call does not require submitting to a congregation's change to error, nor does it allow a pastor to claim a right to turn the congregation from truth to error through his continued service. To attempt the latter through subversive methods without the knowledge of the congregation is most reprehensible.

A distinction must be made, however, between actual departure from a doctrinal position and doubts about its correctness that arise as temptations (*Anfechtung*). When doubts arise, the pastor needs to struggle to allay them with the Word of God, seeking brotherly help through private discussions or at pastoral conferences. While he struggles with his doubts, he will not let them become a factor in his public teaching. Quite different are firm convictions that represent doctrinal change. These disrupt the confessional unity, and honesty calls for resignation.

Summary: Although a pastor will reject thoughts of resignation that would involve unfaithfulness to his divine call, circumstances may arise in which the Lord indicates that resignation is in place. A disabling illness, debility caused by advancing age, loss of a congregation's confidence resulting from tactlessness or legalism, or an actual change in the pastor's confessional convictions are such circumstances.

43

B. Removal from the Ministry

The congregation as the calling body retains the right, for reasons that will be listed, to terminate a pastor's call. The congregation may proceed by asking for the pastor's resignation. If this fails, it may remove him from office. However, it must take great care to remain withing the bounds established by Scripture.

False Doctrine

The Lord Jesus bids His church beware of false prophets (Mt 7:15). St. Paul calls a curse down on those who proclaim "another gospel" than the one he had been sent to preach (Ga 1:6-9). The Thessalonians are admonished to "stand fast, and hold the traditions" which they had been taught (2 Th 2:15). St. John specifically enjoins his "beloved" readers that they are not to "believe every spirit, but test the spirits to see whether they are from God" (1 Jn 4:1 - NASB). The church must separate from those who "cause divisions and offenses contrary to the doctrine which ye have learned" (Ro 16:17). The reason given is the nature of error and its destructive consequences. A congregation thus has the responsibility to watch over the doctrine of its called servants and may not tolerate false doctrine on the part of those who speak in the congregation's name. The congregation may not retain as pastor anyone who perverts the gospel and persists in doing so in spite of admonition.

Works of the Flesh

Whoever impenitently continues in the works of the flesh is subject to exclusion from the congregation. This is also applicable to the impenitent pastor and includes removal from office. Should the pastor repent, the congregation will assure him of the Lord's forgiveness and continue to see in him a brother in Christ. Nevertheless, because of the offense which his sin may have caused both within and outside the congregation, it cannot be taken for granted that he may remain as pastor. The Lord would have his servants be "blameless" (1 Tm 3:2) and "have a good report of them which are without" (1 Tm 3:17). The congregation will have to determine whether these qualifications now are lacking to a degree that makes the pastor's resignation or removal mandatory.

Unfaithfulness

The Lord would have His church require faithfulness of those called to be stewards of His mysteries (1 Cor 4:2). A congregation

44

has a right to expect the pastor faithfully to use whatever gifts the Lord has given him. The pastor who persistently and willfully fails in this, as may be evident through lack of sermon preparation, through neglect of important pastoral duties, failure to visit the sick, etc., or through presumptuous lording it over the congregation, has given sufficient cause for removal from the ministry. His unfaithfulness is a hindrance to the gospel. He is not edifying but harming the Lord's people.

Incompetence

Should it become clearly evident to the congregation that a pastor lacks the necessary gifts for the ministry or the particular gifts without which the work in its midst cannot be done, consideration for the man should not outweigh the welfare of the church. Incompetence may also result from illness or age. Since incompetence does not involve the pastor in conduct worthy of blame, the congregation will with all kindness but firmness seek to lead the pastor to submit his resignation in the interest of the gospel.

Christian Procedure in Cases of Removal

When sin is involved (this would not be the case with incompetence), the erring pastor should be admonished and the dealings should proceed according to Matthew 18. Since the removal of a pastor can become an offensive spectacle to those outside the church and cause divisions within the congregation, great care must be taken to proceed with Christian charity and patience. This should, however, not extend to the point of allowing the erring pastor to continue carrying out the pastoral functions while he is being dealt with by the congregation. It should be self-evident that the congregation continue to support the pastor until the case is settled.

The removal of called personnel is the responsibility of the group that originally issued the call. Hence the removal of a pastor is a congregational matter. While the synodical body through the boards that issue specific calls must assume responsibility for admonition and removal of men with such a call where this becomes necessary, no synodical body or board has the right to remove a pastor called by a congregation.

Although a congregation must make the final decision and has the right to do this without outside advice and help, it will seldom proceed with a removal without consulting with men of Christian maturity and experience. Generally a congregation feels at a loss as to how to proceed and appreciates the assistance which its synodical membership makes available, particularly that of the visiting elder of the conference or of the district president. The protest of the pastor cannot prevent the calling in of synodical assistance, although this should not be done without the knowledge of the pastor. All things should proceed according to good order, with openness and honesty.

The congregation's synodical membership also brings with it the responsibility to give an account of its actions to fellow Christians in the larger fellowship, should that be necessary. A pastor's status as a pastor member of the synod may be involved as well as the question of his eligibility to receive a call to a sister congregation. The disciplinary action of a congregation beyond one's confessional fellowship should also be honored unless careful investigation has led to the conclusion that it has no biblical basis.

When the pastor's competence is in question, a congregation will hardly want to base a final decision solely on its own judgment lest it raise the suspicion that the congregation's demands on the pastor may have gone beyond biblical requirements. The advisability of consulting with men whose Christian knowledge, experience, and judgment are recognized is evident.

If a pastor who has been guilty of false teaching retracts, it may be possible for him to continue serving his congregation unless he has demonstrated a general doctrinal weakness or unless his continued service causes offense to the weak in its midst. In the latter case, a call to another congregation may be the solution, and the district president should be consulted in the matter. The pastor who has fallen into gross sins of the flesh and has lost his "good report of them that are without" will seldom be able to continue as pastor even though the congregation has acknowledged his repentance, assured him of forgiveness, and accepted him back as a brother in Christ. Whether he can serve in another congregation will need to be determined by those to whom the synodical fellowship has given the responsibility of proposing candidates to congregations. More often than not they may conclude that his lapse cannot remain hidden from other congregations and decide against proposing his name.

Should a pastor who in general has adequate gifts for the ministry lack some specific gift essential for work in his particular congregation, the congregation need hardly press for a resignation, but in consultation with the district president can await the time when the Lord opens to him a field that he can adequately serve.

Through the rearrangement of multiple parishes or through the consolidation of congregations the service of one of the pastors may become superfluous. Such changes are not in violation of the biblical concept of the ministry, for the needs of the church in that locality have changed. Since such changes will be made in consultation with synodical representatives, the released pastor can be called into a field where his services are needed. On the other hand, a parish consisting of two or more congregations may decide to separate and become two independent congregations. The pastor who had been jointly called by both congregations will have to decide which of the two congregations he will continue to serve and ask for a release from the other.

Summary: The calling body retains the right to terminate a pastor's call for valid reasons. Such reasons are false doctrine, gross works of the flesh, evident unfaithfulness, and incompetence. Admonition and discipline should proceed according to Matthew 18. Circumstances will need to determine the repentant pastor's future status. Incompetence, not involving sin, may find a solution in voluntary resignation.

For Additional Reading

Fritz, John H. C. *Pastoral Theology.* Chapter 6: "The Call to the Ministry." St. Louis: Concordia, 1932. pp 32-60.

> This chapter, written from the "Missouri" viewpoint of the divine institution of the local congregation and its consequently unique role in calling, presents much practical material, often enriched by references to other sources.

Hoenecke, Adolph. "Das Lehramt." Chapter 68 in vol. IV of *Ev. -Luth. Dogmatik.* Milwaukee: Northwestern, 1909. pp 175-205.

> This doctrinal presentation of the "teaching office" includes a discussion of the divine call, especially under thesis II.

Koehneke, P. F. "The Call into the Holy Ministry." Chapter XVIII in *The Abiding Word,* vol. I. St. Louis: Concordia, 1946. pp 366-388.

> Six theses are discussed with frequent references to essays that appeared during the first hundred years of Missouri Synod history.

That the specific "Missouri" views of church and ministry find expression in this presentation is thus to be expected.

Luther, Martin. "Concerning the Ministry." *Luther's Works*, vol. XL. Philadelphia: Muhlenberg, 1958. pp 7-48.

Luther instructs the Bohemians of Prague concerning their right as Christians to call pastors without ordination from Rome. Luther clearly presents his views about the universal priesthood, the public ministry, and the right of Christians to call pastors.

Reinboth, Oscar H. *Calls and Vacancies*. St. Louis: Concordia, 1967.

A paperback that provides practical guidelines for the pastor considering a call, for the congregation sending a call, and for the ministry during a vacancy. The last point is one not often discussed to the extent that it is treated in this book. Most of the practical suggestions are acceptable.

Schaller, John. *Pastorale Praxis*. Chapter I: "Die Berufung." Milwaukee: Northwestern, 1913. pp 4-14.

Much of the material in this chapter served as a basis for the chapter on the call into the ministry in this volume. The arrangement of the material is thetical with explanatory paragraphs.

Scharf, Erwin. "The Call to the Public Use of the Keys." *Proceedings of the Thirty-Eighth Convention of the Wisconsin Evangelical Lutheran Synod. 1965. pp 53-73.*

This convention essay discusses many practical questions about the call into the ministry in the longest part of the essay entitled "Questions Which Have Arisen Concerning the Call in Recent Years."

Schwermann, Albert H. "The Doctrine of the Call." Chapter VII in *The Pastor at Work*. St. Louis: Concordia, 1960. pp 85-124.

While a remnant of the view that only the local congregation can issue a valid call is present, this chapter covers the many practical aspects of the doctrine of the divine call in accordance with basic scriptural principles.

Walther, C. F. W. *Amerekanisch-Lutherische Pastoraltheologie*. St. Louis: Concordia, 4th ed., 1890. pp 23-58.

Walther's presentation of the call is especially valuable for its many references to Luther's writings. Also the student who has difficulty with German can use the references and check them in an English translation, where this is available.

Zich, August F. "The Doctrine of the Divine Call With Reference to Present Day Abuses." *Wisconsin Lutheran Quarterly*, XXXV (Oct., 1938), 223-245.

After a careful discussion of the divine call as revealed in Scripture, the author warns against abuses. Although the essay was written in 1938, the warnings are still relevant.

3

The Shepherd
Begins His Ministry

"They lay their hands on them"

(Ac 13:3)

I. ORDINATION AND INSTALLATION

A pastor's ministry in a congregation begins with his installation. Although the congregation's call which the pastor accepted makes him pastor of the congregation, the formal entrance upon the ministry customarily occurs through the rite of installation. Until the installation, the vacancy pastor or former pastor, as the case may be, continues to function. The first installation of a man into the ministry is designated as his ordination.

Essentially the Same

There is no essential difference between the ordination and any subsequent installation of the same pastor. The rite of ordination confers the pastoral office on an individual no more than does the rite of installation. The call, not ordination, does this. We view the ordination and every installation as public recognition or confirmation of the validity and legitimacy of the call that was sent and accepted. The Lutheran Confessions similarly state: "Afterwards a bishop . . . was brought in to confirm the election with the laying on of hands; nor was ordination anything more than such confirmation" (*Treatise on the Power and Primacy of the Pope,*

49

70). Hence no ordination should be performed without a preceding call. The church must avoid any practice which could give the impression of agreement with Rome to the effect that ordination is a divinely instituted sacrament which places a person into the state of being a priest or pastor in contrast to the laity and which confers a *character indelebilis* that a man has entirely apart from the church's call.

An Adiaphoron

Neither ordination nor installation are divinely instituted. The custom is, however, an ancient one in the church with traces of it already in Scripture when it speaks of the laying on of hands (Ac 6:6; 13:3; 1 Tm 4:14; 5:22; 2 Tm 1:6). But there is no word of command from God for this custom. It should be noted that the KJV translation "ordain" in Titus 1:5 and Acts 14:23 could be misleading. In the former *kathisteemi* is better translated "appoint" and in the latter *cheirotoneoo* means "to choose by raising hands." Ordination thus is an adiaphoron. Nevertheless, because of the purpose it is to serve we can expect the Lord to bless it. Both Schaller and Walther list the following three purposes: public testimony of the pastor's fitness for the office; public recognition of the call for the reassurance of both pastor and congregation; intercession by the entire congregation.[1] Schaller adds a fourth: public confession to pure doctrine and a promise of faithfulness on the part of the pastor.

Being an adiaphoron, ordination (installation) could be dispensed with without jeopardizing a man's position in the pastoral office. A call does not need such confirmation for its validity. To drop this church rite could, however, result in offense to the weak, might give evidence of an independent, haughty spirit which violates love, and would fail to recognize the value of a custom that goes back to the earliest history of the New Testament church.

The Place

The Lutheran view of ordination as to its essential nature is best preserved by having the ordination performed in the midst of the calling congregation as one rite together with the installation. To separate ordination and installation by having the one per-

1. J. Schaller, *Pastorale Praxis* (Milwaukee: Northwestern, 1913), p 21. C. F. W. Walther, *Americanisch-Lutherische Pastoraltheologie* (St. Louis: Concordia, 1890), p 66.

formed in the home congregation of the pastoral candidate and a subsequent installation in the calling congregation could result in misleading views of ordination. If the home congregation wishes to acknowledge the fact that a young man from its midst is entering the ministry — and such recognition can serve a wholesome purpose — this can be done in other ways than ordination.

In the case of a foreign missionary or chaplain a commissioning service, having the same essential elements as an installation service, is held by those in whose name he is to serve. A candidate's ordination will then become part of this service. A pastor called by the board for home missions to a field where there is as yet no congregation may similarly be commissioned.

The essential parts of the ordination and installation rites are the pastor's solemn obligation to Scripture and the Lutheran Confessions, and his promise of faithfulness in the office. This is followed by a devout laying on of hands on the part of the ordaining (installing) and assisting pastors. The sermon is preached by either the officiating pastor or someone who may have been asked to preach, possibly according to the called pastor's wishes.

Authorization by District President

The WELS constitution assigns to the district president the responsibility for authorizing ordinations and installations. In this way synodical recognition is given to the call as a testimony to the church-at-large. The time for the ordination (installation) and the choice of officiants is generally arrived at by mutual consultation on the part of the district president, the vacancy pastor, the candidate, and the calling congregation.

Summary: Ordination and installation, essentially the same, are not commanded by God but are an ancient church custom that should not unnecessarily be omitted. The performing of such a rite is a public recognition of the validity of the call and the person's fitness for the ministry. In the rite the pastor obligates himself to Scripture and the Lutheran Confessions and promises faithfulness in his ministry. The solemn laying on of hands by the officiating pastors and prayer by the congregation complete the rite. Ordination should be performed in the congregation to which a candidate is called. The district president authorizes ordinations and installations.

II. FIRST DUTIES

The Inaugural Sermon

On the Sunday after his installation the pastor begins his pulpit work with his first sermon, often called an inaugural or initial sermon. (If a special service like a funeral occurs during that week, it is selfevident that he will officiate.) With the Lutheran emphasis on preaching, the pastor's first sermon is of great importance because it gives the people their first, and often quite lasting, impression of him as a preacher. This sermon should not fail to let the gospel shine forth in its full richness. The pastor will preach in a way that is both tactful and truthful. He will speak with a warmth that shows the love he has for the people who have entrusted him with the high responsibility of watching over their souls (He 13:17), for people whom he does not as yet know well personally but loves as the Lord's redeemed.

As text the pastor may find that the scripture selection for the Sunday in the pericope series he has chosen will serve well. If not, there are many suitable texts, as, for example: Psalm 40:9-11; Jeremiah 1:6,7; John 17:20,21; Acts 26:22-29; Romans 1:16,17; 15:29-33; 1 Corinthians 1:21-25; 2:1-5; 4:1,2; 2 Corinthians 1:24; 4:5,6; 5:17-21; 1 Thessalonians 2:13.

The text will determine the specific thrust of the sermon and its contents. The following thoughts may find expression: the call to the pastoral office and how the pastor views his ministry; the importance and responsibility of the ministry; the need to serve God and not merely man; the requirement to preach both law and gospel each according to need; the intention to hold to the Lutheran Confessions as a true exposition of God's Word; the goal of the ministry as the salvation of souls. On the other hand, the pastor may invite the congregation on its part to attend services regularly; to accept the Word in faith; to use the sacraments faithfully; to pray for him as their pastor. The occasion calls for emphasis on the pastor's responsibilities to the congregation. It is not necessary to describe in detail the congregation's duties toward the pastor and his ministry. This can better be done in the installation sermon.

The term "inaugural sermon" should not mislead the pastor into considering it a kind of inaugural address in which he outlines a practical program he plans to carry out in the midst of his congregation and announces changes he believes should be made.

If there are problems in the congregation which already have come to the pastor's attention, this is not the time to make promises or to voice threats.

Getting Acquainted

The pastor should make it his prime concern to learn to know the individual members of the congregation as soon as possible. He must acquaint himself with the way the congregation is organized and functions. He must get to know the community in which he is to live and work.

The Members

Even before the day of installation the pastor will find it helpful to study the list of the congregation's members. In this way the many names he hears on that first day will already sound familiar, and he can concentrate more completely on associating the names with individuals. This can be done by making a conscious effort to remember distinctive characteristics of an individual and associating them with his name. It will, however, help little to remember that Mrs. Brown wore a brown dress on installation day. He may give her a wrong name when he sees her dressed in green.

The best way to get to know people is to see them in their homes. To make a visit into every member's home should have high priority among the pastor's duties. In smaller congregations this should be possible within the first several months. In larger congregations because of the added routine work and the greater number of homes more time is needed, but the visits should not be neglected.

An organized plan is needed to make sure that the visits will be made. The congregational president, the elders, or the church council may assist the pastor in setting up the schedule of visits, since they may know the working schedules of the people, and can help plan visits geographically to avoid spending unnecessary time in travel. In some cases it may be necessary or helpful to schedule the visits in advance by telephone. The sick and shut-ins should receive first consideration because of their specific spiritual needs and because they were unable to be present at the installation.

The pastor will find it helpful to meet the entire family in the home. This gives opportunity not only to observe the home environment, but also to note how the family members relate to one another. By directing the conversation into religious channels and to matters pertaining to the church, the pastor may gain some impressions of the spiritual attitudes and understanding of the members. All of this is helpful for the minister who concerns himself with the needs of the people and will contribute toward sermons that address themselves to the particular flock which called him as pastor. Since these calls are to have a pastoral aspect, it is best if the pastor makes them alone.

A record of the visit, made immediately after the call, can include significant information or observations that will serve the pastor well for future reference. Such a record will be an aid to his memory and will prevent confusing what may have occurred at each place when a series of calls is made. These records are part of the pastor's confidential materials for use by him alone.

The pastor must be on guard lest his visits become an occasion for people to gossip about fellow members or to air grievances, real or imagined, against the former pastor. Special tact and care are called for by a new associate or assistant pastor. He must avoid appearing as a rival or judge of the associate and his ministry. If, however, the people speak well of the former pastor or a present associate, the pastor should recognize this as showing appreciation for the ministry, appreciation that will be shown also for his own faithful service. A warning is in place against people, whether men or women, who seek to ingratiate themselves with the pastor, possibly by flattery, or who assume the role of self-appointed advisers to fill in the pastor on the problems and needs of the congregation.

The Congregation

The pastor can begin to acquaint himself with the congregation's organization and functions by reading the constitution. The file of Sunday bulletins and of newsletters provides informative reading. A perusal of the minutes of council and congregational meetings and of the church records can add to the new pastor's understanding of the congregation's organization, its customs and practices.

Very soon, preferably during the week after installation, the pastor should meet with the church council. These men generally are able to answer any questions that the reading of the constitution, bulletins, etc., raised in the pastor's mind. The various board and committee chairmen on the council are able to give the pastor an insight into their manner of functioning. On the whole, the church council may be the pastor's best resource for gaining an understanding of how the congregation is doing the Lord's business.

If there is a Christian day school, the new pastor will want to meet with the principal and the teaching staff. Details of the school organization can be discussed, and the pastor can determine what his practical responsibilities in the school organization will be. A brief visit in each classroom will demonstrate his interest to the teachers and the children. All of this should provide a good beginning for a harmonious working together of the pastor, the principal, and the teachers.

The pastor may wish to meet with the chairman of each organization within the congregation before attending a meeting for the first time. If an organization has its own constitution, he will do well to acquaint himself with it.

As the pastor learns to know the practices and customs, the organizational structure and mode of procedure, he may discover what he considers weaknesses, areas where changes seem called for. Sometimes a congregation is expecting minor changes with the advent of a new pastor. There are times when the people are looking for changes because the organization has not adjusted to growth or changing circumstances. The pastor can sense when this is the case. Generally, however, he will wisely avoid any rush in suggesting changes. After he has observed the congregation in action for a time, he can better judge whether the change he contemplates will truly be an improvement for that particular congregation. After he has gained the confidence of the members and no longer is thought of as a newcomer, he can more readily suggest practical changes and gain acceptance that is meaningful. Since these will be matters that lie in the area of adiaphora, the pastor can show patience toward practices he thinks could be improved and need not insist on his or his former congregation's way as the only correct one.

The Community

Acceptance of a call generally includes moving to a community that is strange to the pastor and his family. He must, therefore, acquaint himself with the community in which his pastoral work will be carried out and in which he and his family will reside.

A map of the city or area will help the pastor to find his way around in the community. On the map he may locate and mark the homes of members and prospects.

It is well for the pastor to locate the hospitals, convalescent and nursing homes, and other similar institutions before he is called to one or the other for pastoral service. Knowledge of the medical facilities and social service agencies and of the services available, of mental health facilities, of programs for the retarded may serve him well in advising those who come to him for help.

By acquainting himself with the name and location of the churches in the proximity of his congregation, the pastor may be able to anticipate the kind of religious contacts he and his members may make outside the congregation. If certain denominations or religious groups are heavily represented, he may wish to make a special study of them so that he is prepared to answer questions that could arise. Although the need is less pressing if the congregation has a Christian day school, the pastor should know something about the public school system which some or even all the children of the congregation may be attending.

The church is not of the world, but the Lord has placed it into the world, and each congregation lives in a particular community of that world. Since it is the congregation's mission to preach the gospel to the people of that community, an understanding of a community's characteristics is helpful in carrying out the church's work in that place. In his ministry, Paul, e.g., noted the difference between Athens and the cities of Galatia.

The pastor and his family will become citizens of the community in which the congregation is located. Upon arrival, he will arrange for his banking and ought to find out what doctors and medical help are available should an emergency arise in his family. He and the adult members of his family need to register to establish their eligibility for voting. He may want to subscribe to the local newspaper, even if it is only a small weekly publication. From it he may learn about the community things valuable both for his work and for the family's life in it.

The pastor and his family should not be so aloof from the community in which the congregation is located that he, and sometimes his church, is known only to the members. On the other hand, the pastor must guard against seeking to become a leader in the community and its affairs. His priorities are clear. He must proclaim the gospel. "Seek ye first the kingdom of God" applies in a special way to him. If he faithfully performs all responsibilities of his God-given ministry, he will find that to be a full-time position.

Summary: The pastor's pulpit work in a congregation begins with an inaugural sermon in which he stresses his God-given assignment to preach the Word faithfully. As quickly as possible he should get to know the members, especially through visits in their homes. He will acquaint himself with the congregational organization and with the community in which he and his family will reside.

III. MISCELLANEA

If the pastor moves into a new state, he must find out what, if anything, is required of him to qualify for performing marriages. This should be attended to immediately. He should become familiar with marriage and divorce laws, especially those that may have a relationship to his ministry. He will need to remember that his and his family's life is now regulated by state laws that may differ from those he knew in his former state.

- - - - - - - - - -

When moving from one parish to another, sufficient time should be allowed for the move so that the pastor and his family can get well settled in the new location and home before the day of installation. To move only a day or two before the installation will force a pastor to divide his time during the first weeks between his home and congregational duties. The many responsibilities involved in getting to know his new congregation should receive the pastor's concentrated attention as soon as he is installed.

- - - - - - - - - -

The pastor and his family may find some customs in the congregation and the community strange and even odd. To criticize or to ridicule them will not serve to "win friends and influence people." He may soon find them not so strange at all. In such matters the pastor is well advised by St. Paul to become all things to all men.

During the first weeks or months the pastor should not absent himself from his congregation for any longer period of time. Conferences and conventions must indeed be attended. But to begin one's ministry with an early vacation may raise doubts about one's devotion to the congregation and the ministry.

- - - - - - - - - -

A pastor should establish and carefully guard his credit standing in the new community. Some credit accounts are useful for establishing one's credit rating provided the bills are paid promptly. The good reputation the pastor is to have among those outside his congregation should extend also to his demonstration of financial responsibility. Debts cannot always be avoided, but to incur burdensome debts as the result of foolish spending and a standard of living beyond the pastor's modest salary is inexcusable. If debts must be made, it is best, however, not to borrow money from members.

- - - - - - - - - -

A pastor may find that soon after his arrival in a new community he will be invited to join the local ministerial association. Such organizations are not set up to discuss and, on the basis of Scripture, to remove doctrinal differences among the churches of varying confessions. They rather serve, either expressly or by implication, to enable the pastors and through them their congregations to demonstrate to one another and to the world that they can associate and work together in spite of their differences. Frequently they have as one of their objectives the uniting of the churches as a force for social betterment in the community. Joint devotions and the sponsoring of joint services are often part of such organizations. A confessionally minded Lutheran pastor will on the basis of Romans 16:17 reply to such invitations with a polite refusal.

4

The Shepherd
Feeds the Flock

*"Stewards of the
mysteries of God"*
(1 Cor 4:1)

I. THE PASTOR AS PREACHER AND LITURGIST

Manifold as the duties of a pastor may seem to be, they ultimately have one common purpose, that of preaching the Word. This in turn is essentially preaching the gospel, for while the law does have a preparatory and auxiliary function to perform, it is the gospel which alone can produce the results at which the work of the ministry aims.

The pastor is called to act publicly for the church. To the church the Lord has given the assignment to preach ("O Zion, that bringest good tidings . . . lift up thy voice with strength," Is 40:9; "Preach the gospel," Mk 16:15; " . . . that ye should show forth the praises of him who hath called you out of darkness into his marvelous light," 1 Pe 2:9; " . . . teaching them to observe all things whatsoever I have commanded you," Mt 28:20). Therefore the ministers of the church are called heralds (1 Tm 2:7; 2 Tm 1:11; Ro 10:8,14), a term which implies boldness and exactness in relaying a message received from a king; and ambassadors (2 Cor 5:20; Eph 6:20). In Romans 12:7 what they present is called "teaching," in 1 Timothy 4:13,16, "doctrine." Preaching the Word is their one duty, for it includes also their pastoral calls on the one hand, and, on the other, the administration of the sacraments because the Word makes them what they are. While there is scriptural warrant for speaking of the fivefold use of the Word (doctrine, reproof, correction, instruction in righteousness, and comfort), it is evident that doctrine pervades all of the other uses as well. Therefore, as previously indicated, one of the chief requirements for a person in the pastoral office is that he be "apt to teach" (1 Tm 3:2).

The preaching of the Word will center about the preaching of the gospel (Mk 16:15; 2 Cor 5:18-21). This is the heart of New Testament preaching (Jn 1:17). This does not rule out the preaching of the law (witness the example of Jesus Himself and that of His apostles). There can be no appreciation of the gospel until the law has made man realize his sin and lost condition. When the gospel has worked faith and that faith seeks expression in love, it needs and welcomes the law for guidance (Ro 7:22). But the gospel is the mistress, the law is only the handmaiden.

It is only by the preaching of the gospel in public and in private that the pastor can accomplish that at which his ministry is to aim: the conversion of sinners to their God, preservation and strengthening of saving faith, love for God and man, progress in sanctification, and eternal salvation. "I commend you to God, and to the word of his grace, which is able to build you up, and to give you an inheritance among all them which are sanctified" (Ac 20:32). Therefore, on the one hand, the pastor must be ready and able to preach to his people every doctrine of God's Word with the emphasis and frequency which their particular needs indicate. "I have not shunned to declare unto you all the counsel of God" (Ac 20:17). On the other hand, he has no other authority in his congregation than that which comes when he speaks for the Lord by speaking His Word — nor should he want to have more authority than that. He is not to be "self-willed" (Tt 1:7).

The Liturgy

The pastor is a minister of the gospel also when he conducts the liturgical part of the church service. A detailed study of the evangelical nature of our various liturgies is made in the courses in liturgics which are part of a pastor's seminary training. Because leading in the liturgy is also a form of gospel proclamation, the pastor ought to accord to this function the same sense of privilege and respect which he accords to his other pastoral functions. Those parts of his attire which are not covered by the clerical vestments — shirt, tie, trousers, shoes — ought to be subdued and ought not to clash so that the attention of the congregation is diverted from the content of the liturgy to the person of the pastor. His manner ought to be dignified, but not affected. He ought to be sure of the order which is being followed lest by getting mixed up he confuse either the organist or the congregation, or both. His manner ought not to be that of one who is merely rushing through a routine which has to be disposed of, but of one who is fully aware of the sacredness and seriousness of what he is saying and doing. He ought to make sure of the pronunciation of all words which occur in the prayers and readings for the day lest by some incorrect pronunciation he divert the attention of those who know better from the content of what is being read. Enunciation ought to be exact and deliberate so that all may hear and understand. Rushing through the concluding portion of the liturgy because the sermon has exceeded the expected length is to be avoided. Abbreviation of the liturgy is the better solution if time is limited. Liturgical innovations ought never to be introduced just to satisfy some whim of the pastor. If he is convinced that a change would promote the edification of his congregation, it ought to be preceded by consultation with the church council, education of the members both privately and in their various organizations, and eventually by a decision of the congregation itself. It would be tragic if a liturgy were to irritate and anger instead of aiding in worship. In order that proper consideration might also be shown for sister congregations, it would also be well that a congregation which is contemplating a liturgical change solicit the reaction of the Commission on Worship of the WELS.

The Sermon

In an ordinary week the pastor reaches the summit of his activity as a minister of the gospel when he preaches a sermon to his assembled congregation. His courses in homiletics at the seminary served to prepare him for this activity as far as its formal side is concerned. For the material side, the content of his preaching, he needed the full scope of seminary and preseminary training and still needs continuing intensive study of the Bible. For us the sermon is the climax in the worship service of a congregation, the hub about which all else centers. Unlike Rome and certain liturgical extremists, we consider a service complete without the celebration of the Lord's Supper, but not without the sermon. An exception might be made in the case of the children's Christmas Eve service or a similar service where the recitation of Scripture passages and the gospel in song provide material for edification.

Frequency of Services

How many services are to be held on a Sunday or during the week is something which a congregation will have to decide in consultation with its pastor. If exceptional circumstances make it impossible for a congregation to have preaching services every week, it would be unwarranted judging to accuse it of despising God's Word. On the other hand, if the congregation expresses a desire for an additional service, a pastor ought to be happy to accede if it is physically possible for him to do so. For a pastor to decide to introduce additional services on his own without consultation with his congregation is both autocratic and unwise, since he must have the good will of his people if he is to have hearers at the planned additional services. He has no right to command people to attend. To cite the Third Commandment to compel them to attend would be legalistic. Nor should he forget that it is the congregation which will have to pay the additional expenses for fuel, light, and the like, which would be involved.

The Language Question

With the Pentecost miracle the Lord taught that the gospel is to be preached to people in a language which they can understand. This principle is important in shaping policy especially in our mission fields. The attitude no longer prevails that if people want to hear the gospel they should learn the language with which the preacher is familiar. Rather, the principle is that if the preacher wants to reach people with the gospel, it is his duty to learn the language with which the people whom he wants to reach are familiar.

Concern for communicating the Lord's message to people in a language which they can understand also raises the question about the use in public worship of a Bible translation which can readily be understood by people. The decision to use a translation in contemporary English ought not to be made unilaterally on the part of the pastor. Rather, the same cautions which were previously mentioned concerning liturgical innovations ought also to be observed in this matter. Moreover, since there are modern translations which contain doctrinal errors or go beyond the scope of translation by introducing the translator's interpretation, extreme caution needs to be shown in choosing a contemporary translation for use in worship services lest more harm than good result.

Hymns

The choice of fitting hymns for the worship service is considered the responsibility of the pastor since at least two of the hymns are related to the sermon. If he is to make good selections, he must know his hymnal. He will have acquired an acquaintance with a wide range of hymns during the course of his training. He can add to this knowledge if he makes the singing of hymns part of the daily devotions in his home. He will also need to explore the range of the familiarity which his members have with the hymn tunes lest he detract from their participation in the service by overloading them with unfamiliar hymns. New tunes can be introduced gradually, if possible after some practice either on the part of the choir or on the part of the entire congregation after a service. The hymn before the sermon has traditionally been considered the sermon hymn, intended to prepare the mind of the hearers for some of the thoughts of the sermon. The hymn after the sermon was considered the response of the congregation to the sermon. If only one hymn can be located which fits with the sermon, it would be wiser to save it for after the sermon to reinforce the impression left by the sermon and to aid the hearers in carrying it along into life. The choice of hymns for festivals and special occasions should cause no problem since festival hymns, like the sermon, all emphasize the prevailing thought of the day.

The Robe

Lutheran congregations expect their pastors to wear a pulpit robe. For a pastor to refuse to wear one under ordinary circumstances would cause unnecessary confusion and would thus be an abuse of Christian liberty. Furthermore, they expect their pastor to wear the kind of robe which they have been accustomed to see their pastors wear. Again, it would be unwise and uncharitable for a pastor to appear before his congregation in ornate trappings without first having discussed the matter with the congregation on as many levels as possible. Without previous instruction, people are apt to regard the wearing of alb, surplice, and stole as Romanism. On the other hand, if they have become accustomed to the more elaborate vestments, it would be unwise for a pastor because of personal preference to refuse offhand to wear them. These matters are too minor to warrant disturbing a single soul. What has been said here also applies *mutatis mutandis* to the use of the clerical collar.

When the robe is to be worn will be determined by what a congregation is accustomed to. We doubt whether there are many, if any, congregations which still demand the use of the robe at private communions or baptisms. If the decision is left to the pastor, he will restrict the wearing of the robe to the church building. Since many pastors greet their members as they leave the church and have not had time to remove their robe, it would be going too far to insist that the pulpit robe belongs only in the chancel area.

The Sacristy

The equipment and size of the sacristy vary greatly. As a minimum there ought to be clothing hooks and hangers, a mirror, a table to hold comb and brush and books, and at least one chair. It is highly desirable that there also be toilet facilities and a wash basin. At all events the sacristy ought to be clean, lest a room so close to the sanctuary stand in horrible contrast to it. If the pastor smokes, he ought to be able to curb his habit sufficiently to keep from smoking in the sacristy. The smell of smoke emanating from the sacristy into the church is inappropriate, while the smell of tobacco on the pastor's breath or on the hand that distributes the communion wafer can for some be nauseating.

Summary: While all of a pastor's ministry centers about the preaching of the gospel, in a sense this activity reaches its climax in the public worship services of his congregation. Decorum and dignity, efficiency and order in the chancel and pulpit are to be cultivated so that the attention of the worshiping congregation may remain focused on the content of the order of service and of the sermon.

II. BAPTISM

The pastor, according to the call he has received from his congregation, is to administer the sacrament of baptism in its midst. He must assure himself that it is performed in a manner which includes everything essential for a valid baptism. He must determine to whom the sacrament is to be administered. He will show discretion in following ecclesiastical customs associated with the baptismal rite.

A. Administering a Valid Baptism

In the Name of the Triune God

In instituting baptism, the Lord commanded that it be done "in the name of the Father, and of the Son, and of the Holy Ghost" (Mt 28:19). It is essential to a valid baptism to perform it in the name of the only true God revealed in Scripture, the triune God. A Christian congregation, which confesses the triune God, calls its pastor to administer baptism in the name of the God it confesses. It should thus be self-evident for the pastor in baptizing to use the trinitarian formula contained in Jesus' institution. This can reassure the recipient throughout his life that there is no question about his having received baptism in the name of the Trinity as Jesus prescribed.

The three references in the book of Acts (2:38; 10:48; 19:5) to baptism in the name of the Lord Jesus Christ do not compel the conclusion that the apostles used a formula in the baptismal rite which included only Jesus' name. Luke simply wants to show that these baptisms were performed by the command of the Lord Jesus and in accordance with His institution. Nevertheless, should a Christian congregation that confesses itself to the Father, Son, and Holy Ghost as the one true God baptize with the briefer formulation, "in the name of the Lord Jesus Christ," such a baptism would not for that reason have to be considered invalid. In naming Jesus, they cannot but include the Father who sent Him as Mediator, and the Holy Spirit who testifies to Him as the Redeemer from sin, even if they are not specifically named.

65

The trinitarian form must not be looked on as a ritualistic incantation of magical words according to a specific form. If this were the case, the words would need to be spoken in the original language used by Jesus, and any grammatical error or slip of the tongue in pronouncing the words would make the baptism doubtful.

What determines whether a baptism is truly performed in the name of the triune God is not only the formulation of the rite, but the content of the words spoken. Since words do not always have the same meaning for all people, the congregation that baptizes will through its confession show what content the words it uses in the formula have for them and reveal whether this is in agreement with Scripture's original meaning.

A church, however, which knows the triune God as the only true God will want to use a form that most clearly expresses this confession. There is no better way of doing this than by using the trinitarian form our Savior spoke at the time of institution. Any departure from this, while it would not invalidate the baptism as such, could at some time raise doubts and questions for the recipient. This possibility must be avoided.

Water

According to Christ's institution the use of water is essential to a valid baptism. The term used by Jesus, *baptizein*, means "to dip, immerse," or "wash" (*baptismos*, a washing or cleansing) in a religious rite. Although the term is used figuratively when Scripture speaks of being baptized with the Holy Ghost (Mk 1:5; Jn 1:33; Ac 1:5) or with fire (Mt 3:11; Lk 3:16), the meaning in connection with the sacrament instituted by Christ can only be that of a literal washing with water (cf Jn 3:5; Eph 5:26; Ac 10:47). Since water seldom is found in a pure state, the fact that other substances may be mixed with the water does not prevent its use in baptism. Whatever commonly is recognized as water may be used. However, any substance or liquid not known as water should not be used even if it does contain some moisture (water in that sense). At best, its use would raise great doubt about the validity of the sacrament. Scripture leads to the simple conclusion: without water there is no baptism. Under normal conditions the pastor will arrange for clean, warm water for baptism.

Jesus gave no express command about the manner of applying the water, whether by immersion, pouring, or sprinkling. *Bap-*

66

tizein can refer to any manner of ceremonial washing as is evident from Mark 7:4. Scripture sees symbolical significance in the various methods of applying water in baptism. Immersion best symbolizes being "buried with him by baptism into death" (Ro 6:3), while pouring symbolizes well the washing away of sins (*apolouoo*) spoken of in Acts 22:16. The purpose of water in baptism is not to cleanse the body. Its use symbolizes cleansing of the soul (cf 1 Pe 3:21). Thus the cleansing power of baptism does not depend on the quantity of water used nor on the manner of its application. Pouring, or sprinkling, water with the hand on the head is the common method used among Lutherans. A baptismal shell may be found convenient, since there is less need for the pastor to dry his hand after its use.

The Lord does not specify how often the water is to be applied. The usual custom of applying the water three times shows symbolically that the baptism is in the name of the triune God. However, a single application of water does not invalidate a baptism. But application of water there must be. The pastor will do well to use enough so that no question about the validity of the baptism can arise.

The One Who Baptizes

Scripture in no way makes the validity of baptism dependent on the person who baptizes. Since the congregation has called a pastor to administer the means of grace, good order requires that he will normally function as the one who does the baptizing. However, a baptism performed in an emergency by any lay person is equally valid if nothing that is essential is omitted. The ratification of a lay baptism in a public service does not serve to validate the baptism but is to give certainty that what is essential for a valid baptism was duly carried out. Even if the person who performed the baptismal act should be an unbeliever, the baptism is valid if Christ's institution was followed in all essential factors.

Summary: According to Jesus' institution, it is necessary for a valid baptism to apply water in some manner in the name of the Father, Son, and Holy Ghost. Any "baptism" that does not employ water or is not performed in the name of the one true God, the triune God, is not a true baptism. The manner and frequency of applying the water are adiaphora. The validity of the baptism is not affected by the person who performs the baptismal act.

B. Persons to Be Baptized

The Unbaptized

Baptism is to be administered only once. Unlike the Lord's Supper, there is no command to baptize the same person repeatedly nor is there any example of such practice in Scripture. Acts 19:5 does not speak of rebaptizing, but rather of baptizing those whose baptism was found to be questionable or invalid. Thus the pastor must determine not only whether a baptism of some kind was ever performed, but whether it was a valid one.

An Invalid Baptism Is No Baptism

Those are to be considered as unbaptized who received a baptism that was not according to Jesus' institution. Any religious group that as a matter of public confession denies what is essential to the sacrament is not carrying out Jesus' command and is not administering a valid baptism. What was said above must be noted here again: Not the faith or unbelief of the individual who performs the baptismal act determines its validity. If it did, one could never gain certainty, for the baptism performed by a hypocrite would be invalid. Baptism is a gift bestowed not by the officiant, but by the Lord Jesus. The Lord has given it to His church to be administered according to His institution. Whether a church is doing this will be evident from its confession. Any religious group that openly as a matter of confession denies the triune God, and with it the divinity and lordship of Jesus, has no Word of God and reveals that an essential factor of a valid baptism is lacking. Even if such a group should use a form that follows the external wording as found in Scripture, one must remember that not the mere sound of the words spoken, but their meaning, or content, are determinative. The god whom they serve is an idol even if they may choose in baptizing to use the same outward sounds in referring to him. The Lord Jesus and His Word are not present with a religious group that has denied Him. He has not entrusted His sacrament to them. They do not perform His works, no matter how much they may cry out, "Lord, Lord" (Mt 7:21-23).

Thus in determining the validity of a baptism the pastor examines not the faith of the one who performed it, but the confession of the religious group for whom the individual was acting. Their confession does not create or destroy baptism but reveals whether Jesus' Word, which alone establishes a valid baptism, was present and being followed.

Among those who clearly deny the Trinity are the Jehovah's Witnesses, the Mormons, the Christian Scientists, the Unitarian-Universalists, the Jews. Because of the increasing vagueness and meaninglessness of the confession of many churches, it is sometimes difficult to become certain as to their true position with respect to God and Christ Jesus. False doctrine, however, even in regard to baptism, which does not destroy the essentials of baptism does not invalidate the sacrament, as, for example, unbiblical teachings of Reformed churches about the purpose and efficacy of baptism, and the ecclesiastical traditions, often involving superstition, which Rome associates with it.

When There Is Doubt

Those about whose baptism there is doubt are to be considered as unbaptized. Faith cannot find an anchor in baptism if the baptism itself is in doubt. This includes not only doubt about its validity, but also about its ever having taken place.

The baptism of an abandoned child that is found with nothing more than an anonymous note affirming its having been baptized remains doubtful. An emergency baptism performed without the presence of witnesses could give rise to doubt. If an adult vaguely remembers having been told by now deceased parents that he was baptized but has no certificate, and no church records to corroborate his memory can be found, a strong element of doubt is present. To baptize oneself (se-baptism) is a doubtful practice, since everything Scripture says about administering baptism does not fit in with it.

When there is doubt about an earlier baptism, the pastor proceeds the same as with any unbaptized person. Luther rejects the Roman practice of administering a conditional baptism ("If you have not been baptized, I baptize you," etc.) as one that gives no certainty to the recipient since it does not dispel the doubt about the earlier baptism and with its condition makes the second similarly doubtful.[1] The question can properly be asked whether a conditional baptism is a baptism at all.

Only living persons should be baptized, since only for those whose time of grace has not come to an end through death can

1. St. L. X, 2135.

baptism be a washing of regeneration (Tt 3:5). This excludes the stillborn child. To baptize an unborn infant is not possible, since the water should be applied to the child's body and not merely to that of the mother. Whatever is born and has life, though grossly deformed, may be considered to be a person with a soul and should be baptized.[2] The principle remains: When in doubt, baptize.

Adults

Adults are to be instructed in preparation for baptism. This was the practice among the apostles, whom Jesus instructed and sent out. It was only after a lengthy sermon had had its effect that those who gladly received the Word were baptized on Pentecost day (Ac 2:14-41). Likewise the Ethiopian eunuch (Ac 8:35-37), Cornelius (Ac 10:34-48), and the jailer at Philippi (Ac 16:30-33) were instructed and gave evidence that the Word had successfully worked in their hearts before they were baptized.

How much instruction is necessary before baptism? Scripture does not give a direct, detailed answer. A cursory reading of the examples from Acts may give the impression that the instruction was very brief, since baptism occurred on the same day as the instruction. However, in almost all cases (the jailer may be an exception) the apostles were addressing such who knew and believed the Old Testament with its Messianic promises and needed only further instruction to identify Jesus as the fulfillment. An examination of Peter's Pentecost sermon, for example, removes any thought that the apostles proceeded in a superficial manner, particularly when we remember that the account in Acts is no doubt only a summary of what was said. It should also be noted that in the postapostolic age, when an increasing number of converts had little if any previous knowledge of Scripture, a catechumenate of up to two or three years often preceded baptism.

Generally the same basic understanding of Christian doctrine is advisable for adult baptism as for adult confirmation (cf the chapter on Education, pp 124-126). Through baptism or confirmation the individual becomes a member of the congregation. One should not baptize anyone into a faith he does not adequately know. One should not receive anyone into membership who

2. In 1973 a two-headed baby boy was born in Argentina. The decision to perform two baptisms appears to have been a good one. *Milwaukee Sentinel*, April 27, 1973.

does not know the confession of the congregation. To delay baptism until the way of salvation and basic Christian doctrine has been learned is not to despise this gift of God. To rush into baptism without adequate preparation could result in casting "pearls before swine" (Mt 7:6). The faith that is worked and nourished by the gospel in which the adult receives instruction already lays hold of eternal life. On the other hand, when terminal illness restricts the time available for instruction, the pastor may arrange his instruction in such a way that the adult may receive baptism very soon as an added comfort in the face of death and eternity.

The Holy Spirit must work the desire for baptism through the Word of salvation. The pastor must guard against permitting family or other considerations to exert the kind of pressure that could in fact hinder the free working of the Spirit. Special care is in place when a marriage is conditioned on the reception of baptism by the non-Christian party.

The pastor may wish to encourage adults to receive baptism in a regular service of the congregation. The congregation will hear the confession of faith and rejoice that another sinner has come to repentance and is receiving the washing away of sins in Holy Baptism. This ought, however, not to be encouraged in such a way that a person receives the impression that such a public ceremony is necessary and withdraws from baptism entirely because of his shyness. There should be the option of a privately administered baptism. Witnesses, however, should be present even though this is not essential for a valid baptism. These witnesses may be the congregation's elders, representing the congregation into whose membership the adult is being received.

The question may be asked at what age children should begin to receive instruction in preparation for baptism. This will have to be determined by the mental development of each child. The amount of instruction can be adjusted according to the child's ability to comprehend. If some instruction is possible, it should not be neglected lest baptism appear to the child as a meaningless ceremony.

Children

The Lutheran Confessions assert: "Children, too, should be baptized" (AC, IX, 2). It is not the intention here to establish the scriptural correctness of this statement, since that is done in sys-

71

tematic theology. Suffice it merely to say that God's command to baptize "all nations" must be understood to include children unless it is shown from Scripture that God Himself excludes them from it. This God has not done. The pastor thus has been called to baptize also children.

Who Decides?

Since children are incapable of making the choice for themselves, the question arises as to who is to decide on baptism for them. The Lord has made the parents responsible for rearing their children and calls on children to be obedient to their parents (Col 3:20,21; Pr 1:8,9; 13:24). This parental responsibility extends also to the religious training of the children (Gn 17:23,25; Mk 10:13-16; Eph 6:4). It is thus the parents, or the guardians who may have replaced them, who are responsible for making the decision and bringing their children to baptism. The decision of one parent is adequate, but may be difficult to carry out if there is violent objection on the part of the other. It is to be hoped that the objecting parent may be brought around at least so far as to permit the baptism even if he does not desire it, especially if this involves the father, who is head of the family.

After a child has reached sufficient maturity and understanding, the child's decision may be accepted even against the parents' will. The pastor will have to accept the child's decision to obey God rather than man. If parents have permitted or even requested the church to instruct their child, and this instruction leads the child to desire baptism, the parents should realize that they have forfeited the right to object.

Under no circumstances should the pastor become a party to or tacitly permit the use of deception in baptizing a child. The end does not justify the means.

When?

Scripture does not designate the exact time when baptism is to be administered. Under the Old Testament law God required circumcision on the eighth day. The New Testament has no such law for baptism. However, the child's need because it is flesh born of flesh (Jn 3:6) and God's promise that baptism is a "washing of re-

72

generation" (Tt 3:5) should lead parents to recognize the importance of avoiding delay.

Generally the church administers this sacrament in connection with its public worship. The parents should be urged to arrange for baptism in the first service possible. If there is any question about the child's health, immediate baptism is called for.

Should We Refuse Baptism?

Baptism as a "washing of regeneration" is a means of grace and brings immediate blessing. It is not administered in the hope that sometime in the future the gospel as it is taught to the child will work faith. Hence the pastor should not categorically refuse to baptize a child if the parents do not promise that the child will in the future receive biblical instruction. Since this question arises primarily with unchurched parents, the pastor should point out that through baptism their child becomes a member of the church, and the church recognizes its responsibility for teaching and will expect to carry this out even though the parents are not ready to make any promises. Should the parents upon hearing the church's claim withdraw their request for the child's baptism, the responsibility remains entirely theirs.

When a child is baptized, its name should immediately be entered on the cradle roll of the congregation. This should help to maintain regular contact with the child and its parents as the church consciously follows through on its responsibility toward a baptized member.

Summary: According to Scripture an individual is to be baptized only once. The pastor will determine whether an individual seeking baptism has been baptized previously, and, if so, whether his baptism was a valid one. If there is doubt about a baptism having taken place or about its validity, baptism is to be administered. Adults are baptized subsequent to instruction in the Word of God which enables them to confess their faith and to be received into membership. Children receive baptism at the request of their parents or guardians, whom God has made responsible also for their religious training. They should be baptized without delay and receive instruction in God's Word as mental growth permits.

C. Baptismal Customs

Whatever in the baptismal ceremony goes beyond the essentials of Christ's institution falls into the category of adiaphora. This does not mean that these additions may not be useful and beneficial, but that they are not necessary for a valid baptism. It also does not mean that the pastor should feel free to change them solely on his own initiative, since he is acting for the congregation in performing a baptism. The Formula of Concord points out "that the community of God of every locality and every age has authority to change such ceremonies according to circumstances, as it may be most profitable and edifying to the community of God" (Ep X, 4). For a pastor to make changes at will, however, could result in misunderstanding and even cause offense to the poorly informed.

The Baptismal Rite

In the beginning the apostolic church in its baptismal rite simply used the words of institution in Matthew. By the second century the rite received additions meant to enrich the act with meaningful symbols in order to demonstrate the significance and power of baptism. However, some of these took on sacramental significance.and an importance that in time detracted from the baptism itself. In his German "Order of Baptism" of 1523 Luther still retained most of these accretions but warned:

> Now remember, too, that in baptism the external things are the least important, such as blowing under the eyes, signing with the cross, putting salt into the mouth, putting spittle and clay into the ears and nose, anointing the breast and shoulders with oil, signing the crown of the head with the chrism, putting on the christening robe, placing a burning candle in the hand, and whatever else has been added by man to embellish baptism. For most assuredly baptism can be performed without all these."[3]

Luther stresses the use of the Word of God and prayer in the rite: " . . . listen to God's Word, and earnestly join in prayer."[4] At the time, Luther, as he said, "did not want to make any marked changes in the order of baptism. . . . The human additions do not

3. L.W. LIII, 102.
4. *Ibid.*, p 102.

matter very much, as long as baptism itself is administered with God's Word, true faith, and serious prayer."[5]

In "The Order of Baptism Newly Revised" of 1526 Luther eliminated many of these additions. By this time the churches that followed the Lutheran Reformation were ready for these changes. Luther's views of the baptismal rite and its various parts and his way of making changes reveal a pastoral heart concerned about the people and can serve as an example to the Lutheran pastor today.

The use of the Word of God and of prayer in the baptismal rite has genuine value. They are worthwhile additions to the simple formula of Matthew. These also require little explanation. Their value lies in that they instruct and edify.

Symbolical actions need explaining and must not be permitted to assume an almost magical significance. Making the sign of the cross on the forehead and breast is explained in the words the pastor speaks, "in token that thou hast been redeemed by Christ the Crucified."[6] The laying on of hands during prayer and a benediction should not be understood as conferring a special supernatural blessing, but as a direct way of showing that the petitions and blessing apply to this child.

Problems in understanding may arise especially in connection with the questions addressed to the child and answered by its sponsors for the child. These involve the *abrenuntiatio* and the *credo*. The significance of the questions is easily lost if the introducing words are not carefully noted: "to signify thereby what God in and through Baptism works in him."[7]

That any or all of these ceremonial elements may be dropped when an emergency situation arises is self-evident. The pastor will instruct his members as to what is essential for a valid baptism in case of emergency. On the last page of *The Lutheran Hymnal* there is "A Short Form of Holy Baptism in Cases of Necessity."

Sponsors

A custom of long standing is the use of sponsors in baptism. It originated in connection with adult baptism in the early Chris-

5. *Ibid.*, p 103.
6. *The Lutheran Agenda* (St. Louis: Concordia, 1949), p 2.
7. *Ibid.*, p 7.

tian church when the sponsor literally "sponsored" the person to be baptized, assuring the church of the person's fidelity. This was to prevent infiltration of such who were hostile to the church at a time when the church was still under persecution. With the decrease of adult baptisms and the growing number of infant baptisms, the custom was retained with a changed purpose. The "Exhortation to the Sponsors" in *The Lutheran Agenda* reminds sponsors of the role assigned to them by the church: To confess "in this sacred act the faith of the Christian Church in the Triune God"; "to bear witness publicly in the *child's* stead that by Holy Baptism as a means of grace *he* obtains and possesses the saving faith in the one true God and renounces the devil and his wicked works"; to pray for the child, remind him of his baptism, and aid, if necessary, that the child "may be brought up in the true knowledge and fear of God, according to the teachings of the Lutheran Church and faithfully keep the baptismal covenant unto the end."[8]

These responsibilities distinguish a sponsor from a mere witness. Any responsible person may serve as a witness to testify to the fact that water was applied in the name of the Father, Son, and Holy Ghost. Nevertheless, those who are openly hostile to the church, avowed unbelievers, or atheists are hardly desirable as witnesses, since even this kind of participation at the ceremony on their part could give the impression of disrespect for the Lord's sacrament.

The role the church has assigned to sponsors limits the choice of persons to those who can in good conscience be expected to assume the role and perform its responsibilities. This excludes not only unbelievers, but all who belong to heretical churches, and limits the choice to those who are in confessional agreement with the church that administers the baptism. While the custom of having sponsors is an adiaphoron, the choice of the persons, in view of the role they are to serve, is not. The Word of God, e.g., Romans 16:17 and 2 Corinthians 6:14, must find application in the choice of those who are to assume spiritual, Christian responsibilities for the church's members.

The pastor does well to instruct parents in advance about the choice of proper sponsors. Once the parents have made their choice and asked someone to serve, practical and emotional

8. *Ibid.*, p 4.

factors often make a reversal of the invitation difficult. As a practical solution the pastor may then advise use of a baptismal rite without sponsors so that those who have been asked serve simply as witnesses. If this is proposed and explained to the parents in a tactful manner, this solution generally is acceptable. The pastor does well to avoid a serious confrontation with members on a custom that in itself is an adiaphoron. To gain an objective hearing on the fellowship question involved in the choice of persons is often difficult at a time when practical difficulties and emotional factors can becloud objective judgment.

Some congregations have sought to solve the problems involved in the choice of sponsors by adopting revised baptismal rites that abandon the customary concept of sponsorship (e.g., by having the parents bring the child to the font and speaking for it). The question is in place whether the custom of having sponsors is more of a tradition than a practical necessity and whether changes can be made that will be in keeping with the needs and circumstances of the present. A pastor and congregation should, however, remember that their brotherly relationship with sister congregations may make it inadvisable simply to make major changes in this custom independently, lest there be a proliferation of baptismal rites that could become confusing and offensive.

No baptism ought to be delayed so that the chosen sponsors can be present. Proxies can replace the official sponsors at the ceremony. Since they witness the baptism, also their names should be entered in the record of the baptism.

In the case of adults or of children who are able to answer for themselves at the time of baptism, sponsors are not needed to speak for them. Witnesses ought, however, still to be present.

Practical Suggestions

The custom of announcing the birth of a child in a service and of calling on the congregation to join in prayer is a good one and should be encouraged. If the parents do not initiate the request for such an announcement and prayer, the pastor may solicit it when the birth is announced to him.

The pastor should not fail to visit the mother in the hospital. This gives him a natural opportunity to speak about the child's baptism and the choice of sponsors, and about parental responsibility for the soul God has entrusted to their care. If the child's health is in question or if it is born with some defect, the parents should receive the pastor's special concern.

It is well to get all necessary information for the baptismal certificate and for the church records at the time arrangements for the baptism are made. Particular care is in order to insure the accurate spelling of all names. An application form for baptism (see Appendix) will prove helpful in securing such information. The information should be entered into the permanent church records without delay after the baptism.

There is no fixed time in the service for baptism. It is, however, generally preferable not to delay the baptism until after the sermon. The service may begin with a baptismal hymn with the baptism following immediately. Or the baptism may follow the Scripture readings, replacing the Creed, which is included in the baptism ceremony. An usher may show the participants (sponsors, witnesses, parents) where they may conveniently sit during the service, lead them to the font for the ceremony and back to their seats after the baptism.

The pastor will avoid embarrassment from a possible lapse of memory if he has the child's name in written form before him. This may be on a slip of paper in the agenda or on the envelope of the certificate that can be placed on the font. If the pastor is doubtful about how the parents wish a certain name to be pronounced, he should consult them. He may find it convenient to give the certificate to the sponsors immediately after the baptism. In any case, it is advisable to prepare the certificate in advance and to see to it that the parents receive it on the day of the baptism.

If there is more than one baptism, the pastor should inform the participants as to the order in which the baptisms will be performed. An alphabetical sequence appears convenient.

The pastor must guard against becoming the cause for delaying a baptism. If the pastor is absent for a Sunday, the guest pastor can perform the baptism. Any suggestion by the people to delay the baptism until the pastor's return should be rejected.

The pastor who has numerous baptisms must take care lest they become a commonplace routine for him and must guard against reading the baptismal ceremony in a mechanical, monotonous manner. Let him not lose his joy over every sinner to whom the Lord through his ministry grants the washing of regeneration and assurance of eternal life.

Summary: Over the centuries, baptismal customs have developed and the order of baptism has received numerous additions. These, however, must be recognized as adiaphora in that they are not necessary for a valid baptism. They can, however, serve a good purpose and edify if they are properly used and understood. The use of sponsors, too, is an adiaphoron, even though it is an ancient custom. Because of the role sponsors have been asked to assume, they should be in confessional agreement with the church that administers the baptism. Others may serve as witnesses. The pastor will guard against careless errors, especially in the pronunciation and spelling of names as he performs the baptism and enters it in the congregation's records. Let him recognize the importance of every baptism.

III. THE LORD'S SUPPER

While the gospel is to be preached to "all nations," the Lord's Supper is intended only for certain Christians. It was given to nourish and strengthen those who already know Christ as their Savior. The Lord has placed restrictions on its use. These the church is to observe lest someone receive the sacrament unworthily and bring judgment on himself. Scripture leads to a practice that is called "close communion."[9]

The pastor, called as steward of God's mysteries (1 Cor 4:1), administers the Lord's Supper for the congregation. The Lord bids him watch for the souls of the flock (He 13:17) and warn them against sin (Eze 3:17-21), responsibilities that he must remember in his stewardship of this sacrament. Thus the pastor must know who according to Scripture may be admitted. He will follow practices that encourage worthy and frequent reception of the sacrament. He lets the Word of God alone be normative for the manner of its celebration.

A. Who May Be Admitted

The Baptized

Through baptism God establishes a covenant with the individual and identifies him as His own. In baptism the individual

---

9. Both terms, "close" and "closed" communion, are applied to this practice. The former stresses that those who are one in faith enter into this intimate fellowship in communion. The other stresses that the communion is "closed" against those outside the fellowship. The former is the preferable term, listed in the dictionary.

79

puts on Christ (Ga 3:27). Only those who have become identified with the Lord through baptism may receive Holy Communion. That this was the practice in the apostolic church is evident, e.g., from Acts 2:41f and from 1 Corinthians 11. This is analogous also to the requirement of circumcision for those admitted to the Passover meal (Ex 12:48).

Those Who Examine Themselves

However, even among the baptized only those who can and do "examine" themselves (1 Cor 11:27-29) are to eat and drink in the sacrament. This means that they recognize and condemn sin in themselves and that they, as Paul puts it, "discern the Lord's body." They know and believe that Jesus' death on the cross is the atonement for sin and that in the sacrament they receive His body and blood as pledge and assurance of God's grace toward them. "Discerning the Lord's body" thus involves more than belief in the bare doctrine of the real presence.

Not all baptized Christians are able to examine themselves. Children do not have the maturity or understanding for such self-examination. At what point in their development and education this ability can be assumed to be present Scripture does not state directly. Most often the rite of confirmation has been used among Lutherans as a practical dividing point.[10] Some mental retardates may never reach the point of self-examination for the reception of communion.

It can also happen that individuals again lose the ability to examine themselves. Mental illness may result in loss of contact with reality. Senility may lead to utter confusion and forgetfulness. The pastor must, however, remember that such people may have lucid moments when they may receive the sacrament worthily. With those who are in a coma or unconscious one must await consciousness before giving the sacrament. The deaf and dumb, on the other hand, should not be turned away because of their handicaps. With them there may indeed be a problem of communication, but this can be solved. Their handicap does not as such make them unable to examine themselves.

10. This is discussed in greater detail in the chapter on "Education," where also changes made by some Lutheran bodies in their position are examined.

Eating and Drinking Unworthily

Not all who are baptized and have the necessary maturity and understanding do in fact examine themselves in the sense of 1 Corinthians 11:28. Theirs is an unworthy eating and drinking, "not discerning the Lord's body." They are "guilty of the body and blood of the Lord." Such a person "eats and drinks judgment to himself" (1 Cor 11:29-NASB). This is impenitence. The impenitent eats and drinks unworthily.

Neither the church nor its pastor has the ability or the right to examine and judge hearts. The pastor will accept the confession of the mouth and dare not judge a person to be impenitent on the basis of feelings the pastor has about that person's sincerity. But when impenitence has become outwardly evident, the pastor must avoid becoming a partaker of another's sin by knowingly giving communion to the openly impenitent (1 Tm 5:22). Withholding communion is then a forceful preaching of the law to call the sinner to repentance. Likewise such withholding will avoid public offense which could result from giving communion to one whose sin is public and whose impenitence is evident. If, however, the sin and impenitence are known only to the pastor, he can only warn the impenitent sinner against receiving communion as a judgment. Should such a person appear at the Lord's table in spite of the warning, passing him by would be to reprove him openly. Such reproof must wait until the whole matter has become public.

To prevent offense, repentance for gross sin that is public knowledge should somehow have become public before the penitent sinner receives communion. How public the repentance must be cannot categorically be determined for every situation. How widely known was the sin? Will a public confession in fact publicize the sin? How great is the possibility for offense? Will receiving the person back to the Lord's Table possibly in itself be recognized by the congregation as evidence of repentance? The answers to such questions can guide the pastor to a course of action that avoids giving the impression that public confession prior to communion is a necessary satisfaction for sin.

It should be noted that there is no particular list of sins that automatically exclude from Holy Communion. Not sin in itself results in unworthy reception of communion. If that were the case, who could receive it worthily? But impenitence, sin that is not repented of, results in unworthy eating and drinking.

Recognizing Impenitence

Those who persist publicly in works of the flesh (cf Ga 5:19-21) with no evident effort or desire to avoid them must be told the judgment of Scripture that "they which do such things shall not inherit the kingdom of God." To refuse reconciliation and forgiveness toward anyone is a sign of unbelief (Mt 5:23-25; 18:21,22, 28-34). Whoever is unforgiving loses the Lord's forgiveness and unworthily uses the sacrament of Christ's body and blood, the pledge of the Lord's forgiveness. Hatred, failure to forgive, refusal of reconciliation may become evident by a lawsuit (1 Cor 6:1-7), especially if it is against a fellow Christian. Christians should be able to settle their differences among themselves and should be willing to suffer loss in the process, if necessary. This hardly applies, however, to a "friendly suit" the only purpose of which may be, for example, to establish the application of the law so that an insurance company will know and carry out its responsibility under the policy. In such a case, refusal of reconciliation may not be involved at all. Repentance furthermore includes bringing forth fruits "in keeping with your repentance" (Mt 3:8-NASB; Ac 26:20). What these fruits must be is not always evident, and the pastor must guard against making demands arbitrarily. Scripture does, however, show that repentance includes the effort at restitution when this is possible (Lk 19:8). Refusal even to attempt meliorating the evil consequences of one's sin hardly is evidence of true repentance.

Communion as an Expression of Fellowship

Although in communion the Lord gives the individual His body and blood for the personal assurance of forgiveness, receiving this blessing at the same altar with others has further implications. St. Paul writes: "We being many are one bread, and one body; for we are all partakers of that one bread" (1 Cor 10:17). Those who partake of the sacrament together thereby express that they are one body in Christ. Fellowship in the sacrament is an expression of confessional fellowship, evidence of unity of faith.

The pastor must therefore not only ask who may receive communion at all, but also who may receive communion in fellowship with his congregation. Normally the pastor communes the members of his congregation. They have called him to serve them in

82

this way (Ac 20:28; 1 Pe 5:2). Anyone else must establish his confessional unity with the congregation before being received as a guest communicant.

Membership in a sister congregation generally suffices for this. The pastor must, however, be sure that his receiving the guest communicant does not violate another pastor's call or interfere with his ministry. Members who will be absent from their home congregation for longer periods of time, like students or servicemen, may be given communion cards that identify them and commend them to sister churches as communion guests.

Whoever holds membership in a heretical church must first clarify his confessional position before being received at the Lord's table. It must be clear that he cannot promiscuously receive communion in two churches with diverging confessions.

Encouraging Frequent Communion

The fact that not everyone is to receive communion and that the pastor has the responsibility of withholding this sacrament under certain circumstances should not lead him to think primarily of keeping the unworthy from it. He recognizes the blessing the Lord would give through this sacrament and will encourage faithful use of it.

In providing encouragement, the impression must not be given that to receive communion a specific number of times is necessary as a part of fulfilling one's Christian duty. The Lord does not by law require communion attendance. But He does graciously invite sinners to His Supper for the comfort and healing it offers. Let the pastor work toward more frequent use of this sacrament by fanning the flame of desire for it. This includes demonstrating the need for it by exposing sin and by reminding his hearers that the fruits of Jesus' death are offered to the sinner personally and directly as he eats and drinks Jesus' body and blood.

The Pastor as Communicant

The pastor receives communion at conferences and conventions. He, however, is a communicant of his congregation and may wish to commune in fellowship with the members and thus supplement the less frequent opportunities which conferences provide. For him to commune himself cannot simply be rejected as a practice that violates Scripture and the Confessions and that invalidates the sacrament. The self-communion rejected in the Smalcald Articles (II,II,8) was that which occurred apart from the congregation in Rome's private mass. Nevertheless, a better solution so that the pastor may receive communion with his congregation is for the congregation to designate someone to serve the pastor. This can be a layman, perhaps a member of the church council. Where there is a Christian day school the congregation may wish to assign this responsibility to one of the male teachers.[11] Whatever course is chosen, the pastor must assure himself of the full understanding of the congregation.

Summary: Baptism precedes admission to Holy Communion. Only such baptized Christians who can and do examine themselves according to 1 Corinthians 11:27-29 are to receive the sacrament. Children must first acquire this ability; others like the mentally ill and the senile may again lose it. The impenitent fail to examine themselves, eating and drinking unworthily, not discerning the Lord's body. The pastor must guard against giving communion to those whose impenitence is openly evident lest he become partaker of their sin. However, he is not to attempt to judge hearts, but must limit his judgment to what can be openly observed. Joint communion is an expression of fellowship and is to be practiced among those who are one in their confession. The pastor will encourage faithful attendance at the Lord's Table and seek a solution for his own communing that will be understood by the people.

B. Practices that Encourage Worthy and Frequent Communion

Communion Announcement

Lutheran churches that practice close communion have followed some form of communion announcement. While close communion has a biblical basis (Mt 7:6; 1 Cor 5:11,13; 2 Th 3:6; Ro 16:17), the custom of announcing one's intention of receiving com-

---

11. For a complete discussion of this subject, see I. Habeck, "Who May Officiate at the Lord's Supper?" W.L.Q. LXV (July 1969), 187-205.

munion to the pastor arose within the church, has no divine command, and thus is an adiaphoron. It does, however, serve useful purposes and can contribute toward worthy reception of the sacrament and toward its being administered according to the will of God.

Purpose

By requiring announcement prior to the communion service the pastor can to some extent control admission to the sacrament he distributes. This does not mean that communion announcement should enable the pastor finally to begin discipline with a delinquent member. The pastor should warn and admonish as the need arises and not wait until communion announcement. Besides, the limited time available during the announcement hardly is suited to disciplinary admonition. But the custom of announcing does allow the pastor to know in advance who will appear before the altar for communion and gives him opportunity to intervene should a member who is under discipline plan to attend.

By announcing in the communion service, either verbally or in the service bulletin, that the congregation practices close communion, and by adding a brief explanation of the requirement for communion announcement, the pastor may deter strangers from approaching the Lord's Table unannounced. Without such an explanation visitors, especially from churches that have open communion, may take it for granted that they may receive the sacrament. To pass anyone by, once he is at the altar, has its difficulties. It involves a split-second decision that becomes all the more difficult if the pastor does not as yet know all the congregation members well. It becomes virtually impossible when two pastors officiate. Most often the bread is distributed by the man least familiar with the congregation. Once the communicant has received the bread, the cup should not be withheld. And if the bread has been withheld, this information must be given to the other pastor so that he can withhold the cup also. It is to be hoped that the practice of communion announcement can be used in such a way that such decisions will not confront the pastor during distribution.

Communion announcement can serve also a more directly spiritual purpose. An extensive discussion with each individual about

85

sin, the way of salvation, and the sacrament is generally not possible or necessary. The few minutes that can be allowed for each communicant, especially in a larger congregation, do not permit the kind of *Exploratio* that was encouraged in past generations.[12] However, it may give the pastor an opportunity to touch on some point that seems called for in the case of a particular member, or the parishioner may take the opportunity to ask a question which may have been on his mind for some time. If more time is needed, the pastor can make an appointment for a more extensive discussion. Apart from such opportunities to speak with individuals to meet their specific needs, the pastor will do well to prepare a few words that can be spoken in an informal way to all who come to announce. These words can center on the blessings of the sacrament for the sinner and can be varied to fit the seasons of the church year. There is always time for the pastor to wish the communicant the Lord's blessing in the sacrament.

The custom of having a confessional address or a special confessional service for the communicants has passed out of existence almost entirely. Some pastors have found a replacement in connection with communion announcement. Each half hour during the times designated for announcement a short (5 to 10 minute) address is presented in the church for those who have announced during that period. This gives opportunity for a more extensive presentation than the few words the pastor may be able to speak to each individual.

Whether communion announcement will serve a spiritual purpose will depend on the pastor. Practical circumstances have made a meaningful practice difficult. It will require initiative and imagination on the part of the pastor to find ways of overcoming the difficulties. But the effort is not in vain since the Word of God that is used can lead to more worthy and even more frequent reception of Holy Communion.

Communion announcement enables the pastor to keep an accurate record of attendance at the sacrament. Such a record may alert the pastor to the need for pastoral attention. If an indivi-

12. Schaller, for example, lists five points that may receive consideration in the *Exploratio*. However, he points out that such an *Exploratio* need not be carried out with each member each time. *Pastorale Praxis*, p 42.

dual fails to attend communion as frequently as in the past, the pastor will feel concern. In this way the member may be calling for help even if he is not doing so with conscious intent. Generally, regular communion attendance can be assumed to indicate spiritual health, for the only means to spiritual health, the gospel in Word and sacrament, is finding application.

Methods

Communion announcement can be carried out in various ways. Personal announcement during designated hours lends itself best to making it part of meaningful preparation for communion. It provides for personal contact between the pastor and individual members. It can become time-consuming, especially in a large congregation where communion is celebrated in at least one of the services several times a month. However, the advantages of personal announcement merit effort to retain this form of announcing.

With the wide use of the telephone for communication, its use for communion announcement is inevitable. It does retain a degree of personal contact, but does not lend itself as well to a spiritual message as does announcement in person. However, also over the telephone a few words directing the thoughts to the blessings of the sacrament are possible if the pastor answers the telephone personally. If the pastor's wife or a secretary receives the calls, the personal contact with the pastor is lost, and all that remains is a recording of the names for the pastor.

Especially larger congregations have found communion cards a convenient and time-saving method of registering communicants. This naturally eliminates personal contact and makes of it no more than registration. The same is true of any method of "signing up" for communion in a book conveniently located in the church. The problem with these methods is that they frequently become no more than a record of those who have attended rather than an announcement record of those who intend to come to communion. If cards are used, they should be given to the pastor in advance so that he may know who will come to the sacrament and remain in responsible control.

A congregation may find it advisable to use a combination of methods. Where cards are used, opportunity for personal announcement may be retained. By making the personal announcement meaningful, the pastor may find that there are those who use this method with appreciation. At the same time the telephone or cards provide for those who find personal announcement difficult or impossible.

Communion announcement should not be made so difficult that people are kept from the sacrament. Nevertheless, hurried, last minute registration before the service should be discouraged. If a member at some time attends communion without announcing, the pastor will remember that the custom is an adiaphoron and not make it a matter for serious admonition. In general, the methods adopted for communion registration should be such that the purpose for it is best served according to the practical circumstances facing the congregation and its pastor. Multiple parishes naturally present their own scheduling problems for the pastor.

Confession

There is a close connection between confession and Holy Communion. Repentance is central for worthy communing. The penitent sinner confesses his sin and receives absolution. This means first of all confessing to God in contrite faith. Without this there can be no salutary use of the sacrament.

The church has very properly included confession and absolution as a significant part of communion preparation, either in a separate confessional service, or, as is most common now, as part of the order of service with Holy Communion. The congregation joins in making a public, general confession to God. The pastor, as the called servant of God, announces the free and unconditional forgiveness of all sins through the blood of Christ. When communion is included in services that use the order for matins or vespers, the pastor must remember to add the confession and absolution, possibly after the sermon before the communion liturgy. Likewise in giving private communion, confession and absolution should be part of the preparation for the sacrament.

Private confession and absolution is particularly comforting when specific sins trouble the conscience. Our Lutheran Confessions state that "our churches teach that private absolution should be retained in the churches" (AC XI, 1), however, not as a mandatory enumeration of sins required at least once each year. The pastor will encourage the use of this means of receiving comfort through direct and personal application of the gospel to the individual. Such private absolution is not limited to the preparation for Holy Communion. The pastor may experience that it more often becomes a part of his *Seelsorge* with people as he ministers to them in their anxieties, trials, and sickness.

The pastor must guard the privacy of confession. Whatever sins are confessed to him must remain in confidence. He will share such information neither with his wife nor with any member. If another person is suffering innocently for a crime confessed to the pastor, he must try to convince the one who confessed to correct the wrong. Even according to state laws the pastor is not allowed to reveal such privileged information without the consent of the person who confessed.

Summary: The practice of close communion is served by requiring communicants to register for communion. In this way the pastor can to some extent exercise responsible control over who comes to the Lord's Table, can prepare the people with a spiritual message, and can keep an accurate record of attendance that may reveal problems which need his attention. Personal communion announcement has definite advantages in fulfilling these purposes. The telephone and communion cards are convenient methods that must not, however, lose sight of the purpose of announcing. Confession and absolution is a fitting preparation for worthy reception of communion and should be included whenever communion is celebrated. A general, public confession to God is regularly used. Private confession is available to those who feel the need for it and desire the personal comfort which it brings. Whatever is confessed in private must remain confidential.

C. The Communion Service

The Elements

According to Christ's institution bread and wine are the visible elements. The pastor must make it his concern that they will be on hand in sufficient quantity. He will procure them for the congregation personally or through a responsible, designated person. The pastor should not wait until Saturday to determine whether an adequate supply of both elements for the next day's communion is on hand.

Scripture does not define the bread more closely. It is a matter of Christian liberty whether the bread is made of wheat or some other grain, whether it is leavened or not, whether it is shaped in a loaf or a wafer. Although it is a matter of historical knowledge that unleavened bread was used at the time of institution, it is nowhere mentioned directly or made mandatory. The communion wafers are convenient, and their use has continued partly as a confessional position against the Reformed to demonstrate the liberty the Lord has given in regard to the bread. In an emergency bread in any form may be used.

The other element is simply called the "cup" in the various accounts of the institution. That the content of the cup was wine is again a matter of historical knowledge, although no reference in Scripture to this element ever uses the word *oinos*. The Lord does refer to it as the "fruit of the vine" (Mt 26:29). The church has therefore very properly insisted on *grape* wine. Wine made from any other fruit should not be used. Since the term used for the contents of the cup is "fruit of the vine," the use of unfermented grape juice in case of an emergency cannot be considered invalid. Nevertheless, the church will avoid all doubt on the part of its members by using fermented fruit of the vine and may at times do so also as a confessional action over against anyone who claims that the use of any alcoholic beverage is sin.

The pastor must make the cleanliness and care of the communion ware his concern. An altar guild can render useful service in this area. If its members are responsible for placing the communion ware and the elements on the altar, the pastor may wish to assure himself that everything is in order and that an adequate supply of both elements has been placed on the altar. Besides the ciborium and paten, the flagon and chalice, a perforated spoon may be included with the ware so that any foreign material that may find its way into the wine can readily be removed. A supply of napkins will enable the pastor to wipe the rim of the chalice during the distribution.

The Consecration

Essentially the consecration consists in speaking the words of institution over the visible elements. Its purpose is, first of all, to show that it is the pastor's intention to carry out Jesus' institution and to set the visible elements apart for use in the sacrament. It furthermore serves as a prayer that the Lord may do what He has promised, as a confession that the body and blood of Christ are present in the sacrament, and as an invitation to the communicants to appropriate Jesus' promise by faith.

Such a use of the words of institution in consecrating the visible elements is an ancient custom (cf 1 Cor 10:16), but the words are not to be considered a magic formula that effects a change in the elements. The presence of the body and blood does not depend on the simple repeating of the words but comes about through the gracious working of the Lord, whose promise is connected with the words. The real presence is therefore also not dependent on the faith of the man who speaks the words. In this connection it should be noted that it was of the bread which the disciples took and ate that Jesus said, "This is my body," and of the cup as they drank of it that Jesus said, "This is my blood."

Not being a magic formula, incidental changes or omissions in the wording do not invalidate the consecration and its purpose. Nevertheless, the pastor should not speak the words carelessly or take liberties by changing their customary form.

It is important that an adequate supply of both bread and wine is on the altar at the time of consecration so that all communicants can be served. It is not advisable to count out the exact number of wafers for the announced participants. An error in counting (either the wafers or the announcements) or an unannounced communicant would cause a problem. If the common cup is used, 30 to 40 communicants can generally be served from a fifth of wine. With individual cups, as with the wafers, more should be prepared than for the exact number of registrants. Should the supply of either element be exhausted and replenishment be provided, consecrating the new supply will avoid any doubts about the continuing validity of the sacrament. It is customary to use only the words for the particular element that has been replenished. A shortage of several wafers can be overcome by breaking the necessary number of wafers. Let it be said again,

91

however: It is better by far to provide an adequate supply from the very beginning.

Scripture says nothing about the manner of consecration. It is customary after removing the communion veil to place the ciborium and paten on the left side of the altar, the flagon and chalice on the right. The pastor may take hold of the paten and chalice successively as he recites the words of institution, making the sign of the cross when he speaks the words "body" and "blood."

Proper consecration is not dependent on the public call or ordination of the one who speaks the words. Christ's institution and promise stand no matter what Christian speaks them. Nevertheless, since the congregation has called the pastor to administer communion to its members, it would be contrary to good order and disruptive of fellowship for any family or group within the congregation to set up its own communion service. There also is no situation that calls for emergency communion comparable to the emergency baptism of infants, since adults can receive strengthening of faith through the spoken gospel. Emergency communion could easily become in the minds of the people a kind of Lutheran extreme unction. There are few situations where the called pastor cannot satisfy the needs for communion. Should, however, the situation arise, there is no reason why, for example, an unordained vicar cannot conduct the entire communion service, including the consecration of the elements.

The Distribution

In the words spoken during the distribution the congregation confesses itself to the words of institution. The positive assertion, "Take, eat, this is the true body, etc.," expresses the conviction of the Lutheran faith in the real presence. Any wording which could raise doubt about this is unacceptable. After the union of the Lutheran and Reformed churches in Germany in the last century the wording was changed to read, "Take and eat, Christ says, 'This is my body, etc.' " The intent clearly was to allow each communicant to interpret the words to his liking. The words spoken during the distribution must, however, be an unambiguous confession. They are spoken to all communicants as they receive the elements. The pastor must take care lest they sound like a thoughtless, mechanical recitation, especially when they must be repeated several times to each group appearing at the altar.

In distributing the bread the pastor will find it helpful if the communicant brings his tongue forward to the lower lip. The wafer immediately clings to the moist tongue, lessening the possibility that it could drop from the lips to the floor. Should a wafer somehow be dropped, the pastor will pick it up and lay it aside on the altar.

The pastor should be certain that every communicant receives wine from the cup. This must be watched especially when a lady's hat obstructs a clear view of the mouth. The distribution of the wine also calls for considerable care lest some of it spill on a communicant's clothes or on the floor. While unconsumed portions of the bread and wine are not the body and blood of Christ, their falling to the floor can disturb the devotion of the communicants and may give the impression that the pastor is careless about the sacrament.

The cup should be rotated during the distribution so that a different part of it is exposed to the lips of each communicant in a group. The pastor may also find it helpful to carry a napkin in his left hand to wipe the cup after each person drinks. This can help avoid spilling or the accumulation of wine on the outside of the cup. In any case, the chalice should be carefully wiped for each new group that comes to the altar. If a communicant has a disfiguring rash or sores on his face and about the mouth, the pastor may tactfully suggest private communion. This is all the more in place if there is the possibility of contagion. Otherwise it has been found that the silver of the chalice together with the alcoholic content of the wine and the regular wiping of the chalice make the common cup no special carrier of harmful bacteria beyond what is experienced in the various contacts that are part of normal life.[13]

13. A recent letter to one of our pastors from the University of Michigan Medical center states that "most communicable diseases are transmitted through our breathing mechanisms. Diseases transmitted through the intestinal tracts and hence through the sputum or mouth are relatively few in number. The one major exception to this would be hepatitis." Thus special care is called for if one suspects the possibility of infectious hepatitis.

Although the common cup can have symbolical significance and its use in the church has a long tradition behind it, there are no theological reasons for rejecting the use of individual glasses. Even as the bread is not broken at the altar but prepared in individual wafers, so the wine may be apportioned in advance in individual cups without affecting the validity of the sacrament.

The use of individual glasses calls for certain practical decisions. Will the pastor take the glass and serve the communicant or will the communicant take the glass himself? In the latter case, it is not advisable to have the glass pass from the hand of the pastor to the communicant's hand, since such a small glass might easily be dropped in the transfer. If the communicant takes the glass, there is also the question of its return to the tray. The observation of various methods and personal experience suggest that it is most convenient for the pastor to carry the tray on his left arm, serve the communicant personally with his right hand and replace each glass into the tray immediately. Each pastor will have to determine what method is most convenient and the least time consuming for him.

The pastor must observe the utmost care in personal cleanliness when preparing to distribute the elements. A washbasin readily available in or near the sacristy will enable the pastor to wash his hands immediately before the distribution. Pastors who indulge in smoking must avoid distributing communion with hands stained by nicotine and smelling of smoke.

The approach of the communicants to the altar should be arranged so as to avoid confusion and congestion. Each congregation will plan this according to the physical arrangement of the furniture and the aisles. Ushers may be instructed so that they can facilitate a smooth flow of the people to the altar and back to the pews.

The pastor can instruct the future communicants in confirmation instructions in regard to the practical aspects of receiving communion. If practical problems arise, these can be discussed in council and congregational meetings, in the meetings of the various organizations, and in private contacts.

The custom of dismissing the congregation and continuing with a separate communion service is becoming less common since

"The Order of Holy Communion" in *The Lutheran Hymnal* places communion without interruption after the offertory as part of the service. Also those who are not receiving communion can profit from singing the hymns, observing the sacrament, and hearing the Word connected with it. Early departure from the service on the part of those not communing may be disturbing and the pastor may want to discourage the practice by showing the benefits of remaining with the congregation to the conclusion of the service.

What should be done with the consecrated wafers and wine that remain after communion? The premise must stand that apart from the sacrament the elements are only bread and wine. Whatever consecrated visible elements are not used in the sacrament cannot be considered the Lord's body and blood unless one holds to the Roman doctrine of transubstantiation. There is no scriptural reason why they may not be saved for another communion, at which time they will, of course, again be consecrated.

Luther strongly opposed mingling the consecrated elements with the unconsecrated. This rests on the fear that the sacrament would thereby be despised and even lost, and offense be given.[14] He suggests that some of those who communed consume what remains of the bread and wine. If, however, it is clear that there is no despising of the sacrament or questioning of the real presence and offense is avoided, it would appear that the reasons for his position are no longer present.

In our churches the saving of the remaining wafers for a future communion should cause no problem. The wine that remains in the flagon may also be returned to a bottle and saved for future use. What remains in the chalice can be used for private communion, or disposed of in a manner that does not show disrespect for the sacrament or cause offense to the people. Some churches have a drain opening directly into the ground for this purpose.

14. St. Louis, XX, 1606, 1609. Note also Luther's strong insistence that apart from the actual use in the celebration of the sacrament, the elements do not constitute the sacrament (XXIb, No. 3291: "ausserhalb des Gebrauchs nichts ein Sacrament ist"). This shows that Luther's objection to mixing the consecrated with the unconsecrated elements was not based on any idea of transubstantiation or the idea that the real presence continued after the celebration.

Summary: The visible elements in the Lord's Supper are bread and grape wine. These are consecrated by speaking the words of institution over them to show that what the Lord instituted is taking place and to set the elements apart for use in the sacrament. During the distribution the pastor speaks words that clearly confess the real presence of Christ's body and blood. The entire service should be conducted in such a way that due respect and honor are shown the sacrament of Christ's body and blood and the faith of the communicants may find strengthening.

5

The Shepherd's Concern
for Christian Education

"Feed my Lambs"
(Jn 21:15)

I. THE CHURCH'S RESPONSIBILITY

The broad injunction of Jesus to make disciples of all nations includes the command to teach them "to observe all things whatsoever I have commanded you" (Mt 28:20). The risen Lord told Peter, as He restored him to the ranks of the apostles, "Feed my lambs . . . feed my sheep" (Jn 21:12-17). This same Peter, recognizing the continuing need for such feeding, calls on the elders in the congregations to whom he addressed his first letter to "feed the flock of God which is among you" (1 Pe 5:2). St. Paul, too, enjoined the elders in Ephesus "to feed the church of God, which he hath purchased with his own blood" (Ac 20:28). He himself had the desire to journey to Rome to "impart some spiritual gift" to the Romans so that they might be established (Ro 1:11). The church is to train men who will "be able to teach others also" (2 Tm 2:2). All of this points to the responsibility the church and its called pastors have in the field of education. This responsibility of teaching and nourishing is indeed carried out regularly through the Sunday sermon, but it requires also the use of every means and method that can be employed in the educational endeavor.

97

The Scope of the Responsibility

The pastor and congregation need to remember the scriptural scope of the church's educational assignment. Generally education is thought of as applying to the young. Children, young people are to receive education. Jesus, however, told Peter to feed both the sheep and the lambs of His flock. While the church's major educational endeavor will for practical reasons direct itself particularly toward the young, a congregation should not conclude that the adults are outside the scope of this responsibility. Education is a lifelong process, also the education the church provides.

Education is generally thought of as the process of imparting knowledge. The goal of education is to grow in knowledge. Peter calls on the Christians to grow "in the knowledge of our Lord and Savior Jesus Christ" (2 Pe 3:18). To have the knowledge of Christ, of what Scripture teaches about Christ, is important, for "how shall they believe in him of whom they have not heard?" (Ro 10:14.) The church's educational responsibility must concern itself with the content of God's revelation in Holy Scripture.

The education enjoined on the church, however, goes far beyond the intellectual process of growing in knowledge. Growth is not to be limited to an increase in knowledge. Babes in Christ are to grow through the sincere milk of the Word (1 Pe 2:2). They are to grow as Christians, to grow in faith, to be established (Ro 1:11), to grow in the grace of Christ (2 Pe 3:18); they are to learn to observe, and not merely to have knowledge of, all that Christ commanded. Christian education, then, concerns itself with man's total being and life. It is concerned not only with imparting the content of divine revelation but also with molding thinking and feeling and willing, with guiding life through the divinely revealed knowledge.

The key word in education is growth. But the growth at which the church's educational activity aims is effected not merely by mental processes, but by the effective working of the Holy Spirit through the divine message, which is the "power of God unto salvation to everyone that believeth" (Ro 1:16).

Church Does not Replace Parents

The church's involvement in education does not replace the responsibility of the individual or of the parents. The fact that the church teaches the Word of God does not nullify Jesus' directive to every Christian to search the Scriptures. The educational efforts of the church in behalf of children do not absolve the home of its responsibility to "bring them up in the nurture and admonition of the Lord" (Eph 6:4). The example of Timothy's grandmother Lois and his mother Eunice, who taught him the Holy Scriptures from his childhood (2 Tm 3:15), is to be emulated in every Christian home. Parents have a direct personal responsibility here. No efforts on the part of the church can replace the training provided in a Christian home.

At the same time, the church too should not think of its teaching function as replacing that of the parents, or as simply being derived from the parents. The church has its teaching responsibility directly from the Lord, even as do the parents. Neither replaces the other. The church should instruct the parents as to their responsibility, equip them for it, and assist and supplement as needs and opportunity direct. These responsibilities the church has from the Lord.

Pastor and Congregation

The congregation through its call places a broad teaching responsibility on the pastor. Generally he is held accountable for all educational efforts of the congregation, may be required to function in them, or at least to provide leadership and guidance. Besides this, the congregation may call additional workers to specific teaching responsibilities, to supervise and administer a particular educational agency, or even to assume the entire responsibility for a particular educational program. Where more than one person is involved in the congregation's educational program, it becomes necessary to define each person's responsibility for the sake of good order and harmonious cooperation.

The congregation will do well to elect a board of education to work with the pastor and teachers in administering the congregation's entire educational endeavor. Most commonly a congregation's educational program will include a Sunday school, a Christian day school, a vacation Bible school, confirmation and Bible information classes, and Bible study groups. In setting up its program, a congregation will outline its educational objectives, examine the role each agency has in its total program, and set up the curriculum needed to fill this role and attain the objectives. The pastor will need to recognize his particular responsibility in each agency and provide leadership for properly organizing the effort.

General Objectives of the Congregation's Educational Effort

What has so far been said leads to three general objectives which the congregation will keep in mind in carrying out its educational program. First, and basic, is the objective of making people "wise unto salvation through faith in Christ Jesus" (2 Tm 3:15). The importance of this objective is evident from Jesus' question: "What is a man profited if he should gain the whole world and lose his own soul?" (Mt 16:26.) Let the church never lose sight of what God has made its prime educational objective!

Closely related to this first objective is a second, spiritual growth. Babes in Christ are to drink the milk of the Word so that they may grow to maturity (1 Pe 2:2). The Lord gives His church pastors and teachers and various types of ministries in order that the saints may be perfected, not remaining children readily deceived, and may grow up into Christ in all things (Eph 4:11-15). The educational effort of the church has as its objective a maturing faith.

The third objective concerns the Christian's life. Education aims at growth in sanctification. Christians have been called to follow in Jesus' steps in this life (1 Pe 2:21). Christians are to learn not to yield their members as instruments of unrighteousness, but rather to yield themselves to God (Ro 6:13). They must increasingly recognize that through their actions and especially by speaking God's message of sin and grace they are witnesses of Christ and His gospel to sinners in need (Ac 1:8). In all of life's relationships, whether in the home, church, or state, whether at work or play, they are to learn to live as such who are dead to sin and alive to God (Ro 6:11), who are the earth's salt and a light to the world (Mt 5:13,14).

Concerning every educational agency, three questions are relevant: 1. Does this endeavor concern itself with teaching the way of salvation in Christ? 2. Does this agency contribute toward growth and maturing in faith? 3. Is this agency making a contribution toward the Christian's life as a believer? If the answer to all three questions is No, such an agency has no place in the church's educational program.

These general objectives do not preclude more specific objectives and goals which can be brought into focus in connection with the specific educational agencies that will be discussed.

Summary: The Lord has enjoined on His church a broad teaching responsibility that extends to all age groups. It aims not only at imparting Christian knowledge, but also at growth in faith and in the grace of Christ through the power of the gospel. The congregation's educational effort does not free the parents of responsibility, but encourages and equips the parents for their task and supplements their efforts. The pastor is called to supervise and administer the total program in cooperation with a board of education. Inevitably others will have to be called upon to serve in the various agencies. Broad objectives of the total program will be knowledge of salvation, maturing of the faith, and growth in the total life of faith.

II. THE CHRISTIAN DAY SCHOOL

The most comprehensive agency the church has developed for the instruction of its youth is the Christian day school. Its unique strength is that the entire educational process is carried out under the influence of the gospel, so that the instruction in religion does not become merely a small adjunct to the secular education received in a non-religious school.

Its Role in the Total Program

The Christian day school enrollment generally consists primarily of the children of the congregation's members. Even of these children, few congregations have a 100% enrollment. Thus the Christian day school will seldom be the sole agency for Christian education. Other agencies may be expected to attract a larger number of unchurched children than the Christian day school. When, however, such children are enrolled in the Christian day school, there is an added mission opportunity for gaining not only the child, but also the entire family.

Since the Christian day school seldom is the church's only agency for the instruction of its young, its role must not become one of competition but of cooperation with whatever other agencies the congregation may establish. Since its staff has received careful training also in teaching religion courses, the members of its staff are well qualified to assist in improving the quality of

101

teaching in the Sunday school, the vacation Bible school, etc.

Although the Christian day school provides a comprehensive educational program, its role should not be considered one that frees the home of its responsibility. Rather, it should work closely with the parents so that through their joint effort children may receive the best possible training and education for this life and for eternity.

Experience shows that the Christian day school is a fruitful source for recruiting future workers in the church. The added instruction and training by means of the Word of God can inspire a desire for the pastoral or teaching ministry.

Some Specific Objectives

It is self-evident that the general objectives of all Christian educational agencies as outlined above apply to the Christian day school. More specifically, the further objectives of the Christian day school are:

to provide the children with a rich background of Bible history, with a basic understanding of Luther's Small Catechism, and with a fund of memorized material from Scripture, the Catechism, and the hymnal (this also serves to prepare the children for the pastor's confirmation instruction);

to teach all subjects from a viewpoint that finds its roots in Scripture;

to train the children to take their place as Christians in the life of their congregation and synod;

to educate the children for their life as Christians in the world and as Christian citizens of their country.

The Pastor's Role

The congregation in Christian liberty states in its call to the pastor the particular responsibilities it assigns to him. Because his call is broad and comprehensive, it will include responsibility for the work done in the Christian day school. This may be spelled out in detail although more often it is stated only in general terms. The calls of the principal and teachers likewise determine their specific responsibilities. The pastor's call makes him the pastor also of the teaching personnel while their calls establish them as co-workers with the pastor in the Christian day school. The pastor's call will generally not require of him an active teaching role in the school as does the teacher's but makes him in a broad way the "overseer" also of this phase of congregational activity. As such he will visit the school and its various classrooms. Sometimes this may be done casually, at other times after prior announcement. His purpose will be to demonstrate his interest and his availability for counsel and encouragement. He will attend faculty and board of education meetings but avoid dominating them with overly much speaking. He will assure himself that the curriculum of the school best promotes the goals and objectives of the school, that the religion courses are correlated with his confirmation instructions, and that the school is fulfilling its function in relation to the total educational program of the congregation. Although the ultimate responsibility for the supervision of the school remains his, he will recognize the specific responsibility that has been placed on the teachers and the principal.

The pastor will promote the Christian day school, informally in contacts with members, more formally in his sermons and at council and congregational meetings as occasions present themselves, and when discussing the congregation's program with new members. A school may not die immediately because of a pastor's indifference toward it, but it will not long remain healthy. Where there is no school, the pastor can do more than any other individual to promote the opening of a school.[1] Care must be taken not to oversell the Christian day school as a panacea for all spiritual problems facing individuals, families, or the congregation.

The pastor concerns himself with recruiting students for the school. He will help organize an annual school canvass and participate by visiting those homes where a particular problem may call for his attention. An especially helpful tool in planning a canvass and studying and planning the school's future enrollment is a file of all children in the congregation. The pastor can see to it that this file remains current by immediately adding the names of the newly baptized infants and of the children of new members, and by removing the names of those whose membership in the congregation has terminated.

The pastor remains shepherd also of the children in the school, even though the teachers share in shepherding them. It is a part

1. Materials for promoting a Christian day school are available from the Wisconsin Synod's Board for Parish Education. See the bibliography for more information.

of pastoral wisdom to encourage them to see in him a friend and thus to win their confidence. He retains responsibility for counseling and disciplining the children. Because this is a responsibility shared by the teachers, the principal, and the pastor, an orderly procedure should always be followed. The disciplining and counseling should begin with the teachers, who may refer difficult cases to the principal and ultimately to the pastor. Circumstances will indicate how much consulting and sharing of information among the three will best serve a child's welfare. Great care must be practiced by the pastor not to circumvent the teachers and principal in dealing with children or their parents in matters pertaining to the school.

The pastor will in every way seek to work in cooperation with the faculty for their and the school's welfare. He may be called on to help in planning the devotions and assist in preparing the children's Christmas service. If the teachers serve as organists or choir directors, he will provide them with the text of the sermon and the list of hymns in sufficient time that they may plan and prepare for their role in the service. Because of his involvement in all phases of the congregation's program, he can discuss with the teaching staff how certain school activities or programs may help or hinder the total program. Especially newly called teachers should be made to feel welcome by him and informed of the congregation's program and their place in it. He should make it his concern to assure himself that the material needs of the teachers are properly cared for by the congregation. Let him work with the members of the faculty in such a way that they see in him a sympathetic, faithful pastor and co-worker.

Pastor-Teacher Harmony

When a number of people serve the same congregation as its called workers, harmony and cooperation among them is vital for the welfare of the church. Satan can only rejoice when he succeeds in sowing strife among those who are workers together in the church. A pastor will strive for harmony between himself and the teachers, or the associate or assistant pastor, with whom he is called upon to work. He can promote such harmony by his attitudes and by his actions.

By His Attitudes

The pastor will recognize that the teacher too has a divine call into the public ministry. The Lord through the congregation has called both. The difference in the scope of the work does not change the essential nature of the call. This should lead to an attitude of respect, honor, and love toward those who, like the pastor, have been called by the Lord. What is more, he will recognize that through their divine calls the Lord has chosen all the members of the called staff to work together for the welfare of His church.

The pastor should ask the Lord to preserve in him an attitude of humility. The broader responsibilities assigned to the pastor are no cause for pride but can cause it nonetheless. Important as the pastoral ministry is, it should not lead to assuming an air of importance, especially not toward those whose ministry may be restricted in scope. Both received calls that take into account their gifts and training. The pastor will recognize the specialized training of the teacher. Although the pastor's call extends to a broader scope of duties, neither his call nor training make him an expert in everything. To pretend that it does over against those whose call is restricted to the field in which they have received more expert training will not contribute to harmonious relations. Here the word of Paul finds apt application: "Be kindly affectioned one to another with brotherly love; in honor preferring one another" (Ro 12:10).

There is no perfect pastor. There is no perfect principal. There is no perfect teacher. All are still sinners who need the Lord's daily forgiveness, but whom the Lord in grace has called into His service. Remembering this should lead them to work together with a spirit of forgiveness toward one another, always forgiving even as the Lord has forgiven them.

By His Actions

Harmony and cooperation are promoted by keeping an avenue of communication open between the pastor and teacher. Communication builds good rapport. Silence breeds misunderstanding and distrust. Also informal, friendly contacts contribute toward openness. If differences arise, let the pastor and teacher frankly discuss them, but in private. If the differences involve matters of policy or program, they can also be discussed in meetings of the board of education and the church council. But let them strive to agree on proposals and recommendations concerning the school that are to come before the congregation. For the pastor to oppose in a congregational meeting what the principal advocates, or vice versa, could give the appearance of disharmony.

The Eighth Commandment needs scrupulous application in the pastor-teacher relationship. Each will guard against using his tongue to broadcast the weaknesses and faults of the other. Let the pastor not fail to speak well of the work that has been capably done by the teacher. Let his ear not become a ready sounding board for complaints against the teacher in violation of Matthew 18.

Congregations generally acknowledge the pastor's broader scope of responsibility by a larger salary, even as the principal's added duties find reflection in his paycheck. The pastor can prevent such differences from becoming cause for disharmony and jealousy when he does not seek such greater returns for himself but rather shows concern that the teachers may be adequately provided for. The pastor should not permit a situation to arise where the teacher must ask for an increase in salary because the congregation has ignored the teacher's needs. (Cf salary review committee in the chapter on administration, p 319.)

The pastor's faithfulness in his calling can help to inspire faithfulness in others. He will, however, warn a congregation against increasing a teacher's work load by imposing numerous extra assignments that may infringe on the time that should be used in the interest of classroom teaching or for necessary time with his family.

Promoting harmony is the responsibility of all workers. When each called worker strives to be a "workman that needeth not to be ashamed" (2 Tm 2:15), a harmonious working together should result. This should exclude carping criticism and promote constructive help. In this presentation, however, the emphasis has been on what the pastor on his part can do.

Summary: The Christian day school is a congregation's most comprehensive educational agency for the children. Although it will enroll as many of the congregation's children as possible, as well as unchurched children, it will seldom be the sole agency for the education of this age group and will work in cooperation with the other agencies. Its comprehensive program does not free the parents of their responsibility. The pastor by his call has the role of "overseeing" the total program of the school while recognizing the specific roles assigned to the teachers and principal through their calls. He will promote the school, be involved in recruiting students, be available for help in disciplining and counseling, and

106

in every way further the welfare of the school through establishing a helpful spirit of cooperation between himself and the faculty.

III. THE SUNDAY SCHOOL

If the Christian day school is the church's most comprehensive program of education for the children, the Sunday school is the most widely used. Few congregations will be without a Sunday school. Even those congregations that support a Christian day school will generally find it advantageous or necessary to conduct a Sunday school.

Its Role

The Sunday school's role will depend somewhat on the scope of the congregation's total program. If there is no Christian day school, the Sunday school becomes the congregation's chief educational agency for all its children. In addition to this it will serve a major role in bringing unchurched children under the influence of the gospel.

When there is a Christian day school, the Sunday school's role as a mission agency remains the same, but the extent to which it serves the children of the congregation decreases. A congregation will hardly conduct a Sunday school for the children already enrolled in a Christian day school even though it will not prohibit or even discourage them from attending. The Sunday school will, however, receive the additional role of serving as a feeder for the Christian day school.

In either case, the Sunday school should not be viewed as a part of the total program that is, because of its limitations (time, difficulty of finding qualified teachers), merely tolerated. If a Sunday school is part of the church's program, as it generally is, then the congregation and its pastor should strive to make the most of it in spite of its limitations. It is possible to have both a good Christian day school and a good Sunday school. Where there is no Christian day school, the need for a good Sunday school is all the more urgent.

Some Specific Objectives

Even as with the Christian day school, the three objectives of all Christian education also apply to the Sunday school (cf p   ). The larger number of unchurched children will make the objec-

107

tive of teaching the way of salvation all the more important. The specific objectives will be similar to those of the Christian day school, even if they must be less pretentious. They can be stated as follows:

> to provide the children with the necessary background of Bible history and familiarity with the Catechism, including memorization of Bible passages and the chief parts of the Enchiridion (this also serves to prepare the children for the pastor's confirmation instruction);

> to train the children to take their place as Christians in the life of their congregation and synod;

> to educate the children for their life as Christians in the world;

> to develop a Christian world view that looks to Scripture with confidence and that can recognize and resist the secularistic, humanistic influences to which the children are exposed during the week in nonreligious schools.

The Pastor's Role

In most circumstances the pastor will be involved more directly in the Sunday school than in the Christian day school, and his role will be more extensive. Only if the work of supervising the Sunday school can be turned over to a qualified and adequately trained person (e.g., a Christian day school teacher) will the pastor be able to relinquish some of this personal involvement. In some cases his direct involvement will include teaching one of the classes, conducting the opening devotions, or at least visiting classes and remaining in close contact with the children and teachers. More specifically, the pastor's role will involve him in promoting the Sunday school, in securing and training teachers, in setting up and carrying out the curriculum, and in providing organizational leadership.

Promoting the Sunday School

Only with the pastor's active support and encouragement can a Sunday school, with its limitations, begin to reach its objectives. The congregation should know that the pastor is intent on effective work in the Sunday school. The congregation should know that it is expected to support the Sunday school fully in attaining its objectives.

Promotion concerns itself particularly with recruiting pupils. It should be taken for granted that all the children of congregational members who are not attending a Christian day school are expected to attend the Sunday school. An accurate, up-to-date file of the congregation's children with pertinent information has much practical value.

The Sunday school wants to enroll unchurched children. The pastor will seek to gain these through personal visits, arranging canvasses, distributing literature, and training the children of both the Sunday and Christian day school to invite and bring unchurched friends and neighbors to the classes. This can become an effective training in evangelism.

Securing and Training Teachers

The effectiveness of the Sunday school is determined by the quality of its teaching. To secure and train qualified Sunday school teachers will have high priority on the time the pastor devotes to this agency.

Qualified teachers are best secured through invitation or appointment. The pastor, together with the congregation's board of education, may select the teachers for each class and approach them with the church's call to serve in proclaiming the gospel to the congregation's youth. This is more effective than publishing an appeal for volunteers. In the latter case some qualified persons may not take the initiative to volunteer and so their talents are not used, or such may volunteer whose talents do not include an aptitude to teach. Since the Sunday school teacher, like the pastor and the Christian day school teacher, is to proclaim the gospel in the name of the congregation, careful selection of those called is mandatory. The selection may be preceded by a careful consideration of the qualifications to be sought in those to be chosen (cf the procedure used in Jerusalem in choosing deacons, Ac 6).

There are two stages to the training of Sunday school teachers. The one concerns itself with training before they begin teaching, the other is the continued training after they are active.

For effective Sunday school work, no one should be asked to teach who has not received preparatory training. Some congregations have developed a training curriculum that takes up to two years to complete. This should include a course in Bible history, possibly the life of Christ, a course in Christian doctrine, and training in pedagogy.[2] Volunteers for this training program may be solicited. Others may be invited to enroll in the courses. The limited time available in the Sunday school for teaching (generally one hour a week) should emphasize the importance of having well-trained teachers. The pastor may find it particularly advantageous to enlist the help of a Christian day school teacher in the courses on pedagogy. The program may also include observing capable teachers at work and giving practice lessons for critique.

The pastor should provide ongoing training of active Sunday school teachers in regular weekly or biweekly Sunday school teachers' meetings. An important purpose of these meetings is to study and discuss the lessons in advance. Time may be given to a discussion of problems which have arisen in the past. Time may also be allotted for further courses aiming at the spiritual and professional enrichment of the teaching staff. The regular teachers and those who serve as substitutes should be required to attend these meetings. The pastor will prepare well for these meetings and may ask the teachers to study the lessons in advance so that the result is a profitable meeting which no one will want to miss.

Such careful training of the teachers will give them confidence for doing their work. Thus it is not a deterrent to securing teachers, but may actually help. It will upgrade the quality of the teaching and show that the teaching of Sunday school is a responsible privilege.

Setting up and Carrying out the Curriculum

The major portion of the Sunday school curriculum concerns itself with Bible history. The Sunday school material that is used usually determines what stories are studied. The pastor will become familiar with this part of the curriculum because of his involvement in the teachers' meetings. In this way he will know what stories the children have learned so that he can use them as reference material in his confirmation instructions.

The pastor may want to set up the memory work in the Sunday school in such a way that the Bible passages and the parts of the Catechism memorized will correlate with his catechetical course for the confirmands. In this way the objective of preparing the

2. The bibliography contains specific suggestions of courses for Sunday school teacher training.

children for his confirmation class will best be served. On the other hand, he may find that he can attain this objective by simply using the passages included in the Sunday school course.

So that the curriculum can be carried out effectively, the teachers should be provided with whatever teaching aids are found helpful, and trained in their use. Among these are a flannelgraph, especially for the younger classes, maps, pictures, films, together with the necessary projectors, blackboard, tackboard, a file of pictures, and activity materials also for home use. Care must be taken lest these helps assume too great a role. A filmstrip or a movie cannot be allowed to take over the teaching role. They are teaching aids and do not replace the teacher. Too frequent use of the same aid may decrease its effectiveness. Variety will provide increased attention and interest. The pastor's encouragement can do much to induce a congregation to provide the necessary helps and to lead the teachers to use them effectively.

Providing Organizational Leadership

To be effective, the Sunday school effort should be properly organized. The pastor will provide leadership that results in necessary organization of the work without letting the organization become an end in itself. The congregation's board of education will provide valuable help in determining organizational policies and planning their implementation.

Organizing the Staff

Essential on the Sunday school staff are qualified teachers. There are advantages in recruiting as teachers men and women of various age levels. Such recruitment should not begin below the age of a junior in high school. For the preschool classes women who have reared children in their own homes have been found to be especially qualified. Men may be asked to serve the upper grades and the high school classes. Where a Sunday school provides classes for those of high school age, recruitment from this age group may await graduation from high school.

The size of the Sunday school enrollment will determine how extensive an organization is needed. There may be a superintendent, whose duties can include enrolling new children, ordering necessary materials and equipment, following up on absentees. A secretary can keep the records, including each Sunday's attendance. The offerings require a financial secretary or treasurer. In a small Sunday school, all these functions may be assigned to one person. While an individual can be placed in charge of securing substitutes, this often is better left to each teacher. In either case, this should be done from a list of approved substitutes.

Some congregations have found it useful to extend a written "call to teach" to the teacher members of the staff. This may help show the teachers the importance of their responsibility. Induction into office during a Sunday service can serve the same purpose for all members of the staff. This may be done on an annual church education Sunday.

Organizing the Classes

The Sunday school may provide classes for children from the four-year-old preschool children to those in eighth grade. The pastor may encourage extending this through the high school years, or even beyond. The size of each class will differ according to the age of the pupils. It has been found useful to limit the number of pupils in a class to the numerical age of the pupils, e.g., the four-year-old class to four, the eight-year-old class to eight, etc. If enough qualified teachers are available, it is advisable to limit all classes to a maximum of eight.

Although the cradle roll is not in the strict sense a class, it can be a significant part of the Sunday school organization. All infants should be enrolled in the cradle roll at the time of their baptism. During the years preceding actual attendance in a Sunday school class, the church remains in contact with the parents, periodically providing the parents with religious material suited to the child's growth in understanding. In this way the church can impress especially on unchurched parents its responsibility for the spiritual growth of their baptized children.

In organizing the various classes, the physical facilities available need attention. Each class should be able to function without disturbance from another. The children should be seated in furniture that corresponds to the physical size of the child.

Time

If at all possible, the Sunday school should not meet during a church service. Having the Sunday school meet during a church service prevents the pastor from actively participating in the Sunday school and prevents church attendance on the part of the children. The time allotted to the Sunday school should not be less than an hour. Some teaching time may be saved by having each class conduct its own opening devotion, even if a joint opening service may be desirable where time and space make this possible. Many Sunday schools discontinue classes during the three vacation months in summer. However, where circumstances permit, the pastor can avoid developing the impression in the minds of the church's youth that vacation time includes vacation from the Word of God by continuing the classes throughout the year. Since the time for Sunday school is so limited, whatever time can be made available should be used.

Financing

Most Sunday schools have an offering which is used to cover the expenses of materials and equipment. In this way a Sunday school frequently is financially self-supporting and functions independently of the congregation. Since the Sunday school is one of the educational agencies of the congregation, there are advantages in including its financing in the congregation's budget. This may give the congregation a more direct sense of responsibility for the Sunday school. The offerings of the Sunday school may then be channeled through the congregational treasury. The children may also be given a set of offering envelopes which can be used either in the Sunday school or in the church services. Mission offerings in the Sunday school can serve to stimulate interest in world-wide gospel work.

Miscellanea

An annual parent-teacher meeting may be helpful in inducing parents to support regular attendance and faithful preparation on the part of their children. This can also serve as another helpful contact with unchurched parents.

Special or regular services in which the Sunday school children have a part can lead the children to recognize that church services are also for them. Such services likewise are in the interest of the Sunday school's mission objective. Care must be taken lest preparation for special services infringe on teaching time unduly.

Summary: The Sunday school is the most widely used and sometimes the chief educational agency serving the congregation's children. In addition, it is an effective mission arm. Its inherent limitations should not lead the pastor merely to tolerate its presence, but rather to help make it as effective as possible in spite of its limitations. The pastor will promote the Sunday school in the congregation and among the unchurched. He will have an important part in securing qualified teachers, in training them in preparation for their teaching responsibility, and continuing their training after they are teaching. He will be concerned that the curriculum serves to prepare the children for his confirmation class. He will provide organizational leadership for the Sunday school in all its practical aspects. Financing the Sunday school through the congregational treasury may increase the congregation's interest in and concern for this agency.

IV. VACATION BIBLE SCHOOL

Among the part-time weekday schools, the vacation Bible school has gained considerable popularity. While it cannot replace either the Christian day school or the Sunday school as the chief agency of education, its specific role is sufficiently important in the total program to deserve the congregation's and the pastor's support.

Its Role in the Congregation

A new mission or a congregation with a high percentage of unchurched people in its neighborhood will find the vacation Bible school particularly useful in opening doors into the homes of mission prospects. It can become the first contact children from these homes have with the gospel. It can be a means of bringing the children into continuing contact with the saving gospel by directing them into the Sunday school or the Christian day school.

A congregation whose area appears to be well-churched will find its vacation Bible school serving particularly its own children as an agency providing daily additional instruction in the Word of God during a period when no other school preempts the children's time. However, even under such circumstances one should not lose sight of the mission aspect of the vacation Bible school. There are few communities with a total absence of unchurched children. Besides, the children of delinquents, who have drifted out of the other educational agencies of the congregation, may find a way back to needed contact with the gospel through the vacation Bible school.

114

Its Specific Objectives

The objectives of the vacation Bible school in an area where many of the children are from unchurched homes will be first of all to teach the basics of sin and grace, of the way of salvation, very simply; to instill a desire to hear more, so that it may become a feeder for the Sunday school and the Christian day school; to have the children memorize some hymns, Bible verses, and portions of the Catechism so that the message of salvation may remain before their minds.

For children of the congregation the objectives will be to provide additional instruction in the Word of God and parts of the Catechism, to apply the truths to their daily lives, to instill mission mindedness through the special mission thrust of this agency, and to provide Christian fellowship.

The instructional materials need to be chosen according to the particular objectives to which the type of enrollment directs.

The Pastor's Role

If it is to succeed, the vacation Bible school may require an even greater effort on the part of the pastor than do other agencies. Only if it can be placed into the hands of an experienced Christian day school teacher or vicar can the pastor's direct involvement be reduced. Under all circumstances there are advantages for the pastor to be involved daily in the school by conducting devotions, teaching a class if necessary, remaining in contact with the children in such a way that a beginning is made through him of establishing a bond with the church. In congregations where the pastor's regular confirmation class is limited to one meeting a week during the school year, the daily classes during two or three weeks of vacation Bible school may be used for a final concentrated review with the confirmands.

Enlisting the Congregation

The pastor in inaugurating a vacation Bible school should begin by gaining the support of the congregation for such an undertaking. He can do this through the board of education and the church council, showing them its role and objectives. As the help of more and more people of the congregation is enlisted, the interest in the school will intensify.

Planning the School

Plans for a vacation Bible school should begin as long as six months in advance. The assistance of the congregation's board of education should be enlisted. Early planning will include a decision on the dates for the school, choice of the materials to be used, and the scheduling of meetings and activities involved in preparing for the two or three weeks of school.

Choosing and Training Teachers

What has been said about the size of classes and the securing and training of Sunday school teachers is applicable also here. Not to be overlooked are students from the congregation who are attending the pastor and teacher training schools of the synod. That the Christian day school and Sunday school staffs are a source of experienced personnel is self-evident.

Less experienced teachers will particularly need special training. A full week of meetings (about two hours a day for five days) should provide sufficient time to study the materials and methods of teaching, the schedule, projects, and recreational activities. It will be advisable to work through the entire course, since time for such meetings will usually not be available while the school is in session except to discuss questions and problems.

Other Personnel

The vacation Bible school can enlist considerable lay assistance. Secretarial help is needed to keep records of the enrollment and attendance, of prospects, and to order and distribute supplies. There can be teachers' helpers to assist with the classwork, the projects and the discipline, especially in the lower grades. Others can supervise the playground. An organist will be needed as well as a treasurer. Additional custodial help is called for. If there is a break for refreshments, these must be supplied and served. The pupil recruiting program may require a team to canvass and to distribute literature.

Publicity

Important within the congregation is an early announcement through the church calendar to alert the members of the time for vacation Bible school so that this can be taken into consideration in planning vacations. Further announcements in the Sunday bulletins will remind the members as the time of the opening draws near. Since the VBS has a strong mission objective, publicity must reach out into the community in such a way that the unchurched are invited. A canvass of the neighborhood is the most direct form of publicity. Flyers, doorknob hangers, newspaper releases, announcements on the radio (some stations provide for this on a "community calendar"), posters in stores, a banner on the church property can inform the community in a variety of ways. The children of the day and Sunday schools can be used effectively in finding and bringing the unchurched. Ultimately all the members of the congregation should be conscious of the opportunity the VBS provides in fulfilling in part their evangelism responsibility.

The School Day

Usually the VBS meets for approximately 2-1/2 hours in the morning, Monday through Friday, for two weeks. The day may begin and end with a group devotion. Singing, art projects, and even refreshments, as well as the recess help to break up the morning into short time segments and prevent monotony. It should, however, not be forgotten that the purpose of the school is not to entertain but to teach. Yet the teaching must be done in a way that does not forget that continued attendance at the VBS, especially on the part of the unchurched, is often dependent on retaining the good will and interest of the children.

The final day may include a closing service either at the end of the day's schedule or in the evening. The latter has the advantage of providing an opportunity for the parents to attend. This is especially important in the case of mission prospects. For the same reason, it may be well to have the children learn a hymn they can sing in the following Sunday's service.

Follow-up

Careful records should be kept, listing the unchurched and unbaptized children and families. Follow-up will include efforts to win them for the Sunday school and invite them to the services. It will also include keeping their names on the soul responsibility list so that the congregation's evangelism committee makes them its concern.

117

Financing

Three methods of financing the cost of the vacation Bible school are used. 1. The congregation can include the cost in the budget. This has the advantage of impressing the congregation with the fact that this is a part of its educational program. 2. Children can contribute daily during the opening devotion. If this is intended to finance the school, the money can still be channeled through the congregational treasury. If a congregation provides the financing from its regular budget, such offerings by the children can be directed to a mission project. 3. A registration fee can provide the bulk of the financing. This may result in more regular attendance. On the other hand, the size of the fee may also deter the unchurched from attending.

Summary: The vacation Bible school can supplement other educational agencies of the congregation and serves an important mission role among the unchurched in a congregation's area of responsibility. Its objectives and curriculum may vary according to the background of the children served. The pastor will enlist the early support of the congregation so that there is adequate time for all planning, for choosing the materials, for enlisting and training the teachers, and for securing all other necessary personnel. A variety of methods can be used to publicize the VBS in the community and invite the unchurched. The school day must present a program that retains the good will and interest of the pupils. Various methods of financing its cost are possible although a method that recognizes the congregation's responsibility has its advantages. Careful follow-up is mandatory lest mission prospects be lost.

V. CONFIRMATION

Confirmation is a church rite, not a divinely instituted sacrament. It has neither the command of Christ nor any specific promise of grace. Hence the church can define the concept of confirmation and determine the purpose it is to serve.

Definition

The Lutheran church has had no single, consistent view of confirmation. When Luther rejected the Roman sacrament of confirmation, he did not provide for a replacement. His concern was for the instruction of the youth, as is seen from his preparation of the

Small Catechism. Nevertheless, from 1539 on various Lutheran territories in Germany introduced confirmation rites that represented a variety of views in regard to confirmation. Some emphasized the catechetical instruction in preparation for Holy Communion. Others saw in the prayer and laying on of hands a sacramental act that bestowed the Holy Ghost. Still others made much of the confirmation vow and saw confirmation as the act of receiving the confirmands into the fellowship of the true believers, into the believing congregation. Pietism, which laid great stress on confirmation, saw it as a renewal of the baptismal covenant while rationalism considered it an act of receiving children into the confessing church or into adult church membership. There have been those who viewed confirmation as completing what was begun in baptism, as a supplement to baptism, as a kind of lay ordination. Suffice it to say that any view that gives the impression that baptism is not complete in itself, that the baptismal covenant needs a later renewing on the part of man, that baptism does not already produce the faith that brings one fully into the fellowship of the church, that sees the laying on of hands as having sacramental significance, must be rejected.

A church's confirmation practices will be determined by its definition of confirmation and by the purpose it wants the rite to serve. The following definition sums up the view of confirmation in the Wisconsin Evangelical Lutheran Synod and serves as a basis for its confirmation practices: Confirmation is a church rite in which a congregation gives its catechumens who have been instructed in Christian doctrine according to the Bible and the Lutheran Confessions an opportunity to confess their faith before the church, prays for the children with the laying on of hands, and invites them as such who have sufficient spiritual maturity to participate in the Lord's Supper.

This definition draws attention to the following significant points: 1. the instruction of the children, 2. the opportunity for a public confession of their faith, 3. the prayer of the congregation in their behalf, and 4. the invitation to partake of Holy Communion. This view retains a direct connection between confirmation and the first admission to communion and thus provides a bridge between baptism and Holy Communion. The confirmation instructions and the public confession are seen as important in this relationship.

Some Warnings

The pastor should guard against speaking of confirmation as a renewal of the baptismal covenant. The wording in some liturgies may lead to this way of speaking. The baptismal covenant is one that God makes with the child and is permanent. God need not renew it; man cannot renew it. Nor should we assume that children have fallen away from it and need to return to it in confirmation. Some liturgies also contain the term "renewal of the baptismal *vow*." If by this is meant that the child now for himself speaks the confession and promises spoken in his name by the sponsors in baptism, this is admissible. However, the term appears to be subject to misunderstanding and ought to be avoided.

The confirmation vow to remain faithful and rather suffer death than fall away from the faith that has been confessed should be understood as the intent which a believing Christian should always have. To confess one's faith without the desire to continue in it is an admission of doubt. The pastor must, however, guard against presenting this promise as a formal oath that is to keep the child faithful. The preservation of faith is the work of God. And to use the oath made in confirmation at a later time as a reason for remaining with the church, pointing to the seriousness of breaking an oath, will lead to legalistic practice.

The pastor must take care not to give the impression to the children that he considers confirmation as the conclusion of their formal instruction in religion. It must not be viewed as a kind of graduation. To dismiss the children from Sunday school the Sunday after confirmation could contribute to such an impression. On the other hand, this impression can be avoided by providing Bible classes for at least the teen-age youth during the hour of Sunday school.

"A Report for Study"

A Report for Study[3] prepared by the Joint Commission on Theology and Practice of Confirmation, which consisted of representatives from the three major Lutheran bodies in the United States, recommended in 1967 that "first Communion and confirmation be separated as two distinct acts."[4] This division, ac-

3. Frank W. Klos, *Confirmation and First Communion* (Minneapolis, St. Louis: Augsburg, Concordia, 1968), pp 183-213 contain the *Report*.
4. *Ibid.,* p 199.

cording to the *Report*, "will permit eligible young Christians to partake of the Lord's Supper at an earlier period of their life and also make possible a more effective experience of confirmation at a more mature age."[5] It suggested the fifth grade as the time for admission to communion and the 10th grade for confirmation. The proposal found acceptance in two of the major bodies, the third, The Lutheran Church-Missouri Synod, leaving the choice up to each congregation.

That the church in Christian liberty can make such decisions must be recognized. Whether the new course of action will provide the desired solutions for the problems the commission saw in the present practice is subject to question. That it can add problems is a definite possibility.

One must agree that the confirmation rite should not replace baptism in significance and that the church's educational effort should not terminate with confirmation. Yet a change in form, method, or procedure will not in itself solve such problems. The early communion could, on the other hand, result in a diminution of the instruction in preparation for it, and communion could degenerate into a mere ritualistic act. The separation of confirmation from the first admission to communion may also have this result that a large segment of the membership may neglect confirmation with the added instruction it is to provide, since the earlier admission to communion may give the impression that adequate instruction has already been received. Whatever procedures are followed, there is a continuing need to watch for problems and misconceptions as they occur and for faithful instruction and work to overcome them. At the same time, it should be recognized that a uniform practice within a church body, although not a scriptural "must," nevertheless has much to commend it in view of the high rate of mobility on the part of America's population.

Instruction Prior to Confirmation

Special instructions in preparation for confirmation are conducted by the pastor, generally over a period of two years while the children are in the seventh and eighth grades. Confirmation and admission to communion then corresponds with the completion of the eighth grade of schooling, when the child is 13 or 14

5. *Ibid.*, p 199.

years of age. It must, however, also be recognized that a certain chronological age or the completion of a particular grade in school does not guarantee readiness for communion.

Confirmation instruction should be based on the Bible and Luther's Small Catechism. The Catechism is one of the Confessions of the Lutheran Church, the one with which the laity should be thoroughly familiar. This does not, however, exclude the use of other materials. The advantage of not having the eighth grade course be a simple repetition of the previous year's lessons should be obvious. The pastor should also remember that he is addressing himself not simply to the intellect, but to the heart of the child. Let him approach the confirmation instructions not simply as a teacher of the children, but as their divinely appointed shepherd. The methods and procedures of this instruction are studied as a special course in Catechetics.

The pastor may ask himself how far a child must progress in this instruction before he may be confirmed. If confirmation were to mark the conclusion of all religious learning, a specified broad level of attainment might be considered necessary. With the definition of confirmation given above, the first objective of the instructions will be that the children may grow in faith and Christian maturity through the Word of God so that they can confess their faith with understanding and be received at the Lord's table. Thus a clear understanding of the way of salvation (sin and grace) and of the sacraments is most important. To this minimum requirement for confirmation a broader objective will include memorization of the Enchiridion, of Bible references, and a good understanding of the whole counsel of God. This will serve as a basis on which to build throughout the Christian's life so that he may become ever more mature and complete in Christ. In the case of some children the pastor must content himself with the minimum necessary for being able to receive Holy Communion worthily. This, however, should not become the generally accepted level of growth in knowledge and understanding for all children. Since the instruction concerns itself with the message of God's Word that has eternal importance for the child, the best efforts of both pastor and children are called for.

The Examination

It is customary to examine the children before the assembled congregation as a part of the confirmation procedure. Such an examination is not intended to reveal the intellectual understanding of each child. It is not a final test to determine who will be confirmed. It cannot reveal to the congregation all that the children may have learned. If the examination is understood in these terms, it serves its purpose very poorly.

The examination can, however, serve as an opportunity for the children to give expression to their faith in their own words as they answer the pastor's questions. It prepares for the confession of faith made in the confirmation rite by means of the memorized words of the Creed. It gives evidence to the congregation that the memorized creedal confession is one that is understood and not a mere recitation by rote. It reveals to the congregation that the children are ready for Holy Communion.

The above objectives will determine the extent, content, and procedure of the examination. It is not possible to examine the children on all parts of the Catechism. A mere recitation of long sections of the Catechism is not necessary. The examination each year should concern itself with the law and sin, with the Second Article and redemption, with the sacraments, particularly the Lord's Supper. There may be value in varying the examination from year to year by adding to such basic questions others that concentrate on a particular part of the Catechism in greater detail. The pastor will prepare the examination carefully so that he keeps it moving along the course of a planned outline.

Specific questions should not be assigned in advance to individual pupils. The pastor will endeavor to put the children at ease, proceeding in a somewhat informal manner so that they may be brought to express themselves freely in response to his questions. Naturally questions that require a sentence or two to answer, that call for some kind of thoughtful explanation are better than those that can be answered by a single word or even by a mere yes or no. Let the pastor think of his questions as the means whereby the children are given an opportunity meaningfully to confess and explain their faith as God has worked it in their hearts through His Word.

The examination may take place in the regular service on the Sunday preceding confirmation. In this service it can then replace the sermon. Or it may be conducted in a special service in the afternoon of the preceding Sunday or on some evening during the week before confirmation. Time generally does not permit including it in the service on the day of confirmation. Congregations that have several services each Sunday and large confirmation classes may divide the class so that a portion of it is examined in each service. A half hour's examination should provide sufficient time to carry out the above objectives of the examination. In a larger church the use of a public address system will make the answers more readily audible.

The Confirmation Service

The confirmation service most often takes place in the spring of the year. Palm Sunday, which in some congregations may have become the traditional date, presents its problems, as does Pentecost. Since these are movable church festivals, the time for instruction before confirmation will vary from year to year. This must be taken into consideration when planning the course. There is also the danger of losing the significance of the festival in the church year when confirmation regularly is associated with the same festival. It is preferable to set a particular Sunday in May or early June as the regular confirmation Sunday.

The service can proceed according to suggestions in the agenda. The pastor will prepare the children for the service, since the children should be well acquainted with their part in the service so that confusion does not disturb the devotional atmosphere of the service. The pastor will also have to guard against letting externals draw attention away from the spiritual significance of the occasion. May the children remember, not the clothes they wore, the gifts they received, or the beautifully decorated altar, but rather the message they heard, the confession they made, the memory verse spoken over them, and the joy of being invited to the Lord's Supper!

Time usually does not permit including Holy Communion in the confirmation service. While our definition of confirmation would make this desirable, most often it is necessary to delay communion until a later service. The class may be asked to step forward as a group to receive their first communion together.

Adult Confirmation

Adult converts are received into fellowship with the congregation through the rite of confirmation. By their personally spoken confession, their faith in Christ and their confessional unity with the congregation are expressed, and they are received as communicant members.

The pastor has the responsibility of preparing adults for such reception into the congregation. This is done in a Bible information class. Since those who enter the class can hardly be expected to commit themselves to church membership before the instruction is completed, the term "adult membership class" can be misleading. We invite adults to the Bible information class in the hope that the Holy Spirit through the instruction in God's Word will work and strengthen faith in Christ and lead them to accept the full truth of Scripture and desire fellowship in the church that confesses this truth.

Various manuals are available specifically for such adult classes.[6] These should lead the learner into Scripture rather than replacing it. Luther's Small Catechism should also be drawn in because of its confessional status in the Lutheran Church.

A Bible information course should contain 20 to 25 lessons. This makes it possible to present it twice during the year. If work schedules or other complications do not permit someone to attend evening meetings, special classes can be arranged at convenient hours during the day. The pastor will attempt to accommodate as best he can all who are willing to listen to instruction from God's Word.

The regular order of confirmation for children can be adapted for adult use. The adults may be encouraged to make their confession in a regular service of the congregation. If there is strong hesitation about this, the rite may be performed in the presence of congregational representatives such as the church council or the board of elders. While a public examination of the adults could serve a useful purpose, it generally is omitted.

Those adults who have not been baptized may receive this sacrament at the time of the adult confirmation. They need not subsequently be confirmed in a separate rite.

Adults from Lutheran bodies not in fellowship with the congregation may be received into membership on the basis of their confession of faith without a formal adult confirmation rite. The pastor will need to assure himself of their qualifications for membership in the congregation, especially their agreement with the congregation's confession. In some cases this may become evident very soon. More often it will be desirable for them to attend the Bible information class, not only as a review for their own under-

6. See the bibliography for a listing of recommended manuals.

standing of Bible truth, but also that they may assure themselves that the congregation's teaching and practice are indeed of the kind with which they wish to become identified.

The Mentally Retarded

About three per cent of our nation's population is considered to be mentally retarded. A congregation of 400 souls can expect that about twelve will have an I.Q. of 70 or less. A very large percentage of these can be expected to fall into the educable group (I.Q. 50 to 70), a smaller percentage will be trainable (I.Q. 30-49), the smallest percentage are custodial cases (I.Q. 0 to 19), whose mental age remains between zero and two years and who will remain completely dependent on others throughout their lives.

Some of the educable will be the slow learners in the pastor's regular confirmation class. The pastor will recognize their limitation and take this into consideration in the demands made on them and may need to be satisfied with their reaching the minimum requirement for confirmation.

Others, especially the trainable mentally retarded, will require special classes. The Sunday school should already make provisions for these exceptional children in a special class where materials can be used that are suited to their limitations and where the size of the class (1 to 5) permits much individual work.

The pastor should not assume that whoever cannot fit into the regular confirmation class can never reach the understanding required for communion. Patient work with individuals even in the trainable group will make it possible for some of them to be confirmed and receive Holy Communion. Their mental handicap does not remove the need for the Savior, who reaches out to them too in His means of grace. Let the pastor not neglect these children who too readily are looked upon as "the least" in the kingdom of God!

Summary: Confirmation, as it is practiced among us, is an ecclesiastical rite in which children, upon being instructed in the Word of God as summarized in Luther's Small Catechism, confess their faith before the congregation and are admitted to Holy Communion. Care must be taken lest confirmation assume sacramental characteristics and even appear more important than baptism in the child's thinking. The confirmation instructions

126

should not give the impression that they conclude the study of God's Word, but rather that this is the beginning of a lifelong exposure to Word and sacrament. A public examination precedes the confirmation service, and Holy Communion follows as soon as possible. Adult converts are prepared in a Bible information class for reception into the congregation by confirmation. The mentally retarded need special consideration and can in many cases be brought to at least the minimum requirement for receiving Holy Communion.

VI. ADULT BIBLE STUDY CLASSES

The importance of continued study of the Bible should require no proof in a church that knows Holy Scripture to be God's own Word. The pastor will stimulate personal and group Bible study in every way he can. The Lutheran church, committed as it is to the *sola Scriptura*, should have pastors and people who study and know their Scriptures.

Role of the Bible Class

While various agencies are found in most congregations to teach its youth up to the time of their confirmation, congregations are less committed to providing further education on the adult, that is, post-confirmation, level. Unfortunately this can give the impression that confirmation brings all organized group study of the Bible to a conclusion. The church will want its young people to realize that the instruction up to the time of confirmation lays a foundation on which further instruction is to be built during the rest of the person's life. What is more, the post-confirmation age group contains the great majority of the congregation's souls. The role of the adult Bible class is to meet the needs for continued Bible study on the part of all age groups in the congregation. This is a broad role that frequently is severely limited in its application.

Objectives of the Bible Class

It must not be forgotten that the regular Sunday service does provide instruction in the Word of God for all age levels in the congregation. This is the primary means the church has employed through the centuries for the edification of its members, to build them up in knowledge, understanding, and faith.

The Bible class has objectives that supplement this teaching of the church as done in the Sunday service and that go beyond it.

We may state the specific objectives of the Bible class as follows:

to provide opportunity for growth in Christian knowledge and understanding; the sermon will also provide for this, but places special emphasis on providing inspiration; the Bible class will be inspirational, but aims more directly at growth in knowledge;

to provide opportunity for study of the Bible, its various books, and its truths, in a systematic way that is not readily possible from the pulpit;

to provide opportunity for questions and discussion, which cannot well be included in the Sunday worship.

The Pastor's Role as Leader of the Bible Class

The pastor may find himself with sole and complete responsibility for the Bible class in a congregation. He must stimulate interest in it, organize its class(es), and may be its only teacher. Such total responsibility can unduly limit the scope of Bible class activity.

When the adult Bible study class is recognized as an educational effort of the congregation, its board of education should provide assistance in planning and carrying out the work of adult education in the Bible. The council and the congregation in their meetings can discuss the work of the Bible class and make its success their concern.

The pastor is responsible for all teaching done in the Bible class. In practice he often is the only teacher. Especially in larger congregations this can result in limiting the number of people served through adult Bible classes. If laymen can be found who are "apt to teach" and who are willing to give the necessary time to preparation, the pastor may extend his Bible class effort by including in it the training of these lay teachers. Only laymen whose knowledge and ability help retain the respect of their fellow members should serve. Such assistance may be found most helpful for the teen-age group.

The Pastor As Organizer of the Bible Class

Bible classes conducted during the Sunday school hour may draw the largest enrollment, especially among the high school youth. Bible classes at this hour can also encourage them to conclude that the religious education begun in the Christian day school and the Sunday school should continue in the Bible classes

128

that are part of the congregation's educational program. If the pastor is to teach, practical considerations may, however, require a different time during the week. Consideration may also be given to conducting Bible classes both on Sunday morning and on a weekday evening.

Preferably, weekly meetings will be scheduled in either case. Anything less than a biweekly meeting will lose much of its value. Limiting the class to an hour can help prevent monotony. Unduly long evening meetings that go beyond their scheduled time discourage attendance. The class should begin and end on time.

There is no need to divide classes according to age as in the Sunday school. A division between those of high school age and all adults beyond that age may be sufficient. If this is done, the teen-agers will enter into the discussion more readily than when their parents and elders are present. Parents, too, may be freer in participating when their teen-age children are in a separate class. On the other hand, to group all others together may have its advantages for the participants, since adults of various age levels will participate in the discussions to their mutual growth in understanding. For those living in retirement a Bible class scheduled during the day may find ready acceptance as profitable use of the leisure time now available. A capable layman of this group may attend the pastor's regular Bible class and present the same material to the "golden agers."

A Bible class, if it is true to its name, must involve study of the Bible. Entire books or portions of books can be studied as a unit. A study of what the Bible says on a particular doctrine or on some practical topics and questions can provide variety. A series on notable people in the Bible may prove enlightening and inspirational. The Bible class can devote some time to a study of the Lutheran Confessions, or can offer a course in significant events from church history. Prepared courses are available. At the same time, the pastor will do well also to work out his own material. He may solicit suggestions of topics or courses from the people.

There are advantages in dividing the year's Bible class work into several shorter courses. Each course may consist of between 8 and 10 lessons. A useful division for midweek Bible classes may be to have one course in the fall, concluding with Advent or Christmas. The second can begin after the New Year and conclude with the beginning of Lent. A third course can begin after

129

Easter and continue through May or part of June. Sunday morning Bible classes should continue without interruption even though the division of the year into courses may still find application. Such a division into shorter courses provides several natural opportunities each year to invite attendance when a new topic is announced.

The Pastor as Teacher of the Bible Class

The best encouragement for attendance at the Bible class is a well prepared teacher. Since this most often is the pastor, he will need to provide time in his schedule for careful Bible class preparation. This preparation may require as much time as does the preparation of a sermon, or even more. Where time becomes a factor, the pastor may choose to make the portion of Scripture chosen for the Bible class the object of his private Bible study. A group of pastors may collaborate in preparing material in a smaller study conference. In this way the preparation for the Bible class will become directly rewarding for the pastor himself as well as for his people.

If the pastor uses prepared materials, he must not fail to study and adapt the material so that he is thoroughly acquainted with it and can present it as though it were his own. A cursory reading of the material before the meeting will hardly result in such a presentation.

Various teaching methods can be used in the Bible class. Perhaps the easiest and the one most familiar to the pastor is the lecture method. More difficult may be an inductive method that employs skilled use of questions and discussion. The former may be necessary with large classes; the latter is preferable with teenagers. However, discussion may be provided for large classes too by dividing them into smaller discussion groups under trained leaders for part of the period. An introduction to the discussion can begin the period and a report from the groups after the discussion can result in a profitable conclusion. Such a procedure does, however, require careful planning and preparation. Never must the discussion be permitted to deteriorate into a debate between two people or into a rap session that proceeds aimlessly to no conclusion. The type of material and the time available may also determine the method used.

The assignment of homework that needs to be done as a prerequisite for profitable attendance at the next meeting is hardly

130

possible or advisable. Nevertheless, the Bible class ought to arouse a desire for home Bible reading. A church library of carefully chosen books may profitably serve the avid reader. Books that are useful but that cannot be recommended without reservation should contain a notice to that effect with specific comments relating to the error.

Summary: The Bible class supplements the Sunday sermon in providing opportunity for growth in understanding through a study of God's Word under less formal circumstances that allow for questions and discussion. The pastor most often is the teacher of the class. If laymen are enlisted to assist, the pastor remains responsible for all teaching and will provide instruction and guidance. The Bible class requires no numerous divisions according to age, although a separate class for the teen-age youth is desirable. Whether particular portions of the Bible, biblical topics, or current problems that face the Christian are taken up, the Bible class should lead the people into Scripture itself. Attendance is best stimulated by careful preparation and teaching methods that avoid monotony.

VII. Other Agencies

The specific educational agencies considered in this chapter are those most commonly found in a congregation. This should not prevent a pastor and congregation from using any other agencies that may become available or that local circumstances make possible. Some states have laws that permit local public schools to release children (perhaps for an hour each week) so that they may receive religious instructions in their respective churches. Some congregations conduct a Saturday school or a weekday school on several days. These allow for more teaching time than the one hour a week available in a Sunday school.

A congregation that is able to use such agencies will need to decide how these relate to the other more commonly used agencies and to what extent they meet the objectives of its educational effort. That no part-time agency can replace the Christian day school should be evident. Whether some kind of weekday school can replace the Sunday school will depend on several questions. Will teachers be available in adequate numbers? Will the weekday school serve as a mission agency as well as the Sunday school? Is the time such that it can serve all children of the congregation? The answers to such questions will determine whether a weekday school can replace or merely supplement other agencies.

Generally only few materials are available offering a curriculum prepared specifically for these agencies. It should, however, not be difficult to plan a curriculum for the released time or weekday school by adapting the Bible histories or catechisms used in the Christian day school or by supplementing the Sunday school course.

Let the pastor and congregation spare no effort to set up the best educational program which it is able to carry out with its means and under prevailing circumstances. The Lord's injunction to teach should call the church's best efforts into action.

For Additional Reading

The Board for Parish Education of the Wisconsin Ev. Lutheran Synod has published materials helpful to the pastor in connection with the Christian day school. Among them are the following:

> "A Statement on the Philosophy and Purpose of the Christian Day Schools"
> "An Appraisal of Educational Principles in the Light of Scripture"
> "Starting a Christian Day School"
> "An Evaluation of the World's Philosophy of Education"
> "Suggestions for Building a School"
> "Selected Problems in School Administration & Supervision"
> "Thoughts on Organizing a Parent-Teacher Organization"
> "Responsibilities and Duties of Congregations' Boards of Education"
> "Christian Day School Informational and Promotional Packet"
> "Packet of Aids for New Schools"
> "The Director of Christian Education"

These may be ordered from the Board for Parish Education, 3614 West North Avenue, Milwaukee, Wisconsin 53208.

Concordia Leadership-Training Series. St. Louis: Concordia.
> *Old Testament History*, by A. W. Klinck
> *New Testament History*, by Wm. Arndt
> *Fundamental Christian Beliefs*, by Wm. Arndt
> *The Reformation Era*, by N. S. Tjernagel
> *Home Life in Bible Times*, by A. W. Klinck
> *The Life of Saint Paul*, by Wm. Arndt

These volumes can serve in the training of Sunday school teachers to add to their background-knowledge of the Bible and its times.

132

Drewes, Christopher F. *Introduction to the Books of the Bible*. St. Louis: Concordia, 1929.

This book is designed to acquaint the reader with the background against which the sacred writers wrote, and makes the central message of each book of the Bible clear. This could provide material for a course in Biblical introduction.

Eickmann, Paul E. *The Wonderful Works of God*. Milwaukee: Northwestern, 1970.

This adult manual of 20 lessons treats the chief doctrines of the Christian faith within the framework of Bible history. Each lesson is divided into shorter sections, generally followed by brief statements of the doctrines taught in the Bible passages cited in the discussion. Each section closes with a number of review questions, suggested Bible readings, and pertinent selections from the *Lutheran Hymnal*. This manual encourages working directly with Holy Scripture, treating the doctrines in a Bible history setting.

Eickmann, Paul E. *Gospel Gems from Isaiah*. Milwaukee: Northwestern, 1973.

In eight lessons for the adult Bible class the author treats familiar prophecies of Isaiah, giving a brief account of the historical setting for the message as well as a concise explanation of the prophecy.

Fischer, William E. *God's Will for Our Lives*. Milwaukee: Northwestern, 1973.

The young adult Bible class can review the 10 commandments on the basis of the 12 lessons in the Pupil's Guide. This should lead to thought provoking discussion in the light of their current experiences. Teacher's Manual available.

Franzmann, Werner H. *The Gospel Banners Forward Go*. Unit 1: "The Gospel Begins its March"; unit 2: "The Gospel Continues its March of Conquest"; unit 3: "The Gospel invades the Gentile World." Milwaukee: Northwestern, 1970.

The three units are based on the first twelve chapters of Acts. They serve to encourage more faithful and effective witnessing for Christ, even in the face of adversities.

Gerlach, Joel. *The Word is Now*. Milwaukee: Northwestern, 1972.

The six topics, creation, ecology, humanism, a Christian's dual citizenship, God's divine design for sex, and abortion, are discussed in six lessons. Each lesson provides material for two one-hour sessions with the young adults Bible class. There is a Pupil's Guide and a Teacher's Manual.

Grunze, Richard. *God's Record of Beginnings*. Milwaukee: Northwestern, 1972.

 The young adult Bible class can dig into the text of the first fourteen chapters of Genesis on the basis of a Pupil's Guide that studies the text by means of questions and cross references. Each of the six lessons concludes with selected thoughts for young people to contemplate and discuss. There is material for 12 one-hour sessions. A Teacher's Manual is also available.

Kolander, Donald E. *The Sermon on the Mount*. Milwaukee: Northwestern, 1973.

 A course for the adult Bible class that recognizes that the Sermon on the Mount is not intended to show how people should live in order to be saved, but how the saved should live. The seven lessons abound in application for Christian living, with the gospel as the constraining power.

Kretzmann, P. E. *Popular Commentary of the Bible*. 4 Vols. St. Louis: Concordia, 1921-24.

 This four-volume commentary of the entire Scriptures is a useful help to the Sunday school and Christian day school teacher.

Lueker, Erwin L. *Concordia Bible Dictionary*. St. Louis: Concordia, 1963.

 A helpful Bible companion for the Sunday school teacher, giving concise, up-to-date definitions of biblical terms in the Old and New Testaments.

The Lutheran Educator. A. F. Fehlauer, Editor-In-Chief. Published by the Board for Parish Education of the Wisconsin Ev. Lutheran Synod. 3614 West North Avenue, Milwaukee, Wisconsin 53208.

 This Lutheran education journal is published especially for the use of pastors and Christian day school teachers. Many of its articles will prove helpful and instructive likewise to Sunday school and vacation Bible school teachers.

Meier, Norbert R. *Jonah, The Unwilling Missionary*. Milwaukee: Northwestern, 1972.

 An adult Bible class course of six lessons that applies the attitudes and work of the prophet Jonah to the mission work of Christians.

Meyer, Arnold C. *Getting Acquainted with Christian Teaching*: An Introduction to Sunday School Teaching. Milwaukee: Northwestern, 1968.

 Can be used for a course in the principles of education and methods of teaching applied to the various departments of the Sunday school.

Miller, E. *Religious Arts and Crafts for Children.* St. Louis: Concordia, 1966.

This volume shows how arts and crafts may be used to enrich religious instruction. Helpful especially for the vacation Bible school.

Panning, Armin J. *The Life of Christ.* Milwaukee: Northwestern, 1971.

This is another unit in the Northwestern Teacher Training Series. Its particular value lies in that it helps the Sunday school teacher see how various episodes in Christ's life, treated in Sunday school, are related to one another and what they mean for our salvation. This book also lends itself well for Bible class and young people's meetings.

Rein, R. C. *Building The Sunday School.* St. Louis: Concordia, 1950.

This is a practical survey of the factors which make for an efficient Sunday school: Equipment, teachers' meetings and training, administration, records, congregational interest, attendance, enrollment.

Riess, Oswald. *What Does the Bible Say?* Detroit: Bethany Lutheran Church Office. Available through Northwestern Publishing House, Milwaukee.

Originally published in 1943, this manual has found wide use in the instruction of adults as well as in Bible classes. The method used in the 24 lessons follows a regular pattern. A question is followed by Scripture passages under the heading, "The Bible Says—" with the biblical answer to the question given under the heading, "From This We Learn—." A worksheet is part of each lesson.

Rupprecht, F. *Bible History References.* Vol. I: Old Testament; Vol. II: New Testament. St. Louis: Concordia, 1934.

A valuable sourcebook that can be placed into the hands of the Sunday school teacher for a study of the Bible history stories. Besides the explanations of the text, it provides numerous geographical, archaeological, and historical references, as well as hymn and Catechism references, Bible readings, maps, and charts.

Schuetze, Armin W. *Basic Doctrines of the Bible.* Milwaukee: Northwestern, 1969.

This is a course in the Northwestern Teacher Training Series for Sunday school teachers. Its 16 lessons present a concise and comprehensive study of the important teachings of the Bible. It may be adapted for use with a Bible class or for adult instruction.

Schuetze, Armin W. *Family Life under Christ.* Milwaukee: Northwestern, 1971.

This manual for the adult Bible study class contains seven lessons that apply Scripture to seven aspects of family living.

Toppe, Carleton. *The Church's Ministry in a Corrupt Society.* Milwaukee: Northwestern, 1972.

In Paul's first epistle to the Corinthians, which reflects the difficulties the young congregation faced in a pagan environment, we have a valuable God-inspired guide for congregational life today. The first eight chapters are covered in as many lessons, each lesson requiring two one-hour sessions. For the adult Bible class.

Wicke, Harold E. *Catechism of Differences.* Milwaukee: Northwestern, Fourth Edition, 1974.

The preface states the purpose of this booklet to be "to examine the differences in doctrine and practice between the various bodies in the pure light of the Word of God, so that error may be recognized as such and may eventually be removed in obedience to the Holy Word." This can serve as a basis for a Bible class unit on the differences among Lutherans.

Wicke, Harold E. *Christ and the Holy Scriptures.* Milwaukee: Northwestern, 1970.

Six lessons demonstrate how Christ used the Scriptures, lived by the Scriptures, and how He wants us to live by them. For the adult Bible class.

Wisconsin Synod Commission on Doctrinal Matters. *This We Believe.* Milwaukee: Northwestern, 1967.

Nine brief chapters present a summary of the doctrinal position of the Wisconsin Ev. Lutheran Synod. Useful for the Bible class or adult work.

Wisconsin Synod Board of Education. Individual Memory Course.

6

The Shepherd
Visits the Sheep

"Ye visited me"
(Mt 25:36)

The pastor has the responsibility to minister not only to the congregation as such, but also to each individual member of his flock in particular as the need for such ministrations arises. This is the area of the ministry to the individual, the care of souls, *Privatseelsorge*. What he does in performing this function is not essentially different from what every Christian ought to do for a fellow believer in the exercise of his spiritual priesthood. In the case of a pastor, however, the performing of these functions is assigned to him either explicitly or implicitly in his call. His very title as pastor implies as much, for a good shepherd is concerned not only about the well-being of his flock as such, but also about that of each individual sheep in his flock according to its needs. A pastor's conscience will be bound by passages like Ezekiel 3:17-21; 33:7-9 (where warning the individual is particularly stressed); Luke 12:42; Acts 20:28; 1 Peter 5:2. In his concern for the spiritual welfare of each individual member of his flock the pastor will be following the example of his Lord Jesus (Mt 9:2; 26:23-25, 50; Lk 15:4; Jn 3:1-21; 4:1-26) and of His apostles (Ac 20:20, 31; 1 Th 2:11; Eph 5:22, 25; 6:1-9).

137

The means with which the pastor will operate in his pastoral care of individuals will be the Word of God, ultimately the gospel. For, if he does find it necessary to apply the law, it will be either to prepare for the gospel by working a knowledge of sin; or to direct sanctification, for which the gospel alone can provide proper motivation. The particular skill which needs to be developed is to diagnose just what Word of God the individual in a particular situation needs and to be able to apply it in a manner which he will understand. This involves taking into consideration age, sex, temperament, social status, education (cf 1 Cor 9:19-23; Tt 2:2-6). Love and a truly evangelical spirit will give the proper tone to a pastor's ministrations. The pastor will find that his knowledge of psychology and pedagogical principles, in fact, his entire educational background provide him with insights which will enable him to size up situations correctly. Witness how St. Paul's varied background enabled him to adapt to various situations in his concern for souls: "I am made all things to all men, that I might by all means save some" (1 Cor 9:22). Furthermore, the pastor ought to know his members well. This fact argues against frequent changes of pastorates. It also explains why normally the pastor of a smaller congregation is less apt to feel burdened in his conscience than one whose charge includes many hundreds of souls or even more. In general it is the realization that he is to care for every individual soul committed to his charge that makes the pastor feel that his is indeed a responsible and difficult assignment. So it is not only in connection with his sermon work that a pastor needs to cultivate fervent and frequent prayer for the Lord's blessing. He will also need to ask for the Lord's guidance in the care of the souls committed to his care by the Lord. It will be his experience that the Lord does hear him and guide him. As he does his work, relying on the Lord's help, he will have frequent occasion to offer up for his congregation and its individual members prayers of thanksgiving similar to those found so frequently in the epistles of St. Paul.

I. PASTORAL CALLS IN GENERAL

Need

In order to learn to know his congregation better and better and to remain in contact with each individual member the pastor will consider it part of his continuing obligation to endeavor to visit his members in their homes. There are, of course, occasions when circumstances demand that a pastor visit a member, as, for example, illness, calamity, or when personal admonition is called for. But even apart from these special occasions a pastor's call as shepherd of Christ's flock makes it necessary for him to visit his members systematically and regularly in order to learn to know them better and to gain their confidence. There can be a sense of distance and strangeness over against the pastor if his people know him only from seeing him in the pulpit. If, however, he has contacted them in their homes and they have learned to know him as a friend who takes a personal interest in them, it will be much easier for them to accept his ministrations in a time of trial, or to go to him for help when a problem arises in their personal life, or when they are looking for an answer to questions which they have concerning matters of doctrine and practice. The Lord Jesus says of a good shepherd: "He calleth his own sheep by name" (Jn 10:3), and says of Himself: "I know them (My sheep)" (Jn 10:27). The Apostle Paul, whom we might well call a model pastor, says of himself: "I . . . have taught you publicly, and from house to house" (Ac 20:20). And again: "We exhorted and comforted and charged every one of you" (1 Th 2:11). Making house calls in our day presents more problems than it did in previous generations. Split shifts, working wives, involvement in scheduled recreation, and the like often make it difficult to find members at home. As a result it often becomes advisable to try to make an appointment before endeavoring to visit members in their home.

Beside the fact that learning to know one another better involves a degree of regularity and frequency of contact, the pastor will have to reckon with the fact that things do change. His members are exposed to temptation and error from without and, besides, have their own sinful flesh to contend with. Hence the fact that everything seemed to be in order in a home when it was last visited is no guarantee that on his next visit the pastor won't encounter doubts, questions, or problems. The weaker members, who may perhaps be in the greater danger, are the ones who will be least apt to contact the pastor if they have a problem. If he, however, visits them periodically, the fact that the pastor was concerned about them enough to visit them will set them at ease in his presence and make them willing to "open up."

139

Relation to Church Attendance

A pastor may not content himself with the thought that in his preaching he covers the whole spectrum of doctrine and practice in the course of time, for beside the fact that not all of his members hear his every sermon it is also true that not all will apply to themselves what they have heard. In pastoral calls the specific needs of people can be supplied. Furthermore, there is much truth to the statement: "The true pastor finds the themes of his sermons among his people." This may not be true of the homiletical form of his sermons, but points up the fact that the better he knows his people, their thinking and their problems, the more practical will be the applications in his sermons. There is also some truth in the old adage: "A housegoing pastor makes a churchgoing people," partly because the pastor in his visits tacitly or expressly will encourage church attendance and partly because some may respond to the fact that he by his visit has shown a concern for them by going to hear him preach to them. Regular churchgoing on the part of all is always the ideal, for by it the edification of Christians is furthered. House calls do not supplant, they only supplement church attendance.

Frequency

No flat rule can be laid down as to how often a pastor ought to visit his members. Once a year might be considered the ideal, but definitely not a law, since the size of a congregation will have much to do with determining whether a pastor can reach the ideal. We are not bound by the Calvinistic prescription that a pastor must visit his members regularly because he is a watchdog over their progress in sanctification. Furthermore, "there are diversities of gifts" (1 Cor 12:4). Some men can drive themselves harder than others, some can accomplish more in ten minutes than others in half an hour. *Ultra posse nemo obligatur.* Certainly a pastor will have to guard against making so many calls which are largely social or recreational in nature that he uses up time which ought to be devoted to careful preparation of his sermons. If the pastor faithfully makes every call for which there is a distinct need, he need not let his conscience be troubled by his inability to do as much general calling as he would like to do because of the demands upon his time by the varied requirements of his office. There will be weeks when he can make no general pastoral calls, while there will be others in which the opportunity is there to make a goodly number. He will do what he can and trust the Lord to lead him when he is specifically needed by some soul of whom he had not thought when he planned his schedule.

System

While system dare never be an end in itself, it will be an aid to efficiency and regularity in making calls. As much as possible, each day's calls ought to be restricted to some geographical section of the congregation lest by flitting hither and yon the pastor waste precious time. A record ought to be kept of calls that have been made, not only to arrive at statistical totals, but also to indicate when homes have been visited so that on subsequent rounds those who have not been visited for the longest period may be visited first. Opinions vary as to what is to be listed as a call. A casual encounter with a member is certainly not to be considered a pastoral call. An earnest conversation on a street corner which was truly pastoral in nature might well be so listed, however. One record system provides columns for listing sick, pastoral, mission, social, and office calls. This may be as good a system as any.

Purpose

The pastor's purpose in making house calls is to exercise his pastoral concern. He is the shepherd moving among his flock, displaying in his person the loving concern of the Good Shepherd. To serve under Him is a high privilege, but also involves a solemn responsibility. The faithful pastor will therefore hardly be satisfied with just getting into a home and out again as quickly as possible as though he were performing an irksome duty, nor with just having engaged in small talk. He will be alert for openings in the conversation which might give him an insight into the degree of knowledge which his people possess or into their particular problems. At the same time he will also be alert for opportunities to share with his people spiritual insights which have been granted to him. Not always will people be ready to speak about spiritual matters, nor be at ease in doing so. But even when that circumstance makes it appear as though there were no immediate results in a given visit, the very fact that the pastor has displayed an interest in his member will serve to build up the member's confidence and make him more ready to speak of what is in his heart when the pastor visits him again.

141

Cautions

A pastor will have to be circumspect at all times when making calls in the homes of his people. It is not enough for him to know that his motives are honorable, he will also need to be careful not to give wrong impressions. Let him be guided by the principle which the apostle expressed in a different context: "We have regard for what is honorable, not only in the sight of the Lord, but also in the sight of men" (2 Cor 8:21-NASB). Especially in his contacts with the women of his congregation must he be guided by the apostle's caution: "With all purity" (1 Tim 5:2). A pastor's position and a woman's profession of Christian sincerity do not guarantee that some woman member may not be tempted to try to exercise her coquettish wiles upon him. History and experience show that feminine enthusiasm for certain members of the clergy at times has had elements of an erotic nature in it. When a pastor suspects that such might be the case, no better advice can be given him than to imitate the turtle and withdraw into his shell. If additional calls upon such a misguided soul become necessary, it may be wise for the pastor to augment his own wariness by asking his wife or a reliable member to accompany him. He needs to bear in mind the general advice: "Considering thyself, lest thou also be tempted" (Ga 6:1), and the specific advice given by Paul to Pastor Timothy: "Flee youthful lusts" (2 Tm 2:22).

Furthermore, the pastor must be careful not to give the impression that he spends more time with the well-to-do, or with those who show him special favors, or with special groups than with the other members. This does not mean that he may not accept social invitations from his members if he has the time. Not only is he entitled to some social life, but he will also find that even at meals or on social visits occasions frequently arise to "preach the Word . . . out of season" (2 Tm 4:2). Furthermore, he will recognize the good will shown by such invitations and "quench not the Spirit" (1 Th 5:19). He will, however, need to be careful not to give the impression that he accepts only such invitations which come from a good cook or an entertaining conversationalist, but always be strictly impartial. In this connection the question may arise whether he may reciprocate by inviting members who have shown hospitality to him to be guests in his home on occasion. Why not? But he will need to realize that he is taking a calculated risk, for in a congregation of any size he will not be able to invite everyone, and there is always the possibility that those who were invi-

142

ted might boast of the fact while those who were not invited might take it amiss. After he has learned to know his congregation and has won the confidence of all of his members, he will be able to feel his way in this matter of inviting members to be guests in his home. There is no need to extend a return invitation; it is generally not expected.

Use of the Word

The effectiveness and fruitfulness of pastoral calls depend upon bringing and applying the Word of God. It has been traditional to speak of the fivefold use of the Word on the basis of 2 Timothy 3:16 and Romans 15:4: doctrine, reproof, correction, instruction in righteousness, and comfort. A sixth use must not be overlooked when we consider that a pastor's house calls take him not only into the homes of his members, but also into the homes of the unchurched and other prospects for membership. We are referring to its use for conversion, its missionary use.

Seldom will a pastor's use of the Word be restricted to one or the other of the above-mentioned categories. He will be alert to the need which confronts him in each new situation and seek to supply that need. Nevertheless, it is well to refer to the fivefold use of the Word to indicate how varied and rich ministering to individuals can be. Mission calls will be discussed later in this chapter.

Doctrine will be supplied when a pastor discovers that a member is so ignorant concerning some fundamental gospel truth that his faith is in danger, or concerning the Lord's will for Christian living that he is in danger of becoming estranged from his Lord or of undermining the harmony and good order of the congregation. While the pastor will try to remove any lack of knowledge which comes to his attention, he dare not burden himself with the feeling that it is his responsibility to eliminate every last trace of spiritual ignorance among his members. Such an ideal will not be attained in this life.

It is the same with *reproof,* a term which actually covers every exposure of error, whether it be in doctrine or in moral standards. Traditionally, it has been restricted to the former. It is well to note that in the New Testament this term is used only in the area of religion. People may have strange ideas about many things, but if they involve only secular matters, the pastor will not consider it his duty to try to set people straight. If, however, a member ex-

143

presses false doctrine, the pastor will have to expose it for what it is. If this involves a weak brother who is willing to be instructed in the truth, the pastor will be patient in dealing with him. If, however, it should become evident that the member is a persistent errorist who tenaciously clings to his false views and even seeks to spread them, gentleness will have to be coupled with firmness, and if there is no change, separation must follow (Tt 3:10). But a pastor is not to be a heresy hunter. He will have more than enough to do in combating the false views which come to his attention as he goes about among his people.

The use of the Word for *correction* goes hand in hand with its use for reproof. While the latter by use of the Word exposes error in doctrine or in moral standards for what they are, the former aims at pointing out the right way and encouraging that it be followed. In the traditional division of the fivefold use of the Word correction refers to the entire area of dealing with sin as distinguished from false doctrine. As God's called representative the pastor dare never condone any sin and thus give the impression that his standards are more relaxed than the Lord's. Nor dare he hesitate to register his disapproval of sin and thus give the impression that he lacks courage to speak up. On the other hand, he will show patience and understanding and not immediately thunder down the threat that the offender will have to be taken into church discipline unless he repents at once. Often a disapproving shaking of the head will suffice to call forth an apology or other indication of repentance on the part of the offender. Church discipline itself will be treated in a later chapter.

While sin on the part of his members will confront a pastor in various ways, one area which will be his constant concern is that of the so-called delinquent members. In seeking to win them from the error of their ways the pastor, especially in a larger congregation, may have to enlist the cooperation of the elders of the congregation. Perhaps the simplest way of determining which members are in this area of concern is to check the records of Communion attendance, for generally neglect of the Lord's Supper goes hand in hand with neglect of church attendance and with niggardly giving. A pastor's flesh may shrink from making disciplinary calls, but love for the Lord who has called him and love for the souls whom He bought with His blood will give him strength to overcome his flesh. The Lord gives him the encouraging reminder: "Brethren, if any of you do err from the truth, and one convert him; let him know, that he which converteth the sinner from the error of his way shall save a soul from death, and shall hide a multitude of sins" (Jas 5:19,20).

The very term *instruction in righteousness* brings the reminder that we are dealing with imperfect Christians who are in constant need of instruction and education so that they might be helped along to an ever higher level of knowledge and consecration. The Word supplies both the goals toward which Christians are to strive and the motivation for such striving, love for the Savior and gratitude for His blessings. Hence the faithful pastor will be alert for opportunities to present the Word. "Preach the word, be instant in season, out of season" (2 Tm 4:2).

The use of the Word for *comfort* has been called the most difficult but also the most beautiful facet of the pastor's care for the individual. It is difficult, for his own heart will be torn by grief when he sees people whom he loves ravaged by pain, approaching death, or crushed by some grief or calamity. He will feel the need for being comforted himself and wonder whether he is adequate for performing the duty of love which is set before him. But when he sees the power of the Word to help people to smile in spite of their pain, to die triumphantly, or to submit to the Lord's chastisements patiently, he will thank the Lord that he has been entrusted with the ministry of comfort.

In general, especially the younger pastor would do well to prepare for his calls by reviewing what the Word of God has to say about the situation which he expects to encounter. Since he is dealing with individuals he will also try to anticipate the objections or questions which a particular person is apt to raise and what he as pastor will say on the basis of the Word. This kind of preparation can be only relative, however. To try to plan a visit in detail and to force it to follow a preconceived pattern could lead to legalism, artificiality, and a failure to try to understand the thinking of an individual and to meet him on his ground as is the way of love. The thorough training which a pastor has received is intended to give him a reservoir of knowledge upon which he can draw on the spur of the moment if need be. *Mutatis mutandis* the pastor may apply to himself the Lord's promise to His disciples: "When they deliver you up, take no thought how or what ye shall speak: for it shall be given you in that same hour what ye shall speak" (Mt 10:19). This points up the privilege of praying for help and wisdom before making a call. When situations arise which call for repeated visits because of a baffling problem, a pastor does well to remember that he has another resource available to him in the advice of experienced brethren in his vicinity.

Summary: The making of pastoral calls is a duty which is inherent in the pastor's position as shepherd of a flock. His concern is for both the flock as such and for each individual member of the flock. Therefore he will endeavor to remain in contact with the individual member both in order that he may learn to know him and his needs, and in order that the member may learn to know his pastor and to feel at ease with him. Various factors will determine the frequency with which calls can be made. System will be an aid to efficiency. Certain cautions will need to be observed when calls are made. As the pastor meets with varying circumstances while making his calls, he will employ one or more of the traditional fivefold uses of the Word. The pastor will do as much as he can to prepare for his calls but will endeavor to remain flexible enough to react appropriately if the call develops differently from what he expected.

II. THE MINISTRY OF COMFORT

We now turn to a more detailed discussion of the ministry of comfort. In it the pastor needs to be especially faithful and conscientious, and to it he ought to give a high priority in his schedule. This ministry involves calls which need to be made to comfort members in physical or spiritual distress, and especially when they are ill or death is approaching.

Neither the church in its corporate activity nor the pastor has a specific call to minister to the physical needs of the members of a congregation, all talk about the "total ministry to the total man" to the contrary notwithstanding.[1] The pastor in obedience to the law of love will indeed also provide whatever help he can in cases of physical distress and will also bring them to the attention of his people. But his main concern, in line with his call, will be the

1. A fuller presentation of the authors' position on this matter may be found in two essays which appeared in the *Wisconsin Lutheran Quarterly*:

Habeck, Irwin J. "An Evaluation of the Term 'Christ's Ministry to the Whole Man.'" WLQ, Jan. 1969, LXVI, 50-58.

Schuetze, Armin W. "Scriptural Principles with Respect to the Church's Mission and Christian Welfare Work." WLQ, July 1973, LXX, 194-208.

special spiritual needs of his people when calamity has overtaken them, since it is at such times that the temptation to murmur, doubt, or despair is especially strong. He will not take it for granted that at least his stronger members will come through a time of trial unscathed. He will show his concern for all of his members when they are afflicted by bringing them the comfort which they need (1 Th 5:14; 2 Cor 1:4).

Prisoners

Before we proceed to a discussion of cases which most frequently call for the ministry of comfort, mention should be made of the fact that members who are jailed because they have run afoul of the law dare not be bypassed but rather are especially in need of spiritual ministrations. If the member admits his guilt and expresses his repentance, the pastor will try to determine whether he is sorry only because he was caught and got himself into trouble, or whether he is sorry because he has sinned against his God (Ps 51:3,4). If there is every indication that the repentance is genuine, the law has already done its work and it behooves the pastor to proclaim the gospel in all of its fullness, both by means of the promises of grace and by examples of this grace in action, as, for example, in the case of David or the prodigal son. The pastor will show that in this situation it is a fruit of faith patiently to submit to the sentence which the Lord in His providence has let the authorities impose. He will caution his member against thinking that serving the sentence helps to remove his guilt before God. The prisoner may be paying his debt to society, as the expression goes, but his debt to God was paid on the cross.

If the prisoner attempts to explain or even to defend or justify his crime, the pastor will indeed be a sympathetic listener, but in the end will have to show him that he is accountable to God for his behavior and that the way to peace is to confess his sin and to cast himself upon the Savior's mercy. Where there is only circumstantial evidence and the prisoner steadfastly affirms his innocence, the pastor will take him at his word and in all sincerity comfort his member and encourage him to be patient in his time of great trial. The pastor dare not be governed by his own suspicions, although he may feel constrained to point out the spiritual danger in trying to hide one's guilt from God (Ps 32:3,4). If the prisoner privately admits his guilt to the pastor but publicly pleads innocent, the pastor will have to respect the confessional

147

seal, but in his private ministrations warn about the consequences of living in sin.

The rehabilitation of released prisoners will be a matter of special concern for the loving pastor. He will need to encourage the man not to hesitate to take his place in the congregation, in public services, and at the Lord's Table at the side of all other penitent sinners. On the other hand, he will carefully try to counteract any evidence of the elder-brother attitude which might come to light among his members.

Spiritual Nature of Sick Calls

The time of sickness and especially of approaching death can be a time of spiritual danger for any Christian. There is the temptation to doubt God's love, to murmur, to despair. Even the most mature Christian cannot be counted upon to know to which portion of Scripture to turn for comfort and strength. It is one of the pastor's chief duties and privileges to meet the needs of his people at such a time. And that is what the members expect of a pastor when he visits at their sickbed. Incidentally he also is a friend. If there is a material need to be met, he will either help or call in someone else and then gracefully step into the background. As a wise cobbler he will stick to his last and not try to practice medicine, although there may be times when he will advise calling a doctor or going to the hospital.

The pastor will have to counteract the expectation that his prayers and ministrations are going to effect a physical cure. This could happen; the age of miracles is not past. But it will not always happen, and if a pastor does anything to encourage the expectation that he will help the patient recover and recovery does not follow, confidence in his entire ministry may be undermined. It is not the pastor's calling and concern to effect physical healing, but to minister to the soul by encouraging patience, supplying comfort, and strengthening the hope of eternal life. Since his ministrations are on the high spiritual plane, he will not downgrade them by requesting or encouraging a gift for his services. There may be times, however, when to refuse to accept a token of appreciation spontaneously offered might do more harm than good.

Even if it were not a specific function assigned to him in his call, the pastor would still consider it his duty and his privilege to visit the sick. For among the good works to which the Lord Jesus will point as evidence of saving faith He mentions: "I was sick, and ye visited me" (Mt 25:36). And St. James writes: "Is any sick among you? let him call for the elders of the church" (5:14). The sickness which we have in mind when we speak of calling on the sick does not include minor, passing ailments like a bad cold or stomach flu, or, in the case of children, measles, mumps, or chicken pox. On the other hand, the sickness does not have to be a matter of life and death. If hospitalization is required, except briefly for tests, there ought to be no question about the pastor's duty to visit his member as soon as possible. A visit before surgery is especially necessary to provide needed comfort and assurance. In any event it is better to err in the direction of being overly concerned than in the direction of being indifferent.

Various Cases

The pastor's obligation to visit the sick involves all of the members of his flock without exception and without respect of persons. Members who might be under church discipline but with whom the process has not been concluded ought not to be bypassed. The Lord may be using affliction to soften a stubborn heart. Sick children ought not to be overlooked. If they are old enough to understand simple words of comfort, they will as a rule be very receptive. If they are still infants, the parents and family will not only be in need of comfort, but will also appreciate the fact that they can be present when their pastor prays for their child.

Patients in a maternity ward ought to be visited. If a mother has been blessed with the gift of a healthy child, her pastor will want to lead her in a prayer of thanksgiving. His visit will also give him an opportunity to encourage the choice of responsible sponsors of our confessional fellowship. If there has been a stillborn child, the pastor in his ministry of comfort will encourage the mother to submit patiently to the will of the Lord. If the child is physically or mentally defective, the pastor will encourage the mother to commend herself and her child to the care of a gracious Father and a loving Savior.

If an unchurched person who is sick requests the services of a pastor, the pastor will welcome the opportunity to do mission work. The extent of his ministrations will depend upon the patient's reaction. If he is requested to visit an unchurched sick person, the pastor will not insist that the request come from the patient, but simply go. If others have requested the visit, the pastor will soon discover as he speaks to the patient whether his ministrations are welcomed or considered a nuisance, and guide himself accordingly.

If a pastor chances upon a patient who is a member of another congregation, whether it be of his fellowship or not, he will direct him to his own pastor to avoid becoming "a busybody in other men's matters" (1 Pe 4:15). Even what he considers only a friendly neighborly call could expose him to suspicion. If, however, death appears to be imminent so that it may seem to be too late to call the patient's pastor, the pastor will feel constrained by the duty of love to do for the patient what can be done under the circumstances.

Showing Pastoral Concern

Sick calls are made in the home, in nursing homes, in public institutions, and especially in hospitals. Where there is a large hospital or a concentration of hospitals there may be an institutional missionary who has been called to minister to the sick of his confessional fellowship and to the unchurched. The pastor of a congregation will call upon the hospitalized of his congregation and upon others to whom he has been requested to minister. If he comes upon a member of a sister congregation whose pastor has not been informed about the patient, he will show his brother the favor of informing him. Where it is evident that such a patient is being neglected by his own pastor, the pastor may well feel constrained to forget technicalities and give the patient the spiritual care for which he yearns. If a member of his congregation must be hospitalized in a distant hospital, a pastor ought not to be satisfied with giving the family the name of the pastor or institutional missionary in that city — he will write to the man or phone him himself. Pastoral concern will make a pastor want to be sure that his patient is receiving spiritual care in his time of trial. Nor should he be too ready to shift the entire responsibility for visiting his patient upon other shoulders. If at all possible he ought to try to make even a long trip at least at intervals to visit his patient himself. If this cannot be done, one expedient which will help to manifest his concern for his patient is to write him a letter of comfort and encouragement from time to time. When he learns that the patient has returned to his home, the pastor ought to make a special effort to see him as soon as possible.

150

Emergency Situations

When a pastor is called to visit a sick member who is suddenly stricken with what appears to be a critical illness or whose condition has taken a sudden turn for the worse, he will respond as soon as is humanly possible, by day or night, in fair weather or foul. He will never want a dying member to remain without comfort due to his negligence. Since emergencies of this nature can happen at any time, it is advisable for the pastor as a general practice to leave information as to where he can be contacted, with his wife, the church secretary, or some designated member, when he is out making calls or away from his home or office.

Scope

Routine sick calls are to be made at a time which is convenient for the home or the hospital, not too early in the morning nor too late at night. Members of a congregation need to be trained to inform their pastor as soon as possible when sickness occurs in the family. Even when the illness is not critical and no immediate visit is indicated, this information will help a pastor in his stewardship of time so that he can schedule his calls in geographical areas instead of scattering each day's calls over a wide area. No pastor, however, ought to make it a rule that he will visit the sick only when called and only as often as he is called. Spiritually weaker members in particular may not think of calling the pastor. Since, however, they are the ones who especially need his spiritual care, he will immediately call on them if he hears that they are ill. A faithful pastor will also not hesitate to call upon members who are afflicted with a contagious disease, for they too need the ministrations of their pastor. It goes without saying that the pastor will use whatever antiseptic measures are indicated to safeguard others to whom he will be ministering, his family, and himself.

A faithful pastor will not neglect to visit a patient even though the sight of a person in the last stages of cancer, or of a body badly mangled by an accident, or covered with horrible burns would tend to nauseate him. He will stifle his own reactions and consider his patient's desperate need for comfort, even as our Lord Jesus did not consult His own convenience but regarded our need (Php 2:4,5).

151

Length and Frequency

The patient's condition will to some extent determine the length of the visit. If he is hovering on the threshold of consciousness, the visit will be very brief. If he is under sedation or in great pain, the visit will perforce be brief. If the patient is fairly comfortable, the visit may be longer. But even under favorable circumstances the visit ought not to exceed twenty or thirty minutes in length. The frequency of calls will generally be in inverse ratio to their length. If the call must be kept brief because of the critical condition of the patient, it will be necessary to visit him every day. As his condition improves, the call may last longer and the visits may become less frequent, every other day, twice a week, once a week. The final call will be used by the pastor to direct his patient to thank the Lord for his recovery and to dedicate his regained strength to serving his Lord. Once the patient is able to come to church, the necessity of calling on him has ended.

Shut-Ins

When patients never fully recover and are unable to come to church, or the infirmities of age lead to the same situation, they generally are classified as shut-ins. In the case of shut-ins a regular schedule of calls is indicated, both to serve them with the Word and to give them the Lord's Supper. The size of a congregation and the number of shut-ins will determine the frequency with which calls on shut-ins can be made. Since we expect our members to come to church every week, the ideal would be to visit shut-ins every week. But in a congregation of any size this ideal is beyond reach and the pastor may be hard pressed to visit his shut-ins once per month. Some system of rotation will have to be devised so that no one is forgotten and all are treated equally. Having members play taped services to the shut-ins will supplement, but dare not supplant the pastor's personal ministrations. Among the shut-ins it is well to include the mentally retarded, whether they are children or adults. The pastor's concern for them represents the Lord's, an assurance which they particularly need because they otherwise feel "left out." Their families too need continuing comfort in this type of affliction.

Nature of the Visit

The background of training which a pastor receives ought to equip him with a reservoir of comforting Bible passages and hymn stanzas upon which he can draw in his ministry to the sick. In the early years of his ministry he may want to write out the devotions which he intends to use with his patients until such a time when experience has developed the faculty of drawing from his store of memory a text which is particularly appropriate and of applying it. The pastor will pray that the Lord might endow him with wisdom, tact, and love as he ministers to his patients. It has rightly been said that the entrance of a pastor into a sickroom ought to be like letting in a ray of sunshine. If members of the patient's family or other visitors are present, their offer to leave the pastor alone with his patient ought not to be accepted unless there are circumstances which demand privacy. The family is also going through a time of trial and needs not only an expression of sympathy, but above all comfort. A visitor hearing the pastor's devotion may under the Lord's guidance turn out to be a mission prospect. In no event ought a pastor allow humility or timidity to keep him from ministering to his patient because he does not want to interrupt the visitors. Patients expect their pastor to bring them comfort from the Word of God.

The Devotion

Honest concern for the patient will lead the pastor to inquire about the patient's condition unless the circumstances are such that the patient's attention span is extremely brief. It is well to let him talk, since what he says may often afford an insight into his spiritual state. This does not mean that the pastor needs to use up his time listening to the medical history or life history of a patient who rambles on and on. His concern is to discover whether his patient has any particular spiritual problems or whether he is submitting patiently to the Lord's will, knows his sinfulness, is sure of his salvation, is not afraid to die, is not worrying. His remarks will be tailored to fit the patient's state. There are times when only a brief Scripture passage or prayer can be used. In less extreme cases the application of a passage is always desirable even when the condition of the patient is not serious or he is well on the road to recovery. While a devotion ably prepared by another may be used occasionally, original work generally is more spontaneous and direct.

The pastor's fund of appropriate texts will grow with experience. He will be alert for them in his own devotional reading of the Word. Often a portion of his most recent sermon can be adapted, and a text which led to a sermon which emphasized comfort may become one to which the pastor will subsequently often revert. The length of the devotion itself will be determined by the condition of the patient, but should rarely exceed ten minutes. Where repeated calls are necessary, it is well to keep a record of texts that have been used. Memory is tricky. Since the Bible is full of fitting texts, there is no need for repetition. Usually devotions are welcomed. If, however, there appears to be apathy, calls are still to be repeated as often as the situation of the patient demands, and the pastor will trust that the Spirit will work when and where He wills. In his devotions with the sick the pastor ought always to take the patient to the foot of the cross. He will not just tell him that because he is a child of God all is well, or that a child of God is patient. Rather, he will remind him that it was for a sinner like him that Jesus died; that the death of Jesus for him is proof that God loves him; that the Savior who loves him has promised to be with him and is leading him at all times in wisdom and love.

Speaking about Death

If the condition of a patient does not appear to be serious, there is no warrant to alarm him needlessly by dwelling upon the subject of death. Still every sickness is a reminder of human frailty and mortality, sudden turns for the worse are not unusual, and therefore it is well tactfully to refer also to the hope that is ours. If it seems that the patient is nearing his end, the pastor will direct his thoughts more and more to death and eternity in order to help him to be ready to depart and to be with Christ, and to die triumphantly. He usually does not need to tell the patient bluntly that he is dying — the patient usually senses it anyhow — but on the other hand he will not be deterred from facing the facts by suggestions to the contrary on the part of the attending physician or the family.

Use of Prayer

Usually the devotion is concluded with a prayer. While prayers written by others may be used, especially early in a man's ministry, a pastor will gradually try to develop the art of using *ex corde* prayers. It is well to conclude with the Lord's Prayer; the patient will often join in. The use of the first person singular or plural in prayers seems to make them more intimate as the pastor speaks for the patient in his weakness. Only in exceptional cases ought the devotion to consist of only a prayer. Prayer is not a means of grace — the Word is!

Even if a patient appears to be unconscious, comatose, delirious, or heavily sedated, his pastor ought not to leave him without addressing something brief to him, e.g., John 3:16; 1:29; 1 Timothy 1:15; "Jesus, Thy blood and righteousness"; "O Christ, Thou Lamb of God." Sometimes patients realize what is going on without being able to respond; sometimes they may even react with an unexpected flicker of recognition. A pastor ought to be careful about what he says about such patients to others who may be in the room — the patient may be able to hear and remember an inconsiderate remark.

Private Communion

If a pastor has been called to visit a sick member, it may be well to ask him whether he would like to receive the Lord's Supper. Often the suggestion is welcomed. If the patient hesitates because he has the mistaken notion that private Communion is something like extreme unction and only for the dying, the pastor will be quick to assure him that the Lord's Supper is the Lord's special means for strengthening faith and giving assurance of forgiveness, both of which benefits we need in the time of trial. But undue pressure is to be avoided.

If a table and napkin are available, good; if not, they are not essential. The form in the agenda may need to be shortened if the attention span of the patient is short. The sacrament is not to be administered to those who are unconscious or delirious since they are in no position to examine themselves. At times only a minimal amount of the wafer and wine can be used; at times intinction is necessary. Sometimes when the pastor distributes the elements he will have to raise the patient's head if he is lying down. As a general rule it is wise to restrict private Communion to patients who cannot come to church lest members of the family who are not of our confessional fellowship for sentimental reasons ask to be included. After Communion has been given, the pastor will address a few parting words to his patient and leave without lapsing into generalities so that the patient may meditate upon the comfort which he has received. The pastor of a larger congregation may find that he can save time by carrying his private communion set with him whenever he is out making calls. This is

155

advisable, since in the course of making his calls he may be contacted to make an emergency call, may discover that a patient has taken a turn for the worse and requests the Lord's Supper, or may receive a similar request from one of his shut-ins.

Summary: The ministry of comfort is concerned with ministering to the spiritual needs of those members who are afflicted and distressed. While a member who has been arrested and jailed may not always belong in this category, he is in need of special spiritual care. The sick, the dying, and the shut-ins, however, are always to be counted among those who are afflicted and distressed. The pastor's prime concern is to supply their spiritual needs. Visiting sick members is, in fact, one of his specific duties. He is to respond to emergencies, but also to be faithful in making regular calls upon his sick and shut-ins. Circumstances will determine their frequency. The pastor will supply comfort from the Word of God and by the use of prayer. At times his ministrations will include private Communion.

III. SPECIAL CASES
A. Mental Illness
Symptoms

A detailed discussion of mental illness is beyond the scope of this book. Nevertheless it is desirable that the pastor know something about the nature and symptoms of mental illness. Psychiatrists distinguish between neurosis and psychosis. The neurotic maintains contact with real life. Some of the symptoms of neurosis are feeling unloved, inferior, and inadequate; excessive shyness; constant sense of guilt, dread, and fear; chronic tiredness and nervous tension; sleeplessness; the constant fear of physical illness; pronounced phobias such as fear of high or closed-in places. It has been said: "All of us have some of these feelings some of the time, but the neurotic person has them to a greater degree most of the time."[2]

The psychotic has lost contact with some or all aspects of reality; he lives in a world of his own. Some of the symptoms are: hearing voices; feeling that people are plotting against him; being highly excited; depression; abuse of alcohol; loss of memory;

2. *Some Things You Should Know about Mental and Emotional Illness* (National Association for Mental Health), p 4.

156

carelessness about appearance or being overly concerned; talking to himself; imagining visions or ailments; acting out his psychosis in ways that endanger his own life or that of others; feeling that something terrible is about to happen to him or that he has committed a dreadful crime; imagining that he has magical powers or is a famous person; assuming one position for incredible periods of time; repeating one motion or phrase over and over; being unable to see or to walk, with no physiological cause for the blindness or paralysis. "The self-absorbed are so involved with their thoughts and fancies that they pay no attention to eating, drinking, sleeping, or elimination; the restless are too busy to stop for them; the senile are too absent minded or befuddled."[3] Psychotics "may see or hear what is not there (hallucinations), misinterpret what is there (illusions), or invent fantastic new things (delusions)."[4]

Senility is characterized "by personality deterioration, progressive loss of memory, eccentricity, and irritability."[5]

Use of This Knowledge

It has been said that a little knowledge is a dangerous thing. The fact that he has some knowledge about mental illness dare not mislead the pastor into thinking that he is competent to treat and cure it any more than he is able to treat and cure physical illness. His concern is the spiritual well being of his member. The knowledge which he has about mental illness may, however, enable him to diagnose a case while members of a family still are at a loss to explain what has happened to one of their own. Then he faces a duty which charity will not permit him to shirk. He must confront the family with the painful facts of the case and urge them to seek psychiatric help. He will tell them that mental illness is no more a disgrace than physical illness; that both are a chastisement from the Lord; that anyone afflicted with mental illness may become violent or develop suicidal tendencies; that any delay in seeking professional help may lead to grave consequences; that not every case of mental illness is incurable, for psychiatric science has made great progress especially in the dis-

3. Edith M. Stern, *Mental Illness, a Guide for the Family* (National Association for Mental Health, 1962), p 26.
4. Rev. Henry H. Wiesbauer, M.S.S., *Pastoral Help in Serious Mental Illness* (National Association for Mental Health, 1960), p 5.
5. Mary W. Holand ed., *Doors to Daylight* (Milwaukee County Association for Mental Health, 1965), p 2.

covery and use of effective medication, and has been used by the Lord to help many patients to return to normal living; that treatment in the early stages of mental illness has the best prospects of being effective. Only if he can discover no alternatives will a pastor, constrained by his love for the patient and for society, sign a petition for a sanity hearing.

Spiritual Care

In his contacts with his mentally ill patient the pastor will make a special effort to reflect the love and concern of the Savior. He will not allow himself to feel rebuffed by apparent hostility on the part of the patient nor fall into the trap of being pitted against the doctor by the patient. He will be a sympathetic listener even to ramblings. He will not feel frustrated if the patient continues to gravitate toward his obsessions. If he can, he will hold a devotion; if that doesn't work, he will find some way of leaving something of the Word of God with the patient. The pastor will have to use sanctified judgment in determining whether a member who is mentally ill may receive the Lord's Supper. There are cases of senility in which the member will stop his ramblings and be alert while he receives private Communion, while in other cases it will become evident that he is no longer capable of the lucidity and concentration which are necessary for self-examination and receiving the Lord's Supper with blessing. In some cases of mental illness there are longer periods of lucidity. In others there is normal thinking in all areas except in that of one obsession. In other cases there are only confusion and irrationality. Hence each case will have to be dealt with on its own merits.

It needs to be borne in mind that mental illness does not ordinarily respond to treatment as quickly as physical illness. Even if the patient is institutionalized and distance makes it necessary to refer the regular care of the patient to an institutional missionary, a pastor should still make the effort to visit his member. These contacts are valuable also later when the patient is released and may feel shy or ashamed about moving among people again. Since the pastor stood at his side during his illness, the member will feel free to go to him if he is disturbed about anything. This will enable him to reenter the life of the church and community more confidently.

B. Alcoholism, Drug Addiction, Sexual Perversion

We cannot go along with the current thinking that those who are enmeshed in one of the evils mentioned in the subtitle are merely "sick," are in need only of psychiatric help, and are not to be charged with any moral lapse. Scripture speaks too plainly about sexual perversion and the excessive use of alcohol in passages like 1 Corinthians 6:9,10; Galatians 5:19-21; and Ephesians 5:18. While it is difficult if not impossible to find a direct reference to the drug abuse which is such an alarming evil in our day, since the effects produced by drugs parallel and exceed those produced by alcohol, passages which refer to drunkenness are applicable. The use of such passages is also pertinent because competent medical authorities classify alcohol as a drug. Likewise applicable are the Fifth Commandment and the law of love, which one who uses drugs illegitimately violates over against himself, his family, his community, and society in general. Since those who sink into these vices show a weakness which has made them unwilling to face up to reality, the pastor will approach them with understanding, loving concern, and the desire to win them from the error of their ways. But he will not mitigate the seriousness of sin. If there is evidence of repentance, but the penitent laments that he just can not break with his sin, the need for psychiatric help may be indicated. But the more important means upon which the pastor will depend and upon which he will lead his member to depend are the power of the Word and God's promise to answer prayer.

C. Demoniac Possession

Older textbooks of pastoral theology go to some length in discussing this phenomenon. That it can still appear is beyond question. We know from the gospels that the symptoms resembled those of insanity. But both the term and our Lord's treatment of the cases with which He met show that demoniac posession was different, due not to natural causes but to direct intervention of the devil. If a pastor were to encounter a case where a supernatural cause seems indicated, his resort will be prayer both on his part and on the part of his congregation.

D. Spiritual Distress

It can happen in the life of any Christian that his own sinful heart, abetted by the Tempter himself, will give rise to doubts

159

about the truth of the Word, uncertainty about his own salvation, or to blasphemous and even suicidal thoughts. Young people who are going through the transition from simply believing what has been told them by their parents, pastors, and teachers to independent conviction based upon evidence in the Word are especially apt to be assailed by questions and doubts. But spiritual distress can also be caused by others as they try to get a Christian to doubt the truth or to embrace error, or tempt him to sin. The pastor will welcome it if a distressed member reposes enough confidence in him to tell him what is bothering him. For that very reason if a young person, for example, asks his pastor how he can know that the Bible is true, the pastor dare not thunder down upon the person, "You ought to be ashamed of yourself for even asking such a question. Didn't you pay attention in confirmation class?" Rather, he will endeavor to be empathic and seek to restore the troubled soul to conviction or consecration by the use of the Word of God and prayer in the spirit of Galatians 6:1: "Brethren, if a man be overtaken in a fault, ye which are spiritual, restore such an one in the spirit of meekness; considering thyself, lest thou also be tempted."

Summary: While it will be of some value for the pastor to know something about the symptoms of mental illness and the patterns of behavior which result from it, his prime concern in ministering to his members who have been afflicted with it will be to supply their spiritual needs as much as their condition permits. In cases of alcoholism, drug addiction, and sexual perversion the pastor will recognize that a specific sin is the root problem, and by use of the Word seek to work repentance, the assurance of forgiveness, and the determination to bring forth the fruits of repentance. If he should encounter a bona fide case of demoniac possession, the pastor will fervently pray for the deliverance of his afflicted member. He will treat cases of spiritual distress with sympathetic understanding and supply guidance and comfort from the Word of God.

IV. MISSION CALLS

Mission calls are distinct from the types of pastoral calls which have been discussed in the foregoing. In making mission calls the pastor is not dealing with those under his pastoral care, but is involved in missionary outreach on the local level. The pastor, whether in a mission congregation or a self-supporting congregation, will always consider himself a missionary. Self-evidently the Great Commission (Mt 28:18-20) applies to him, too.

Purpose

The purpose of mission calls is to preach the gospel in the hope of winning souls for Christ (Mk 16:15,16; 2 Tm 2:10). If the pastor bears in mind that his sole responsibility is to tell the good news and that the producing of results is entirely in the Lord's hands, he will not feel frustrated over an apparent lack of results, nor will he be inclined to boast if the Lord grants him many visible results. There is always the danger that the complexity of the organizational church might induce a pastor to substitute inferior goals. He may want to increase the membership figures of his church either to impress a mission board or to enhance his own reputation. He may want to swell the number of contributors or add to the prestige of his congregation by adding some prominent person to its ranks. These and other by-products may follow, but preaching the gospel is the main matter. For that reason, too, respect of persons must carefully be avoided. It is easy to be influenced to regard renters, apartment dwellers, the poor, or people low on the social ladder as less desirable prospects than their opposites.

Means

From the foregoing it is evident that the one means upon which the pastor as missionary will rely is the Word. To get people to join his church he will not, for example, use as a sales pitch the consideration that other members of the family or close friends belong or that as a member the prospect could make contacts which would be to his advantage. Nor will the pastor rely upon pat answers to common excuses to break down the prospect's sales resistance.

Since first impressions are important, especially in the case of those whose contacts with the organized church have been limited or nonexistent, the pastor when making mission calls ought to make a special effort to be neat in appearance, to display good manners, and to be friendly. He must not allow himself to become ruffled if he encounters an initially hostile attitude. Since our church body has a reputation for "strictness," prospects may want to start an argument about our practice in one area or the other.

161

Then it is well to remember that we are called, not to argue, but to testify. At the same time the pastor will let the prospect know that he is perfectly willing to answer all questions in due time, but that his immediate concern is to tell his prospect good news which he needs to hear. Beyond that it will be a matter of "playing it by ear." Each situation is different, and each pastor is different. But the man to man contact is basic. Witness our Savior's way with Nicodemus (Jn 3:1-21) and with the Samaritan woman (Jn 4:1-42). The invitation to come to church and later to attend an adult information class will follow at the proper time. Even if there has been little initial success, because of the eternal importance of the undertaking it is well to heed the old adage: "If at first you don't succeed, try, try again." Many a pastor can relate instances in which such persistence led to an eventual happy outcome.

Prospects

Prospects can come to a pastor's attention in various ways. In new areas convassing is indicated. Where there is a nucleus or an organized congregation, leads to prospects can often be found in the congregation itself: an unchurched husband or wife; or unchurched parents of children on the cradle roll, in the Christian day school, the Sunday school, the vacation Bible school. Premarital counseling where one party is not a church member presents an opportunity. Members may tell the pastor of prospects. If the address of visitors who sign the guest register shows that they live in the neighborhood and they indicate no church affiliation, that lead ought to be followed immediately. If they indicate a church affiliation, but in a church at some distance, a visit may still be in place. Care must, however, be taken not to become guilty of proselytizing, of violating an existing pastor-member relationship and with it the Tenth Commandment. The case of members of a non-Christian group is different — they are mission material. A pastor may also be led to prospects at social gatherings in connection with baptisms, confirmations, weddings, and funerals. Here the ability to mingle with people is an asset. The organized evangelism efforts of a congregation will be discussed in another chapter.

When mission calls have succeeded in bringing a soul to Christ and winning a member for the church, the new member becomes the object of the ongoing pastoral care which is the main subject of this book.

Summary: Every pastor will consider it his privilege and responsibility to bring the gospel to the unchurched. He will need to be careful to look upon the preaching of repentance and remission of sins as his primary concern and to let his entire manner reflect his sincere desire for the salvation of souls. By virtue of his position he will have a variety of opportunities to discover prospects for his missionary outreach.

For Additional Reading

Publications of the National Association for Mental Health, 10 Columbus Circle, New York, N.Y. 10019.

> *The Clergy and Mental Health*, 1960. Based on an article "The Minister and Mental Hygiene — His Opportunity and Responsibility" by Charles Kemp which originally appeared in *Mental Hygiene.*

> *Some Things You Should Know about Mental and Emotional Illness.*
> This leaflet supplies a brief description of mental illness.

> Stern, Edith H. *Mental Illness, a Guide for the Family*, 1962.

> Ward, Archibald F., Jr., Ph. D. and Granville L. Jones, M.D. *Ministering to the Families of the Mentally Ill*, 1962.

> Wiesbauer, Rev. Henry H., M.S.S. *Pastoral Help in Serious Mental Illness*, 1960.
> Full of valuable information and suggestions.

Others

Holand, Mary W., ed. *Doors to Daylight*, distributed by Milwaukee County Association for Mental Health. Milwaukee: Inland Press, 1965.
A handbook of definitions, laws, resources relating to mental illness and the maintenance of mental health.

Milt, Harry. *Basic Facts about Mental Illness.* Fair Haven, New Jersey: Scientific Aids Publications, 1962.

7

The Shepherd
Seeks the Straying Sheep

"If thy brother shall trespass"
(Mt 18:15)

I. BROTHERLY ADMONITION

The Duty

To speak to a sinner about his sin and to urge him to forsake his sinful way is a moral duty. This duty is set forth already in the Old Testament (Lv 19:17). It is repeated in various ways in the New Testament (Mt 18:15; Lk 17:3; Ga 6:1). The performance of this duty therefore is part of Christian sanctification. Its main purpose is to bring the sinner to repentance. Because of its importance the pastor will by word and example encourage the exercise of brotherly admonition. While he will counteract the notion that admonition is a prerogative of the pastor's office or, at the most, one shared with the church council, he will himself be diligent in supplying admonition when it is called for. But he will also set the example of being one who is willing to accept well-meant admonition when he himself needs it.

Who Is To Be Admonished

Admonition is a duty which we owe to our neighbor. In the case of the unbeliever our main concern must be to admonish him because of his greatest sin, the failure to accept Jesus as his Savior

165

(Jn 16:8,9). To admonish an unbeliever about his cursing, for example, and perhaps even to get him to quit his cursing could result in his being in a worse state afterward than before. He could become self-righteous because his language would then be better than that of some church members. Admonition becomes "brotherly" only when it involves a Christian brother. It is an antidote both against indifference about a brother's spiritual peril and against a legalism which would automatically rule him out of the Christian church because of his sin. The brother need not be a member of the same church as the one who does the admonishing. The term includes all who profess faith in the Lord Jesus as their Savior. Brother will be concerned about brother when the latter by his sin endangers the salvation of his soul. The fact that a person is in a subordinate position which brings with it the duty to show respect should not, for example, prevent a child from admonishing its parent, an employee his employer, or a wife her husband.

Any brother who sins is to be admonished. There are no restrictions. The "against thee" of Matthew 18:15 has weak textual support. To show concern only when we are hurt directly would ill reflect the attitude of the seeking Shepherd who wants none of His sheep to perish. To restrict admonition to cases of "mortal sin" (1 Cor 6:9,10; Ga 5:19-21) is to fail to see in every sin a violation of the majesty of God which calls forth His curse and condemnation. Nor is a brother required to act only if he is the only one who knows of his brother's sin.

The Basis for Admonition

The one who knows of a brother's sin is to do the admonishing. He must be an eye- or earwitness, or have his information by way of confession, or on the basis of unimpeachable evidence. Fellow Christians who want to tell another of a brother's sin are themselves to be admonished because they are sinning against the Eighth Commandment and must be encouraged to show their repentance by themselves speaking to the sinner. Charity demands that newspaper accounts or reports widely circulated among the general public are not to be accepted offhand as a valid basis for admonition. But concern for the brother will move one discreetly and tactfully to confront him with what has been printed or is being said about him and to ask to hear his side of the story. Only if it becomes evident that he is indeed guilty of sin will admonition

166

be in order. A pastor will not accept charges against a member unless the accuser has dealt with the accused personally and before witnesses. Gossip which peddles reports of another's sin to the pastor is a sin and is to be dealt with as such. The pastor will turn a deaf ear to it. A congregation must know that neither its pastor nor his wife are ready to listen to gossip. It is a disgrace if the parsonage is known to be a clearing house for gossip. Nothing will more quickly undermine confidence in the pastor's fairness.

A pastor should not consider himself called upon to ferret out sins. He is not called to be a detective. He will have his hands more than full with cases which are brought to his attention in a legitimate manner. But in such cases he dare not ignore his responsibility by playing the part of an ostrich which hides its head in the sand and pretends that an unpleasant situation does not exist.

The Purpose

Brotherly admonition ought to have only one purpose, that of reclaiming a sinning brother for his own spiritual good and for the glory of the Lord and His church. It ought never to be looked upon as an irksome duty which must be performed, or undertaken to give the offender a tongue lashing for the irritation which he has caused, or to parade one's own superiority. Above all its purpose must not be simply to get rid of a troublesome member. The attitude in which it is to be exercised is to be one of meekness and humility, recognizing one's own weakness and sinfulness, and yearning to help a fallen brother even as one would want his brother to help him if the situation were reversed (Ga 6:1).

The Means

Although many books have been written on the subject of public and interpersonal relations and although it is possible to learn something from the children of this world, the tools essential for admonishing a brother so as to win him are provided only in God's own book. The law needs to be used to expose sin as sin. This use of the law would not be circumvented if the attempt were made to encourage a sinner to repent by reminding him of the peace and comfort which he experienced on a previous occasion when he penitently sought and obtained the Lord's forgiveness. However, an appeal to his pride, urging the sinner to be big enough to admit his sin, or an appeal to his love for his family, re-

167

minding him that his family will be happy if the case is settled, though they may lead to outward results, will not get at the root of the matter.

The Manner

Good judgment, which is one facet of love in action, is very necessary. The temperament of the offending brother needs to be considered so that he may be approached in the manner which promises to be most effective in his case. There is a time and place for everything. Our Lord Himself indicates that admonition is to take place in private and not in the presence of others. Consideration needs to be shown for previous plans and commitments lest the offender become impatient and unwilling to hear the admonishing brother out. Nagging and continual faultfinding are to be avoided. To make a capital offense of a sin into which a brother may have fallen in weakness and about which he has indicated his regrets will serve only to embitter and harden him. There are times when shocked silence or a disapproving shaking of the head will be all the admonition that is needed. One needs to know with whom one is dealing.

II. CHURCH DISCIPLINE

Brotherly admonition leads to church discipline when according to Matthew 18 the case of the sinning brother is brought before the church. The purpose of church discipline is the same as that of private admonition and admonition in the presence of witnesses. It may be initiated only after private admonition and admonition in the presence of witnesses have proved fruitless. According to Matthew 18 it is evident that our Lord considers admonition in the presence of witnesses a private matter. Since church discipline involves exposing and rebuking a sin, the law is being used. But the motivation for practicing it is produced by the gospel, which also leads to its being carried out in an evangelical manner. The training element in the word "discipline" is to be emphasized, not the retributive. Though excommunication may result as the last recourse left for love, it is ill-advised to threaten people with church discipline as though it were a form of punishment which might have to be inflicted. The purpose is to gain a brother, not to clean house by getting rid of a problem member.

The Church

There is nothing in Matthew 18:17 to indicate that the church which is involved in church discipline must be organized in a specific manner. The presence of the church is determined by the fact that the means of grace are in use in the midst of a number of professed believers; that they are gathered in Jesus' name (Mt 18:10), that is, in response to the gospel revelation to perform functions which their Lord has assigned to them. Our Lord's concern is not to grant a special privilege to a group of Christians organized in a specific manner, but to make sure that a sinning brother is given every possible opportunity to be confronted with the seriousness of his sin. To read more into Matthew 18 than is there can lead to a restriction of New Testament liberty and flexibility by the introduction of a ceremonial law, to hierarchical attitudes which consider an excommunication valid only if declared in the presence of a pastor and announced by him, or to an evasion of a duty of love when an offense occurs of which no one in the offender's congregation knows.

Each stage of the admonition outlined in Matthew 18 may be repeated and will often be repeated. Our Lord is not showing us the quickest way to get rid of a sinner, but the lengths to which love will go in order to gain him.

"One or Two More"

The "one or two more" of Matthew 18:16 need not have been eye- or earwitnesses of the sin concerning which a brother has admonished the offender without success. They are to go with him when he repeats his admonition to be able to testify to the church, if need be, of the sinner's impenitence. But the Lord also indicates that they are to join in the admonition. For that reason Christian maturity, understanding, and tact will be looked for in those who are asked to be witnesses. If the pastor is asked to serve at this stage, he may hesitate or decline because his official character could give the impression that admonition is no longer a private matter. But if he has been instructing and urging his people to be faithful in brotherly admonition and to follow the full course of Matthew 18, he may feel that he dare not, by refusing, discourage a brother who asks him to go along. The elders of a congregation are in a similar situation. If the pastor is the one who has done the initial admonishing, he will very likely ask an elder or two to

169

accompany him if private admonition has proved to be fruitless. He need not, however, restrict his choice of partners in that way but choose whomever he has reason to hope will best be able to reach the fallen brother.

The Need for Evidence

Witnesses may be drawn in only if there is definite proof that the sin has been committed or if the sinner defiantly admits his guilt. If the sin is known only to the admonishing brother and he mentions it to witnesses, the offender may well deny his guilt and turn about and accuse the brother of slander. There are cases, then, where the first stage of Matthew 18 will also be the last. The admonishing brother has done what he could. Now the matter rests with the Lord who has said, "Vengeance is mine; I will repay" (Ro 12:19). He has also said: "There is nothing covered, that shall not be revealed; neither hid, that shall not be known" (Lk 12:2). He may well bring secret sins to light and make further dealing with the sinner possible.

Public Offense

In the case of sins which have been committed in the presence of the congregation or are a matter of public knowledge and an offense to the congregation, admonition may still take place privately and in the presence of witnesses if that seems to be the best way of gaining the offending brother. But that in such cases these steps need not precede is evident from Galatians 2:11f and 1 Timothy 5:20. In these cases love for the sinner is decisive. We shall ask ourselves which course in our judgment offers the best prospect of winning the guilty brother.

The Sinner's Congregation Involved

We have already shown that when our Lord in Matthew 18 speaks of the church He means a gathering of professed believers whose character as part of the universal church is evidenced by the fact that in their midst the means of grace are in use and that they are gathered in Jesus' name, that is, in response to His revelation of Himself, to perform functions assigned to them by Him. It is to this church which is closest to the sinning brother that the brother who has admonished him privately and in the presence of witnesses will turn in order that the sinner may hear the united testimony of a greater number of his brethren. This is the additional effort which love will make to win a sinning broth-er. Ordinarily the church will be the congregation of which he is a member. In any event love and order require that at some point this congregation is drawn in even though, because of the nature of the case, disciplinary proceedings may have been initiated else-where. The voters' assembly acts for the congregation (cf Voting Rights in the chapter on Administration). It becomes the church which performs the duty of love assigned to it by our Lord in Mat-thew 18.

Place in Sanctification

Brotherly admonition and church discipline lie in the area of sanctification, in which growth is continually to be fostered. A pastor will seek to do that by reminding his people that these evi-dences of brotherly love are more important for the brother than those which concern only his temporal well-being, since these demonstrate concern about the possible loss of his eternal salva-tion. Jesus went all the way to death on the cross to save the brother. As believers reflect His love, they will not allow carnal considerations to cause them to shrink from practicing brotherly admonition or participating in church discipline. Passages like 1 Corinthians 5:1-5, 13; 2 Thessalonians 3:14,15; Revelation 2:14, 15,20 indicate how important this phase of sanctification is for the well-being of the church. On the other hand, misguided zeal is to be guarded against. A pastor's faithfulness is not to be gauged by the number of excommunications in which he has been involved.

When a Congregation Is To Be Drawn In

There are situations in which a congregation will have to refuse to allow a case to be placed on its agenda. Such is the case if the sinner has not previously been admonished privately and in the presence of witnesses. To do otherwise would be to condone a vio-lation of the Eighth Commandment. Furthermore, the congrega-tion has a call to act only if the case involves a sin. If the fact that a sin has been committed cannot be proved, the congregation has no call to play the role of detective. If the dealings involve an adiaphoron and remain on that level and do not expose an under-lying contempt for the will of God, they do not call for congrega-tional involvement or action.

Scripture does not speak about any intermediate course be-tween admonishing in the presence of witnesses and bringing the

171

matter before the church. But since the emphasis is upon winning the brother, it may in some situations be well if the pastor alone or members of the church council who have not previously been involved make one more effort to gain the brother after they have been informed that an appeal is pending to ask the congregation to act in the matter.

The Desired Outcome

The purpose of admonition, be it by an individual, or by that individual in the company of witnesses, or by the church, is to bring the sinning brother to repentance. As soon as this purpose of love has been attained, the case is closed. This is done by assuring him that the Lord has forgiven him. When David said: "I have sinned against the Lord," Nathan told him: "The Lord also hath put away thy sin" (2 Sm 12:13). The confession must be clearcut without any ifs or buts. But to demand more, to demand, for example, that the confession be made in a prescribed manner, would be legalistic. It would also be legalistic to impose on the penitent a period of probation before his confession would be considered sincere and the absolution would be pronounced.

Fruits of Repentance

On the other hand, it must be borne in mind that Scripture speaks about "fruits meet for repentance" (Mt 3:8). There are cases where repentance for a sin ought to be shown by righting the wrong which has been done (returning stolen goods, apologizing for remarks which hurt a brother or sullied his good name, seeking reconciliation with a rejected spouse, arranging to repay just debts after bankruptcy has been declared). Another principle to be observed is: "Public offense must be publicly removed." We see it applied in our Lord's dealing with Peter (Jn 21:15-17) and in Paul's dealing with Peter (Ga 2:11-18). This procedure will be applied only when the offense is really public, that is, common knowledge in the congregation. If the sinning brother is not well known and his sin even less, it would be a violation of the Eighth Commandment to publish it. "Charity shall cover the multitude of sins" (1 Pe 4:8). If, however, a brother realizes that by his flagrant sin he may have put a stumbling block in the way of the faith or sanctification of his brethren, his repentance will include an eagerness to do what he can to remove the offense. How that can best be done, whether by personal confession in a public service, an announcement by the pastor in a public service, or in a voters' assembly, he will seek to determine in consultation with his pastor and other brethren.

III. EXCOMMUNICATION

Defined

Excommunication is the solemn declaration of the church that a sinner because of his impenitence is no longer a member of the church, that he is to be regarded "as a heathen man and a publican" (Mt 18:17), that his sin is bound upon him on earth and in heaven (Mt 18:18). Exclusion from the visible church takes place because it has become evident that by his impenitence the sinner has excluded himself from the communion of saints. The church declares the Lord's verdict, which stands on its own merits and is not supplemented by any human power or authority. The purpose of excommunication is that this last and most severe preaching of the law might yet bring the sinner to see his error and that he thus may in the end still be saved. All of this implies that the congregation must be as sure as is humanly possible that the sinner is indeed impenitent.

Doctrinal Aberration

A congregation may proceed to excommunication only when a sin is involved, never in the case of *adiaphora* (e.g., refusal to participate in a fund raising drive, refusal to send children to a Christian day school). Where admonition has taken place because of doctrinal deviation, only those are to be excommunicated who persistently adhere to an error which subverts the foundation of faith (denial of the Trinity, the divinity of Jesus, salvation by grace, vicarious atonement, resurrection). In other cases separation is called for (Tt 3:10), i.e., the declaration that the persistent errorist is no longer a confessional brother, but not that he is to be regarded as a heathen man and a publican.

Impenitence the Ground for Excommunication

In cases where the sin was not public, admonition privately and in the presence of witnesses must have preceded excommunication, and in every case admonition by the congregation. Our Lord's concern as it is revealed in Matthew 18 is that a sinner receive every possible opportunity to be instructed and won by

173

God's Word. His impenitence becomes evident when he refuses to bow to this Word of God. It is impenitence which is the ground for excommunication, not the sin which first called forth admonition, for had he repented, he would have been forgiven. We cannot, therefore, make a distinction between sins which can lead to excommunication or those which will not. Impenitence is a refusal to obey God and calls for action by the church no matter what the sin may be of which the sinner refuses to repent.

Restrictions

Since the entire process of admonition and church discipline is to reflect concern for the soul of an individual, mass excommunications are improper even though only a husband and wife or a single family are involved. The individuals who are excommunicated must be such who claim membership in the church (those who have withdrawn from membership to evade church discipline are no longer the responsibility of a congregation, although the consequences of their impenitence will be pointed out to them when they announce their withdrawal); those who are responsible for their actions (not the mentally ill); and those who are in their majority. As a general rule the church considers children competent in spiritual matters after they have received the instruction which precedes confirmation.

The Church Acts

It is the church which is acting in the third stage of admonition and, if admonition is fruitless, in excommunicating. The church which acts will always be only a part of the universal church, whose presence is established by the fact that in the midst of the people who are acting the means of grace are being used. To them individually and therefore collectively the keys of the kingdom of heaven have been entrusted. When a brother sins, the church in whatever form it may be gathered at the time will proceed to admonish him if his offense is public, otherwise after the first two stages of admonition have proved to be fruitless. But it would be a violation of brotherly love if the church as it appears in one form (for example, a synodical board) were to take conclusive action without drawing in the church in another form, that is, the congregation in which the person being disciplined claims membership. Congregations, on the other hand, expect that in brotherly love the entire church will respect their excommunication. If

174

called upon to do so, congregations will be ready to supply evidence of the correctness of an excommunication which they have had to pronounce.

The Pastor's Role

A pastor has no unique or indispensable function in the process of excommunication. He will, of course, see to it that all is done in line with God's Word. He votes, however, not as a pastor, but as a Christian. The words of the third part of the explanation of the Ministry of the Keys in the Small Catechism must be understood in this light, and not vice versa. The pastor by virtue of his call speaks for the congregation, not independently, in announcing an excommunication.

Its Essence

The essence of excommunication is the declaration by the church that the admonished sinner has rejected all exhortation from God's Word, has proved to be impenitent, and may not be considered a member of the Christian church. Nothing new has been done except formally to establish an existing fact (cf scriptural divorce). This fact is then announced to the congregation.

Unanimous Action Required

An excommunication based upon adequate evidence that impenitence actually exists must be respected by all. God's Word has decided the status of the impenitent sinner. For that reason too, the vote to excommunicate must be unanimous. If there is a protest, the one who voices it must be dealt with in order to bring him to conviction. Should he in turn prove to be disobedient to God's Word, he too becomes an object for church discipline. If a greater number of members cannot be brought to the conviction that excommunication is called for, no conclusion can be reached. The pastor can only commit the matter to the Lord, comfort himself with the knowledge that the sinner has heard, also in the presence of the congregation, the admonition which he needed, and continue in his efforts to indoctrinate the congregation.

Valid for the Whole Church

It bears repeating that since it is the church which acted, the church wherever it may appear is expected to abide by the verdict. If there are Christians who for cause, not curiosity, question

175

the validity of an excommunication, they may ask for a review of the case, and in Christian love the body which exercised original jurisdiction will supply the requested information (the sin, the stages of admonition, the evidence of impenitence, the unanimous resolution of the body). The WELS constitution provides courts of appeal and review for such who believe that they have been unjustly excommunicated. Refusal to rescind an invalid excommunication can result in suspension from synodical fellowship for the guilty congregation and its pastor.

Its Purpose

The fact that he has been excommunicated is intended to be for the impenitent sinner a continuing preachment of the law, since the church has only repeated God's verdict of no forgiveness and God in turn has bound Himself to abide by the verdict of the church. "Whatsoever ye shall bind on earth shall be bound in heaven" (Mt 18:18). The purpose of excommunication is that the sinner might be jolted out of his stubborn impenitence by such drastic action and still come to repentance (1 Tm 1:20; 1 Cor 5:5).

Consequences

An excommunicated person is not to be barred from attending church services, for our Lord's command is to preach the gospel to every creature (Mk 16:15). But it is self-evident that he may not receive the Lord's Supper. Nor may he be considered qualified to serve as a sponsor at a baptism. Even to permit him to serve as a witness could cause confusion and offense. Neither is he entitled to receive Christian burial. If he was a voting member, excommunication terminated his legal rights in the congregation, such as the right to vote or to claim a share in the congregation's property or funds.

It behooves all members of the congregation to show by their attitude toward the excommunicated person that excommunication is a very serious matter and that all fraternal relations have been terminated. (Cf 1 Cor 5:9-13; 2 Th 3:6,14). The fact that someone has been excommunicated does not, however, excuse anyone from performing the duties over against him which are involved in relationships which are not dependent upon membership in a Christian congregation, as, for example, the husband-wife, or the child-parent, or the citizen-government relationship.

176

Excommunication terminates a pastor's responsibility toward the one who has been excommunicated. He will have gone the limit in his efforts to win the sinner before excommunication took place. Excommunication is the final word of the church, and this includes the pastor. He need not be coldly aloof. He may still practice the customary social graces to show that he is approachable. But the initiative toward restoring fellowship must be taken by the one who has been excommunicated. Excommunication is never a matter of vindictiveness. Where it has become necessary, that action has been taken for the eternal good of the sinner, seeking to bring him to repentance by this action in a case where words have failed (2 Cor 2:6,7); for the congregation, demonstrating that sin is something serious (1 Cor 5:6; 1 Tm 5:20); and for those outside the congregation, showing them that the congregation means what it confesses (1 Cor 10:32).

If investigation upon appeal were to establish the fact that an excommunication was not valid because one or more of the necessary elements was lacking in the process (sin, impenitence, unanimity), the only God-pleasing course for the excommunicating body to take would be to rescind its action.

"Self-Excommunication"

The term "self-excommunication" is inaccurate. Excommunication implies action by the church which on the basis of evidence that the sinner is impenitent declares that he is excluded from the Christian church. If the sinner has refused to heed the summons to appear before the church to hear its testimony, this refusal is the evidence of his impenitence which becomes the basis for excommunication. There dare be no question as to whether the sinner has received the summons to appear before the church. It may be sent by registered or certified mail or presented orally or in writing by at least two members.

Minutes

Special care ought to be exercised in keeping the minutes of meetings in which discipline cases are an item of business. These minutes will be called for if one who is excommunicated appeals his case. It may also happen that an excommunicated person may apply for membership years after action has been taken against him and after there has been a change in pastors, so that the minutes become the only accurate source of information. It is recommended that the secretary read his notes at the end of the meeting and record that they have been adopted unanimously. In their polished form they will again be read at the time when the minutes of the entire meeting are submitted for adoption.

The Hope for Absolution

It is with a heavy heart that the church acts when it excommunicates an impenitent sinner. If the Lord then uses the preaching of the law which is involved in excommunication to bring the sinner to repentance, there should be no hesitancy on the part of the church to forgive him and receive him back into fellowship (2 Cor 2:6-11). Rather, it will reflect the joy that there is in heaven in the presence of the angels of God "over one sinner that repenteth" (Lk 15:7,10) and count it a blessed privilege and opportunity to forgive and forget and to enjoy again the fellowship of one who "was dead, and is alive again; and was lost, and is found" (Lk 15:32).

Summary: Brotherly admonition reflects a Christian's concern for a brother who by sinning has endangered his eternal welfare. The purpose of such admonition is to restore the sinner by bringing him to repentance. If private efforts seem to be fruitless, the admonishing brother is not to let the matter drop, but to repeat the admonition in the company of one or more brethren. If this course too leads to no favorable results, the case is to be referred to the church in the hope that the united admonition of even more brethren might win the sinner. If he remains impenitent, he is to be excommunicated. This declaration that he by his impenitence has excluded himself from forgiveness and from the church is the final effort which love can make to impress him with the seriousness of his state. If and when he does undergo a change of heart, the church will rejoice to assure him of the Lord's forgiveness.

8

The Shepherd
Counsels the Troubled Sheep

"Bear ye one another's burdens"

(Gal 6:2)

I. WHAT IS PASTORAL COUNSELING?

Dual Background

The term "pastoral counseling" combines two concepts that have distinct meanings. Each of these concepts has its own background and origin. The word pastoral concerns itself with the shepherding that Jesus, the Chief Shepherd (1 Pe 5:4), performed and entrusted to those whom He calls to lead and feed the flock of God (1 Pe 5:2; Ac 20:28) (pastor-shepherd). Shepherding involves "taking the oversight" over a flock and feeding the church of God.

Another term that has become closely associated with that of shepherding is the German word *Seelsorge*, or, when applied to an individual, *Privatseelsorge*. This has been translated into English as "the cure of souls." Since the translation does not carry with it the rich warmth and deep feeling of *Seelsorge*, the German expression finds frequent use in English writings. The German expression speaks of the deep concern which the pastor shows for the needs of the souls entrusted to his care. It speaks of the healing comfort and strength from God's Word of grace that the pastor applies to souls in their need. This feeding and leading which

179

the Lord has solemnly committed to the pastor is an important part of his ministry.

The other word, counseling, literally means "giving advice." However, it has been pointed out that "counseling is not primarily giving advice," leading to the suggestion that "we are in need of a more appropriate term by which to describe it."[1] The term as it is used in the expression "pastoral counseling" has been defined as "a process of encouraging growth from within."[2] This definition has its source in dynamic psychology, developed from the work of Sigmund Freud.[3] Its methods have been developed by the clinical psychologist and psychiatrist. It has thus become a technical term the application of which one writer would like to see limited "only to situations where (1) two persons have knowingly entered into a relationship, (2) in which one attempts to help the other, and (3) where an established series of meetings is arranged for this purpose."[4] Thus counseling has become a technical term for a technique used in working with people. The origin of the term may make the Bible-based pastor wary.

The question is in place: Can counseling in this technical sense become a part of the function of the pastor, who is to shepherd the church of God with the divine Word? Is it proper to combine the two and speak of pastoral counseling?

One view is simply to reject the counseling process because of its origin without giving it a closer look. Scripture, however, reminds the pastor that "the earth is the Lord's and the fulness thereof" (1 Cor 10:26), so that all things are his to use whatever the source, provided they do not violate God's Word. The other extreme is to be so impressed by what the clinical counselor does that his findings are accepted uncritically. Whatever is contrary to Scripture must be rejected however impressive it may appear, again, because "the earth is the Lord's and the fulness thereof." The premises that underlie much of counseling, e.g., that the counselor must help his client simply by drawing on the resources the latter has within himself, must be rejected. The pastor must

1. William E. Hulme, *Counseling and Theology* (Philadelphia: Muhlenberg, 1956), p 23.
2. *Baker's Dictionary of Practical Theology*, ed. Ralph C. Turnbull (Grand Rapids: Baker, 1967), p 193.
3. *Ibid.*, pp 193f.
4. Harold J. Haas, *Pastoral Counseling with People in Distress* (St. Louis: Concordia, 1970), p 59.

know that the best help, the only genuine, enduring help, he can bring to people is to lead them to Christ, using Holy Scripture as the powerful resource for help in their difficulties. But insofar as counseling involves a method of dealing with people, the pastor can appropriate or adapt in his *Seelsorge* whatever is not contrary to Scripture.

A Definition

It was recognized above that counseling has become a technical term for a specific process. According to one author, there are three requirements which must be met before the term can properly apply. He views counseling as a definitely structured and planned method. In this sense, the average pastor may do little counseling, many none at all. It has been well said that "the minister's image of the setting, structure, and process of counseling needs to be much more flexible than the psychotherapist's. To render significant help to the maximum number of people, the clergyman must be able to apply his counseling skills to the host of informal and often chance opportunities which he has to relate to those struggling with complex decisions, staggering loads, and agonizing problems."[5] A definition of pastoral counseling must keep in mind the kind of ministry the pastor has under God. It must be in harmony with his position as *Seelsorger* and the role Scripture gives him. The following definition seeks to do this: *Pastoral counseling is that pastoral care (Seelsorge) of individuals as they face their problems, troubles, griefs, burdens, fears, and illnesses, which involves not simply giving advice, but assisting them to find help from the Word of God.*

This definition recognizes that counseling is a form of *Seelsorge*. This must never be forgotten. The pastor must always remain *Seelsorger*. Reference to individuals should not be pressed in such a way that all counseling with more than one person present is eliminated, thus ruling out counseling with entire families or even with husband and wife together. But the word does point out that counseling is a personal ministry in which the pastor does not address himself to the entire congregation or even large segments of it. Generally it has to do with individuals, even if it may be several at one time. Giving advice is mentioned. This cannot be ruled out if the shepherd is to do the leading and feeding

5. Howard J. Clinebell, *Basic Types of Pastoral Counseling* (Nashville: Abingdon, 1966), p 29.

that the Chief Shepherd calls for. On the other hand, counseling will use every method available to bring the help of God's Word to people in their needs. Finally, the definition concludes with the Word of God. This must remain the great source of help, a fact never to be forgotten by the pastoral counselor.

It has been suggested that the proper emphasis is better expressed if instead of speaking of pastoral counseling one were to speak of the counseling pastor. This has some merit. In the former expression the emphasis is on the noun counseling, with pastoral as a defining adjective. In the latter the emphasis is on the pastor, the called shepherd, adding the fact that he can function in a counseling role and adapt counseling methods to his ministry.

Summary: The term "pastoral counseling" combines two words. The first refers to the shepherding the pastor does under Jesus, the Chief Shepherd. The second, counseling, has become a technical term for a particular process of working with people. Elements of this process may be useful for the pastor. He must, however, reject any unscriptural presuppositions the counseling psychologist or psychiatrist may have.

II. THE PASTOR AS COUNSELOR

Two people are involved in the counseling process, the pastor as the counselor, the person in need as the counselee. In considering the pastor as counselor, we shall first explore the equipment he needs for counseling, then the attitudes that are necessary for effective work. Though no pastor will ever master all of these perfectly, it is necessary that he strive to become aware to an ever greater degree of what is needed for counseling effectively and of the attitudes he is to cultivate.

A. The Equipment of the Counseling Pastor

Faith in Christ and the Power of His Word

There should be little need to mention faith in Christ as a prerequisite for the counseling pastor. This means that the pastor has experienced in his own heart and life the transforming power of the gospel. Thus he knows whereof he speaks. He is confident that through the Word of God the Holy Spirit is active, and so he trusts in the means God has given him to use in his ministry.

Knowledge of Scripture

Since the tool with which the pastor works in his *Seelsorge* is the Word of God, the need for a thorough knowledge of Scripture is beyond question. That this refers first of all to its doctrinal content is self-evident. But he must also know parts of it from memory so that he can cite them when needed. He must be able readily to find pertinent passages. His knowledge of Scripture must enable him to turn to a word of Scripture that is fitting for the situation which has quite unexpectedly confronted him. All of this is, however, not to be a mere intellectual knowledge but must be accompanied by and applied with a deep faith in God's Word.

An Understanding of Human Nature

Since in counseling the pastor is dealing with people, since he is applying the Word of God to human beings, an understanding of human nature should be part of his intellectual equipment. He must learn to diagnose the needs of his parishioner, must recognize where the parishioner as a person stands and what may be the best manner of approaching him.

Such an understanding of human nature comes first of all through a study of *Scripture*. Never to be forgotten is what Scripture says about human nature, its weaknesses and its potentialities. The pastor who forgets that Jesus' death reconciled the world unto the Father will fail to see the true worth of every soul that seeks his help.

Psychology studies the human mind and its processes. Its findings, evaluated in the light of Scripture, can be helpful to the pastor. A course in psychology for future pastors rightly enlarges the definition of psychology to include a "study of man, his nature and behavior, as it is revealed in the Scriptures and in the findings of modern psychological research."[6]

Experience is an invaluable teacher. As the pastor observes people and their reactions to various approaches, as he consciously analyzes his successes and failures in dealing with people, he will grow in the understanding of human nature.

6. Northwestern College Catalog, Watertown, Wisconsin, 1973-74, p 40.

Knowledge of Counseling Methods

The pastor should not fail to appreciate Scripture and the example of his Savior as a source for learning counseling methods. To observe the manner in which Jesus dealt with the rich young man, the Samaritan woman, the woman taken in adultery, fallen Peter, doubting Thomas, the proud Pharisees, is to learn from the master Counselor. At the same time, the pastor will examine, evaluate, and adapt the findings of the professional clinical counselor and psychotherapist. More of this in a separate section on counseling methods.

B. The Attitudes of the Counseling Pastor

Evangelical

It has been said that the traditional pastoral role "is based on moralistic and ethical command."[7] This is, however, at best a caricature of the pastoral role as portrayed in Scripture and as exemplified by Luther. McNeill in his *The History of the Cure of Souls* describes Luther as follows: "He writes . . . as a sinful and tempted Christian who is glad to bring such spiritual remedies as he has learned from Scripture and experience to the aid of those who ask, or need, his brotherly help."[8] "His task is that of a deliverer of troubled consciences."[9] That is what it means to be evangelical. It is an attitude that grows in the heart of the pastor who through personal application of the law and gospel in his own life gains an ever deeper understanding of both, as revealed in Scripture. This eliminates the possibility of the Bible becoming nothing more than a code-book for ethics, to be applied with divine authority. This helps eliminate legalism and moralizing. The pastor who has an evangelical attitude deals with people not simply out of moralistic and ethical interests, but seeks to help troubled souls through Christ in their relationship to God and to encourage sanctification as a fruit of repentance.

Having a Love and Concern For People

Counseling has to do with people. The very term *Seelsorge* includes the thought of loving concern for people. However, the love

7. Robert Lofton Hudson, *Marital Counseling* (Englewood Cliffs: Prentice-Hall, 1963), p 23.
8. John Thomas McNeill, *A History of the Cure of Souls* (New York: Harper, 1951), p 174.
9. *Ibid.*, p 169.

for people that is meant is not only love for such who through their good qualities inspire love. It is rather a love that is inspired by God's love for the sinner, a love that inspires love in the heart of a believer — here the pastor — for fellow-redeemed sinners. The temptation is ever present for the pastor to be annoyed when he must give of his time to people who have made a mess of their lives and do not know where to turn for help. The fact that people have messed up their lives should be all the more reason for the pastor to reach out with Christlike concern, for Jesus came to seek and to save that which was lost. The picture of the good shepherd seeking the one lost sheep should be an inspiration to those entrusted with the flock of God to extend a helping hand to the "lost."

Nonjudgmental — Accepting

The two terms, nonjudgmental and accepting, are closely related. The second refers to a positive attitude that corresponds to an attitude described negatively in the first. Although the pastor cannot be nonjudgmental and accepting in the sense in which the psychiatrist may use the term, there is also a truly biblical nonjudgmental acceptance.

The originator of client-centered, nondirective counseling defines acceptance in this way: "By acceptance I mean a warm regard for him as a person of unconditional self-worth — of value no matter what his condition, his behavior, or his feelings . . . It means an acceptance of and regard for his attitudes of the moment, no matter how negative or positive, no matter how much they may contradict other attitudes he has held in the past."[10] This definition excludes all moral evaluation of the actions, thoughts, or attitudes of the counselee. The pastor can never be nonjudgmental in this sense. Sin remains sin, and the pastor dare never give the impression that he does not regard it as such.

But the pastor should be nonjudgmental in the sense in which Jesus was when He told the woman taken in adultery: "Neither do I condemn thee; go, and sin no more" (Jn 8:11). In telling the woman to go and sin no more He was passing a moral judgment on her past action. At the same time He did not condemn her, thus rejecting her for her sin. The pastor can be "accepting," even as Jesus was when He ate with the publicans. Jesus never gave

10. Carl R. Rogers, *On Becoming a Person* (Boston: Houghton Mifflin, 1962), p 34.

them the impression that He did not consider them sinners. But He did let them know that He did not despise and condemn them as did the Pharisees. Jesus' acceptance of the sinner was like saying: "You have committed a grievous sin and are troubled. I agree with you; what you did was sin. But I do not on that account turn my back on you. Rather, I want you to be Mine, to come to Me. In Me you have forgiveness. I do not condemn you. Go, and sin no more." This attitude of acceptance the pastor must share with the Chief Shepherd.

Such acceptance needs to be communicated in some way to the troubled counselee. He may often think of the pastor as a moralistically judgmental person who, because he condemns sin, will reject him. That may even prevent someone from going to his pastor for *Seelsorge*. Such a person often has already condemned himself and expects the same from the pastor. He thinks the pastor will not want to have anything more to do with him. To be nonjudgmental in the biblical sense means not to share that judgment with him. To be accepting is to refrain from expressing shock and disgust toward the person because of his sin and guilt and to let him sense the helping hand that reaches out to him, ultimately the forgiving, healing hand of Christ.

Genuine

A psychiatrist writes: "I have found that the more that I can be genuine in the relationship, the more helpful it will be."[11] This is not surprising, for his experience taught him what our Savior always demonstrated in His relationship with people.

To be genuine means that the pastor must be himself in his relationship to the other person. He must not put on professional airs, nor hide behind a pastoral facade. It means not saying one thing and thinking and feeling something else. It means that the acceptance spoken of must be genuine, as indeed it must be if the pastor has fully grasped the gospel.

Tactful

It may seem that being tactful does not harmonize with being genuine. To be tactful, however, does not mean being untruthful. It does not mean saying something one does not mean or believe or feel. Tact can be defined as the ability to say the right thing at the right time in the right way.

11. *Ibid.*, p 33.

Tact, to be genuine, involves being sensitive to people's feelings. It involves respect and consideration for other people. Thus it, too, makes an important contribution to a good relationship in *Seelsorge*.

Empathic

Empathy has been called the key to the counseling process.[12] The term had its origin in connection with professional counseling. What it speaks of, however, is not something foreign to the pastor.

What is empathy? How does it differ from sympathy? The difference has been described in this way: "In sympathy we suffer with the other person. Our suffering may even be more painful to us than the actual suffering of the other person. Not so with empathy. Empathy involves the projection of oneself into the other person's situation in an attempt to understand what he is feeling."[13]

Sympathy is more emotional, a feeling toward a person, perhaps sorrow, pity, compassion. It is feeling the hurt the other person is experiencing. In empathy the element of understanding is more prominent. It is understanding how the person feels in his situation. The counseling pastor will do well not only to feel sorry for someone, but also to understand what that person is experiencing, what he is going through, and to let him realize that he is understood.

Perhaps what in psychology was termed empathy has been included under the term sympathy in *Seelsorge*. A pastor may find that after experiencing a serious illness, he can do more for people in his sick calls. He now not only feels compassion, but he can understand how they feel, what they are going through. This is a form of empathy.

If people recognize that the pastor has a genuine understanding of their problem, they will have confidence in his helping ability. If they say: "I don't think he knows what I am going through," they will have little confidence in his effort to help. They may feel that it is not relevant, and they may be right.

Care for people led Paul to say: "Who is weak, and I am not weak? Who is offended, and I burn not?" (2 Cor 11:29.) The empathic attitude is not foreign to Scripture.

12. Rollo May, *The Art of Counseling* (Nashville: Cokesbury, 1939), p 75.
13. Hudson, *Marital Counseling*, pp 31f.

187

Humble, Yet Confident

To be humble is the opposite of being cocky, proud. It is not the opposite of being confident. The sense in which the pastor should be humble is expressed by St. Paul when he writes: "Brethren, if a man be overtaken in a fault, ye which are spiritual restore such an one in the spirit of meekness, considering thyself, lest thou also be tempted" (Ga 6:1). The counseling pastor is a sinner even as the person who comes for help. When the pastor remembers what he is, a sinner who only through the mercy of God has been forgiven, pride over against other sinners will find no room in his heart. He may even pave the way for greater confidence on the part of the counselee by letting him know that this is the way he regards himself.

The humility of the pastor, however, should not be such that casts doubt on the help he can bring. Humility is not uncertainty about God's Word or the call the pastor has to apply the healing power and comfort of the Word. The pastor can be confident, not because of personal ability or superior training, but because the means he uses to help is of divine origin, because the gospel is the vehicle of God's power. He is confident that the Lord has called him to use this means effectively to help man in his deepest needs. It will inspire confidence in the counselee to know that the pastor is a workman of God who uses the Word of God for the counselee's welfare.

Summary: For effective work the counseling pastor needs to be equipped with faith in Christ and the power of His Word, with a good working knowledge of Scripture, with an understanding of human nature, and with knowledge of counseling methods. His attitude will be one that is evangelical, that shows a love and concern for people, that displays acceptance of the sinner. He will be genuine, tactful, empathic, and humbly confident.

III. THE COUNSELEE AND HIS NEEDS

The second person involved in the counseling process is the counselee. This is a person created by God with a body and soul, with a mind and reasoning power, with feelings, with a will. But this is also a person afflicted with original sin, suffering from the profound consequences of the Fall. At the same time this is a person for whom the Lord Jesus brought a priceless sacrifice to redeem him from the damning consequences of sin, so that he might live his life under God both in time and in eternity.

The Counselee's Needs

When a person thus afflicted and thus endowed comes to the pastor for help, his basic need is for faith in Christ, its strengthening, and reassurance and direction from the Word of God. This basic need must never be lost sight of when examining man and his needs in distress more specifically. The question is: How can we break down this one basic need into something more specific and directly practical? What help does this person need in his distress so that his basic need may be most effectively met?

These needs in some respects are of a psychological nature, for God has endowed man with a soul, with a mind that reasons, with emotions that react, with a will that makes decisions. Hence the counseling psychologist or psychiatrist may recognize certain needs of the distressed person and provide perceptive observations useful also to the counseling pastor. Such observations must, however, be scrutinized and judged in the light of Scripture. It is not surprising that the observations of even an unbelieving psychiatrist as to man's problems and needs may in some ways agree with the revelation of Scripture. Scripture speaks about man as he is in reality, for in Scripture He speaks who knows him with perfect insight, the omniscient Creator. The honest observer of man, truthfully recording what he sees, will have to come to similar conclusions. Take as an example the general recognition of man's need to do something about his feelings of guilt. Wherever the observations of man differ from those of Scripture, it will be because of man's limitations and fallibility. Man has failed to observe correctly.

The specific needs of the counselee can be presented in ways that will vary from counselor to counselor. One analysis looks at the matter in a general way, listing four basic personality needs:[14] 1) the need for security, both in reference to life on earth and to man's relationship to God; 2) the need for satisfaction, concerning primarily the drives or the hungers in man; 3) the need of acceptance, to be recognized and loved by others; 4) the need of cosmic relatedness, or more simply, the need for God. Such an analysis of the basic needs of man can be helpful. On the other hand,

14. *The Pastor at Work* (St. Louis: Concordia, 1960), pp 281f.

Hulme in his *Counseling and Theology*[15] looks more directly at the specific needs of the counselee who is in trouble. He sees these as four in number: 1) the need for a listener; 2) the need for confession; 3) the need for understanding; and 4) the need for growth. Since the latter division can be applied more directly to the pastor's role as *Seelsorger*, a more detailed examination of these four needs is in order.

The Need for a Listener

When Scripture says, "Bear ye one another's burdens" (Ga 6:2), it indicates that the person in distress has need for someone to help him. To suffer is grievous; to suffer alone may become unbearable. A first step in finding someone to help bear the burden is to find someone who will listen.

By having someone to talk to the counselee satisfies the need for clarifying his own thinking. Putting his problem into words is a way of facing up to the problem directly and applying his thinking to it.

The pastor can satisfy the need for a listener. More will be said later about how to be a good listener.

The Need for Confession

We have already referred to the universal recognition that almost every counselee is plagued by feelings of guilt. Only self-deception can evade such a feeling. "If we say that we have no sin, we deceive ourselves, and the truth is not in us" (1 Jn 1:8). It is destructive to bear the burden of guilt silently. "When I kept silence, my bones waxed old through my roaring all the day long" (Ps 32:3) is the way David saw the destructive effect of silence when plagued by guilt. There is need for confession. "I said, I will confess my transgressions unto the Lord; and thou forgavest the iniquity of my sin" (v 5).

This speaks of confession to God. James speaks of confessing also to one another: "Confess your faults one to another, and pray one for another, that ye may be healed" (Jas 5:16). Confession, however, consists of more than merely speaking to another person, as, for example, Lamech did when he boasted to his wives: "I have slain a man to my wounding, and a young man to my hurt" (Gn 4:23). Confession includes feeling guilt over one's action and accepting responsibility for it.

15. Hulme, *Counseling and Theology*, pp 19-94.

190

The latter may be hindered by man's proclivity toward rationalization. "The woman thou gavest to be with me" was Adam's rationalization, seeking thereby to evade responsibility for his action. Too often men use the environment, social evils, or even fate as a rationalization whereby to evade responsibility for their sins. Yet, at the same time, a feeling of guilt may still, almost subconsciously, plague them.

Confession accepts responsibility and gives expression to it. This in itself may bring relief. This is spoken of as catharsis. However, this in itself is not enough. Judas accepted the guilt of his betrayal, confessing: "I have sinned in that I have betrayed the innocent blood" (Mt 27:4). Whatever relief he may have felt at having confessed and cast the 30 pieces of silver at the feet of the chief priests and elders brought no healing; he still hanged himself in despair.

The most important part in confession is absolution. This the chief priests and elders, enemies of the atoning Christ, could not speak. To the confessing Judas they proved to be miserable counselors indeed. It is only the word of absolution that brings healing (catharsis in the true sense).

The person in distress needs to confess. The counseling pastor can satisfy this need. But let him remember these three points: 1) He should allow the confession to take its full course and not cut it off before the person has completed it. 2) He must not minimize the guilt. That is not the way to relief unless the person is in fact only imagining guilt. In such a situation the pastor would point out that the specific act about which the person felt guilty was not a violation of God's law. 3) He must bring the counselee the full proclamation of forgiveness in Christ. In this way he not merely attempts to eliminate a guilt complex by allowing it free expression, but removes the guilt through the God-given means, the atonement of Christ.

The Need for Understanding

This refers not to the need on the part of the pastor to understand the problem (necessary as this is) but to the understanding the counselee has of himself and his problem. In Romans 7:15-25 Paul shows such understanding of himself, of the forces active within him, of what was happening in his life.

The psychoanalyst presses this need to its ultimate extreme. He leads his client back into early childhood, into his long repressed subconscious mind in a search for the reasons that have caused his present neuroses, psychoses, fears, inhibitions, etc. The need for such understanding is increasingly being questioned even by many psychiatrists.

The primary understanding the parishioner needs comes from letting the Word of God speak to him about himself and his situation. Luther's recognition that the Christian in this life is both saint and sinner is an important insight that finds its basis in Romans 7 and throws light on the struggle that every Christian sees within himself. But when he understands himself as St. Paul did when he cried out, "O wretched man that I am, who shall deliver me?" he needs to turn with Paul to the only solution: "I thank God, through Jesus Christ, my Lord."

The Need for Growth

Christians are not to remain children in faith, but are to "grow up into him in all things, which is the head, even Christ" (Eph 4:15). They are to proceed from the status of children, who use milk, to that of grown, mature Christians, who can profit from strong meat (He 5:12-14).

As a Christian matures, he gains the ability to cope with what confronts him in life, the evils, troubles, anxieties, the guilt. A child needs to be shown where help is to be found; the mature person may more often find help for himself. Through the afflictions and trials the Lord sends into his life, the Christian grows and matures. Maturing involves learning to turn to the Word of God for help, also without the explicit direction of the pastor.

Growth may be hindered when the pastor simply gives the counselee the solution, simply tells him what to do. A person may never learn to drive well if he at all times is told exactly what to do, when to turn, when to apply the brake, when to turn on the lights. He must learn to decide for himself when to do each of these. Maturing will be accomplished as the pastor leads the parishioner to apply the Word of God to his problem. Through this Word the Holy Spirit enlightens and strengthens. As people are helped to work through their problems by means of God's Word, they can be expected to mature.

Nevertheless, some people will always remain spiritual children. The pastor will not despise them. He will not turn from them because they are not maturing as he wishes. In fact, the need for growth will remain in every Christian to a greater or lesser degree.

Summary: The counselee has certain needs, psychological in nature, that can give direction to the counseling process. A convenient division of these needs lists four: the need for a listener, the need for confession, the need for understanding, and the need for growth.

IV. ESTABLISHING CONTACT

If the troubled parishioner is to be helped by the pastor, the two must be brought together. The pastor can function as *Seelsorger* and bring the healing of the gospel only when he has made contact with those who need the help.

Initiative on the Parishioner's Part

If the counselee-parishioner seeks out the pastor's help a better relationship results from the very beginning than if the pastor must take the initiative for the contact. The former generally is evidence that the counselee recognizes the need for help and wants it. If he does not want help, it is difficult to give it. "They that be whole need not a physician." The alcoholic who denies that he is one cannot be helped. But when he acknowledges his problem and cries out for help, he is ready to grasp the helping hand that is extended to him.

In Time of Crisis

When the cry for help comes, it frequently indicates a crisis situation. Many will not want to "bother" the pastor or do not see the need to seek help until a problem has reached the crisis stage. The wife is suing for divorce, the husband is threatening to leave, the daughter is pregnant, the son has been arrested by the police, a serious illness or accident puts the victim on the critical list. The telephone call announcing the crisis should result in immediate response. A call merely asking for an appointment may indicate a crisis situation even though this is not directly stated. The pastor will need to "probe" sufficiently to determine whether delay from Saturday night to some time Monday is possible. To delay where immediate help is called for sets up a barrier to his *Seelsorge*. A crisis situation must always have priority claim on the pastor's time.

Encouraging People to Come

The pastor will encourage his parishioners to seek him out in their troubles and problems. He must let it be known that he is available. It is debatable how useful it is to have "office hours" during which the parishioners know that the pastor is in his office available for personal consultation. These hours may not be convenient for everyone and could discourage seeking out the pastor at other times. Yet in a large congregation it could encourage some to come who otherwise would not want to preempt the time of their busy pastor. Frequently the best encouragement to people will be indirect, through those who have found the pastor a helpful, sympathetic counselor. Unquestionably, the most fruitful type of contact is established when the pastor projects an image that lets people know that he is available and concerned. When they, as a result, on their own initiative seek him out for help, a favorable relationship for successful *Seelsorge* is likely to be present from the very beginning. Sometimes people may avoid taking the initiative because they see the pastor as a very busy man. If, however, the thought were to gain wide acceptance that the pastor is so busy that one really should not make a claim on his help, the time may come when the pastor is not really so busy at all.

Initiative on the Pastor's Part

Sometimes the pastor needs to take the initiative to establish contact with a troubled parishioner. Signs that something is wrong in a family or in an individual's life call for active concern. The pastor cannot always wait until the people come to him. The existence of problems may be indicated by a decrease in church attendance, by failure to receive communion as regularly as formerly, by diminished giving. Sometimes the contacts a pastor makes in committees and societies will reveal a troubled soul. The problems children have in school may reveal problems in the home. Even what may appear to be a casual remark may be an indirect invitation to the pastor to respond with a helping hand. Certainly when a crisis occurs in a family, an accident, sickness, or death, the pastor need not await the initiative of the parishioner. Also after a crisis situation has seemingly been weathered successfully, the pastor will want to verify appearances. A bereaved person may require the pastor's counsel even more after the funeral than before.

194

For the pastor to take the initiative on the basis of informers who wish to remain anonymous may be in violation of the Eighth Commandment and could make a good counseling relationship difficult. Informers should be encouraged to direct or bring the people involved to the pastor.

How can the pastor establish contact when the initiative is his? He may simply call at the home unannounced. Or he may arrange for an appointment in the home. He may invite the people to come to the church office or his study. The latter has the advantage of avoiding disturbances often present in a home and of gaining privacy. The situation, the persons involved, and even the personality of the pastor may determine which is best.

A special problem when the pastor establishes the contact may be to get the people to desire and accept the offered help. They did not ask for it, may not see the need for it, and may even resent the pastor's concern. This calls for a special measure of pastoral tact, skill, honesty and patience.

Summary: The pastor will encourage his people to seek him out for *Seelsorge* and must not fail to recognize when a call for help indicates a crisis that requires his immediate attention. The pastor may also need to take the initiative in establishing contact with those who need help. Such a situation often calls for great pastoral wisdom and sanctified common sense.

V. THE COUNSELING SESSION

The needs of the counselee as outlined earlier can be helpful in determining the procedures in the counseling sessions and the course which the counseling should take. The points discussed should not force the pastor into a fixed mold, but can give direction to the sessions so that they do not degenerate into aimless conversation or a quasi-social visit.

Establishing Rapport

This is a necessary preliminary. A strained relationship does not lend itself to *Seelsorge*. If a good relationship exists between the pastor and the member involved, little time is needed for such preliminaries. When a member on his own initiative comes to the pastor, this may be evidence that the pastor already enjoys his confidence.

195

Generally it is not advisable to spend much time on small talk in the attempt to establish good rapport. How should I present my problem? What does this parishioner want of me? Why did the pastor want to see me? These and similar questions will be on the mind of the one or the other so that a feeling of uneasiness often continues until the purpose of the meeting has been clearly stated.

Improving rapport will be an ongoing process. But the counselee needs to feel sufficiently safe in the presence of the pastor to expose his problem to the pastor. To encourage this feeling of safeness the pastor will let it be known, perhaps directly say, that whatever is spoken in the meeting is confidential. This means that he will not break such a confidence. What is confessed in counseling is something he will not reveal to his wife or members of his family. He will not use what one spouse confided to him when speaking to the other. If he feels the need for this, consent is required. He must take care not to use what happens in a counseling session as an example in his sermons in such a way that someone can recognize the source of the example. Keeping confidence is a must.

Giving Opportunity for Unburdening

The counselee needs a listener. He needs to be allowed and encouraged to speak. In this way he brings the problem into the open where he and the pastor can look at it. This may take time. The problem he presents first may not be the real problem. He may be using rationalizations, still attempting to evade and cover up his real problem. As he feels safer with the pastor, he will more fully unburden himself. The need he has for confession will seek to be satisfied.

Such confession in itself already brings relief. Finally he is able honestly to confess what has troubled his heart, what has been bottled up and covered over by excuses and rationalizations. He is facing reality honestly. The pastor, however, is never satisfied with that alone as catharsis. He dare not neglect the genuine healing that comes alone through the gospel as it is applied by absolution, whether formal or informal. The importance of absolution for spiritual healing was pointed out in speaking of the counselee's need for confession.

Sometimes this is as far as a pastor needs to proceed with a parishioner. His only problem was a feeling of guilt over some

196

past action. This has been removed. A pastor is, however, mistaken if he concludes that this is as far as he should go in all cases. The pronouncement of absolution has applied the healing of the gospel to the troubled soul. Jesus, however, also looked to the future life of the forgiven sinner. "Go, and sin no more," he told the adulterous woman. The counseling pastor is concerned about the future. A complete solution may require changes in the counselee's life lest the same problems continue. The drunkard must not only receive forgiveness for his past drunkenness but also be helped to avoid future excessive drinking.

Gaining an Understanding of the Problem

The need for understanding was referred to earlier. To overcome a problem, understanding for what caused it may be necessary. This means, for example, proceeding from the fact that a person drinks excessively to the question: Why is he doing this? In family problems the question is: What brought these two people to where they are now? And each spouse should ask himself: What part did I have in this? The presenting problem that brings someone to the pastor may not be the real, source problem. Understanding of the latter needs to be sought.

This need not be an in depth psychoanalysis as carried out by a psychiatrist. The value of such an analysis, often requiring months and years, is questionable, nor is the pastor trained in these procedures. But there is value in knowing the more immediate causes of the problem. They may need attention; possibly they can be removed or mitigated.

It is more helpful for the counselee to gain an understanding of his problem from his own words than to be confronted with accepting the explanation of his problem as given by his pastor, even if the pastor's explanation is obviously correct. A wife may not be ready to have the pastor point out directly that her nagging is driving her husband to drink. But the pastor may succeed in bringing her to that understanding as he leads her to talk about the problem and her own actions in relationship to it. Often understanding grows as the talking progresses. If there is to be direct confrontation, the way must be prepared for it. Nathan prepared David for the blunt accusation: "Thou art the man."

Looking for a Solution

Having gained understanding, the question arises: Where do we go from here? What is the solution? The pastor may have a solution in mind. He may present it to his parishioner, who gratefully accepts and even follows it. However, his need for growth will better be served when the parishioner works on his own solution under the pastor's guidance, whether direct or indirect. Maturing takes place as he assumes this responsibility.

Vital, however, is the application of the Word of God to the problem. The solution must either come from the Word of God or at least not be contrary to it. This may require some educative counseling on the part of the pastor. He needs to point out what the Word of God says or show where a solution violates Scripture. In dealing with Christians who have received adequate biblical instruction, such teaching may be done in an indirect way. The pastor may ask the parishioner to call to mind what he learned in earlier instructions. He may with the counselee search Scripture for what God says that is pertinent to the problem. In this way the troubled Christian may learn to use the Word of God in coping with his problems also in the future, and so the need for growth is met.

Action to Mitigate the Problem

This goes a step beyond looking for a solution. This refers to action that helps to put the solution into effect. A few illustrations will elucidate what is meant. Part of the solution for a counselee is to use the Word of God in his daily life. The pastor can show him how to do this, can assign portions of Scripture as homework between meetings. He can provide a copy of *Meditations*[16] and have the counselee use it for the first time in his presence. If the problem in a marital case is primarily financial, he may have the couple work out a budget that comes to grips with the problem. The action may involve referral to a physician, to a psychiatrist, to a banker or lawyer, depending on the problem that calls for specialized help which the pastor is not trained to provide. Such action is aimed at overcoming the problem and in its own way helps to satisfy the need for growth.

Summary: The counseling session is not to become an aimless discussion. There are specific steps in the counseling procedure that can keep the sessions going in a meaningful direction. Care

16. *Meditations* appears in pamphlet form four times a year and contains a devotion for each day of the year. It is available from Northwestern Publishing House, Milwaukee.

must be taken not to view them as a fixed course that must be taken in the order indicated, nor to consider all of them necessary in every case.

VI. COUNSELING METHODS AND PROCEDURES

Some Externals

Where will the pastor meet with his parishioner? Preferably in the pastor's office or study. This should be so arranged that the counselee need not fear being overheard. Disturbances during the meeting should be reduced to a minimum. The need to answer the telephone can disrupt a conversation at a meaningful point. After the interruption it may be difficult to resume the conversation where it was broken off. Some counselors are quite concerned about the arrangement of the room. "It is my opinion," writes one, "that under no circumstances should the counselor talk across a desk to individuals. It creates the impression of aloofness and a stereotyped business relationship rather than one of friendliness and communication between equals."[17]

Since the pastor cannot always control such externals of arrangement in his member's home, the pastor's office or study is more advantageous for such a meeting. Whatever place is chosen, care must be exercised when meeting with a woman counselee that the arrangements are such that they leave no opening for anyone to start rumors of misconduct.

Should the pastor take notes during the meeting? Opinions vary on this point, but it seems advisable to avoid this practice since it could give the impression of businesslike professionalism. The pastor should, however, keep a personal record for future reference of what occurred during the meeting, especially if he is to meet with the counselee again. These notes should be made immediately after the meeting, if possible. Such notes are classified material and should be kept in a place where they are accessible only to the pastor.

How long should a counseling meeting last? The temptation for the pastor is to attempt too much in one lengthy meeting, especially when called to help in a time of crisis. The following is good advice: "Usually fifty-minute interviews are the best. To spend two or three hours in an interview, even in the home, is not

17. Hudson, *Marital Counseling*, p 51.

advisable. More than an hour or so tires everybody concerned and leads the counselee to think that if the pastor hears the whole story he will come up with a solution in one big package."[18] To schedule meetings for a definite, limited time serves the added purpose of helping avoid using too much time for small talk and nonessentials. Care must be taken that in concluding a meeting, the counselee is not cut off without meeting his needs. Whenever the results are inconclusive, arrangements for another meeting should be made. This allows time for both the pastor and the parishioner to give further thought to and to digest what has occurred at the meeting. Another meeting may be scheduled within a few days in critical situations; or, depending on the circumstances, within a week, several weeks, or even months.

Directive or Nondirective Counseling?

The directive and nondirective methods of counseling represent two opposite extremes. The nondirective, or client-centered, method was developed by psychiatrist Carl Rogers and finds expression in his writings.[19] His presuppositions are significant for an understanding of his method. He rejects original sin and sees man as basically good. Although he does not have "a Pollyanna view of human nature" and recognizes that "individuals can and do behave in ways which are incredibly cruel," he nevertheless finds in such individuals "strongly positive directional tendencies . . . at the deepest levels."[20] Rogers is an existentialist who rejects absolutes. "Life, at its best, is a flowing, changing process in which nothing is fixed."[21] He rejects the idea of helping people through teaching: "No approach which relies upon knowledge, upon training, upon the acceptance of something that is *taught* is of any use."[22]

What kind of counseling methods result from these presuppositions? Rogers writes: "If I can provide a certain type of relationship, the other person will discover within himself the capacity to use that relationship for growth, and change and personal de-

18. *Ibid.*, p 127.
19. Especially two of Rogers books should be noted in this connection. *On Becoming a Person* referred to in note 10 and *Counseling and Psychotherapy* (Boston: Houghton Mifflin, 1942).
20. Rogers, *On Becoming a Person*, pp 26f.
21. *Ibid.*, p 27.
22. *Ibid.*, p 33.

velopment will occur."[23] On the basis of his presuppositions, such methodology makes sense.

But the presuppositions are false. That raises doubts about the method, too.

The pastor, acknowledging the fact of original sin, accepting the absolutes which Scripture reveals, and the importance God places on the teaching of His Truth, must be directive in his counseling role. He cannot abdicate a role Scripture assigns to him.

The question, however, remains whether there is anything in the nondirective method that the pastor can adapt and that will not contradict his necessary presuppositions.

Man's natural reactions against dictatorial, authoritarian methods should lead the pastor to avoid extreme forms of directive counseling. Scripture warns the pastor not to lord it over the flock (1 Pe 5:3).

Are there resources within the counselee that the pastor can hope to draw on and bring into operation in the counseling process? Not, of course, in natural man, as Rogers presupposes. But the pastor generally is working with a Christian. There is within the Christian that which enabled St. Paul to say: "I can do all things through Christ which strengtheneth me" (Php 4:13). This is not a resource the Christian has by nature any more than any other man. But it is a strength the Holy Spirit has worked within the Christian through the gospel. This the pastor will seek to build up. This resource is to be brought into action. In other words, the new man in the Christian is to grow and assert himself in the Christian's life. In bringing this about as he counsels the Christian, the pastor may well assume a less directive stance. The pastor does not want to stunt the growth of the new man through being overly directive. But he also dare not by excessive permissiveness allow the old man to suppress the new. Some of the things Rogers assumes and applies to natural man do have some validity in dealing with the Christian.

A degree of nondirectiveness corresponds also to the inductive method of teaching, the value of which is broadly recognized. It is more convincing to lead someone step by step to a conclusion than to face him with the conclusion in the hope of explaining why he must accept it. The former method, since it to some extent permits the individual to discover the conclusion, makes the con-

23. *Ibid.*, pp 32f.

clusion more acceptable to him. If directive counseling means giving someone the conclusion to his problem in the hope that he will be convinced to follow it, and nondirective means leading him step by step to find the same conclusion for himself, the latter would seem to have greater hope of success.

The pastor then must be directive. But let him be so in a somewhat nondirective way.

Active Listening

The counseling pastor must learn to become a good listener. This is not an ability that he comes by easily, since his training and responsibility make him a better speaker than listener. However, in *Privatseelsorge* listening is important.

Listening involves more than being quiet while another person speaks. A counselee often has a keen sense that tells him when the pastor is not really following and is possibly occupying his mind with what he intends to say in response. Good listening is active listerning.

Active listening means that the pastor somehow communicates to the speaker that he is following and grasping what is being said. This may be nothing more than an occasional nod of the head, or it may be apparent from his facial expression. He may indicate that he is following by briefly repeating what he has heard, by reflecting back what has been said, by asking a question or suggesting a conclusion that will lead the speaker in a significant direction.

How does one get people to talk? A question or two may help the counselee get started. If he refers to his problem, a brief "Tell me more about this" encourages him to continue. If he stops in the midst of his account, repeating his last thought should bring him back from straying thoughts to continue where he left off. On the other hand, when a period of silence ensues, the pastor need not feel that he must fill in immediately with his own remarks lest what to him may appear as an embarrassing silence continue. The counselee is thinking, preparing for what he intends to say next. Sometimes what follows may prove to be of great significance.

Questions have been mentioned as inaugurating and stimulating speaking. Such questions should not give the impression of a cross-examination. If they probe into secrets the counselee is not ready to communicate, they may result in a strained relationship and not serve their intended purpose.

The pastor who has been a good listener may receive expressions of thanks for the help he gave when his chief function was to provide an empathic ear to the outpourings of a troubled heart. He will have helped more than he thought.

The Use of the Word of God

The use of Scripture in counseling should be self-evident for the pastor. This distinguishes the pastor as counselor from every other counselor. The many warnings against preaching in the counseling situation should not intimidate the pastor into avoiding the use of God's Word. While he may properly avoid the preaching method and refer to Scripture in a less formal manner, the use of God's Word is not expendable. Hulme puts it well: "The pastor knows the counselee and his problem and he knows the Scriptures; he ought, therefore, to be able to join the Scriptures with the counselee at the proper spot."[24]

The expression "proper spot" serves to warn against a forced injection of Scripture. To bring the Word into the discussion at an inopportune time before the person is ready for it may serve to satisfy the pastor that he has done his duty more than it helps the counselee. Furthermore, the law and the gospel each must be used according to the particular needs of the counselee and the purpose each serves. To use God's Word must not become a mechanical rule, applied ritualistically, to satisfy the pastor's sense of duty. An alert pastor will not fail to find an appropriate time in the counseling session to apply pertinent Scripture truths to the parishioner's needs as they become evident.

A good suggestion by Hulme is to assign the Word of God as homework for the counselee: "By giving his counselee pertinent selections of Scripture to think about for homework the pastor is attempting to facilitate the procedure by which God has chosen to work his healing power."[25]

The Use of Prayer

When the pastor is called upon to minister to a person in distress, it goes without saying that he will prepare himself by turn-

24. Hulme, *Counseling and Theology*, p 206.
25. *Ibid.*, p 207.

ing to the Lord for help. He needs the Lord's help if he is to help others. In his anxiety over what he will do and say he may forget to go to Him from whom alone he can receive the strength and wisdom needed for his work.

Should the pastor pray with the counselee? To feel that every counseling meeting must begin by praying with the counselee can lead to an awkward, formalistic beginning. This is not to say that a prayer with the counselee for the Lord's help may not at times be very much in place. But it can also be out of place before the pastor understands the needs and problems of the person. A more meaningful prayer can concern itself with the specific needs of the counselee at the close of the meeting. This is possible especially if it is spoken *ex corde*. If the counselee has expressed difficulty with prayer, praying with him can also have educational value.

Reference to Examples

A person in difficulty often thinks that he is alone in his experience. Reference to others who have had similar experiences and have surmounted them with the Lord's help can be reassuring. Care must, however, be used not to betray confidences. If the pastor can show that he has experienced similar problems, the counselee gains confidence in his sympathetic understanding.

Reference to similar examples of suffering must not, however, give the impression of belittling the counselee's problem. The pastor must also guard against talking at length about himself, thus drawing the conversation away from the person he is there to help.

Examining the Options

In searching for the best solution to the problem, the counselee may examine what solutions are open to him, considering the consequences of each. The options must be evaluated in the light of Scripture, to dissuade the counselee against following any that are inherently sinful. Divorce, for example, cannot be considered a possible option if no unfaithfulness or desertion has occurred. But even where divorce might be possible, seeing the consequences of this choice for himself and his family economically, socially, and spiritually may result in a decision to make a genuine attempt at reconciliation.

Teaching Changes of Conduct

This is one form of action that can be used to mitigate a problem, as referred to in the previous section. It may be helpful not only to tell a couple that they should have devotions and pray together. The pastor may in the counseling session teach them how to do this. If a husband and wife have difficulty communicating, useful methods have been devised to teach them how to communicate. The pastor in this way not only suggests what may help toward a solution, but teaches them how to put such suggestions into practice.

Summary: While in his counseling the pastor will need to be directive in such a way that the Word of God finds full application, he will guard against becoming directive in a manner that meets with rejection because it is overly authoritarian. As to methods, the pastor will adopt or adapt whatever methods he finds useful in helping people, remembering, however, that the methods must be compatible with Holy Scripture.

VII. COUNSELING IN SPECIFIC PROBLEM AREAS

A. Marital Problems

This is the primary problem area that calls for pastoral counseling in our day. The pastor will encourage his people to come to him with their marital problems before consulting a lawyer and filing for divorce. The confidence he has inspired during instruction courses, in premarital counseling, and in all his pastoral work and contacts with the people will make him the first choice of those seeking help in an endangered marriage. Let the pastor in general be friendly so that people will feel welcome, without, however, becoming so intimate that people will hesitate to reveal their problems.

Experience shows that there are two periods during which problems most often threaten a marriage. There is the first year, or several years, a period when one or both spouses are unwilling to make the adjustments that have to be made in the face of arising problems. The other period is after 20 to 25 years of married life, and that even in many marriages that up until then may have had a solid basis. These years may find the wife experiencing physical and emotional changes during menopause. There may be the fear of a pregnancy later in life. The children are growing up, possibly have left home, and boredom sets in. The husband may fear declining virility and is tempted to prove his masculinity in an extramarital affair. Whatever the cause, the pastor should not express surprise if he finds a couple he considered well adjusted in their marriage coming to him with problems that threaten divorce.

Most Frequent Problems

There are three prominent areas in which trouble arises. 1) A mixed marriage confronts a husband and wife with unresolved religious differences. Experience teaches that a mixed marriage has considerably less hope of success than one where their religious faith is a uniting bond between the spouses. 2) Sex is a frequent source of trouble even though the Lord gave this "becoming one flesh" as a deep, satisfying expression of oneness. The problem most often is not a physical one, or ignorance of "good" techniques in intercourse, but is caused by emotional and mental factors. 3) The third most common cause for marital discord is finances. Lack of money, differences in spending habits, the question of financial control, the wife's earning power to help support the family, saving for retirement are examples of areas in which financial problems can arise early, or even later, in marriage.

In-laws can be a source of trouble, especially when finances are involved. For the newly married couple for economic reasons to reside under the same roof with the in-laws can invite trouble. Children can be the source of difficulty. Whether and how to limit the number of children, a strong desire for children when the marriage has produced no progeny, questions of discipline all provide occasions for troublesome differences. Difficult working hours, an unsatisfactory job, drunkenness, a quarrelsome nature are all further sources of trouble.

On a broader scale, a pastor is called upon for counseling in family problems that do not necessarily threaten separation of husband and wife, but of parents and children. Parents may seek help when there is a breakdown in the parent-child relationship. Children may approach the pastor for help when they believe they see a real or imagined generation gap and feel that little parental love is being shown.

The pastor needs to be aware of the fact that the problem that brings the member of a family or a couple to him for *Seelsorge* (the presenting problem) may not be the real cause of the difficulty. The source problem may be quite another and may not become immediately evident. The husband's drunkenness may be the immediate problem that, however, in turn is caused by an unsatisfactory sex life. On the other hand, a couple's unsatisfactory sex life may be caused by emotional problems that are present because of frequent quarrels about finances. What in one case may be the presenting problem may in another prove to be the source problem and vice versa.

Reasons for Failure

Problems will arise in every marriage. When they lead to marital discord and divorce, it is because a couple is not able successfully to cope with them. What are the reasons for such failure?

Basic is the failure of couples to let the Word of God guide them, as individuals and jointly, in their marriage. Marital discord often reveals itself through a decrease in church attendance. If a husband and wife attempt to put into practice what God reveals in His Word about their respective roles in marriage, if they approach each other in the spirit of forgiveness that is inspired by the forgiveness God in love grants the sinner through Christ, the marital problems that they will face in a world of sin should not prove insurmountable. It is self-evident that the pastor must work toward that end.

Another frequent reason for a couple's failure to resolve differences is a lack of communication. This results when a spouse clams up, not even attempting to communicate a grievance. It results when one will not listen to what the other is saying, when there is no attempt at understanding and possibly even an angry response. The lack of communication may be not only a failure to discuss problems, but a general breakdown of communication in all areas. The two have nothing much to say to one another about anything significant. This easily leads to a loss of common interests. We have so little in common, may be the resulting complaint. Recognizing this as a reason for a couple's troubles, the pastor can help them learn to communicate with understanding.

Finally, emotional instability or lack of maturity may prevent a couple from coping with problems successfully. A quick temper, or uncontrolled anger on the part of one or both spouses, leaves little possibility for working out problems together. Irresponsibility may be a sign of immaturity. The pastor will need great patience in an effort to effect growth in the face of these deficiencies.

Sometimes emotional instability may require medical or psychiatric help.

Some Practical Suggestions

There is no simple blueprint for a pastor to follow in dealing with marital problems. Much of what was said about the counseling pastor will find application here. Without undue duplication of what has been said, the following suggestions may prove helpful to the young pastor as he gains experience in counseling the troubled family. Through these suggestions he may be able to learn from the experience of others and avoid the mistakes that led to some of these suggestions.

Meet with the couple in the pastor's office or study, not in the people's home. Those who are interested in help will keep the appointment to come to the office.

Come to the point quickly. If people come to the office, they are there for a purpose which is not simply to engage in pleasant chitchat.

Meet with each spouse alone, then with the two together. But in meeting with each alone, avoid taking sides or committing yourself prematurely. In the case of a mixed marriage, it is often difficult to establish contact with the nonmember or, if there is contact, to counsel with a person who does not share the pastor's faith. In such cases special care is in order to remain objective lest the pastor simply takes the side of his member or appears to be doing so.

Do not let a session become too long. Make an appointment for another meeting, except where an immediate crisis remains completely unresolved. This will help to avoid making hasty, sometimes ill-advised decisions.

Counsel with the children if there are any that are involved. This can be individual counseling as well as with the family as a group.

Church attendance should be strongly encouraged on the part of those being counseled. Unless the couple through their church attendance shows willingness to let the Word of God become influential in their lives, there is little hope of success.

Do not make promises that you cannot keep. Do not give the impression that you have an easy solution ready, but do lead the couple to listen confidently to the promises of God from Holy Scripture.

Do not counsel with anyone while he is under the influence of liquor or drugs. Such a person is not in a mental state suitable for counseling.

Show genuine interest and concern. Involved is not only the continued existence of a marriage, but the welfare of immortal souls.

Do not let apparent failure raise doubts about the power of God's Word. The Spirit works where and when it pleases God and can be resisted.

If divorce results, seek to bring the guilty to repentance. In many cases it may mean bringing each spouse to repent of his contribution to the failure of the marriage. What Scripture says on marriage and divorce (cf the chapter on "Marriage") will need to find application in the counseling.

The pastor may find that some of these marital cases, especially those involving divorce, become complicated and that a satisfactory solution is hard to find. The advice of Luther is pertinent and may be of comfort to the pastor when confronted with confused cases:

> And wherever so strange or unusual a case occurs . . . that it cannot be decided on the basis of some writing or book, then one should seek the advice and opinion of one or two good, pious men in the case; and after they have given their advice and opinion, their judgment and advice should be followed without any wavering or doubt. For although they may not always meet with the strictest demands of the law, so slight a fault will do no harm, and it is better at last to have peace and quiet with this drawback and less justice than to have to keep on seeking the most pointed and severe justice, with endless discord and unrest. It is not necessary for a good marksman always to hit the bull's-eye; one must concede that he who comes close to it or hits the target is a good shot . . .
>
> So, even if these pious men should err a little in such confused cases, God will be satisfied with their error, because their intentions are sincere and true, and they are not seeking advantage for themselves or knowingly speaking against the established laws, and he will bury it all in the Lord's Prayer when we say, "Forgive us our trespasses."[26]

26. L.W., XLVI, 287-88.

Summary: The pastor will welcome the opportunity to counsel with a couple or family where disruptive problems have arisen. He will recognize that the presenting problem that has brought the people to him for counsel is not necessarily the real source problem. God's will regarding marriage as revealed in Scripture will find application in the counseling. Although marital problems frequently are involved and generally no one person bears all the blame for the troubles, the pastor will seek to reestablish good communication between the spouses, leading each to repent of his wrongs and to forgive the other.

B. Family Planning

Both in premarital and in family counseling the subject of family planning frequently calls for consideration. May a newly married couple delay conception of the first child? May parents determine the exact number of children in their family? May they take steps to space their children at will? May they practice birth control, perhaps better called conception control? Is abortion ever permissible? These questions confront husband and wife ever more directly in a society that is aiming at zero-population growth, that views the "population explosion" as a threat to man's existence in his limited environment on earth, that even in its lawmaking is threatening to limit man's freedom of conception while demanding unlimited sexual freedom.

Scripture does not directly address itself to the above questions. The one example in Scripture of preventing conception is that of Onan, Genesis 38:6-10. However, God's displeasure at the birth control practices of Onan must be viewed in its context. "The thing which he (Onan) did displeased the Lord" because he refused to raise up seed for his deceased brother. The conclusion that this proves God's displeasure with any and all conception control is too broad.

There are, nevertheless, related points in Scripture that will help Christians in considering the above questions. These the pastor will draw to their attention as they seek God-pleasing answers to questions about family planning in their personal lives.

A Blessing of God

People's attitudes toward having children need to be brought into harmony with those of Scripture. God gives children as a blessing. Besides telling of man's creation as male and female

210

which implies the union of the sexes in cohabitation (Gn 2:24), Scripture also says in Genesis 1:28: "And God blessed them, and God said unto them, Be fruitful and multiply, and replenish the earth." Procreation was established in the beginning as a divine blessing. "God blessed them." The imperative, "Be fruitful," was the command of God putting this blessing into effect, even as "Let there be light" brought light into existence. To consider this simply as a command to have as many children as possible does not do justice to the context in which God spoke. God blessed man with procreation. Let that be man's attitude toward having a part in the miracle of producing a new life. Cf also Psalms 127 and 128.

Looking upon children as a blessing of the Lord eliminates an arbitrary approach to family planning. A couple cannot say, "We will rule out this blessing from our marriage for the first several years because that is the way we want it." Selfish reasons, contrived by man's fleshly mind, for limiting the number of children in a family are thus rejected. This means that if there is to be a limitation to the blessing, God's Word must lead the way to it.

With Understanding

Peter writes: "You husbands likewise, live with your wives in an understanding way, as with a weaker vessel, since she is a woman; and grant her honor as a fellow-heir of the grace of life" (1 Pe 3:7-NASB). *Gnoosis*, used without a qualifying genitive as in this passage, simply means knowledge, judgment, understanding. *Kata gnoosin* can be translated "wisely." The husband in living with his wife should apply good judgment that takes into account that she is the weaker vessel. Hence, he will not make excessive demands on the wife sexually nor in the bearing of children. For a husband to insist that his wife bear a child every year would in most cases not be *kata gnoosin*. However, the *kata gnoosin* sets up no simple rule, generally applicable, but calls for wise judgment and understanding applied in accordance with God's Word by each couple in the circumstances that confront them. God's Word must guide them, for they are "heirs together of the grace of life."

The Fifth Commandment

God's will expressed in the Fifth Commandment will guide that judgment. Nothing will be undertaken that is known to be injurious to the wife's health. To ignore sound medical advice may be tempting the Lord rather than an expression of faith. Mental health needs consideration no less than the physical. Let the couple be warned, however, not to allow "health" to become a justification behind which selfish motives hide. A self-diagnosis in determining questions of health will hardly have the validity of a competent doctor's advice.

If health calls for restriction or cessation of child-bearing while normal sexual relations are possible, 1 Corinthians 7:5 warns against prolonged abstinence "lest Satan tempt you because of your lack of self-control" (NASB). The close companionship which intercourse provides by divine institution may continue while the couple must forego the blessing of procreation through some means of contraception.

Economic Reasons

How valid are economic reasons for practicing birth control? That parents are to provide for their children is self-evident. Scripture does not, however, say that this must be possible according to an arbitrarily chosen standard of living. Scripture calls for contentment with the simple necessities of life (1 Tm 6:8), warns against covetousness (Eph 5:3), and calls for trusting the heavenly Father to provide as He does for the birds and the flowers (Mt 6:25-34). These passages greatly limit the possibility of economic reasons being decisive for practicing birth control, especially in a country that is experiencing economic prosperity.

If scripturally valid considerations require longer periods between pregnancies or the cessation of procreation, the method of preventing conception is an adiaphoron provided it is not harmful or otherwise objectionable. There still is a question as to the harmlessness of the "pill." The intrauterine device (IUD) appears to be a chronic abortion when life begins and thus at best questionable. Sterilization, whether of the man or woman, is a form of voluntary mutilation that hardly seems to accord with the Fifth Commandment. Since it more often than not is irreversible, serious regrets can result when an earlier decision is changed, and it can have psychologically harmful effects. A medically indicated hysterectomy, while resulting in sterility, is not voluntary mutilation.

The pastor must reject abortion as a solution to an undesired pregnancy. Not to consider the unborn fetus human life belonging to a newly formed person makes John the Baptist's prenatal leaping in the womb meaningless (Lk 1:44) and not an act of joyful faith in his Savior, likewise still in the womb of Mary. "Thou shalt not kill" protects human life against destruction, also in the womb. Whether abortion should be performed to save a mother's life will have to be determined by considering all facts and options in the light of God's Word. Fortunately medical developments have greatly reduced the need for such therapeutic abortions.

Summary: In counseling people on family planning, attitudes need to be brought into harmony with Holy Scripture. The fact that procreation is a blessing of God rules out any arbitrary approach to family planning. God's Word must remain the guide. Even though Scripture does not speak directly on this subject, the Fifth Commandment points to health as an important consideration. Economic factors can enter in only under unusual conditions. Where Scripture leads to some kind of limitation, the method used is an adiaphoron, provided it is not harmful and does not destroy life that has already begun.

C. Extramarital Pregnancy

The woman who finds herself pregnant outside of wedlock will, it is to be hoped, seek out her pastor for Christian counseling. Quite often, especially if she is still young and living under the parental roof, the parents will be drawn in if it is not they who actually bring their daughter for counseling. Furthermore, the man responsible for the pregnancy no less than the woman is in need of the pastor's counsel.

For the pastor to express shock over the confessed sin against the Sixth Commandment and the resulting pregnancy will hardly set the stage for sympathetic counseling. An attitude of acceptance toward the person as exemplified by Jesus is called for, without giving the impression of denying the sinfulness of what has happened.

Repentance and Reconciliation

The pastor's great concern is the spiritual condition of the young woman. He will look for repentance. If she is overwhelmed by feelings of guilt and remorse over her sin, the pastor dare not withhold the comfort of absolution based on the atoning death of Christ. Jesus died also for her specific sin. If, on the other hand, a permissive attitude toward sex has blurred the sinfulness of the act, the sin must be exposed for what it is on the basis of God's law. Does she recognize that she sinned against God? Is she sorry only because of the consequent pregnancy? Does she attempt to excuse her action ("Others are doing it." "What I did wasn't so bad, but the trouble is the way people look at it and talk." "We're living in different times.")?

But sorrow over sin is never an end in itself. It serves to prepare the way for the gospel. Repentance is contrition and faith in the gospel that proclaims absolution.

What is said about the pregnant woman applies similarly to the man involved.

Reconciliation is a further goal of any counseling with the pastor. Through their sinful conduct the man and the woman have brought injury to their families. They will seek forgiveness and reconciliation (Mt 5:23,24). The parents on their part will forgive the penitent son or daughter even as Christ forgives them their sins (Mt 6:14,15). Such repentance and reconciliation will greatly aid the search for solutions to the practical problems the pregnancy caused.

Marriage?

The first question that demands an answer is whether there will be a marriage. If the couple was engaged, the answer should be affirmative. Under such conditions they can be expected to desire marriage. For either to refuse marriage when the cohabitation occurred after firm marriage commitments had been made is tantamount to breaking a marriage bond.

That every pregnancy must result in marriage cannot be asserted. The requirement of marriage if a man was found lying with a virgin (Dt 22:28,29) was a law given to theocratic Israel and was not imposed in the New Testament. Not cohabitation but consent establishes the marriage bond. The man and woman who have jointly produced the life growing in the womb can be encouraged to give that child what should be its rightful home. If, however, there is no love but a strong resistance against making a lifelong marriage commitment, to force the latter may result in greater problems than it is intended to solve.

214

Reconciliation between the man and the woman, especially if a marriage is to take place, is important for the success of the future marriage. The one may in his heart blame the other for the pregnancy and in time of conflict raise charges. Let each forgive the other and solemnly promise never to raise charges during their married life.

The Child

If there is no marriage, the future of the child comes into question. Should the mother keep the child or give it up for adoption? There is no single answer applicable to all situations. What is best for the future of the child? Can the mother support the child? Can she compensate for the lack of a father in the home? Will a possible future husband accept the child? Especially important is the question: What provisions will there be for the child's religious training should it be given up for adoption? These and other questions will be discussed as an answer is sought to this difficult question. Except in the case of very young girls, the decision must finally be made by the mother. It is to be hoped that she will show or develop the kind of Christian maturity that is needed to make a responsible decision.

Even after the various questions have found an answer and regular counseling ceases, the pastor will through occasional contact make himself available in case further help is needed.

Summary: In the case of an extramarital pregnancy the pastor's first concern will be repentance toward God of both the man and the woman, and reconciliation among those who have suffered injury as a result of the sin. Unless the couple had a marriage commitment, the pastor cannot assume that a marriage must take place, even though he will encourage marriage, wherever possible, for the sake of the child. If there is no marriage, the mother needs to consider carefully whether to keep the child or not, giving special thought to the child's future spiritual welfare.

D. Alcoholism and Drug Abuse

Although the national statistics of the incidence of alcoholism and drug abuse cause great concern, the frequency of these problems among church members is considerably lower. Nevertheless, the pastor will have occasion to counsel with people who have a drinking or drug problem. Such counseling can become time-consuming if it is to be effective and bring the Word of God to bear on the problem with adequate thoroughness. That the pastor must take the time when his help is called for is self-evident.

What is Alcoholism?

Habits vary as to the use of alcoholic beverages. Some people are teetotalers as a matter of principle, others only by habit. A large segment of our population and of our members, no doubt, does not hesitate to drink socially and in moderation. Some people get drunk on occasion. A smaller number drinks to excess and uses alcohol quite regularly as an escape from problems. They are referred to as problem drinkers. Finally there are those for whom drinking has become a problem beyond their control. Once they take a drink, they cannot stop at will. These are considered alcoholics.

Scripture does not require general, total abstinence. To claim that it does will make Jesus' first miracle at the wedding in Cana reprehensible. It would fail to acknowledge Paul's advice to Timothy involving the therapeutic use of wine (1 Tm 5:23).

Drunkenness, however, is sin. Scripture has numerous proscriptions against drunkenness (e.g., Pr 23:29-35; Is 5:11; Eph 5:18; Ga 5:21). All drunkenness is sin, whether of the occasional reveler, of the problem drinker, or of the alcoholic. It is an abuse of the body which was redeemed by Christ and is a temple of the Holy Ghost. It is poor stewardship of God's blessings. It frequently does injury to or endangers other persons. According to Scripture, drunkenness is morally reprehensible. To ignore this is to ignore what Scripture says of it.

At the same time, the alcoholic is a sick person, psychologically and possibly physically. He cannot control his consumption of alcohol. Some believe that his biochemistry is such that once he begins drinking he cannot stop. To call an alcoholic sick does not, however, eleminate his responsibility to God for the sinfulness of his excessive drinking.

The pastor may be called upon to deal as a *Seelsorger* with people who in various ways have fallen into the sin of drunkenness. The alcoholic, however, presents the greatest difficulty, particularly until he has accepted the fact that he is an alcoholic

216

with all that that implies, and genuinely desires help. The pastor should acquaint himself with the progressive symptoms of alcoholism and with the alcoholic's psychological make-up, and with constructive ways of approaching him.[27]

The pastor may be called upon for help during a crisis resulting from drunkenness, but effective *Seelsorge* must await sobriety. The person may be overwhelmed by feelings of guilt for which the only divinely appointed solution is the riches of God's forgiveness in Christ. The alcoholic is powerless in the face of his problem. The pastor knows the power of God's Word and promises. He knows that the Holy Spirit works effectually through them. With earnestness born of this conviction he will urge these reassuring promises upon the soul that in desperation is reaching out for help. God promises help and strength in the battle also against alcoholism. His promises likewise apply to the problems, fears, and tensions that are part of life and that contributed to the alcoholic's present degradation. Frequent, perhaps daily, supportive counseling is needed and will require much patience over a long period of time.

Alcoholics Anonymous

Alcoholics Anonymous has been called "the most effective referral resource available today."[28] This statement is based on its success with many thousands of alcoholics. Since one of its Traditions is that "each Group should be autonomous, except in matters affecting other groups or AA as a whole,"[29] the pastor's knowledge of a local group and the people included in it will help him determine whether referral may be considered. An important step in AA is the alcoholic's recognition of his own helplessness and his need to rely upon a higher power outside himself for help. Scripture, too, teaches this but also reveals who that higher power is. That deistic teaching could find entrance into a group is possible and would make such a group unacceptable to a Christian.

---

27. Some useful volumes are Clinebell's *Understanding and Counseling the Alcoholic*, Keller's *Ministering to Alcoholics*, and the pocket counsel book, *Drinking Problem?* by Keller. Study of such material will give the pastor some insights into the psychology of an alcoholic so that he may apply the Word of God with better understanding and avoid some pitfalls.
28. Clinebell, p 110.
29. Clinebell, p 139.

The church member also needs to be warned against joining in promiscuous prayer, if that finds entrance into the meetings. One of the favorable features of AA, contributing greatly to its success, is the support an alcoholic receives from those who have experienced his problem. This kind of help may be difficult to find anywhere else. If a member joins the AA for help, the pastor should continue his counseling, directing his member to the only source of genuine strength, Christ Jesus, his Savior, as promised in Scripture.

Since the alcoholic must practice total abstinence in order to surmount his problem (he is never really cured in the sense of being able to engage in controlled drinking), the question arises about his receiving wine in Holy Communion. The use of unfermented grape juice in private communion is not excluded theologically. Nevertheless, pastors have found that the small amount of wine received in the context of the Lord's sacrament, with trust in the Lord's help and strength, causes no difficulty for the alcoholic. In fact, he may thus receive added assurance that his Savior is indeed his help and stay in his problem.

The Alcoholic's Family

The entire family of the alcoholic or the heavy drinker suffers as a result of his actions. At the same time, his family can help the alcoholic toward recovery. Thus the pastor will counsel with the family, strengthening them from Scripture so that they may bear the anxieties, doubts, fears, and privations they may be encountering. He will advise and encourage them so that they may know how best to help the alcoholic member of the family. Family counseling is frequently occasioned by an alcoholism problem. Books on counseling the alcoholic generally contain a chapter on counseling the family.[30]

Help for the spouse and adult members of the alcoholic's family is available through Al-Anon. For teenagers in the family an Alateen group may be helpful. These groups, through contact with others having the same experiences, can help the members of the family while the alcoholic himself receives help from AA. These organizations must be regarded as additional means of

30. Cf the volumes referred to in note 27.

finding help, but not as replacing the spiritual support which the pastor provides through God's Word.

The Drug Problem

During the decade of the 1960's drug abuse became a major problem, particularly among the nation's youth, even the very young. That the church's youth would remain totally immune to it was not to be expected. Since alcohol too is a drug, the change was that other drugs, some with greater potential for harm, have been added to the abuse which alcohol had experienced for a long time.

The comparative newness of widespread drug abuse and the publicity it has received may contribute to a somewhat shocked reaction when the pastor is first confronted with a case of drug abuse on the part of one of his members. Such a reaction will make no positive contribution to effective *Seelsorge* with the "drug abuser."

What leads to drug abuse? The reasons will often be similar to those that lead to the abuse of alcohol. Children feel unloved, insecure, lonely, estranged from their parents. They see little meaning in life, are disillusioned with those whom they previously trusted. Or they may simply be looking for a new thrill, or be doing what others are doing.

Until the one who uses drugs wants help, little can be done for him. That help is desired by the person who voluntarily contacts the pastor can be assumed. Considerably more difficult is the case where the family or circumstances "force" the pastor's attention on a drug user. An accepting, sympathetic (empathic) approach is called for, which, however, in no way gives the impression that the abuse is acceptable. That this is sin cannot be disregarded. To what extent it needs enunciating in a given case will vary. The pastor's efforts must first direct themselves at bringing about a desire for help. It is further necessary to find the reason why this member is turning to drugs. What problem is he trying to evade or solve? From Scripture the pastor can show the true meaning of life and the riches of God's love. Since drug abuse is most often found among the children in a family, family counseling will seek to effect the kind of Christian relationship in the family that will remove whatever in the family may have contributed to the abuse

and make the family a source of help to the son or daughter enmeshed in this destructive habit or addiction. The pastor will
never want to forget the power of the Word of God and prayer.

To evaluate the seriousness of the problem and what may be
needed to overcome it, the pastor needs some knowledge of the
different kinds of drugs and their characteristics.[31] In the case of
marijuana the pastor may decide to carry out the counseling
without medical help. LSD, the most potent and best known of
the hallucinogens, presents a much more serious problem. The
use of this drug sometimes even has religious overtones. While its
discontinuance does not result in withdrawal symptoms, intensive
users may experience a "flashback," a recurrence of some of the
features of the LSD state days or months after the last dose.
Stimulants or sedatives may serve a useful purpose when taken
under medical direction. Their abuse is dangerous and withdrawal requires medical help. Heroin, the most widely used of the nar-
cotics, or opiates, is highly addictive. Withdrawal sickness is
painful and can be terrifying. This calls for skilled medical help.
Wherever medical help is required, the pastor will insist on referral to a physician. The latter may, in turn, recommend further referral to an agency that provides specialized help for those with a
drug problem. At the same time, the pastor should acquaint himself with whatever programs or medical facilities the state or
community provides for helping such who have become involved
in drug abuse.

While the seriousness of the problem may be determined by the
kind of drug involved, the fact that a drug is prohibited by law
will have to be acknowledged and makes its use wrong, regardless
of the individual's judgment of the law's wisdom.

Summary: Alcoholism and drug abuse call for empathic concern on the part of the pastor. Counseling in such cases can be

---

31. *A Federal Source Book: Answers to the most frequently asked questions about drug abuse* is an informative pamphlet issued by the federal government. It is revised periodically "as new facts — and new
answers — are discovered." This and other materials are available
from the Superintendent of Documents, US Government Printing
Office, Washington, D.C. 10401, or from the National Clearinghouse
for Drug Abuse Information, Box 1080, Washington, D.C. 20013. A
description of the most commonly used drugs, the pros and cons of
their use so far as this is known, is found also in *The Christian Encounters Drugs and Drug Abuse* by James Cassens (St. Louis: Concordia, 1970).

time-consuming. The pastor will seek to help remove the circumstances that contributed to the problem, apply the healing power of the Word, and refer the parishioner to additional help that may be needed. Such referral does not free the pastor of his responsibility to continue counseling the parishioner on the basis of the Word of God.

For Additional Reading

Adams, Jay E. *Competent To Counsel*. Grand Rapids: Baker, 1970.

This volume on counseling will interest the pastor because its thesis is "that qualified Christian counselors properly trained in the Scriptures are competent to counsel — more competent than psychiatrists or anyone else." Without sharing some of the author's extreme views and his Reformed theology, a pastor will find encouragement to use his Scriptural training for Christ-centered counseling.

Cassens, James. *The Christian Encounters Drugs and Drug Abuse*. St. Louis: Concordia, 1970.

The greater part of this volume describes the drug problem and the types of drugs involved. The final chapter, "A Christian Perspective on Drugs," provides food for thought even though it is a limited presentation.

Clinebell, Howard J. *Basic types of Pastoral Counseling*. Nashville: Abingdon, 1966.

"This well-rounded survey of the entire field of pastoral counseling suggests a revised model beamed directly to the needs and capabilities of the average parish minister" (description on book jacket). Includes a useful chapter on the "Methods of Informal and Short-term Counseling."

Clinebell, Howard J. *Understanding and Counseling the Alcoholic*. Nashville: Abingdon, 1956.

After defining alcoholism and examining its causes, the author in the second part describes the various religious approaches that have been and are used. The final and longest part discusses the minister's approach to alcoholism. Worthy of critical study.

221

Dunn, Jerry G. *God Is for the Alcoholic.* Chicago: Moody, 1965.

From personal experience the author knows that "God is for the Alcoholic." The pastor will appreciate the extensive use of Scripture by the author.

A Federal Source Book: Answers to the most frequently asked questions about drug abuse. Washington, D.C. 20402. Revised, 1971.

A pamphlet that contains information on the various drugs of abuse, their characteristics and effects, as gathered by the various governmental agencies. An excellent source of drug abuse information for the pastor.

Haas, Harold J. *Pastoral Counseling with People in Distress.* St. Louis: Concordia, 1970.

Although the volume concerns itself especially with counseling the mentally distressed and thus contains a basic outline of mental and emotional problems, it can serve also as an introduction to counseling in general.

Habeck, Irwin J. "Responsible Parenthood." *Northwestern Lutheran,* March 2, 1969. LVI, 73-74.

A brief article on the popular level that should prove helpful in counseling members on family planning.

Hulme, William E. *Counseling and Theology.* Philadelphia: Muhlenberg, 1956.

Hulme devotes a great part of his presentation to a discussion of the four needs of the counselee (for a listener, for confession, for understanding, and for growth). Good in its presentation of the doctrine of justification as the means for removal of guilt.

Hulme, William E. *How To Start Counseling.* Nashville: Abingdon, 1955.

Twelve chapters treat various practical aspects that confront the pastor when he starts or wants to start counseling. Concerns itself also with the pastor's own spiritual life, his scholarship, and his own household.

Keller, John E. *Drinking Problem?* Philadelphia: Fortress, 1971.

Useful for gaining information about alcoholism and counseling methods. Scripture finds little direct application in the volume.

Keller, John E. *Ministering to Alcoholics*. Minneapolis: Augsburg, 1966.

    The author has had extensive experience counseling in hospitals with alcoholics. Read with discernment, this volume can give the pastor an understanding of the alcoholic's problems and provide him with practical help for counseling with the alcoholic and his spouse.

Kirsten, Hans. "Birth Control as Ethical and Pastoral Problem." *Wisconsin Lutheran Quarterly*, Jan. 1968. LXV, 24-42.

    This article presents the biblical considerations that are applicable to the subject of family planning.

McNeill, John Thomas. *A History of the Cure of Souls*. New York: Harper, 1951.

    That the cure of souls has not first become the church's concern with the advent of "counseling" is evident from this volume. Particularly interesting is the description of Luther's pastoral concern for souls.

Oates, Wayne E., Ed. *An Introduction to Pastoral Counseling*. Nashville: Broadman, 1959.

    A textbook prepared by the teachers in the field of counseling in the Southern Baptist Convention seminaries. A practical and comprehensive introduction to the subject.

The Pastor at Work. Chapter XVII, "The Pastor and the Burdened Soul." pp. 275-298. St. Louis: Concordia, 1960.

    This chapter provides a brief introduction to pastoral counseling with a section devoted to each of the counseling situations a pastor may encounter (the adolescent, the senile, the bereaved, the mentally disturbed, etc.).

Rogers, Carl R. *On Becoming a Person*. Boston: Houghton Mifflin, 1962.

    Rogers outlines his nondirective method of counseling and reveals the principles on which it is based. These principles do not accord with Scripture.

Wrange, Karl Horst. *Children — Choice or Chance*. Philadelphia: Fortress, 1969.

    It will be difficult for a pastor to find a volume on the subject of family planning with which he can agree fully. This volume is no exception. The author's definite rejection of abortion and sterilization will be appreciated. The volume can be a source of information on the various methods of contraception, discussed by a German medical doctor.

9

The Shepherd Reaches
Out to the Unchurched

*"Preach the gospel
to every creature"*
(Mk 16:15)

I. DEFINITION AND BASIS

Evangelism is a derivative of the Greek word *evangelizoo*. Thus evangelism concerns itself with the gospel, the good message of salvation through Christ. In its broadest sense, it is everything that the church and its individual members do to testify to the gospel of Christ.

The total work of the church as it relates to the proclamation of the gospel can be called evangelism. The church's presence in a community, its regular worship services, the appearance of its property, its membership in a synod, and its support of the synod's mission program, all its educational efforts, its various ministrations are evangelism in a broad sense.

Likewise the individual Christian in his whole life lets his light shine among men so that they may be brought to glorify God (Mt 5:14-16). A wife's Christian conduct may draw an unbelieving husband to the gospel (1 Pe 3:1,2). A Christian's honest labor, his neighborly helpfulness, his chaste language, his regular church attendance reflect favorably on the gospel, provide a setting for

225

its proclamation, and manifest its power. This, too, is evangelism in a broad sense.

However, not only deeds but also words are called for by our Savior. The Christian is to tell people about Christ and His significance for them. The Christian is to preach the gospel to every creature, for it is the gospel alone through which the Holy Spirit works faith in the unbeliever. Hence for a Christian to speak of Christ to another person is evangelism in the narrow sense. The church carries out evangelism in this sense when it has an ongoing program for training and sending out laymen as personal witnesses to Christ. Without forgetting the broad concept of evangelism, the chief emphasis in this chapter will be on the narrow sense of the church's and the individual's evangelism.

God's revelation in Scripture forces evangelism on the Christian, not legalistically, but with compelling urgency. What Scripture says about the nature of man, the nature of the gospel, and the nature of the Christian forms the theological basis for evangelism.[1]

Since the Fall human nature is corrupt (Ps 51:5; 1 Jn 1:8). This is true of all men (Ro 3:23; Ps 14:2,3). The result is that all men are under the just condemnation of God (Ro 5:18; 6:23). The fact of the universal depravity and eternal condemnation of man is unequivocally asserted in Scripture.

The gospel is the good news of salvation from sin through Christ (Is 53:4-6; Jn 3:16). This is the only way of salvation (Ac 4:12). The gospel proclaims salvation prepared for all the world (2 Cor 5:19; 1 Jn 2:2). It, however, benefits only those who receive it by faith (Mt 16:16; Ro 3:28). This faith the Holy Spirit works through the gospel as it is proclaimed and heard (Mk 16:15,16; Ro 10:17; 1:16; 1 Cor 12:3). Scripture reveals a unique, powerful message of salvation, inclusive, yet exclusive — one that offers salvation and works the faith by which it is received. This gospel because it is the heart of evangelism gives its name to it.

The nature of the Christian as revealed in Scripture is one totally different from that of natural man. Believers are sons of God (1 Jn 3:1), invigorated by the power of Christ as branches in Him, the vine (Jn 15:5), temples of the Holy Ghost (1 Cor 6:19,20), so that they will glorify Him while living in this body.

1. Cf *"We Believe"* — *The Theology of Evangelism*, (*Proceedings*, 1971, pp 43-54), an essay read by A. Schuetze at the convention of the Wisconsin Evangelical Lutheran Synod.

They are priests of their King, the Lord Jesus (1 Pe 2:9), proclaiming His praises. Christians cannot but speak of the things which they have seen and heard (Ac 4:20). They are Christ's witnesses (Ac 1:8).

The nature of man reveals a compelling need on man's part for help; the nature of the gospel makes its application to man's need compelling; the nature of the Christian compels him to proclaim the gospel which has made him what he is.

Summary: Evangelism in its broad sense concerns itself with all aspects of gospel witnessing by the church or individual Christians. In a more restricted sense it refers to the verbal testimony to Christ given by a Christian to an unchurched neighbor. The congregation's evangelism program will promote such testimony. What Scripture says about the nature of man, of the gospel, and of the Christian will compel the Christian to follow Christ's command to preach the gospel to every creature.

II. THE PASTOR'S ROLE

The pastor, like all his members, belongs to the universal priesthood. In addition, he has been called into the public ministry. He is a servant of God, called through the congregation to preach the gospel in its behalf and for its benefit.

Both as a royal priest and as a called minister he has the responsibility of bringing the gospel to the unbelieving world. Among the calls the pastor makes are "mission calls" (cf the chapter on "The Shepherd Visits the Sheep," part IV). The congregation's diploma of vocation to the pastor generally contains a statement to the effect that he should be "ever zealous for the winning of souls for Christ's kingdom."

Nevertheless, this is not his only and generally, according to the diploma of vocation, not his first assignment. A pastor is called to do what Paul refers to in his address to the Ephesian elders: he is to take heed "to the flock over the which the Holy Ghost hath made you overseers, to feed the church of God, which he hath purchased with his own blood" (Ac 20:28). Peter was commissioned to feed the sheep and lambs of Jesus (Jn 21:15-17). The pastor must preach the word in season and out of season, conduct services, visit the sick, counsel the troubled, admonish the erring in his flock. The pastor who neglects to "reprove, rebuke, exhort with all longsuffering and doctrine" (2 Tm 4:2) the flock placed into his charge so that he may devote himself more fully to those still outside the church, needs to ask himself whether he is being faithful to his call from the congregation. His zeal for the salvation of souls must reach out into all directions, also into the congregation (cf the broad concept of evangelism). When he successfully calls a sinning member to repentance, "thou hast gained thy brother" (Mt 18:15). When he restores the erring brother, he shall save a soul from death (Jas 5:20). This he will do without, however, forgetting to preach the gospel to the unbelieving world so that the Lord may add to His church "such as should be saved" (Ac 2:47).

Ephesians 4:12 reveals another important responsibility which God has laid upon the pastor in connection with the congregation's evangelism effort. The ascended Lord gives the church pastors, teachers, etc., "for equipping of the saints for the work of service" (NASB). The pastor is called to equip the saints, the members of his flock, for the task of ministering, the ministering they are to do as saints of God, as universal priests. An important part of that is to show forth the Lord's praises by promoting and speaking the gospel. The pastor's role in a congregation's evangelism responsibility is to train its members to be good witnesses of Christ.

How the pastor carries out his role will to a great extent depend on the kind of field he is serving. If the congregation is a new mission with only a small flock, the feeding of the flock will require a minimum of time and the pastor will personally make many of the "mission calls." He will at the same time begin to train the members of his small flock for their task of ministering as witnesses of Christ. As the congregation grows, the pastoral "feeding" will preempt more of his time. He will personally make fewer mission calls. But he will continue to equip the "saints" in his congregation so that there is an ever growing number of those who minister to the unchurched with the gospel. In this way the large size of a congregation does not hinder the evangelism outreach, but increases the number of those who "go and tell." While the pastor may find it difficult personally to make numerous mission calls, his role of equipping the saints is part of his feeding responsibility and at the same time advances the congregation's evangelism effort.

Whether the pastor personally makes the mission calls or not, the fact remains that he more than any other individual represents his congregation to the community. The image he presents to the community will advance or hinder any evangelism effort. Let the pastor be friendly, without becoming a saccharine back slapper. Let him command respect for being a man of principle, without carrying a chip on his shoulder. Let him follow scriptural fellowship practices, without ignoring his neighbors in the world. Let him show warmth and love toward people, without condoning their sins. Let him be himself, without breeding contempt by his familiarity. Let him display confidence and joy in his labors, without acting self-righteous and self-sufficient. In short, let him be as Christlike as possible, knowing that he has been sent by Jesus as His ambassador. Jesus was not a pietistic showoff like the Pharisees. He had come to seek and to save that which was lost, and His warm outreach to people, whom He loved unto death, drew the multitudes to Him. Let the image of the pastor be a reflection of Christ. That will in the truest sense be good public relations for his church in the community and benefit his congregation's evangelism thrust.

Summary: Although the pastor is called to feed a specific flock, his call also includes "winning souls for Christ's kingdom." He will do this personally, but he has also the special call to equip the lay members for such ministration. The pastor's total public image in the community will reflect on the congregation and can affect its evangelism effort.

III. EQUIPPING THE INDIVIDUAL SAINT

All application of the gospel to the saints of God serves also to equip them for their ministry as universal priests. The pastor will, however, directly and consciously seek to prepare his members for gospel witnessing to their neighbors. This begins by implanting zeal for the gospel in their hearts and a deep consciousness of their responsibility for spreading it among men everywhere.

Inspiration

The pastor who himself is on fire with the gospel should have little difficulty igniting his members with zeal for witnessing. Inspiration is contagious and so is the lack of it. The inspiration we seek, however, is one that results not merely from stirred up emotions, but one that is ignited and fueled by the gospel itself. Can a Christian think through the words of John 3:16 and Matthew

28:19 with all they imply without being inspired to go and tell? By means of example and the Word the pastor will provide inspiration for evangelism.

In doing this, the pastor, and the members too, will recognize that each member in the church, the body of Christ, will serve according to the gifts the Lord has given. All Christians are witnesses, but not in the same way. Each will serve according to the measure of faith given to him and the gifts the Holy Spirit has bestowed. Some may witness primarily through their exemplary Christian life. Or it may be their faithful attendance at services that will testify to the gospel and its power. There are those who may have the special gift of meeting strangers and can go out to make contacts in the world. There are those who have the gift of speaking ably of Christ to the unknowing. The pastor will cultivate these various gifts as best he can. He must, however, guard against any attempt to force all members to give witness to Christ in the same manner. Inspiration should move each to do his part according to the gifts God has given. The pastor must avoid causing consciences to be troubled over failure to serve in ways for which the gifts are lacking. Nevertheless, let the pastor not underestimate the God-given abilities of his members. Let the members not underestimate their own talents.

Special consideration must be given to equipping those who will be sent out to speak about the Savior to those outside the congregation. This involves deepening the understanding of the message (indoctrination) and training in techniques.

Indoctrination

A witness is always expected to speak the truth. He is not to be a false witness. Only he who tells the truth about Christ is truly His witness. Lest members avoid speaking to others about their Savior for fear that what they say may not be true, they need thorough indoctrination. For effective witnessing they need the confidence that they are presenting the true message of Christ, for that message alone is the saving one.

The various educational agencies of the congregation as well as the regular Sunday services all aim toward a well-indoctrinated congregation. However, special indoctrination in communicating the gospel to unbelievers is valuable preparation. *Study to be "Witnesses unto Me"* can serve as a means of such special indoctrination.[2] Members can be encouraged to equip themselves by memorizing some of the copious Scripture references in this pamphlet. The pastor may select those passages he has found most useful in witnessing.

Indoctrination can also provide scripturally faithful responses to questions frequently raised by "outsiders." Indoctrination enables the member to begin an answer not with "I think," but with "God tells us in the Bible." Unless the witnessing member can do the latter, he had better delay speaking.

Training in Techniques

Inspiration creates the desire to go. Indoctrination provides the message. But a prospective witness may still hesitate for lack of knowing how to make an evangelism call. Equipping saints for their evangelism ministry includes instruction in the goals and methods of such calls.

By Teaching

The pamphlet *Train to be "Witnesses unto Me"*[3] can serve as a helpful aid to the pastor in training his members in the techniques of the evangelism visit. To learn the externals of such a visit may require no lengthy training, even though they are sufficiently important not to be neglected. More important is teaching the visitors the purpose of the call and what to do to reach the intended goal.

One purpose is to gain information. This requires asking questions. The religious attitudes and beliefs of all members in the household, their church background and present membership, if any, are important to know. Calls made in a religious survey have information as their primary goal. Visitors for a survey with this limited goal in mind can be trained in a minimum of time. While these visitors will not avoid giving testimony to the gospel when a favorable opportunity presents itself, the visitor does not initiate the opportunity. Hence these visits have been referred to as pre-evangelism calls.

2. *Study to be Witnesses unto Me* was prepared by the Commission on Evangelism of the WELS.
3. This is a companion pamphlet to the one mentioned in note 2, also prepared by the WELS Commission on Evangelism. Graf's *The Church in the Community* also has many helpful practical suggestions.

Evangelism visits properly so called have the purpose of presenting the gospel message simply and clearly to the unknowing. This means speaking of sin and grace — man's sin and God's grace in Christ. The pastor must impress on the visitors to remain with these simple facts and not to be sidetracked into a peripheral, sometimes controversial, discussion. He must put the visiting members on guard against presenting a "cheap" view of God's love and grace by minimizing sin and its consequences. The pastor may want to set up an outline of a sin-grace presentation with pertinent Scripture references that can guide the witnessing member in his early visits. The two questions used in the Coral Ridge Program developed by D. J. Kennedy can lead to a penetrating discussion of sin and grace.[4] These two questions in a somewhat revised form are also used in the WELS Evangelism Commission's new evangelism manual, *Talk About the Saviour*. The first question in this manual reads: "If you died today do you know for sure where you'd be?" The second follows: "If you died today and God asked you 'Why should I let you into heaven?' What would you say?" The discussion of these questions can lead to a discussion of sin and grace, which in this manual is conveniently grouped around six passages. Whatever methods of presentation the pastor proposes, he must guard against their becoming a fixed form that puts shackles on the free testimony of the individual Christian. They must be seen as useful aids, especially until someone has gained confidence in his ability to do effective witnessing.

The goal of the evangelism visit is faith in Christ. However, the visitor must realize that he cannot work that faith, that the Holy Spirit invites and works faith through the Word and does this where and when it pleases God (AC V). Because so much evangelism literature stresses the goal of receiving a commitment to Christ, the term "commitment" is best avoided.[5] This term gives

4. The two questions are: 1) "Have you come to a place in your spiritual life where you know for certain that if you were to die today you would go to heaven?" 2) "Suppose that you were to die tonight and stand before God and He were to say to you, 'Why should I let you into My heaven?' what would you say?" The purpose and use of the two questions is explained in *Evangelism Explosion*, pp 61-76.
5. This is where the program in *Evangelism Explosion* goes awry. The entire discussion of the commitment, pp 51ff and 76ff, makes Jesus' entrance into the heart dependent on man's sincere desire for it and his willingness to give his life over to Christ. Even Kettner in *Ad-*

the impression that man can make a decision for Christ. Rather than a commitment, a confession that gives expression to the faith God works through the gospel is sought. Like Paul, we shall invite the response of faith by saying, "Believe on the Lord Jesus Christ and thou shalt be saved" (Ac 16:31). Like Jesus, we may encourage a confession by asking, "Believest thou this?" (Jn 11:26).

An evangelism call can also serve the purpose of allowing people to give expression to their "grievances" against the church, to their religious "hangups," to the obstacles that have kept them from active association with Christianity. The pastor will train the visitors in the technique of being good listeners. He will attempt to anticipate questions and suggest scriptural, tactful responses aimed at overcoming the obstacles most often encountered. *Train to be "Witnesses unto Me"* has a helpful section entitled "Give an Answer" (pp 16-31), listing 20 possible objections with suggestions for biblically based responses.[6]

Finally, an evangelism call is intended to lead to specific action. This may be enrolling a child in the Sunday school, attendance at the pastor's adult information class, or church attendance. The action must aim at bringing the person into a continuing contact with the gospel. Finally this should lead to the action of joining the congregation. The purpose of this is not to make the statistics of the congregation look good. But fellowship with a group of Christians in a congregation is part of healthy Christianity (cf Ac 2:42-47; He 10:25). Soliciting a promise of specific action must be carefully distinguished from a so-called commitment to Christ. Hence the term "commitment" is best avoided when speaking to the unchurched. The pastor will do well to equip his members who are sent out to witness with a clear understanding of the doctrine of the means of grace and conversion. This is necessary lest subtle shades of synergism in applying the techniques eclipse the noon-day brightness of the *sola gratia*.

---

ventures in Evangelism is confusing in the matter of commitment (e.g., p 98).

6. *Train to Be "Witnesses unto Me"* contains practical suggestions on the various aspects of an evangelism call. Kennedy's *Evangelism Explosion* contains the dialog as carried out on a call according to his program. Kettner's *Adventures in Evangelism* also contains sample conversations. Similarly Graf's *The Church in the Community*.

As much as possible, the evangelism call should end on a positive note, leaving an opening for future contacts. A tract, suited to the situation as revealed during the visit, can give the people something to read and think about and may provide a good opening for another call and discussion. Follow-up calls are generally necessary before all the goals of evangelism visitation can be reached under God. Since the working of the Spirit is like the wind, which "bloweth where it listeth, and thou hearest the sound thereof, but canst not tell whence it cometh, and whither it goeth" (Jn 3:8), much patience is required. Follow-up work must continue even if the goals are not reached as quickly as desired by the visitor or in the exact manner desired.

By Demonstration and Practice

The teaching of techniques may include demonstration of an evangelism visit before the group of trainees through role-playing. Each member of the group may be given an opportunity to "practice" making a call before the group, with a subsequent exchange of constructive criticism. Although such demonstration and practice can be a helpful form of instruction (like the theological student's practice sermons and catecheses), a simulated call will not fully correspond to the "live" situation when a call is made.

To have a trainee accompany an experienced visitor (the pastor or one of the experienced lay visitors) on actual evangelism visits has obvious advantages over "pretended calls" and is especially instructive. As the trainee gains confidence, he can actively participate in the call until he feels ready to lead the discussion during the visit. This method of training in the techniques of making an evangelism call finds emphasis in some evangelism literature and has merit.[7] It corresponds to the teaching-learning method for seminary students during a year of vicarship in a congregation under an experienced pastor.

Summary: The pastor must inspire his members to bear witness to Christ according to the gifts the Holy Spirit gives them. He will indoctrinate so that the witnessing will correspond faithfully to Scripture. He will instruct by word and example in the tech-

7. This method of teaching is a significant part of the Coral Ridge Program as outlined in *Evangelism Explosion*. Coleman in *The Master Plan of Evangelism* also stresses the thorough training of a select group patterned after Jesus' training of His disciples. This is the method used also in the evangelism manual entitled *Talk About the Saviour*.

234

niques and goals of visits, whether these are pre-evangelism, evangelism, or follow-up calls.

IV. ORGANIZING FOR EVANGELISM

The pastor's leadership role includes organizing a congregation's evangelism effort. Jesus did not outline an organizational scheme for carrying out His command to evangelize. But His broad plan is clear, that His disciples are His witnesses (Ac 1:8), that the gospel testimony of believers leads those who hear to faith (Jn 17:20). In accordance with 1 Corinthians 14:40, the pastor will encourage good organization so far as that is helpful toward an efficient and purposeful evangelism effort on the part of the congregation.

Evangelism manuals like *Organize to be "Witnesses unto Me"* supply many practical suggestions for organizing a congregation for evangelism work.[8] The pastor will study and adapt these suggestions to his congregation's situation.

The pastor who has the responsibility of organizing the congregation's evangelism effort may decide that the best way to start is by recruiting one or several consecrated laymen to accompany him on mission calls. In this way the pastor is training his first lay visitors, who in turn will be helpful in recruiting and training additional visitors. Soon these beginning efforts may progress to the point where the creation of a congregational evangelism committee is indicated. Such a natural development of an organization appears preferable to setting up a full-scale organization to begin the effort. In the latter case the danger exists of placing undue emphasis on the organization, with an effort to pattern it simply on what seems theoretically ideal rather than on what is actually needed.

The evangelism committee with its chairman can help the pastor in studying the congregation's past performance[9] and evaluating its future potential. They can supervise a religious survey of the neighborhood and recruit visitors. They can help organize visits and keep records. Their reports to the church council and the

8. *Organize to be "Witnesses unto Me"* is the third evangelism pamphlet (cf Notes 2 and 3) prepared by the WELS Commission on Evangelism. Graf's *The Church in the Community* should also be mentioned in this connection.
9. *"Therefore We Speak"* — *Evangelism in Practice*, a WELS synodical essay by Daniel W. Malchow (*Proceedings*, 1971, pp 55-66) contains a checklist for a congregation's self-evaluation (p 64).

congregation will stimulate the congregation's interest in evangelism.

Good organization calls for setting up a prospective member file or soul responsibility list. The most likely prospects may be those who registered in the congregation's guest book or those whose names have been submitted by congregation members. Nevertheless, no means of securing names of prospects should be neglected. The file will, however, serve its purpose only if it is carefully kept and faithfully used.[10]

The congregation and its pastor will recognize their particular responsibility to do concentrated work within a specified radius of their house of worship. In setting up an area of responsibility, care will be taken not to encroach on a sister congregation's field of activity. The congregation will want to know the religious status of the people in every home within its area of responsibility. This information can best be secured through a religious survey.[11] Because of the high mobility rate of population, especially in urban and suburban areas, a survey may be needed every few years to keep the information fairly current. The unchurched discovered in this way will form a part of the congregation's soul responsibility list.

The congregation that has developed a corps of lay visitors will need to organize its visitation program, determining who is to visit each prospect so that no one is missed and there is no duplication of effort. The date of each visit should be recorded together with significant information that may determine the time and nature of another call.

There are times when an organized evangelism "drive" satisfies an urgent need. It may help to draw the entire congregation's attention to this important work. A religious survey of the community calls for an organized program involving special effort at a given time. Nevertheless, the goal is to develop an ongoing evangelism program that will see intensified effort in the weeks before the beginning of a new adult instruction class, but one that still reaches out to the unchurched with the gospel "in season and out of season."

10. Pp 11-13 of *Organize to be "Witnesses unto Me"* outlines the sources and the systematic use of the prospective member file.
11. A brochure, "The Religious Survey," included in "Duties of the Evangelism Chairman," outlines in detail the mechanics of conducting a survey.

Sometimes religious surveys and evangelism programs are sponsored by a local ministerial association or, on a national scale, by interchurch evangelism associations. Since evangelism concerns itself with preaching the gospel, the pastor and congregation may unite in evangelism efforts only with those who are united with them in faith (Ro 16:17; 2 Jn 10,11). While participating in a religious survey may appear as nothing more than cooperating in externals, the evangelism activity of the congregation is in danger of suffering through the requirement of sharing the gathered information with all participating churches.

Evangelism must be carried on in such a way that it does not seek to make converts of those who are active members in a Christian church. The pastor himself will avoid proselytizing and warn his members against it. Those people who are members of a church that confesses the one true God (the triune God, including recognition of Jesus as God) and acknowledge redemption through Christ cannot be considered "unchurched." Treating them as prospects is to interfere in another church's ministry (Ac 20:28; 1 Pe 4:15). When, however, members of erring Christian churches seek information in their search for the truth, a forthright answer must follow without fear that this could raise the charge of proselytizing (1 Pe 3:15).

On the other hand, any religious group that denies the divinity of Christ does not know the true God (Jn 8:19; 2 Jn 9). Members of such groups (e.g., Jehovah's Witnesses, Mormons, Christian Scientists) are properly considered unchurched. Unfortunately, the confessional deterioration in many so-called Christian churches causes increasing difficulty in determining their Christian status.

Summary: The pastor may begin a congregation's organized program by personally training several consecrated laymen in making visits. As the situation requires, he will organize an evangelism committee, which with its chairman can help organize the visits, keep records, supervise religious surveys, etc. While a given situation may call for an evangelism "drive," the goal will be to develop an ongoing program. Care must be taken to avoid proselytizing.

V. THE CONGREGATION'S WORLDWIDE MISSION

It is incumbent upon the pastor to impress on a congregation its responsibilities beyond its immediate environs. The Holy Spirit gave the disciples power to witness in Jerusalem, but also in all of Judea, in the neighboring country of Samaria, and "unto the uttermost part of the earth" (Ac 1:8). The congregation that is inspired to carry the gospel into the homes of its neighborhood will also recognize its worldwide mission; and conversely, interest in worldwide mission work must be accompanied by concern for the unchurched neighbor. The two cannot be separated. Souls are souls, precious and blood-bought, wherever they are.

A congregation carries out its worldwide mission responsibility through the synod it has joined. The WELS home mission program provides for expansion in the United States and Canada. The work "unto the uttermost part of the earth" is administered for the congregation by the Synod's board for world missions. Apart from intercessory prayers in behalf of this worldwide work, a congregation's participation will consist largely of its financial support. The relationship of a congregation to the Synod and its obligations of financial support will be discussed further in the chapters on "The Shepherd's Place in the Synodical Flock" and on "The Shepherd Trains Christian Stewards."

Occasionally congregations find it possible to further their gospel outreach by organizing daughter congregations. This should be encouraged where the mother congregation can provide financial support until the daughter matures to self-support. In undertaking such a venture, the pastor and congregation should work in consultation with the board for home missions during conception and birth of the daughter lest there be a duplication of effort.

The pastor will use every available means to encourage the Synod's mission program in his congregation. Unless he provides strong leadership, the support will lag. The congregation's delegates at conferences and conventions should be given opportunity to report on what they heard and learned, especially in the area of missions. The tradition of annual mission festivals with guest speakers is continuing, even if it has lost some of its effectiveness. Such a festival should never lead to the conclusion that the subject of missions can be taken care of on one day annually. Missionaries from foreign fields home on leave can inspire interest and support through lectures and sermons. The mission fair has been found an effective means of involving a large part of the congregation actively in gathering and spreading the message of missions locally. The time and effort required in organizing a good mission fair preclude the possibility of doing this annually.

Let the pastor remember that it is most important that constant encouragement come from him. Criticism of the Synod's program, especially if the pastor lets the congregation feel that he thinks the Synod is asking too much for missions, will soon result in lagging enthusiasm and support. On the other hand, the pastor's earnest, persistent encouragement, based on Scripture and on what the Lord is doing through the church, will not fail to show the results of the Holy Spirit's power, active through the Word. Since the world is our mission field, opportunities are unlimited. Time, however, is not. The pastor must convey the urgency of total support for worldwide gospel work "while it is day."

Summary: Besides encouraging and organizing the local evangelism effort, the pastor will impress on his congregation its worldwide mission responsibility. This responsibility is carried out through the home and world mission program of the Synod, occasionally also through establishing a daughter congregation. The pastor will use every available means to encourage interest and procure financial support for a mission which is unlimited in scope.

For Additional Reading

Coleman, Robert E. *The Master Plan of Evangelism.* Westwood, N.J.: Fleming H. Revell, 1964.

Eight points (Selection, Association, Consecration, Impartation, Demonstration, Delegation, Supervision, Reproduction) are outlined from Scripture as constituting Jesus' strategy for evangelism. There is good emphasis on personal training of men. The weak part is placing emphasis on men in such a way that the power of the Word seems to regress into the background.

Graf, Arthur E. *The Church in the Community.* Grand Rapids: Eerdmans, 1965.

The entire subject of evangelism in a congregation is covered from its motivation and theological background to samples of various forms for keeping records. Contains many practical suggestions.

Kennedy, D. James. *Evangelism Explosion.* Wheaton: Tyndale House, fifth ed. 1971.

The successful evangelism program of the Coral Ridge Presbyterian Church of Ft. Lauderdale, Florida, is outlined in detail. There is good emphasis on man's sinfulness and salvation by grace alone. However, Reformed theology comes into evidence in the matter of conversion.

Kettner, Elmer A. *Adventures in Evangelism.* St. Louis: Concordia, 1964.

Useful as supplementary material. The chapters on "Opportunities" and on "Getting Started" can prove helpful in encouraging those who are hesitant to speak about their Savior to others.

Malchow, Daniel W. *"Therefore We Speak" — Evangelism in Practice. Proceedings,* WELS, 1971. pp 55-66.

As the title states, this convention essay concerns itself with the practical application of the theology of evangelism. This is presented under the three headings: I. Preparation; II. Program; and III. Passion.

Mallough, Don. *Grassroots Evangelism.* Grand Rapids: Baker, 1971.

The emphasis is on training the individual layman (grassroots) for evangelism. Scripture comes to its full rights, even though one does not agree with every interpretation. The presentation is simple and practical.

Michigan District Committee on Evangelism. *Duties of the Evangelism Chairman.* Available from the Committee at 10729 Worden, Detroit, Michigan 48224.

Besides outlining the duties of the chairman, detailed instructions on how to organize a religious survey are included.

Schuetze, Armin W. *"We Believe" — The Theology of Evangelism. Proceedings,* WELS, 1971, pp 43-54.

This convention essay aims at presenting the biblical basis for evangelism and encourages its application.

WELS Commission on Evangelism. *Study to be "Witnesses unto Me," Train to be "Witnesses unto Me,"* and *Organize to be "Witnesses unto Me."* Milwaukee: Northwestern, 1963.

Three practical pamphlets for developing interest in evangelism and for organizing a program. The first two will be useful for discussion or meetings of organizations and for training lay visitors. The third will be useful in organizing an evangelism committee.

- - - - -. *Talk About the Saviour.* Detroit: The Evangelism Bookshop, 1972.

This manual is intended to train individual lay people to "talk about the Savior." The value of the program lies in the training method in which the trainee accompanies an experienced "evangelist" on visits. He learns how to get into and how to carry on a discussion of sin and grace.

10

The Shepherd
Trains Christian Stewards

*"Present your bodies
a living sacrifice"*

(Ro 12:1)

Stewardship is as old as Christianity. It was encouraged and practiced by early Christians, as recorded in Scripture. What is meant by stewardship in the church must therefore be determined by God's Word.

Background

That the understanding of the concept of stewardship should have suffered under European state-church arrangements is understandable. This is true especially in regard to the stewardship of money. Since state taxes supported the church, whatever offerings were gathered were either for the support of missions or of the poor. It was in the support of mission societies that stewardship often found practical application, even if the term was not used. On the whole, books on pastoral theology published in Europe referred only incidentally to this area of Christian sanctification.

In America, where the church was dependent on the gifts of its members for support, the emphasis on stewardship had a very practical reason. Even so, Walther in his *Pastorale* refers to the collection of funds for the church's support only in passing. Fritz's *Pastoral Theology*, in many respects based on Walther's earlier work, does include a chapter on "Christian Stewardship." Concordia's more recent publication, *The Pastor at Work*, contains two chapters, one on "Stewardship in General," another on "The Stewardship of Money." This shows the growth of concern for an understanding of the concept and for its practical application.

Schaller's *Pastorale-Praxis*, which appeared between the time of Walther's and Fritz's books, uses the broad concept of joint works of love (*gemeinsame Liebesdienste*) to speak of a congregation's stewardship responsibilities. That the individual must perform works of love Schaller considers as self-evident, for a Christian must bear the fruits of faith. Among these self-evident works of love Schaller includes the personal preaching of the gospel to unbelievers. However, greater efforts are possible by works of love done jointly through the congregation and the synod. Such joint work requires the financial support of the congregation and the synod on the part of the individual. Included in Schaller's presentation are several pages of practical suggestions that show the gospel approach to congregational giving and include warnings against letting the law intrude itself in a manner that results in legalism. Although his presentation is not worked out in the detail found in later stewardship treatises, the treatment under "works of love" and congregational support has much that is akin to what is being said today in discussing the term stewardship.[1] The greater amount of attention stewardship is receiving should result in the recruiting of more laymen for increased activity in the congregation. However, a congregation must be on guard lest lay activity result in shallow activism, in decreased concern for true doctrine, or in downgrading the public ministry as instituted by Christ.

I. STEWARDSHIP ACCORDING TO SCRIPTURE

A steward, in Greek *oikonomos*, is a manager. Frequently the steward was "a kind of chief slave who superintended the house-

1. A history of the development of the stewardship concept in Christian churches outside the former Ev. Luth. Synodical Conference is found in chapter one of Brattgard's *God's Stewards*, (Minneapolis: Augsburg, 1963), pp 1-21.

hold, and even the whole property of his master."[2] In biblical times the steward was often one of the slaves so that in Luke 12:42 the *oikonomos* is also called a *doulos*. How broad a responsibility was placed on the steward is seen in the parable of the unjust steward (Lk 16). He was not charged with having exceeded his authority when he arbitrarily lowered the debtors' bills. But the master did expect wise administration of entrusted goods, an administration that would be to his advantage. The steward was only called to give an accounting when it was reported that he had wasted his master's goods. St. Paul thus makes the general observation that in stewards it is required that a man be found faithful (1 Cor 4:2). To what extent do these various aspects of stewardship apply to the Christian when he is called a steward of God?

Slave — Son

Christians are *douloi*, slaves. They are not hired managers. Rather, the Lord chooses as His stewards such on whom He has a claim of ownership because of the price He paid for them.

The Christian is what he is because the Lord Jesus redeemed him from sin with His precious blood — blood "as of a lamb without blemish and without spot" (1 Pe 1:18,19). According to the riches of God's grace in Christ, the Christian has "redemption through His blood, the forgiveness of sin" (Eph 1:7). Luther aptly expresses the meaning of redemption so that even the simplest Christian can understand when he says that Jesus "purchased and won me, not with gold or silver, but with His holy precious blood and with His innocent sufferings and death."

In 1 Corinthians 6:19,20 Paul draws the conclusion that must properly follow upon this act of redemption, or purchase. He writes: "What? know ye not that your body is the temple of the Holy Ghost which is in you, which ye have of God, and ye are not your own? For ye are bought with a price." Peter similarly calls Christians "a chosen race . . . a people for God's own possession" (1 Pe 2:9-NASB).

Christians, thus, belong to the Lord Jesus because He paid a tremendous price for them. Even their bodies they cannot claim

2. Gerhard Friedrich, *Theological Dictionary of the New Testament* (Kittel), trans. by Geoffrey W. Bromeley (Grand Rapids: Eerdmans, 1967), V, 149.

as their own. Body and soul, they belong to their Redeemer. He has a total claim on them.

This includes their total life. Having been bought with a price, Christians are not to be servants of men (1 Cor 7:23). The life they now live in the flesh they are to live by faith in the Son of God, who loved them, and gave Himself for them (Ga 2:20). As such who through baptism have been buried with Christ into death, Christians are to walk in newness of life (Ro 6:4-6; 2 Cor 5:15). They are to yield their members "as slaves to righteousness, resulting in sanctification" (Ro 6:19-NASB). Indeed, their reasoned service is to present their bodies a living sacrifice, holy, acceptable unto God (Ro 12:1). In this sense they can be called "slaves," not as the result of repressive coercion, but because they were drawn into this slavery by the grace and mercy of God.

Christians, however, are slaves who at the same time are God's adopted children. "Ye are all the children of God by faith in Christ Jesus" (Ga 3:26). Thus in the case of Christians the Lord chooses as stewards those who as His slaves owe Him total obedience, and as His adopted sons, total love.

Entrusted with Gifts

A slave or son becomes a steward when he is entrusted with gifts that he is to "manage." Peter refers to Christians "as stewards of the manifold grace of God" (1 Pe 4:10).

The manifold grace of God, *poikilee charis*, refers to "the aggregate of the extremely diverse powers and gifts granted to Christians."[3] That these gifts are "manifold" will be evident to all but the thoughtless and thankless. There is the entire catalog of gifts the Father or Creator gives to mankind in general as listed by Luther in explaining the first Article of the Creed — body and soul, eyes and ears, etc. There are special gifts in which one person differs from another, whether this is a sharp intellect, a native aptitude, or a pleasing personality. Other gifts are such as are developed and acquired through education and training — the skill of the physician or the carpenter, of the mechanic or scientist or business man. Scripture speaks particularly of the spiritual gifts centering in the gospel, which the Holy Spirit divides "to every

3. Joseph Henry Thayer, *A Greek-English Lexicon of the New Testament* (New York: American Book Co., 1889), p 666.

244

man severally as he will" (1 Cor 12). As man's body has many members, so the church, the body of Christ, also has many members, differently endowed. However different the gifts may be, they all come from the same Spirit and are all important since they are His gifts. How true is what Paul writes: "For who maketh thee to differ from another? and what hast thou that thou didst not receive?" (1 Cor 4:7)!

Frequently God's varied gifts have conveniently been grouped under the three T's: time, talent, and treasure. Time is a gift of God, a certain portion entrusted to each person. Talent can cover a broad spectrum of native, acquired, general or particular abilities and skills. Treasure is generally thought of as including all forms of material possessions and wealth entrusted to man during his time on earth. We can include here also the spiritual wealth granted the Christian. This threefold division is convenient so long as it does not prevent the Christian from seeing how manifold the gifts are which are entrusted to him by the Lord.

Most important of all God's gifts is the gospel and everything connected with it, forgiveness, faith, love, hope, peace, joy, etc. All other gifts become important according to their relationship to the gospel. The importance of the gospel and its use receives separate consideration under Evangelism.

Unique in some respects is the gift of wealth, especially in the form of money. Money is the chief means of exchange. It enables the Christian to apply his gifts in the worldwide interest of the gospel in ways that would otherwise be impossible. The Christian's gift of time and talents can be converted into money, which can be converted back into time by supporting a missionary to preach the gospel, or it can provide a place of worship in a distant city, or support the many functions missionaries carry out in behalf of those who send them. Money as a means of exchange makes it possible for the Christian to take part in a broad area of gospel work. If money receives much attention in stewardship, this may be because of its unique role as a means of exchange.

All of these many gifts are indeed a trust. The Lord gives the Christian authority and power to use them. He appoints His slaves, His sons by faith, as stewards or managers over these manifold gifts entrusted to them.

Faithful Use

It is faithfulness above all that is required of stewards. The Christian, as a steward, is entrusted with manifold gifts. He must be faithful to his trust.

Faithful stewardship means using God's gifts for the purpose for which He intended them. The Lord gives to each what he needs for his body and life. Jesus taught us to pray, "Give us this day our daily bread." What the Lord gives in response to this prayer — more often than not before we ask — is given to preserve our life during the time of grace He grants. The Christian is also to support his family. Paul writes to Timothy: "If any provide not for his own, and specially for those of his own house, he hath denied the faith, and is worse than an infidel" (1 Tm 5:8). The Christian will use his gifts for the welfare of his neighbor, of the needy in the world. He is to "do good unto all men, especially unto them who are of the household of faith" (Ga 6:10). He is to work "with his hands the thing which is good, that he may have to give to him that needeth" (Eph 4:28). These are all valid considerations as the Christian functions in his stewardship of God's gifts.

If the above stewardship responsibilities are mentioned first, it is because they are so obvious. For the same reason, however, they frequently receive not only first but, unfortunately, even exclusive attention. The Christian must remember that preserving this life is not an end in itself, but that God has a purpose in mind in prolonging a person's time of grace on earth. This purpose centers in the gospel. Christian stewardship must make the gospel proclamation its prime concern.

When Jesus sent out the seventy, He expected that they would be provided with food and lodging by those whom they served (Lk 10:7). The principle that those who preach the gospel should get their living from the gospel (1 Cor 9:14) makes congregational support (for this is nothing else than supporting the preaching of the Word) an important part of good stewardship. Similarly, the command to preach the gospel throughout the world carries with it the responsibility to support that work with the gifts that make it possible. God expects the Christian steward to use the entrusted gifts for his own and his neighbor's spiritual welfare, that is, in the interest of His kingdom. Christian stewardship takes into full account God's plan for the gospel.

246

Faithfulness in stewardship calls for wisdom in administering God's gifts. The parable of the unjust steward is to teach wisdom in administering one's trust, using time, opportunities, and gifts to the best advantage (Lk 16), not unjustly as the steward in the parable, but nevertheless wisely. And true wisdom, as Jesus points out, will keep concern for the "eternal habitations" paramount (Lk 16:9).

Summary: The Christian has been purchased by Christ with the price of His blood. He belongs to God, body and soul. As such the Lord entrusts him with manifold gifts which he as a good steward is to manage faithfully and wisely for the purposes for which they were given. Central is the carrying out of God's worldwide plan for the gospel. Briefly stated, stewardship can be defined as "the Christian using himself and what God has given him in grace to accomplish God's saving purpose in the world."[4]

II. ENCOURAGING FAITHFUL STEWARDSHIP

Good stewardship is a part of the Christian's sanctification. The two have at times been identified. It does appear that many areas of the Christian's life of sanctification involve stewardship in some way.

The Christian's stewardship, even as his sanctification, never reaches perfection on earth. But God does look for growth. The pastor has the responsibility of helping the members of his flock grow and mature as Christian stewards. This calls for instruction in the biblical concept of stewardship. It requires the proper application of the Word of God, the law and the gospel, to this area of Christian living. The law and the gospel must each be put to use in accordance with its God-intended purpose.

The Gospel Motivates

The gospel must provide the incentive and motivation, the power and ability to practice faithful stewardship. Jesus' parable of the good tree and its fruit (Mt 7:16-18; 22,23) leads to the conclusion that if there is to be the fruit of good stewardship, the Christian must first become a good tree. The gospel works this renewal in the Christian and provides strength to bear fruit. "I can do all things through Christ which strengtheneth me" (Php 4:13). "The

4. James P. Schaefer, *Stewardship Workbook* (prepared for the Wis. Ev. Luth. Synod by the Stewardship Office, 1971), p 7.

love of Christ constraineth us" (2 Cor 5:14), writes Paul. This merely acknowledges what Jesus already had said: "Without me ye can do nothing" (Jn 15:5). The mercies of God produce the kind of heart that is willing to bring the body as a living sacrifice to God (Ro 12:1).

The pastor will provide the motivation for stewardship by his faithful preaching of the gospel Sunday after Sunday. By proclaiming the mercy and grace of Christ in all his ministrations he is using the only means that makes Christians fruitful. The extent to which the gospel permeates his entire ministry determines the extent to which the people are prepared to live as God's stewards. Where ongoing application of the gospel is lacking, reference to gospel motivation during a special stewardship program will hardly be an adequate substitute. On the other hand, where the pastor's whole ministry has centered on the crucified Christ, even a brief reference to the gift of redemption will draw on the gospel motivation which by faith has captured the heart.

The Law Convicts and Guides

Should the pastor use the law in encouraging faithful stewardship? Certainly not to effect by the law's coercion what was not accomplished through gospel motivation. The law does, however, serve a purpose in the Christian's sanctification, and so in stewardship. The pastor must not neglect to use it according to its intended purpose.

The Christian's stewardship life on earth will always lack perfection. The flesh lusts against the spirit so that the Christian does not do the good that he would (Ro 7:19-23). The law exposes sin, also the Christian's unfaithfulness as a steward. The law coerces the unwilling flesh. The Christian, whose new man desires nothing else than to be a faithful steward, welcomes this means of suppressing his unwilling flesh. The law reveals the will of God as a guide also in the Christian's life as God's steward. The Christian will listen to it lest his flesh mislead him to consider that good which still misses the mark of God's holy will.

Thus the proper use of both law and gospel is vital in encouraging good stewardship. The distinct purpose of each must remain clear, however. Whenever people are told what they must do, or whenever a goal for giving is placed before them as a guide — the law is in action. It has its place, but only according to its divinely intended purpose. It dare not be used as a substitute for

248

gospel motivation. It is the gospel that strengthens the Christian and moves him to action by holding before him God's gift in Christ — what God has done. The gospel is the power that makes willing, joyful stewards. The pastor's task of encouraging faithful stewardship calls for great wisdom in the use of both law and gospel. To omit the law can lead only to self-righteousness and self-deception; to misuse it, only to legalism. To omit the gospel is to remove the power unto salvation, the only power that produces godly works.

The Pastor's Example

When Peter calls on the elders, the pastors, to be examples of the flock (1 Pe 5:3), this applies also to stewardship. The pastor who zealously applies his varied talents to the gospel ministry will ask for and generally receive a like response from members. The pastor who does his work in season and out of season, forgetting the time clock, will have members whose leisure hours will be available for the Lord's work. Conversely, lazy pastors will produce lazy congregations.

What about the pastor's stewardship of money? He has dedicated his entire life, all his energies and time, to service in Christ's kingdom. The salary he receives is only the result of applying the principle that the preacher of the gospel should get his living from the gospel. Would not his support of the congregation he serves simply be contributing to his own salary? It is true, if his support consisted simply of personal gifts from each member to the pastor, the pastor would hardly make such a gift to himself. And if the gifts to the congregation were intended only to support the pastor, gifts to the congregation by the pastor might still seem to be given to himself. However, the congregational treasury supports the total congregational program. The pastor and his family as members of the congregation he serves should be exemplary stewards, setting a good example of giving "as the Lord prospers," both for local needs and for broader purposes, especially for the synodical program.

Summary: The pastor is responsible for encouraging faithful stewardship. He will teach the congregation members what Scripture says about stewardship. He will properly apply law and gospel to this area of sanctification. He will strive to be a good example to the flock.

III. STEWARDSHIP IN THE CHURCH

Stewardship concerns itself with a Christian's management of his entire life, all his time and talents, all his financial resources. The Christian is to be a good steward of his "manifold gifts" in his work, in the family, applying good stewardship even in his recreation. However, stewardship involves the Christian also directly with the church. He is called upon to place a portion of his time, talents, and treasure into the direct service of the Lord through His church. The pastor has the particular responsibility to encourage this direct giving to the church.

Priorities

This confronts the Christian with the task of setting up priorities in his stewardship life. He needs to apportion his "manifold gifts" according to the responsibilities God places before him. There may be times when a mother should look after her household duties and family rather than serve on several church committees. The husband may not be practicing wise stewardship of his talents if he devotes so much time to "church work" that his business goes bankrupt. Parents can hardly justify starving their children in order to make large church contributions. However, most often such are not the problems that face the pastor. Most often the difficulty lies in getting people to apply in their lives the priority Jesus sets up for the Christian when He says: "Seek ye first the kingdom of God, and his righteousness; and all these things shall be added unto you" (Mt 6:33).

Because of the importance of money, as a means of exchange, for the work of the church, the pastor's efforts toward good stewardship will inevitably include encouragement of faithful monetary support of the church's work. The church is not becoming materialistic or unspiritual when it asks for generous gifts of money so that the preaching of the gospel can proceed on an ever broader scale. The pastor need not apologize when he gives biblical instruction in the stewardship of wealth and encourages increased fruits of faith in the form of money. When people resent "money talk" in the church, the reason may be that the pastor has proceeded legalistically or that the people do not want to part with the "mammon of unrighteousness" which has become their idol. The pastor must guard against legalism and must warn against idolatry.

250

Scriptural Principles for Giving

The New Testament establishes the principles that will guide the pastor in the congregation's stewardship training. Particularly 1 Corinthians 16:1-4 and 2 Corinthians 8 and 9 contain biblical discourses on Christian giving. Although the occasion was a gathering of an offering among the churches of Macedonia and Achaia for the saints at Jerusalem who suffered want, what is said applies to all giving for the work which the church does. A restudy of these sections of the Corinthian letters will prove rewarding for both pastor and people whenever they plan a congregational stewardship program. In these chapters we find what God has to say about Christian giving.

The Grace of Giving

The churches of Macedonia had given bountifully toward the offering for Jerusalem. This was "the grace of God bestowed" on them (2 Cor 8:1). Their generosity was a gift God gave them. The Corinthians abounded in many spiritual gifts: faith, utterance, knowledge, diligence, love. Paul encourages them to "abound in this grace also," that is, in taking part in the offering (v 7). Thus their giving was a gift God worked in them. Generous giving is not something simply produced by the Christian, but a gift, or grace, of God to the Christian. What is true of every fruit of faith is true also of giving. It is God who works in the Christian "both to will and to do of his good pleasure" (Php 2:13).

For this reason the pastor must be careful how he speaks of giving as a Christian duty. That giving is a duty is in itself true, but the pastor must realize that this is a law statement. He may thus use it to reveal neglect and sin, but not as a means of encouraging growth. Giving and growth in giving is a grace the Lord bestows with His gospel. Paul encourages the giving in Corinth not "by commandment," but by referring to the "grace of our Lord Jesus Christ" (2 Cor 8:8,9).

Voluntary — Cheerful

The fact that God bestows the grace of giving on the Christian does not make the Christian an object that unthinkingly moves according to God's will. The Christian's will, renewed by the gospel, is active in giving. The Macedonian churches, although themselves poor, gave liberally, being "willing of themselves" to do this (2 Cor 8:3). In fact, because of their poverty, Paul was hesi-

251

tant to accept so generous a gift from them, but they begged him with much entreaty that he would receive the gift (v 4). They wanted to do this. Christian giving thus is done voluntarily, and that means also cheerfully. Paul sums this thought up in 2 Corinthians 9:7: "Every man according as he purposeth in his heart, so let him give; not grudgingly, or of necessity: for God loveth a cheerful giver." As the new man in the Christian becomes victorious over the unwilling flesh (old man), voluntary, cheerful gifts will follow.

Expression of Love

That the Macedonians had given generously and cheerfully was because they "first gave their own selves to the Lord and to us by the will of God" (2 Cor 8:5). They loved the Lord. They loved their fellow believers. They expressed their love by giving. Similarly the Corinthians were to give not because of a command from Paul, but as a test of "the sincerity of your love" (v 8). Their love would express itself in their giving, and in some respects this giving would be a measure of their love (cf also Lk 7:36-47). This, however, does not allow the pastor to rate the greatness of each member's love by the size of the member's gift to the church. Too many factors are involved, many beyond the pastor's perception, so that he dare not set himself up as a judge of the people's love. But he will seek to inspire ever greater love for God and the neighbor and call upon that love to express itself ever more fully also in generous giving.

Firstfruits

That gifts to the Lord should be firstfruits is an important point to remember and again raises the question of priorities in the Christian's life. The Christian who seeks the kingdom of God first, knowing that food and clothing and all material necessities will be provided by the Lord (Mt 6:33), will recognize that the Lord is to receive the firstfruits, not the leftovers. Abel already recognized that the Lord should receive "the firstlings of his flocks" (Gn 4:4), and Solomon considered it godly wisdom to "honor the Lord . . . with the firstfruits of all thine increase" (Pr 3:9). Paul implies this also when he advises the Corinthians that they should on the first day of the week lay aside and store up (*tithetoo theesaurizoon*) what was intended for the collection (1

252

Cor 16:2). In setting up a budget for himself or his family, a Christian will first consider what to "lay aside" for the Lord's work.

As the Lord Prospers

A principle for determining the size of the gift to the Lord is contained in the words, "as God hath prospered him" (1 Cor 16:2). Paul gives a more complete picture when he writes: "For if there be first a willing mind, it is accepted according to that a man hath and not according to that he hath not" (2 Cor 8:12). By assuming a "willing mind," Paul recognizes that the measure of Christian love helps determine giving. Greater love and faith will produce greater fruit. But when the gospel has worked willingness, giving will correspond under God also to the measure of one's prosperity.

Two factors are involved when measuring the prosperity God grants. One is the size of the income, the other consists of the financial responsibilities God imposes on the individual. A smaller income with fewer responsibilities may result in greater prosperity than a larger income with very heavy financial responsibilities. All of this needs to be taken into account when Scripture says, "as God hath prospered him." That the Macedonian churches gave "beyond their power" (v 3) is not to be construed as a pattern that all must necessarily follow. The Macedonians had done something unusual. However, the chief failing of many Christians in prosperous America is that they do not recognize how greatly the Lord has prospered them materially because of the high standard of living which they look upon as "necessary."

The New Testament leaves no room for compulsory tithing as a principle for determining how much to give. It nowhere encourages the use of the tithe but does criticize those who used it self-righteously (Mt 23:23; Lk 18:12). Although a Christian is free to use the tithe as a guide for himself, ten per cent for some Christians may be giving well "beyond their power" while for others it represents far less than is possible according to the prosperity the Lord gives. In place of the tithe, the New Testament presents a twofold measure for determining one's gifts: the measure of a Christian's love and the measure of his prosperity. The latter is determined by his income as it relates to his God-given responsibilities.

Encouragement by Example

When Paul encouraged the Macedonian congregations to participate in the collection for Jerusalem, he was able to report that Corinth (Achaia) was ready a year ago to undertake this offering. He tells the Corinthians that their zeal had encouraged many (2 Cor 9:2). Now he is able in turn to report on the bountiful giving of the Macedonian churches to encourage the Corinthians, whose collection had lagged in the meantime because of problems in the congregation (2 Cor 8:1-6). It is entirely proper that the example of one Christian congregation serve as an encouragement to another.

In using examples, Paul is careful to avoid any appeal to fleshly pride or self-righteousness. He does not present the examples in a way that leads to one judging another harshly. The emphasis remains on what the grace of God has accomplished in the examples cited.

The pastor will recognize the value of pointing to examples where the gospel has brought forth rich fruit in giving. On the other hand, he will exercise great care lest the encouragement address itself to the flesh instead of to faith and lest it lead to making odious comparisons and result in uncharitable judging.

Good Order

What Paul says about doing all things "decently and in order" in the church applies also to the collecting of gifts for the Lord. When the apostle tells the Corinthians that "upon the first day of the week" each is to lay something aside for the offering, he is calling for regular, orderly giving. He sent Titus and two other "brethren" to help Corinth complete its collection with dispatch. He arranged for an orderly delivery of the offering to Jerusalem by men chosen by the contributing congregations. Although this was the first major financial effort we know of that involved an entire group of congregations in the early church, we see the orderly way in which they proceeded from the outset.

To have a systematic, well-organized method of receiving gifts for the Lord's work is not contrary to free, voluntary giving as a fruit of faith. The two are not mutually exclusive. To develop a stewardship "program" in the interest of good order is in keeping with Scripture so long as it is not applied legalistically, forcing Christians into patterns of conduct not required by God.

Promise of Reward

Paul uses the comparison of the sower. Bountiful sowing results in a bountiful harvest (2 Cor 9:6). Dropping the comparison, we can say that bountiful giving receives a bountiful reward. Similarly, Paul writes to the Galatians: "Let us not be weary in well doing: for in due season we shall reap, if we faint not" (Ga 6:9). Scripture encourages bountiful giving in opposition to covetousness by showing that bountiful giving has its reward of God. The Christian, however, always realizes that this is a reward that flows from the grace of God, not a merited reward.

The pastor will guard against the thought that a reward can be purchased through bountiful giving. This injects the idea of merit. This appeals to the flesh and deals with the promise of reward from the viewpoint of the law.

However, to point to God's gracious promises of reward, also material reward, as an encouragement to faith is in keeping with Scripture. Above all, the spiritual enrichment that God grants as a "reward" should be stressed (2 Cor 9:11).

Summary: While the Christian is a steward of God's "manifold gifts" in all of life's roles, good stewardship finds direct application also in the life of the church. The pastor will not fail to show the high priority which concern for Christ's kingdom must have for the Christian in his stewardship. Because of the unique function of money, financial contributions will be an important part of the Christian's congregational stewardship. The pastor must encourage the giving of money in keeping with the principles outlined in Scripture, especially in the two Corinthian letters.

IV. SOME PRACTICAL QUESTIONS

The Role of Need in Giving

The gospel, not need, is the motive for good stewardship. However, an understanding of the needs that require attention is necessary for intelligent, responsible stewardship. The gospel motivates; but need serves as a guide as to where the gospel motivation should result in action. If there had been no need in Jerusalem, the congregations of Macedonia and Achaia would not have directed their gifts there.

Since good stewardship involves weighing priorities, the guidance which need can give is important. The Macedonian Chris-

255

tians judged that the needs of Jerusalem so far outweighed their own that they gave "beyond their power." And yet, it was not simply the need, but their joy in the gospel that moved them to such generosity.

The New Testament does not call upon Christians to give to the Lord without considering the purpose for which the money will be used. Christians are called upon to be wise and faithful stewards, but not indiscriminate givers.

The pastor will keep the members informed of the needs in the congregation and the synod. The great need of spreading the gospel at home and abroad must receive due emphasis as well as the extensive financial support this requires. As the members weigh these needs in relation to all their God-given financial obligations, they can intelligently function as good stewards of God's gifts.

Sacrificial Giving

All Christian giving will be sacrificial. The only sacrifice the New Testament calls for is the sacrifice of thanksgiving. Whatever is given as a fruit of faith will be such a sacrifice of thanksgiving.

The term sacrificial giving may be misunderstood or misused, as meaning that giving must entail some kind of deprivation for the Christian, or that it means giving until it hurts.

The latter expression can be applied only to the Christian's old Adam. It hurt Judas' covetous flesh to see Mary anoint Jesus with the costly ointment (Jn 12:3-7). On the other hand, the generous Macedonians felt no hurt from their giving although they deprived themselves even of necessities. Because it was a fruit of faith, it was a joy to them. Thus sacrificial giving is not determined by the extent to which it deprives the giver or hurts, but by the fact that it is a joyful sacrifice of thanksgiving flowing from faith. Addressing ourselves to the Christian's faith, we can say: Give until it makes you happy.

Pledging

A pledge or subscription (statement of intent) is a promise to give at regular intervals a designated gift to the Lord. It is a financial commitment the Christian steward makes to his Savior. While pledging should not inhibit the Christian in the freedom enjoyed in the New Testament under Christ, while it should not be forced on an unwilling congregation or individual, the Christian who has first of all given himself to the Lord (2 Cor 8:5) should find joy in promising Him also a specified part of his income. Although Scripture does not require a particular pledging system, some form of financial commitment corresponds well with the concept of firstfruits given regularly and in an orderly manner. It is wholesome for the Christian in arriving at his pledge to be confronted with the need to make a stewardship decision. In addition, it can facilitate orderly planning of a congregation's or synod's kingdom work.

The principle of giving as the Lord prospers seems best served by a percentage pledge, which takes account of income fluctuations. For practical purposes the percentage pledge can be converted into an estimated average weekly amount.[5] The pledge should not be viewed as a legal responsibility so that the report of his giving to the individual takes on the aspect of a "bill" when the giving has been deficient. It should be self-evident that if the Lord sends an unusual change in a person's financial circumstances, the pledge is subject to revision, up or down.

The sealed pledge has been used to accentuate the fact that the promise is made to the Lord.[6] The pledge remains sealed in an envelope during the year. At the conclusion of the year the sealed pledge is returned to the donor for him to open and privately in the fear of God evaluate his performance in the light of his promise.

There may be circumstances under which the secret pledge is called for. On the other hand, the open pledge is not a public pledge and need be known only to the men elected by the congregation to handle its finances. The fact that fellow Christians are informed of the pledge makes it no less a pledge to the Lord. Each congregation can in Christian liberty set up a pledging method according to its circumstances. That opportunities for legalistic coercion and Pharisaism should be avoided is self-evident.

5. Werning in *The Stewardship Call* (St. Louis: Concordia, 1965) suggests a pledge card that combines the percentage pledge with a weekly figure *"according to my expected income,"* p 151.
6. For a discussion of the sealed pledge by an enthusiastic supporter of it, see Berner, *The Power of Pure Stewardship* (St. Louis: Concordia, 1970), pp 99ff.

The Financial Report

The congregation will keep an accurate record of all contributions and provide each contributor with a report of his giving. The question arises whether a general report listing all names and contributions should be distributed to all members. A report of this kind can serve the purpose of mutual encouragement by example. Such a report is misused if it leads to uncharitable judging or pharisaic pride. Where reports of this kind are in use, the pastor will warn against such abuses. If he finds that the abuses prevail and outweigh any advantages, he will work toward the elimination of this type of report.

An alternative to the complete report as described above is an anonymous report that lists only envelope numbers or giving units. This retains the advantage of providing mutual encouragement. However, the pastor must point out to the congregation that no report can give a complete picture, that circumstances vary greatly from family to family so that one must be wary of drawing sweeping conclusions from any report, whatever its form. Nevertheless, some type of report is in order, and an anonymous form appears preferable.

The Unified Budget

The unified budget is a method of gathering offerings in which the gifts for all purposes are combined into one offering to the Lord. The apportionment of the one offering is determined on a percentage basis for the various purposes by the voters' assembly. The aim of the unified budget is to place less emphasis on need and to avoid gathering special offerings for many different purposes. It aims at stressing the Christian's total commitment to the Lord in his stewardship. On the practical side, with only one offering for all purposes there is no need for numerous envelopes, simplifying bookkeeping for the financial secretary.

In considering the use of a unified budget, a congregation will, however, have to determine whether it is advisable to shift all responsibility for apportioning one's contributions to various purposes from the individual donor to the voters' assembly. To determine the use to which one's gifts will be put, at least in a general way, can be part of responsible, intelligent stewardship. By having at least several broad categories (the home operating fund, the building fund, the synod and missions, and charities) the Christian can apportion his total giving without becoming involved in decisions that apply to many small funds which he may know little about. When a unified budget is used, some provision should be made for those who wish to give more for a particular purpose than the congregational allotment provides for. Particularly should the unified budget not be a hindrance to added support for worldwide mission work (the synod's total program) beyond the percentage designated under the unified budget.

A problem can arise under the unified budget when the giving is less than anticipated so that the percentage allotted to the congregation's operating expenses does not result in adequate funds for this purpose. The solution should not be sought in withholding the percentage for outside purposes to meet local expenses. Such a procedure is a misuse of the unified budget and gives the impression that mission work can be carried on with "leftovers," if there are any.

Fund-Raising Agencies

Professional fund raisers have developed organizational skills and techniques that may assist a congregation, especially when a major project calls for an intensified, united stewardship effort. By securing professional aid in organizing and programing a stewardship effort a congregation can be supplied with the organizational skill which neither the pastor nor anyone in the congregation may possess. It should be noted that reputable professionals will determine their fee not on the basis of the money or subscriptions secured, but on the basis of the time required and the services rendered.

When using professional help of this kind, the pastor and congregation must insist that those who provide the professional services have no role in the religious realm, e.g., in providing motivation for giving. The congregation is purchasing organizational skill, not spiritual growth. The pastor must recognize his responsibility to remain in control, censoring all literature, and retaining together with the congregation the right of decision on all aspects of the program lest methods not compatible with the gospel gain entrance. The impression must also be avoided that the congregation is turning to professional help to effect results which the gospel was not able to produce. The method and organization do not replace the gospel and the motivation it provides, but are put into its service.

Money-Making Projects

"Hence along with the steady increase of freewill offerings we have witnessed the gradual disappearance of sales and suppers, bazaars and lotteries."[7] It is to be hoped that this observation made in 1956 is still true and will prove to be increasingly so. The pastor will work toward that end. Why?

The reason is not that suppers and sales can be called sin in themselves. We are speaking here of practices that are not contrary to state law and do not involve gambling. In opposing money-making projects the pastor must be careful not to overstate his case. Very often when the question is asked why a particular project is desired, the motivation that makes it objectionable will become evident. Frequently the reason for a project is one that conflicts with good stewardship practices. For a congregation to depend on the proceeds of a sale or supper to do, at least in part, what the freewill gifts of Christians are to accomplish will be destructive of Christian stewardship. To invite nonmembers to a supper the purpose of which is profit is to seek support for the church where it should not be looked for. The unbeliever may even be hardened in his self-righteousness by thinking he is doing his duty to God by paying the price of a dinner ticket. Generally also the donated time and goods are poorly rewarded so that the profit is more seeming than real.

On the other hand, the supper that is arranged for fellowship within a congregation and incidentally shows a profit can hardly be considered destructive of Christian stewardship. Nor need a so-called "bargain center" that makes usable second-hand clothing and goods available to the poor at a minimal price do injury to good stewardship even if it distributes its profits to charities which are normally supported by freewill offerings. Categorically to reject every supper or sale without regard to motivation leads to legalism and a failure to examine carefully the reasons that make so many of these practices unwise if not wrong.

Training in stewardship according to biblical principles is the most effective way to rid the congregation of undesirable practices for gain. Our opening quotation saw the increase in freewill giving as the reason for a decline in suppers, sales, bazaars, and lotteries.

7. T. A. Kantonen, *A Theology for Christian Stewardship* (Philadelphia: Muhlenberg, 1956), p 5.

The Every Member Visit

The most effective way for a congregation to reach its total membership with the stewardship message is the "every member visit." Programs can also be planned that are carried out by mail, in Sunday worship services, by church meetings, or by small groups. A congregation wisely decides on the method each year according to the congregation's needs and objectives. The *Stewardship Workbook*[8] of the Wisconsin Evangelical Lutheran Synod is a manual that provides the necessary information for developing a program in the local congregation. The stewardship office of the WELS each year provides congregations with materials for a stewardship program that keeps the work of the Synod before the members. While each congregation will adapt the materials and programs to its situation, the complete elimination of all stewardship training in a congregation with the assertion that the gospel should bring about a spontaneous outpouring of gifts fails to recognize the need to guide the person, instructed by the gospel, to action that also accords with God's Word. Scripture itself provides stewardship training. A program that effectively brings this training into every home of the congregation can expect divine blessings.

Summary: Many practical questions arise in connection with stewardship training and programs. The pastor will never fail to evaluate them and guide all practices in the congregation so that gospel motivation prevails and all things are done to the glory of God.

For Additional Reading

Berner, Carl W., Sr. *The Power of Pure Stewardship*. St. Louis: Concordia, 1970.

> This is a kind of autobiography of the author and his stewardship experiences in the congregations he served in California. It is written with great enthusiasm and makes many good points in favor of "pure stewardship." Unfortunately some of the methods strongly advocated, e.g., a unified budget and tithing, are encouraged almost as though they represented "God's way," or "God's principle." There also is undue emphasis on the material rewards of pure stewardship.

8. Cf note 4.

Brattgard, Helge. *God's Stewards*. Minneapolis: Augsburg, 1963.

This is "a theological study of the principles and practices of stewardship," as the subtitle informs the reader. A lengthy chapter on what the Scriptures reveal about stewardship will deepen the reader's understanding of this concept. The first chapter presents a historical account of the development to the present emphasis on stewardship.

Kantonen, T. A. *A Theology for Christian Stewardship*. Philadelphia: Muhlenberg, 1956.

One of the earlier books written on the theology of stewardship. This relates six major Christian doctrines to Stewardship. On the whole a good presentation that can deepen one's concept of stewardship on the basis of the Word. Some weaknesses in the chapter on "Stewardship and The Word of God" and "The Holy Spirit and the Church."

Meyer, Joh. P. *Ministers of Christ*. Milwaukee: Northwestern, 1963.

The exposition of chapters 8 and 9 of Second Corinthians, pp 164-220, contains much valuable material for a scriptural understanding of giving.

Rein, R. C. *Adventures in Christian Stewardship*. St. Louis: Concordia, 1955.

Eight chapters contain as many lessons on stewardship for use in organizations, Bible classes, or privately. The material abounds in Scripture references. Each chapter concludes with "Questions for Discussion" and "For Further Consideration."

Schaefer, James P. *Stewardship Workbook*. Prepared for the Wis. Ev. Luth. Synod by the Stewardship Office, 3512 W. North Avenue, Milwaukee, Wis. 53208. 1971.

An essay, "The Cross — the Center of Stewardship," by Norman W. Berg presents the biblical basis for stewardship. The remaining chapters outline the practical steps required to design and conduct a stewardship program in a local congregation. This workbook merits careful study by all pastors and congregation stewardship committees.

Werning, Waldo J. *The Stewardship Call*. St. Louis: Concordia, 1965.

This volume has the subtitle "An approach to personal and group stewardship based on the concept of Christian vocation." It presents the theology, message, and method of stewardship. A study of this volume should help develop or retain the scriptural concept of stewardship in the practical methods that are put to use.

11

The Shepherd's Concern
for Christian Marriage

"What God hath joined together"

(Mt 19:6)

I. THE INSTITUTION OF MARRIAGE

An Institution of God

Marriage, or matrimony, is an institution established for mankind as part of life in this world. It has no direct connection with the gospel, the proclamation of which is the specific responsibility of the church. In fact, marriage was instituted (Gn 2:24) before the first proclamation of the gospel (Gn 3:15). Like the institution of civil government, it concerns itself only with temporal relationships. It was not instituted in the interest of the sinner's eternal salvation. The blessings promised through marriage are purely temporal (Mt 22:30). It is not a sacrament committed to the church, but an institution established for life in the world.

Hence the church has no inherent right to exercise authority over this institution, to make laws pertaining to it, or to claim a role in performing a marriage in order to make it valid. The Roman Catholic claim that marriage is a sacrament and that the church must regulate this institution by means of canon law has no basis in the Scriptures.

263

At the same time it must be recognized that marriage is an institution of God and not a sociological development. God instituted marriage, pronounced a blessing on it, and protects it in the Sixth Commandment.

The Lord Jesus showed a special concern for this institution. Although He declined to pass judgment in an inheritance case (Lk 12:13f) and declared that His kingdom is not of this world (Jn 18:36), He did not hesitate to give an immediate answer when questioned about principles that apply to marriage and divorce (Mt 19:3ff). St. Paul too at various times was led to write about this institution, particularly in 1 Corinthians 7. Consequently the answers to many questions pertaining to marriage can and should be sought by the Christian in Holy Scripture. The pastor will instruct his congregation in everything Scripture says on this subject and will show pastoral concern that this may find application in the lives of his members.

The Role of the State

Since marriage was instituted for mankind in general, society as such has a vital interest in preserving this institution in accordance with the Sixth Commandment, the content of which to a greater or lesser degree is recognized by all mankind as part of the inscribed law in natural man's heart. Since a breakdown of this institution affects all of society adversely, the government has the responsibility of exercising control over marriage matters through its legislative and judicial functions. The state cannot indeed command what God prohibits. But it may pass marriage laws that are more restrictive than Scripture, and it may be forced to allow what God prohibits, even as Moses because of the hardness of their hearts allowed the Israelite men to put away their wives (Mt 19:8). It must be understood, however, that such permission does not give moral sanction to an action. The Christian will recognize, on the one hand, that obedience to his government will require accepting whatever restrictions go beyond Scripture and, on the other hand, that he cannot apply in his own life practices allowed by the state but prohibited by God. Human permission does not set aside divine restrictions.

The pastor will thus need to know what Scripture says about marriage as well as the marriage laws of the state in which he is serving. The latter is also necessary since the state grants him the legal right to perform a valid marriage. The pastor will consider it one of his first duties in a new parish to meet the legal requirements of his state for performing marriages[1] and to acquaint himself with the state's family laws, particularly where they speak on marriage and divorce. A congregation has every right to expect that the pastor in the performance of marriages and in counseling with people on marriage problems knows first of all what Scripture says on these matters, but also what the pertinent laws of the state are.

Monogamy

Marriage as instituted by God at the time of creation was to be a lifelong union of one man and one woman. God created a monogamous relationship. That the original institution is to be understood in this manner becomes evident when Jesus, referring to Genesis 2:24, concludes with the words, "and the two shall become one flesh" (Mt 19:5-NASB). Paul quotes Genesis 2:24 in the same manner (Eph 5:31) and in Romans 7:2,3 calls the woman who takes a second husband an adulteress. The marriage relationship involves two people. The fact that God-fearing men like Jacob and David were involved in polygamous marriages and divine disapproval in their cases is not directly evident does not change God's original institution, reaffirmed in the New Testament.

Whether polygamy is ever permissible for a Christian is only an academic question for the pastor serving in countries where monogamy is enforced by law. Polygamy then becomes a criminal offense against the laws of the state. The situation is more difficult in a foreign mission field where polygamy is acceptable according to local customs and laws. While God may have permitted exceptions to His institution, for a pastor to sanction an exception will undermine faith in the full authority of Scripture. If the pastor can grant a "dispensation" from the biblical concept of marriage as monogamous, the door has been opened for departure from Scripture in other practices that present practical difficulties. The pastor has no authority over Scripture. He must take great care lest he give even the impression that Scripture is sub-

1. In Wisconsin, for example, the law reads that "before any clergyman . . . is authorized to solemnize a marriage, he shall file credentials of ordination . . . with the clerk of the circuit court of some county in this state in which is located a church under his ministry."

ject to his manipulation. Nevertheless, great patience will be shown in seeking for a solution under difficult circumstances.

The Purpose of Marriage

God, recognizing that "it is not good for the man to be alone," created woman as "a helper suitable for him" (Gn 2:18-NASB). The closest human bonds were to be those established in the life-long union in which a man leaves his father and his mother and cleaves to his wife, and they become one flesh (Gn 2:24). An important purpose of marriage thus is the close companionship of man and woman which reaches its most intimate expression when the two become one flesh in sexual union. This intimate expression of love is a part of the marriage institution and is not to be practiced outside of it.

A second purpose of marriage was established at the time of creation when God added a blessing to the sexual union of man and woman. "So God blessed them, and God said unto them, Be fruitful, and multiply, and replenish the earth" (Gn 1:28). Thus God provided for the propagation of the human race through the institution of marriage.

Since the fall of man into sin, marriage serves a third purpose. Because man now has a heart blind to God's holy will, a heart from which "proceed evil thoughts, murders, adulteries, fornication" (Mt 15:19), each man is to have his own wife and the woman her own husband (1 Cor 7:2). If each fulfills his sexual duty, the temptations to adultery and fornication can better be resisted.

Summary: Marriage is an institution of God for man's life in this world and is subject to the controls and laws of the state. Nevertheless, God sets up the moral principles that are to be applied to this institution by the Christian. A pastor will impress these on the members of his congregation, also where Scripture is more restrictive than the laws of the state.

II. IMPEDIMENTS TO MARRIAGE

Kinds of Impediments

Since the pastor has been given the right to perform a legal marriage, he must know when a marriage is possible according to the laws of the state. Since he is a servant of the Word, he can perform no marriage that might violate scriptural principles.

There are legal impediments, those involving the laws of the state, and moral impediments, those involving God's will as revealed in Scripture. In some, both legal and moral factors are involved. It is to be noted, however, that even legal impediments involve the moral issue of obedience to "the powers that be."

The state's marriage license authorizes the pastor to perform a particular marriage. No marriage should be performed until the pastor has received the license. Generally the license will be sufficient evidence that there are no legal impediments to the marriage. If, however, the pastor knows that the license contains false information, thereby evading legal impediments, he may not proceed with the ceremony.

The pastor's contacts with his members will give occasion to discover any moral impediments to a marriage that may go beyond the laws of the state. It is thus inadvisable to officiate at the marriage of total strangers. Generally, at least one of the parties to the marriage should be one of the pastor's parishioners.

Another useful distinction recognizes that some impediments prohibit entrance upon a marriage without allowing the dissolution of one already solemnized. Other impediments either allow dissolution or render a marriage null and void. Whether the impediment is of the latter kind will be determined, at least to a great extent, by the laws of the state.

An Existing Marriage Bond

Only such who are not bound by a previous marriage bond that is still in force are free to marry. Since state laws require monogamous marriages, an existing marriage is a legal impediment to another marriage. Since Scripture, too, requires monogamy, an existing marriage bond is also a moral impediment to a further marriage. God, of course, dissolves a marriage bond through death.

Age — Parental Consent

Although Scripture imposes no age requirements on marriage, state laws designate the age previous to which marriage is not permitted, as well as the age during which parental consent is a legal requirement. Honor and esteem for his parents according to the Fourth Commandment will move the Christian to desire his parents' consent even when state law no longer requires it. In the latter case, arbitrary or malicious refusal of parental consent

267

does not constitute a moral impediment, and the governmental consent may be accepted in lieu of the denied parental approval.

Health

State law may prohibit a marriage "if either party has such want of understanding as renders him incapable of assenting to marriage whether by reason of insanity, idiocy or other causes."[2] Most states require an antenuptial physical examination and blood test to determine that the parties to a marriage are free of venereal disease. Since the presence of venereal disease is almost always the result of unchastity, this will call for pastoral concern (repentance — absolution) even apart from the immediate marriage in question. A physical condition (injury, deformity, or impotence) that results in a person's permanent inability to engage in intercourse prevents the consummation of marriage in its complete sense. It is an impediment to a normal marriage, although it cannot be considered an impediment in the absolute sense. Nevertheless, those who knowingly contemplate a marriage under such conditions must be warned of the strain this places on their marriage and the serious temptations toward unchastity which the one party may experience. Whatever health problems arise after a marriage is in effect, even if they prevent sexual intercourse permanently, do not nullify a marriage nor are they a biblical reason for its dissolution.

Impairment of Mental Powers

A marriage vow should not be made while one or both of the parties are not enjoying responsible use of their mind and will. This may be during intoxication, while under the influence of drugs, or while suffering from an illness that prevents the use of the mind for making a morally binding decision. While a vow made under such conditions is subject to annulment, the burden of proof lies with the person claiming to have been victimized.

Coercion

Inherent in a valid promise is that it is given willingly. Although Scripture does not address itself to this point directly, it is evident that the leaving of father and mother and cleaving to one's spouse according to Genesis 2:24 is a voluntary action. Re-

2. Wis. Family Code, 245.03.

bekah was asked about her willingness to leave her homeland and family in order to marry Isaac (Gn 24:58). A pastor will not solemnize a marriage where coercion is in evidence. State laws permit an annulment of a marriage if force or coercion were present at the time of the marriage "unless the marriage has been confirmed by the acts of the injured party."[3] Whoever subsequent to the coercion that forced him into a marriage practices marital privileges voluntarily is viewed as thereby giving his willing consent. What constitutes coercion the state laws may well determine. When coercion can be proved, the church too can acknowledge this as evidence that no valid marriage bond came into existence.

Deception

Deception, or fraud, is an impediment to a valid marriage promise. Such deception may involve the essence of marriage itself (e.g., known impotence or known sterility) or related matters (e.g., claiming a particular social or financial status). What turns out to be a mistaken judgment about a spouse's wealth or beauty or desirable qualities cannot subsequently be called fraud.

A pastor cannot solemnize a marriage if he knows deception is involved. If he knows that false information on the marriage license made the securing of the license possible, he must refuse to officiate. When the pastor solemnizes such a marriage knowingly, he becomes a party to the deception. Any deception known to the pastor must be cleared up before proceeding with the marriage.

Since fraud used in securing a promise nullifies one's obligation to it, state laws permit the annulment of marriages that came into existence through deception. The church may acknowledge such an annulment without expressly requiring it. Continued voluntary practice of marital rights after discovering the fraud validates the marriage vows and removes the right to annulment.

Consanguinity

State laws prohibit marriage between close blood relatives, e.g., Wisconsin law states that "no marriage shall be contracted . . . between persons who are nearer of kin than second cousins excepting that marriage may be contracted between first cousins where the female has attained the age of 55 years."[4] Christians

3. Wis. Family Code, 247.02.
4. Wis. Family Code, 245.03.

will consider themselves bound by whatever laws of this kind the state in which they reside has made.

To what extent does Scripture set up forbidden degrees of consanguinity? Leviticus 18 is most often adduced to determine the exact degrees of consanguinity or affinity that prohibit marriage in the eyes of God. The convenient rule taken from Leviticus 18:6 that relationship up to the second degree prohibits marriage is based on translating *she'er besaro* "flesh of his flesh" and interpreting that to mean the second degree of consanguinity. However the two Hebrew nouns are joined through the construct state and here have a superlative meaning, best translated simply "nearest of kin," with no degree indicated. It is also to be noted that the New Testament in speaking of marriage nowhere refers to Leviticus 18. The Mosaic code, of which Leviticus 18 is a part, has no direct application to New Testament Christians (cf Luther's "How Christians Should Regard Moses").[5] The pastor needs to look elsewhere, particularly into the New Testament, for God's will on this point as it applies to all men and thus to the New Testament children of God.

God does have something to say on this point in 1 Corinthians 5:1: "It is reported commonly that there is fornication among you, and such fornication as is not so much as named among the Gentiles, that one should have his father's wife." Paul severely takes the congregation to task for its failure to discipline this incestuous man. Paul, however, does not quote Leviticus 18:8 in the reproof, but mentions that this incestuous relationship (whether she was his mother or step-mother is not clear) is not "so much as named among the Gentiles." Here was a transgression not against the Mosaic code as imposed on Israel, but against the sense of right and wrong which even the gentiles through their natural knowledge of the law had. Beyond this, the New Testament is silent on forbidden degrees. By and large, the pastor will not go wrong by simply following the prohibitions as found in the state laws; they are generally even stricter than those imposed on Israel in Leviticus 18.

In the past, the only type of case not covered by state law that caused concern was the marriage with an in-law (*Schwagerehe*). May, for example, a man marry his deceased brother's wife? This

---

5. *Luther's Works* (St. Louis/Philadelphia: Concordia/Fortress, 1955-), XXXV, 155-174.

was considered prohibited consanguinity or affinity, on the basis of Leviticus 18:6,16,18 and 20:21. Since there is nothing outside the Mosaic code that leads to the conclusion that such a marriage must be avoided and since Deuteronomy 25:5 presents the circumstances under which such a marriage was in fact commanded, the prohibition of marriage with an in-law can hardly be considered part of God's immutable will for all men.[6]

Race

That a difference in race or color between the bride and groom is an impediment to marriage cannot be established from Scripture. Nevertheless, the specific problems that an interracial marriage presents in a particular society, country, or family will need to be faced and should become the subject for premarital counseling by the pastor. Whatever state laws prescribe regarding interracial marriages must be recognized by the pastor, regardless of what his personal views of such laws may be.

Adultery

Is adultery a permanent impediment to another marriage?

That an adulterer may marry after the death of the injured spouse is self-evident. But is this possible while the party who suffered injury is still alive? Under the Mosaic code adultery was a capital offense. Thus this question could not arise. Although the death penalty does not appear to have been imposed in New Testament times (Mt 1:19; Jn 8:1ff), there is no clear directive in Scripture that forces the conclusion that marriage must be denied to the adulterer for the duration of the injured spouse's life. The fact that reconciliation might still be possible so long as the injured party has not entered into another marriage is not decisive once the injured party has rejected all attempts at reestablishing the marriage. Scripture does not impose lifelong celibacy on the penitent adulterer as a kind of penance.

As far as the church is concerned, there must be clear evidence of repentance on the part of the adulterer. This includes bringing forth the fruits of repentance. Such fruits will include attempts at restitution, at correcting the wrongs committed and any injuries resulting from the sin. However, when it is no longer possible to

6. Two unpublished essays discuss the subject of *Schwagerehe* and come to conclusions similar to those presented here. See the articles by O. Eckert and P. Peters in the bibliography.

reestablish the marriage with the injured spouse, the fruits of repentance called for in a specific case do not necessarily consist of lifelong abstinence.

1 Corinthians 7:2 and 9 may well apply to this question. Marriage as a help to resist further temptations of the flesh can hardly be permanently rejected. Luther advises that sin and vice must be reproved and punished, but not by prohibiting marriage.[7]

Of great concern to the pastor and the church, however, must be the question of offense. For the church to give the impression that adultery, or fornication, is not a serious sin (cf 1 Cor 5:1,2) may cause the weak to stumble and fall. The moral laxness of the world calls for a strong testimony from the church.

Religious Differences

A mixed marriage is any marriage where husband and wife do not confess the true Christian faith with one heart and mind. This includes marriages where the husband and wife are members of differing Christian denominations as well as a marriage between a Christian and someone who adheres to a non-Christian religion, or is an unbeliever or an atheist. Included here is a marriage with a member of a lodge with deistic, antichristian religious views. Each type of mixed marriage will have its own specific problems.

Since marriage has no direct connection with the gospel, but is an institution for this life, a difference in religion is not as such an impediment to marriage. The Old Testament prohibitions (Ex 34:16; Dt 7:2f; Ne 13:25) had special significance during the theocracy and cannot simply be applied to Christians today. Nevertheless, the reason for the prohibition, lest the sons and daughters of Israel be turned to worship other gods, stands as a warning against mixed marriages which also New Testament Christians need to take to heart. Experience has shown that a mixture of religion in the home can result in growing indifference and even defection from the truth. There is no question but that the joyful union of two people in marriage will lack a vital ingredient if they do not have in common the Christian faith, which should have first place in a Christian's heart. Basic questions of life, of marriage itself, questions that have to do with rearing a family, even financial and social problems will find harmonious

7. *Luthers Saemmtliche Schriften* (St. Louis, 1880-1910), X, 717.

answers and solutions most readily where the Christian faith is shared.

A mixed marriage raises the troublesome question: In what religion shall the children be brought up? The pastor must warn his member against consenting to have his children taught a false religion or an erroneous form of Christianity. Such consent does injury to one's own faith. It endangers the children's eternal future.

The latter problem arises particularly in a mixed marriage with a Roman Catholic. Rome considers marriage a sacrament and states that "a marriage between baptized Christians is only valid when it is a sacrament."[8] Then too, "the Roman Catholic Church considers itself to be the Church founded by Christ and the lawfully established Church of the New Testament."[9] These two claims raise problems in regard to the marriage itself and the education of future children. The one problem is that a priest must somewhere be involved in the marriage so that it may be a sacrament and hence valid. The other pertains to the education of the children in view of Rome's claim to be the one divinely established New Testament Church. It appears that Rome is finding ways of acknowledging the validity of marriages performed in Protestant churches. It also no longer requires the non-Catholic party to sign an antenuptial agreement in which consent is given for the Roman Catholic education of all children. Nevertheless, such consent may be sought verbally and the continued insistence on it during the marriage by both the Catholic spouse and his church can be expected. Rome's new, ecumenical stance has not eliminated the specific problems of a mixed marriage with a Roman Catholic. Its seeming greater flexibility only makes dealing with the problem more difficult.

The pastor's responsibility calls for advance instruction about and warnings against the dangers of mixed marriages, already in confirmation classes and later as opportunities can be found. The pastor must seek to counsel with his people before they enter into any final marriage agreements. A major point will be to show that in a mixed marriage the true believer is losing something and is in fact placing himself into a situation that can be a danger to his faith, to his soul's salvation.

8. *The Church and Ecumenism*, vol. IV of *Concilium* (New York: Paulist Press, 1965), p 118.
9. *Ibid.*, pp 118f.

Once a man and a woman have made a firm commitment for marriage to one another, the pastor will not feel free to advise against marriage. (See also p 275f.) There may be circumstances, however, under which he finds it impossible personally to officiate, especially when he knows that promises which a faithful Christian cannot make with a good conscience are involved. A call to repentance is then in order.

In warning against mixed marriages the pastor must, however, guard against an extremism that goes beyond Scripture. Both St. Paul (1 Cor 7:16) and St. Peter (1 Pe 3:1,2) hold out the prospect to the believing husband or wife that they may through their conduct win the unbelieving spouse to the Christian faith. The pastor must take care not to alienate either his own member or the unbelieving spouse lest he prove a hindrance to such a possibility.

Prohibited Times

Lutheranism has no canon law that prohibits marriage during certain portions of the church year, for example, during Advent or Lent. Nevertheless, it has been felt that joyful celebrations, such as weddings generally are, do not harmonize with the character of these seasons. Generally there are few marriages during these weeks.

How soon after the death of a spouse a widow or widower may marry is not answered in Holy Scripture. Some countries have had laws calling for a year of mourning. Our states have no such laws. A too hasty marriage may, however, give rise to suspicion that plans for the marriage were already beginning before the death of the spouse. The pastor may well warn against too hasty a marriage without setting down as a fixed rule the exact length of time between the death of a spouse and another marriage.

Summary: A pastor will note both the moral and the legal impediments that may prohibit solemnization of a marriage and will exercise his right to perform marriages accordingly. He will also take care not to add impediments according to his own thinking where there are none that are based on Scripture or on state laws. The pastor has the right to refuse to officiate at a marriage which he considers inadvisable but must practice this right with responsible judgment.

274

III. ESTABLISHING THE MARRIAGE BOND

The Marriage Bond in its Essential Nature

"Therefore shall a man leave his father and his mother, and shall cleave unto his wife: and they shall be one flesh" (Gn 2:24). That these words constitute God's institution of marriage is evident from Jesus' use of them. Referring to them, Jesus says: "What God hath joined together, let not man put asunder" (Mt 19:6). In marriage a man and a woman forsake the previous intimacy of family life with father and mother, cleave to one another, and thus set up a new family. This cleaving, according to Jesus, is to continue so long as both live. Where this permanent relationship has been established, the two become one flesh through the sexual act. The latter does not establish the marriage but is the practice of it.

That this is a permanent bond, a lifelong "cleaving," is established before God and man only by the promises made to that effect. Hence we say that consent, not cohabitation, establishes a marriage bond (consensus facit matrimonium). This is clear from 1 Corinthians 6:16, where the man who has sexual relations with a harlot becomes one body with her, but does not become her husband. Cf also John 4:18. The importance of the promise finds expression in the term wedlock (wed – pledge). The government likewise pronounces a man and a woman husband and wife on the basis of the promises they have given. They are considered bound by their pledge, even before cohabitation. God too, in the Mosaic code, gave laws that treated betrothal the same as marriage (Dt 22.22-29). And in the New Testament, Mary and Joseph on the basis of the betrothal "before they came together" are referred to as husband and wife (Mt 1:18-20). The essential factor in the marriage bond is the mutual consent.

Consent Binds Before God

Before God a binding relationship is established when a man and a woman who are free to do so unconditionally promise to live together as husband and wife. We have already concerned ourselves with the fact that such consent must be free of coercion and should, according to the Fourth Commandment, include the consent of the parents.

In view of this, it was often said that before God engagement is the same as marriage. This can be properly understood. However, the term engagement is used and understood in different ways. It may be viewed as another way of saying that two people are "going steady." Some consider it as still subject to conditions. This must be kept in mind by the pastor lest he consider every so-called breaking of an "engagement" as tantamount to the breaking of a marriage. It may often be difficult to discipline for the breaking of an engagement since the claim may be made that it was not viewed as a firm and final pledge. A secret engagement without parental knowledge, especially by such who are still quite young, or an engagement made in jest, can hardly be considered binding.

However, at whatever point prior to the public wedding ceremony the man and the woman with the consent of their parents make their commitment to each other unconditional (without such a commitment wedding plans will hardly be undertaken seriously) they should consider themselves bound before God according to the essential factors of Genesis 2:24. To those bound by such a firm commitment the words of Jesus apply, "Let not man put asunder" (Mt 19:6). Where such a commitment is broken, the pastor must reprove the sin and call for repentance.

Practicing Marital Rights

Although before God consent establishes the bond, marital rights may not be practiced until the public recognition of the unconditional commitment has taken place before the world according to the laws of the government. While the duly engaged man and woman who consummate their marriage through cohabitation before the legal wedding ceremony are not guilty of fornication as such, they have offended against good order and the laws of the state, are guilty of unchastity, and are practicing deception when at the time of the legal ceremony the impression is given that no cohabitation has taken place. Since marriage is an earthly matter and God has placed the Christian under established government, its laws dare not be ignored. Marital rights may not be practiced until the state's requirements have also been met.

The Pastor's Responsibility to Teach

The difficulty of disciplining in the case of a "broken engagement" has already been noted. This makes it all the more important for the pastor to instruct the young about the seriousness of making a marital promise. He should warn them against hasty and frivolous promises and in particular instruct them on the true nature of an unconditional commitment (engagement in this sense) so that they make it in the true fear of God. Such mutual promises may not be broken simply by one individual or even by the joint action of the two people involved. God joins two people in a lifelong bond through their mutual promises, and man (and this includes the two who make the promises) is not to break this bond. At the same time, the young must be shown that sexual intercourse may not begin until all requirements for marriage, both divine and legal, have been met. This is important in view of the growing sentiment that sexual enjoyment is an inalienable right of every individual in or outside of marriage so long as there is a mutual commitment to that particular act.

Summary: Consent, not cohabitation, establishes a marriage bond. Christians should recognize that once they have given a firm commitment to marriage they ought to consider themselves bound to this before God for the rest of their lives. However, sexual relations may begin only after the state's requirements for marriage have also been met. The pastor needs to inculcate all of this on the youth of the congregation as they approach the age of marriage.

IV. THE MARRIAGE SERVICE

The Pastor Serves His Members

The state has given the pastor the legal right to solemnize a marriage without determining for him whom he is to serve or the particular form the ceremony should take as long as legal requirements are met. The church has called the pastor to sanctify this temporal institution with the Word of God and with prayer. While the pastor has the legal right to perform the ceremony for any man and woman for whose marriage the state has issued a license, as pastor he should remember that the church has not called him to serve the public in solemnizing marriages, but the members of the church, who desire the Lord's blessing on their union. Hence, in general at least one of the parties to the marriage will be one of his members. Most often the bride's pastor is the officiant. Good order requires that the pastor solemnize a marriage for those who are not his own members only with the knowledge and consent of their called pastor. The pastor may, of course, serve those who as mission prospects call upon him for spiritual service.

Announcement and Prayer

The *Lutheran Liturgy* has a form for publishing the banns of marriage. This custom stems from the established or state churches in Europe, where this was a requirement. For several Sundays prior to the marriage the intention of the betrothed was announced, inviting any who could show just cause why the parties involved should not be joined together in marriage to voice their objection, and calling on the congregation to intercede in prayer for the betrothed. State laws in the United States have no such requirement. However, to announce the marriage and invite the congregation to join in a prayer for the betrothed is a good custom that merits continued use. Difficulties arise in announcing mixed marriages, particularly with unbelievers. The prayer may need to be modified lest it contain statements that are not in harmony with the facts.

The Marriage Ceremony

The ceremony itself will proceed according to the order found in an approved Lutheran agenda. Generally an agenda provides several "Orders of a Marriage," each allowing some options (e.g., the repeating of the vows, the use of one or two rings). The pastor will agree with the couple in advance on the particular rite to be used. Requests for changes that go beyond those provided for in an agenda will need to be judged on the basis of Scripture. The pastor cannot permit the admission of unscriptural elements or the arbitrary elimination of what is scriptural (e.g., dropping the bride's promise to obey).

While a wedding address by the pastor is not necessary for a valid marriage and may be omitted in private ceremonies, it should be considered a self-evident part of the public marriage service in the sanctuary. Scripture provides material for these addresses in the many texts that speak of the sanctity of marriage, of its obligation and joys, and of the blessings of a Christian home. The pastor must, however, remember that he is a preacher of the gospel and not the purveyor of sage marital advice. Sin and grace must remain central in this address too. Let the pastor point to sin as the corrosive element in marriage and the gospel of forgiveness in Christ as the source of blessing. The address should be kept short; ten minutes is a good length.

Music will very likely have no part in a private wedding ceremony. A church wedding will generally include the use of the organ and some form of singing. It is good practice to have the congregation's organist serve even as the congregation's pastor normally officiates. Any exception to this should be arranged with the understanding that only such who are in confessional fellowship with the congregation may come into consideration. The singing can be provided by the congregation, a choir, or a soloist. Here, too, it should be taken for granted that only those in confessional unity with the congregation can serve as soloists, thus leading the congregation in worship.

If all concerned remember that the marriage service is a church service, a service in which Christians look to God for blessings through His Word and turn to Him in intercession, worship, and praise, theatricals and pomp will be avoided. The impropriety of secular music, whose sentiments may even conflict with Scripture, is readily evident. "Lohengrin" and "I Love You Truly" make no positive contribution to a church service, but can detract. Flashing cameras and an ostentatious photographer do not add to the worshipful atmosphere.

Should the Lord's Supper be given to the bridal pair in the wedding service? In answering this, one must remember that Jesus instituted the Lord's Supper as a common meal for the church. Hence the Lord's Supper is not celebrated by families in their homes. When it is observed by the church, all who are eligible to receive Communion are invited to participate. Private communion is practiced only when someone for valid reasons cannot join in the church's public administration in a service. To have a private communion for only two people in a public service is not compatible with this concept of the Lord's Supper. There is the danger too that the observance of Communion in a wedding ceremony, which is so susceptible to display and ceremonialism, will degenerate into a decorative ceremonial. The Roman Catholic bridal mass, associated with the sacrament of marriage, is added reason to avoid this practice, lest sacramental views intrude themselves into the institution of marriage.

The pastor will find it helpful to invite his people to discuss the marriage service with him before they proceed to invite an organist and soloist, choose music and songs, instruct the photographer and florist. He can arrange for this when the couple first contacts him about the wedding. (See "Marriage Arrangements," Appendix.) It may seem convenient for the pastor to have fixed congregational "rules" that apply to various practices. They may be a helpful guide to people, but should not lead to legalistic procedures, forcing people into unwilling submission resulting in resentment. The pastor's role is that of a teacher, also here, instructing the people so that they may be brought to follow good practices with understanding. Particular care must be taken not to create resentment and antagonism by that which in itself is an adiaphoron. However, where Scripture directs the course, the pastor must remain firm, in kindness showing that he is bound by a higher authority.

The Wedding Rehearsal

Generally the pastor will be in charge of the wedding rehearsal. If he has consulted with the bride and groom and agreed with them about all the arrangements and procedures, the rehearsal can proceed with dispatch and without too many irrelevant or inappropriate suggestions on the part of relatives and friends present at the rehearsal. The pastor needs to have some understanding for good customs and etiquette and for what is practical in the church building of his congregation. However, the pastor's interest in the rehearsal is not to "stage a good show," but to instruct all participants so that no disruptive annoyances disturb the solemnity of the wedding service.

It will be helpful to the pastor if he instructs the couple to turn the marriage license over to him no later than at the rehearsal.

The Wedding Anniversary

The pastor may be called upon to help a Christian couple observe a wedding anniversary, especially the 25th or 50th. The *Lutheran Agenda* contains an "Order for the Anniversary of a Marriage." This is particularly useful if a service in the church is desired. At other times a devotion in the home may be requested. The latter may limit itself to Scripture reading, address, prayer, and benediction. Texts for such occasions will readily come to mind in accordance with the circumstances. The repetition of the marriage vows by the husband and wife in a solemn ceremony has little purpose and could be misunderstood.

280

Summary: The pastor will help plan and carry out the wedding ceremony with the bridal couple in such a manner that improprieties do not detract from the character of the ceremony as a religious service. He will advise the couple on the choice of music, organist, and soloist so that everything proceeds in a way that is in harmony with good practice based on Holy Scripture.

V. THE DISSOLUTION OF A MARRIAGE

God Dissolves The Marriage Bond

The marriage bond involves the two spouses in a lifelong union. It is not only the man and woman who through their vows established the bond, but it is God who joined them together in marriage. God has reserved for Himself the right to dissolve it. Jesus, referring to the institution of marriage in Genesis 2:24, concludes with the words: "What therefore God hath joined together, let not man put asunder" (Mt 19:6).

God dissolves the marriage bond when He intervenes through death. A woman, Paul points out, is bound to her husband as long as he lives. Upon his death she is loosed from that bond and is free to marry again. Taking another husband then does not make her an adulteress (Ro 7:2f). When her spouse dies, "she is at liberty to be married to whom she will" (1 Cor 7:39). The same is, of course, true of the man if his wife dies. Scripture refers to only this one manner by which God dissolves a marriage.

Any dissolution of a marriage bond during the life of both husband and wife comes about through man's sin. In some way sin is always involved in a divorce. As far as the legal divorce by the court is concerned, it may, on the one hand, merely establish the fact that one party to the marriage has in effect already broken the bond. On the other hand, the securing of a legal divorce may be the action through which the marriage is being broken by one or both of the spouses. But in either case, sin has brought about the dissolution of the marriage.

Passages Having a Bearing on Divorce

To gain a complete picture of what Scripture says about divorce, those passages having a bearing on it need to be studied with care. They must not be made to say less, or more, than they are intended to say. Care must be exercised lest in translation they appear to say something different from what is conveyed through the original Greek in the New Testament. The passages that especially come into consideration are Matthew 5:32; 19:3-9; Mark 10:2-12; Luke 16:18 and 1 Corinthians 7:10-15. Some pertinent points and exegetical problems in these references require special consideration.

Whosoever Puts Away

That the man or the woman who puts away his spouse and marries another is guilty of adultery all three evangelists record (Mt 19:9; Mk 10:11; Lk 16:18). To secure a divorce, except where the reason is that the other party has already become unfaithful to the marriage bond, is to bring about its dissolution. The pastor must reprove such action from the Word of God. Care must be taken not to let reason and sentiment hide the fact that this is sin. Reason wants to conclude that it does not make sense to force two people who quarrel and don't want to live together any longer to continue their marriage. Sentiment would allow separation where love has ceased. The pastor must be Jesus' mouthpiece: "Let not man put asunder."

Except for Fornication

Twice in Matthew (5:32 and 19:9) Jesus is recorded as adding the words: "Except for fornication." Put positively, what Jesus says is this: "When a woman is guilty of fornication, a man may put her away without becoming guilty of breaking the marriage." Extramarital intercourse on the part of one spouse breaks the marriage bond; the innocent party may secure a divorce to establish the fact of the broken marriage legally. In that sense one can say that the Bible looks upon fornication as a cause for divorce.

Fornication speaks of a sexual act in this context, and not of the adultery that takes place in the heart according to Matthew 5:28. Certainly the mere suspicion of unfaithfulness, or rumors and common gossip, persistent though they be, cannot replace the requirement for proof that an act of fornication has occurred.

The question may arise whether homosexual relations are included under the "except for fornication." According to Romans 1:26,27 the unnatural form of intercourse as it occurs between two people of the same sex is portrayed as most reprehensible. For a man to leave his wife and seek satisfaction through the unnatural intercourse with another man is no less a breaking of his

282

marriage bond than it is when this infidelity involves another woman.

Jesus' word, permitting divorce in case of fornication, is not to be considered a command. There is nothing to prevent the innocent party from forgiving the erring spouse and reestablishing the former relationship. The pastor may find it advisable to work toward a reconciliation, especially if the case is not publicly known and if children are involved. Care must, however, be taken lest the injured party's conscience be burdened with the thought that forgiveness must inevitably result in reestablishing the marriage bond.

Should the innocent party consent to continued sexual intercourse after the infidelity has become known, such an action reestablishes the marriage bond. The former infidelity cannot subsequently be used as a basis for divorce.

Malicious Desertion

St. Paul addresses himself to the subject of desertion in 1 Corinthians 7. He points out that the Lord has given the command: "Let not the wife depart from her husband" (1 Cor 7:10). That is the way it should be among Christian spouses. If, however, she departs, he advises her to remain unmarried or to be reconciled. He does not want a Christian to make the separation permanent.

If two Christians in their marriage find themselves at odds with one another, quarreling, unable to live together in peace, the solution may be separation, not, however, one that is permanent as in a divorce, not one in which either marries another, which makes the separation permanent. The hope is that their living apart will make them realize the need they have for one another so that a reconciliation can come about. Since both are Christians, both will recognize the will of God that their marriage remain intact. There are circumstances under which a pastor may advise such a separation of two Christians whose marriage is experiencing difficulty. This, however, is not to be a separation thought of as a first step toward divorce.

A Christian may, on the other hand, be married to an unbeliever. Our Savior gave no advice for such a situation. But Paul addresses himself to it in writing to the Corinthians. Since he wrote by inspiration of the Holy Ghost, the church recognizes his words on this subject as authoritative. The Christian will not for-

283

sake an unbelieving spouse. But what should be done when the unbelieving husband departs? Verse 15 gives the answer: "If the unbelieving depart, let him depart. A brother or a sister is not under bondage in such cases." Through such desertion, the departing husband or wife is breaking the marriage bond and the deserted person is free, that is, free to marry another. Naturally, before that freedom can be put into practice, a divorce through the courts will need to establish the fact that the marriage no longer has legal status.

Paul speaks here of an unbelieving spouse departing. What about the spouse that professes Christianity? The pastor will admonish the professing Christian and advise him against any unscriptural action. He will warn him against deserting his wife permanently by securing a divorce and opening up the possibility of marriage to another. If he persists in his course, Luther correctly points out that through his action he reveals himself as a false Christian and concludes that "what St. Paul here says of the heathen spouse is to be understood as applying also to the false Christian."[10] He becomes guilty of breaking the marriage through malicious desertion.

Forms of Malicious Desertion

The most direct form of malicious desertion is local separation. It is desertion when a husband or wife moves out of the house, literally deserts living under the same roof with the other. However, this must occur without the consent of the spouse. It must occur for reasons within the deserter's control. If business and job requirements result in temporary separation, if the man is called into the armed forces of his country, if he is sent to prison, such separation cannot be viewed as malicious desertion. Nor should the departure of one spouse in anger after a quarrel immediately be construed as desertion. State laws will generally determine when a desertion is of such a nature that the deserted spouse may gain legal freedom for another marriage.

The Greek word that is used in 1 Corinthians 7:15, *choorizesthai*, however, does not refer only to local separation. (Cf its use, for example, in Ro 8:35 and He 7:26.) Its meaning is to separate, divide, part, in whatever way this occurs: Here it would refer to a

10. St. L., VIII, 1062.

desertion of the marriage vow in whatever way this comes into evidence.

Permanent refusal of sexual intercourse is a departure from the marriage promise. Such refusal thus constitutes another form of malicious desertion. However, if illness, incarceration, reasons beyond the person's control, force cessation of intercourse, this cannot be considered desertion, even if the illness, e.g., results in sexual intercourse ceasing for the remainder of the spouse's life. This may be a cross that the healthy person needs to bear, and he may not use it as a reason for divorce or infidelity on his part. The deprived person will need to pray God to give him strength to remain chaste while remaining faithful to the union God has established.

Persistent actions that make life together in the same home impossible are another form of malicious desertion. The husband who continues to threaten his wife, who resorts to physical violence, endangering the life of his wife and family, who maliciously continues to refuse support is thereby deserting his marriage promise. Concern for the preservation of life and limb may force the wife to live apart, but it is the action of the husband that has caused the separation. Care must be exercised lest one conclude too hastily that desertion has occurred. Patient counseling and pastoral exhortation should be used to effect correction and reconciliation. Nevertheless, the person who persistently refuses correction from the Word of God and continues in his course of action finally proves himself a deserter from the marriage relationship. He has broken the marriage and the deserted one may secure a divorce so that the union is also legally dissolved.

Not to be included under desertion are incompatibility, disappointment over the fact that the marriage is not living up to one's romantic hopes, or even loss of love for the spouse. Desertion takes place not only in the heart, but through definite and persistent action. It does not occur by common consent, but is the sinful breaking away from the marriage on the part of one in spite of the efforts on the part of the other to maintain the relationship. There finally comes a time when the Christian can say: "Let him depart."

Exegetical Difficulties

Some exegetical difficulties arise in Matthew 5:32 and 19:9. The question is properly asked: How is it that Jesus says that the woman who is put away by her husband "commits adultery" as well as the one who marries her? Without going into all the textual problems involved, especially into the fact that some of the statements are omitted in various manuscripts, it should be pointed out that the Greek verb form that is translated "commits adultery" is a passive form, *moicheutheenai*. This is preferable to the *moichasthai* found in some manuscripts. Since *moicheuoo* is not a deponent verb, the passive form should not be translated with the active "commits adultery," as is done in many English versions. She does not actively commit adultery, but she passively has something happen to her; she "suffers adultery" is suggested by Thayer. Similarly the one who marries her does not actively commit adultery, but the verb used (a middle-passive form) in this context following the previous passive verb can also be taken to be passive. Schaller's explanation in his *Pastorale Praxis* accords with this quite well when he writes: "For an understanding of Matthew 5:32 and 19:9: That the innocent party and the person who subsequently marries her breaks the marriage does not happen *formaliter* (for through the adulterous action of the other the marriage is in fact dissolved), but it happens *materialiter*, i.e., the innocent party is drawn into a broken marriage as also the person who marries the innocent divorcee."[11]

A further problem arises in Luke 16:18. There Jesus quite plainly states that "whosoever marrieth her that is put away from her husband committeth adultery." In this case the verb form, *moicheuei*, is unquestionably active, the same form used in this verse concerning the man who puts away his wife. Jesus here is speaking against the Pharisees, who were attempting to justify their practices and were deriding Him. The free manner in which marriage and divorce were viewed by them and accepted by all made everyone involved in such practice guilty. The man who married the woman who had been put away did so, not because he considered her innocent, but because he accepted these loose practices in regard to divorce. Under such circumstances everyone was guilty. A similar situation exists today when people freely marry, divorce, and remarry and accept that as perfectly proper, regardless of the reasons. When this occurs, all involved are guilty of adulterous action over against the biblical views of the marriage relationship.

11. John Schaller, *Pastorale Praxis* (Milwaukee: Northwestern, 1913), p 89.

Summary: God joins the husband and wife together in marriage; God dissolves such a union through death. Whenever man puts asunder what God has joined together, sin is involved. Through fornication and malicious desertion the marriage bond is broken. A divorce by the court may be secured to establish this legally. Under any other circumstances, the divorce itself breaks the marriage and is contrary to Scripture.

VI. PREMARITAL COUNSELING

An Ongoing Responsibility

Ideally the home should provide the necessary preparation, guidance, and instruction required by youth for what must be considered one of the most important steps in their lives on earth, that is, marriage. The home will influence the children's views of the marriage relationship, whether for good or evil. The church cannot replace the parents in what are their responsibilities.

The church must, however, teach its people, the fathers and mothers as well as the children, what God's Word says about marriage, family life, and the respective responsibilities of husband, wife, and children in a home. In doing this it will seek to build Christian homes where children will by example and precept receive the kind of preparation for marriage that is needed. At the same time, the children will themselves learn from the Word of God what considerations and attitudes should be prominent as they approach the choice of a spouse and marriage.

The pastor will in his instruction classes, in young people's groups, and wherever opportunity makes it possible seek to provide additional guidance to the youth of the congregation for eventual marriage. He has the ongoing responsibility of teaching proper Christian attitudes toward sex, courtship, and marriage.

Specific Guidance Before Marriage

The church today is faced by an increasing number of homes torn by troubles. The erosion of the family and the growing divorce rate are evident also among the church's members. Counseling with those who are experiencing a crisis in the family requires a great amount of the pastor's time. This points up the importance of providing specific premarital counseling for those about to enter into wedlock.

Such premarital counseling can serve a dual purpose. By directing the bride and groom to the Word of God, by showing them what the Word of God says about marriage and family life, the pastor can hope to establish a solid union under God, one that with divine help can cope with problems as they arise. The Christian bride and groom should be most receptive to such teaching at a time when they can see the immediate relevance of it in their lives. They desire a good marriage, and instruction from the Word of God can do more than anything else to make it such.

That problems will nevertheless arise is beyond question. Sin will still have its evil effects within the new family. Premarital guidance therefore serves a second purpose, that of establishing good rapport between the couple and the pastor with a view to the future. The manner in which he has helped them prepare for their married life can influence the couple, when problems arise, to think of the pastor as one to whom they can turn with confidence.

Areas of Concern

The pastor here too will recognize his educational role. He will, however, remember that what he must teach has its origin in Scripture. The Bible says much that is pertinent and practical for a man and woman as they unite their lives in matrimony. Scripture speaks on the permanent union God establishes in marriage so that divorce should not be considered as a solution to a marital problem by the Christian. God has something to say as regards the responsibility of each spouse in family life, about begetting and rearing children. Sex can be discussed as frankly as is done in Scripture, showing this to be a gift of God, whereby two people not only find physical and emotional satisfaction but also enter into that closest relationship with one another, spoken of in Scripture as becoming one flesh. Family finances need careful planning lest they become a source of friction. Important is the proper attitude toward material wealth, taught in Scripture when it warns against covetousness and calls for contentment. Good stewardship, including the support of the Lord's work, may be aided by setting up a budget. The relationship toward the father and mother whom each is leaving to form the new family can be discussed in the light of Scripture. Finally, the pastor will want to show the need for continued use of the Word of God in the home, suggesting devotional material and instructing the couple in its use. Scripture references like Genesis 1:27,28; 2:18-25; Psalm 127:3-5, Proverbs 22:6; Matthew 5:32; 19:6-9; 1 Corinthians 7:2 5,15,39; Ephesians 5:22-33; Colossians 3:16-21; Hebrews 13:4-6; 1 Peter 3:1-7 provide much material for discussing these subjects and allow for practical applications that take note of the society and culture in which the Christian lives his life.

The pastor's role in premarital counseling is also diagnostic. In the course of the discussions and by means of tools that have been developed for that purpose the pastor may be able to recognize problems that could become troublesome and dangerous to the marriage union. A mixed marriage or a premarital pregnancy calls for special consideration. Conflicting attitudes toward sex, birth control, finances, differences in cultural backgrounds are only some of the sources of possible friction after the emotionally stimulating festivities of the wedding are followed by normal, everyday life. The couple may find that to be forewarned about such problem areas is to be forearmed. On the other hand, the sympathetic, tactful manner in which the pastor has discussed such problems in the light of God's Word may bridge the gap of hesitancy and fear to approach the pastor when disruption threatens the marriage bond.

Mechanics and Materials

How much time is required for premarital counseling and how shall the meetings be set up? A minimum of three meetings of one and a half hours each is considered necessary by many pastors to carry out an effective program. Marriages that require the use of the church building generally are arranged with the pastor well in advance so that dates for counseling meetings can be agreed upon. If it has become known that the pastor carries out a program of premarital counseling and its value has been attested to by those who have received such counseling, there should be little difficulty in arranging for the meetings. In larger congregations where the number of marriages and the pastor's limited time cause difficulty, the couples can be taken in groups, at least for the educational part of the counseling. One meeting privately with each couple still is advisable. Some pastors have also found it helpful to have one separate meeting with each party to the marriage.

That the Bible will be the chief source for premarital counseling should be self-evident. The pastor may feel most comfortable teaching with materials he has himself prepared from Scripture. Helpful books and pamphlets may assist the pastor in this.[12]

Many tools, inventories, counseling cards, guides have been developed for use in premarital counseling.[13] Such tools serve a diagnostic purpose, helping the couple and the pastor to recognize troublesome areas in the relationship of the bride and groom, and provide opportunity for a discussion of those problems. The pastor will supply the necessary biblical basis for the discussions. In this manner the teaching function of the pastor may be combined with the use of such tools.

Summary: Although the home should prepare children for marriage, the church through its pastor will consider teaching parents and children what the Word of God says about sex, courtship, and marriage as an ongoing responsibility. Because of the erosion of family life also among church members, premarital counseling with the individual couple can provide opportunity for special instruction from the Word of God at a time when it is most relevant. The counseling may reveal specific problems that could become troublesome and provides opportunity for discussing them in the light of Scripture.

Marital counseling is discussed in the chapter on counseling.

For Additional Reading

Boeckle, Franz. "Mixed Marriages: A Catholic View." In *Concilium*, IV, 115-122. New York: Paulist Press, 1965.

   This presents the theology involved in Roman Catholic views of mixed marriages. Helpful to evaluate practical modifications that Rome may be willing to make.

Eckert, Otto J. *Is Marriage to a Deceased Spouse's Brother or Sister Forbidden?* An essay delivered at various conferences in Michigan between 1942 and 1947.

   The author examines the passages that have traditionally been adduced as prohibiting *Schwagerehe* and comes to the conclusion that there is no clear prohibition against it.

12. See the bibliography for suggestions.
13. See the bibliography for suggestions.

Feucht, Oscar E. *Family Relationships and the Church.* St. Louis: Concordia, 1970.

This volume in the *Marriage and Family Research Series* has the descriptive subtitle: A sociological, historical, and theological study of family structures, roles, and relationships. Reference to it here is not an endorsement of its entire content.

Fritze, Edwin J. "Premarital Education." Chapter 17 in *Helping Families Through the Church.* St. Louis: Concordia, revised ed., 1971. Pp 181-192.

Stresses the need for premarital education and provides practical suggestions. Acceptance of birth control appears to be taken for granted. Pp 323-327 contain also a "Premarital Counseling Guide for Pastors," prepared by Granger E. Westberg of Hamma School of Theology.

Geiseman, O. A. *Make Yours a Happy Marriage.* St. Louis: Concordia, 1946.

Although published in 1946, this little volume is still in print. It can serve as a guide for the pastor who wishes to prepare his own premarital counseling material. It can be given to the couple for profitable reading. In a simple and winning manner it applies Scripture truth to the marriage relationship.

Graf, Arthur E. *A Marriage Manual for Church Weddings.* Jefferson City, Mo.: Faith Publications. Revised 1970.

This manual of 33 pages is intended to be given to the bride and groom to guide them in planning the wedding. Contains helpful suggestions for appropriate music. An inventory for premarital counseling is included.

Marriage Counseling Cards. St. Louis: Concordia.

This set contains 44 cards to be used for premarital counseling. Helpful in diagnosing the strengths and weaknesses in the relationship of the bride and groom and gives occasion to discuss them, drawing in Holy Scripture.

Morris, J. Kenneth. *Premarital Counseling.* Englewood Cliffs; Prentice-Hall, 1960.

Contains much material from which the pastor can adopt and adapt whatever fits into his program in accordance with scriptural principles.

Peters, Paul. *Die Schwagerehe.* An unpublished essay delivered at Milwaukee City Conference, April 1948.

Although the title is in German, the essay is in English. The question that is explored involves the application of Moses to N.T. times. The concluding statement reads: "Therefore, before laying down the law to our people we will have to be convinced that the *Schwagerehe* is unlawful, not because Moses says so, but because God says so."

291

Schaller, John. *Pastorale Praxis*. Milwaukee: Northwestern, 1913. *"Ehe-fragen,"* pp 75-93.

This material was widely consulted in preparing the present chapter on "Marriage."

Schuetze, A. W. *Family Life under Christ*. Milwaukee: Northwestern, 1971.

A pamphlet in the *Bible Study Series*. It lends itself for use in premarital counseling, or may be helpful in preparing one's own material.

Sohn, Otto F. "The Church and Mixed Marriage." *Concordia Theological Monthly*, XXXIV (Sept., 1963), 517-540.

A study of all aspects of mixed marriages with special emphasis on one with a Roman Catholic. Biblical principles find due application.

12

The Shepherd
Comforts the Bereaved

*"Though he were dead,
yet shall he live."*
(Jn 11:25)

There is no explicit command in Scripture to bury the dead. There are, however, passages which take burial for granted, for example, John 5:28,29; 1 Corinthians 15:42-44. Likewise, not to be buried was considered the ultimate disgrace, cf 2 Kings 9:10. Cremation seems to have been connected with judgment (cf Jos 7:25). Still, David did not reprove, but rather commended those who cremated the bodies of Saul and his sons before they buried their ashes (1 Sm 31:12,13; 2 Sm 2:5). In our times cremation is often associated with unbelief, especially when the ashes are scattered, challenging the Lord to restore and bring back to life the remains. We dare not, however, be sweeping in our judgments. The motive behind the act determines its moral character. Cremation might be requested for a variety of reasons: economy, ease of transportation of the remains, a notion that burial involves health hazards or unwarranted land use. The request of the deceased that his body be cremated does not therefore automatically become grounds for a pastor to refuse Christian burial. If he does officiate, he will change the words in the form for committal to: "We commit his body to the elements in the hope of restoration to eternal life."

293

Nowhere in Scripture are we told that believers had any kind of religious service in connection with the burial of their dead (cf Mt 14:12; 27:59-61; Ac 8:2). The church is exercising Christian liberty when it sanctifies a funeral and burial with the Word of God and prayer. An excellent opportunity for a confession of Christian hope and faith is also involved. For that very reason, however, care must be taken that nothing connected with the burial contradicts this testimony. Otherwise the pastor will in general adapt himself to the customs prevailing in his congregation. He would not, for example, cause a big stir by objecting to placing flowers instead of earth upon the casket when the words "earth to earth, ashes to ashes, dust to dust" are spoken at the committal.

It ought to go without saying that the general features of the funeral service ought to be the same in every case without respect of persons. In the case of a suicide to whom a pastor must give the benefit of the doubt by granting him a Christian burial the time-honored custom, *ohne Sang und Klang* (no tolling or singing), ought to be adhered to in order to avoid offending one who is emotionally or spiritually weak by giving him the impression that to murder oneself is not a serious sin after all. In the case of infants the family itself may desire a more simple service.

It is questionable whether much space needs to be devoted in a book of this nature to the matter of church cemeteries. Economic considerations will preclude the establishment of many new ones, and most of those which do exist are no longer administered by the congregation as such, but by a separate affiliated corporation. While the sale of lots may be restricted to members, to restrict the use of lots can lead to unbecoming squabbles about property rights and the appearance of vengefulness which can only reflect unfavorably upon a Christian congregation.

The Pastor's Role

We have already mentioned that in the exercise of its Christian liberty the church has adopted and retained the custom of connecting religious features with the burial of its members who have died. It has done so for the purpose of bringing comfort to the survivors by confessing the hope which we have concerning our dead. Since the pastor by virtue of his call into the public ministry speaks for the church, he will be in charge of the funeral services.

Under normal conditions he will endeavor to visit the bereaved family as soon as possible after he has been informed that a death has occurred. His immediate purpose will be to speak preliminary words of comfort and, if circumstances warrant, to accompany them with a brief prayer. He will also discuss funeral arrangements as far as his participation is involved. (See "Funeral Arrangements," Appendix.) A time for the funeral must be set. He may want to ascertain whether the family has any preference as far as the text of the funeral sermon is concerned. If there is to be a soloist, he will direct the choice to one who is in confessional fellowship since any involvement in conducting a service indicates confessional fellowship. The pastor will tactfully direct the family to selections which give positive expression to the Christian hope and are not just sweetly sentimental. If it is customary to read an obituary in connection with the funeral service, the pastor will obtain the pertinent information. While funeral directors often supply him with some information, it is mainly secular in nature and does not cover items which the pastor might want to include: date and place of baptism, confirmation, marriage, officiating pastors, special service to the congregation or church at large, and the like.

While the pastor will at all times endeavor to maintain good public relations with the funeral director, he will at the same time tactfully but firmly maintain the principle that as far as the religious features connected with the funeral are concerned, they are his domain. He acts at the request of the family, not at the request of the funeral director, although the latter may under circumstances relay the request. If there is to be a monetary gift in appreciation of the pastor's services, it is a gift from the family to the pastor and not part of the fixed charges which the funeral director collects. In his conversation with the family the pastor may tactfully suggest that they encourage memorial contributions for some phase of the church's work instead of a lavish display of flowers. Often funeral directors will insert such requests in the death notices which they prepare for the public press.

Commonly accepted etiquette in many areas seems to require that the pastor make a brief appearance at the funeral home while the body is lying in state. Since people at the time of bereavement are sensitive and sentimental, a pastor will show good tact by conforming to practice even though he can ill afford the time. If he cannot make an appearance, he might excuse himself in advance.

For a long time it was accepted as a matter of course that funeral services for a member of a congregation be held in church at an early afternoon hour, and exceptions were rare. Lately, in at least some areas, a trend has been developing to have the funeral service in the evening, with the committal following the next morning. More common is the trend to have the funeral service of even longtime and faithful members of a congregation in a funeral home. The decision will have to be left to the family since the place of the service is an adiaphoron.

The Funeral Service

In the funeral service the content of the sermon is of prime importance. It is not to be a eulogy. This does not mean that faithful and exceptional service rendered to the congregation may not be acknowledged, that the example which the departed had given of some phase of Christian living or dying may not be mentioned. But these are not to be the main matter. A pastor must make very sure to remain true to the facts when he refers to the life of the deceased, lest by saying something that is not true he lead his hearers to doubt the truth of his entire message or lay himself open to the suspicion that he is angling for a lucrative fee for his services. His sermon is to be a sermon of comfort and must carefully avoid descending into a sickly sentimentality aimed at causing tears. His aim is to dry tears, not to produce them.

There are several main facets to the comfort which the pastor will try to offer: 1. The Lord's purpose in permitting this death to occur when it did and as it did was a purpose of love (Ro 8:28). 2. Those who die believing in their Savior go to be with their Lord in heaven as soon as the soul leaves the body, and that is far better (Php 1:23). 3. We bury our dead in the hope of a resurrection to everlasting life (1 Th 4:16,17). 4. The Lord will according to His promise be with the bereaved to comfort them, guide them, provide for them, and receive them too into glory at last. At the same time such preaching will serve to strengthen the faith of other believers and will be a testimony of their distinctive hope to non-believers who may be attending the funeral to show their respect for the deceased. Just because such people may be present at a funeral, special care must be taken clearly to preach sin and grace. Even though the truths concerning death and the resurrection are familiar to the pastor, he dare never hold back from repeating them at every funeral for fear that he is becoming trite.

While the survivors who are to be comforted may long since have learned these truths objectively, they take on new meaning when the time comes for them to apply them to their own situation. Nor dare we forget that the faith of every Christian in these truths needs constant strengthening, for the fact of the restoration, vivification, and glorification of the body flies in the face of reason.

Normally the committal takes place after the service in the church or funeral home. For the committal service the pastor will follow the order in the agenda or the order which has been in vogue in his congregation. This is also the case with the main service. In both cases brevity is desirable because the immediate mourners are under an emotional strain. The pastor, however, will avoid any appearance of being in a hurry to finish a service or to get away after the committal lest he hurt the feelings of the survivors.

After the Funeral

If there are close survivors who are under his spiritual care, the pastor will not consider his ministrations finished on the day of the funeral. Often the full impact of the loss of a dear one is experienced only after the excitement and bustle connected with the funeral have subsided. The pastor ought therefore to make an effort to visit the survivors during the weeks immediately following the funeral. He will show himself truly sympathetic, mindful of the injunction: "Weep with them that weep" (Ro 12:15). If people want to apologize for their tears, he will let them know that he understands and, what is much more important, that Jesus understands (Jn 11:35). Above all, he will review the comforting truths of our Christian faith. His evaluation of individual cases will indicate whether further visits are needed. James 1:27 indicates that widows and their children ought to receive special attention.

Substituting for Other Pastors

Up to this point we have been discussing the normal situation in which a pastor by virtue of his call officiates at the funeral of a member of his own congregation. He will follow the same procedure when he officiates for a brother pastor at his request when he for valid reasons is not able to officiate himself. This will also be the case when for geographical reasons a brother pastor asks him to officiate when the funeral is being held at a considerable distance from the place where the deceased last resided. A pastor will not cross confessional lines to officiate at a funeral, nor will he presume to officiate at the funeral of a member of a sister congregation unless he is requested to do so by its pastor.

Nonmembers

If a pastor is asked to minister to an unchurched person during his last illness and has heard a confession of faith in the Savior from him, he will be ready to officiate at the funeral if he is asked to do so, and use the opportunity to extol the grace of the Lord and our Christian hope in death. The same principle will apply in the case of one to whom the pastor has been ministering, let us say in an adult class, but who dies before he is formally received into membership in the congregation. There could also be the case of a forgotten old person who because of physical or mental disability could not maintain contact himself, whose name was allowed to disappear from the church roster, and whose family showed no concern about spiritual ministrations for him until he died, but then come to the current pastor of the congregation and ask him to officiate at the funeral. If investigation establishes the fact that during the period of his competence the deceased had been a faithful Christian, the pastor may consent to serve. In all such cases, however, the pastor will have to be careful to insist that all religious features connected with the funeral are to be under his control. Even in the case of his members he may at times have to stress this point since there are civic organizations which offer a quasi-religious "service" at the funeral of their members.

Whether the church may be used for the funeral service of nonmembers lies within the option of a congregation. Some congregations take the attitude that if their pastor may officiate, he may also have the funeral in church; others, however, restrict the use of their church to the members of the congregation. When a pastor does find it possible to officiate at the funeral of a nonmember, he will do well to inform at least the members of his church council of his reasons for doing so even though his people may have the confidence in him that he is a man of principle. He will show the same consideration to his people in cases where there was some doubt whether it would be proper for him to officiate at the funeral of a member.

Refusal to Officiate

From the foregoing it is evident that a pastor may officiate at a funeral only when he can in good conscience confess concerning the deceased that he is being buried in the hope of the resurrection to eternal life. Membership in a Christian congregation implies a confession of faith in the Savior. In other cases the confession must have been given to the pastor. Where he has no knowledge of either kind of confession, he may not officiate. The pastor who is guided by this principle may come under attack when he refuses to officiate at a funeral. He may be accused of uncharitable judging. But the fact of the matter is that he is merely saying that he has no evidence upon which to base the hope which is expressed in connection with Christian burial, namely, the hope that the departed has died as a believer and will rise to everlasting life. The Word of God knows of no other way to life. To give the impression that there is another is tantamount to denying the very Lord whose public spokesman the pastor has been called to be.

Again, the pastor who refuses to officiate at a funeral may be charged with being loveless. "You can't bury a man like a dog." This skirts the issue. No one objects to using the services of a funeral director or a florist. More is being demanded than a decent burial; a denial of the truth is involved. Of this the pastor will not make himself guilty. If he has qualms about being hardhearted, he will do well to remember that his Lord was ready to allow one unbeliever to receive "the burial of an ass" (Jr 22:18,19). More apropos is the heroic utterance of our Lord Jesus about being too much concerned about the kind of burial which anyone and everyone receives: "Let the dead bury their dead" (Mt 8:22).

Then there is the argument that we are preaching to the living, not to the dead, and that no opportunity ought to be bypassed to preach the gospel. But the fact remains that we are burying the dead in the hope of the resurrection to everlasting life. If we can not express that hope, we had best be silent. No matter what might be said in the funeral sermon to safeguard our position, our actions proclaim that we have given the deceased a Christian burial. We can preach also by refusing to officiate, for our very refusal tells people: "Faith cometh by hearing" (Ro 10:17), and "He that believeth not shall be damned" (Mk 16:16).

Then there are those trying situations in which the deceased was not a member of the congregation, but his family is. Well indoctrinated members may not even ask their pastor to officiate in order not to put him on the spot. But in many instances the request is made. Does the pastor not owe it to his members to address words of comfort to them? By all means — but not at the funeral. May he have a sermon for them, but not in the same room with the casket, either before or after the committal? The danger of offense is still very real. The general impression will be that the pastor officiated at the funeral. Private ministrations to his members will supply their need and safeguard his position and principles. If there is some resentment, he will put up with it patiently, aware of the stress under which his members have been put. As he continues to manifest a loving concern, in most cases the resentment will gradually disappear.

Suicides

In the foregoing there were several intimations that there are cases when it becomes problematical whether a pastor may officiate at the burial of a member of his congregation. One of such cases arises when a member commits suicide. Suicide is murder. For Christians this is axiomatic: "Ye know that no murderer hath eternal life abiding in him" (1 Jn 3:15). Of the suicide Judas we are told that he went "to his own place" (Ac 1:25). To bury a murderer in the hope of the resurrection to eternal life is to contradict God. But are not all suicides out of their right mind? The three suicides of whom the Bible tells us were not: Saul, Ahithophel, Judas. Nor were the Romans who followed the philosophy: "One need not live." Nor were the Japanese who practiced hara-kiri. In many cases suicide is the fruit of unbelief. "Out of the heart . . . proceed . . . murders" (Mt 15:19). It is of suicide deliberately committed that we have been speaking. On the other hand, it cannot be denied that there are those who commit suicide because they are mentally ill. Early treatment of mental illness is urged because people with a psychosis often develop suicidal tendencies. If therefore there is evidence upon which we can give a suicide the benefit of the doubt, we can in charity assume that he acted while he was not mentally responsible. Then the prohibition of Christian burial no longer holds. As was said previously, the old custom of conducting such a burial in a more subdued manner (*ohne Sang und Klang*) is still a sound one. The horribleness of murder is not tempered and those who are weak are less apt to be led to think that suicide in itself is not sin. What

300

was involved in the subdued externals in connection with such a burial included omitting of tolling at the time of death and again at the time of the funeral (*Klang*), no singing at the funeral (*Sang*), no church service, no announcement of the death on the Sunday following the funeral. Circumstances will indicate to what extent all of this should be applied in a given case.

Doubtful Cases

The suicide whose death is immediate has no opportunity for repentance. The case of a member who dies in the act of committing a gross sin other than self-murder, as, for example, adultery, robbery, drunkenness (1 Cor 6:9,10), may present a parallel problem. Much will hinge upon the question whether death was instantaneous or whether there were intervening moments of consciousness in which repentance might have been possible. If it is possible to give the dead the benefit of the doubt, it will have to be done; if not, the verdict of God will have to be confessed by refusing to officiate (Eze 33:13).

A pastor may be confronted with the situation that someone dies whose name still appears upon the membership roster of his congregation although he has long been delinquent in hearing the Word, receiving the Lord's Supper, and contributing for the support of the Lord's work. If the pastor were to be asked to officiate at the funeral of one who at one time was a member of the Lutheran church but has fallen away, he would refuse to function because there is no current evidence on the basis of which he could express the hope that the deceased will rise to everlasting life. But in the case of one who is still listed as a member, while there is no apparent difference between his conduct and that of the person just referred to, there is still the flimsy evidence of formal membership in a Christian congregation. The time for admonition, and for action if impenitence had been established, has passed. The pastor has little choice but to officiate, giving the man the benefit of the doubt that his was a case of severe weakness, but not of stubborn impenitence. Problems of this nature can be avoided if the pastor and his congregation are diligent in practicing brotherly admonition and church discipline.

Lodge Members

There have been cases where a pastor did not discover that a member belonged to a lodge until the member died. The question

301

then arises whether it was a case of ignorance or of deliberate deception. If it was the latter, the pastor will refuse to officiate; if it was the former, he will give the deceased the benefit of the doubt. "Charity believeth all things" (1 Cor 13:7). Furthermore, there may be cases of a deathbed conversion in which because of the exigencies of the situation the pastor had to concentrate upon bringing the dying man to a knowledge of his sin and to the assurance that Jesus died for him to save him from his sin, and to look for a simple confession of faith. The situation did not allow him to delve into the man's background, so that it was not until after he died that the pastor learned that he was a lodge member. If he is asked to officiate at the funeral, he will. To avoid confusion and offense the pastor will, however, seek to prevail upon the family to omit mentioning the lodge membership of the deceased in the published death notice. In such cases where the pastor in good conscience can agree to officiate at the funeral of a lodge member, it must be with the clear understanding that the lodge will have no part in the services. Nowhere does the antichristian character of the lodge reveal itself more clearly than in its burial ritual, which declares that the departed member has gone to the grand lodge above because of his good works and character and his adherence to the moral principles of the lodge. Heaven through the merits of Jesus alone and heaven earned by good works are mutually exclusive. Compromise is impossible. "He that is not with me is against me" (Mt 12:30). Even the appearance of lodge members in their regalia at the funeral ought not to be permitted. In this connection it might also be noted that some congregations in their bylaws prohibit the display at a funeral of the regalia or emblems of any organization except those of a governmental unit or the American flag.

We might sum up the principles governing sound Lutheran burial practice in the following two statements: We grant Christian burial to members of our congregations unless there is a compelling reason not to do so. We shall not grant Christian burial to those who are not members of our congregation unless there is a compelling reason to do so.

The Privilege

While it was necessary to refer to problems which may arise in connection with our burial practice, in the great majority of cases things will run smoothly and the pastor will find that the ministry of comfort which he is permitted to perform in connection with the death and burial of his members is a precious portion of his total ministry. The fact that it was he through whom the Lord brought comfort to the members of a family at the time of their bereavement will give him a special place in their hearts and in their prayers. As such cases multiply, the bond between pastor and people will be more and more firmly cemented. Above all, it is at Christian burials that the pastor has the privilege of serving as the ambassador of "the God of all comfort" (2 Cor 1:3).

Summary: Christian burial involves both acknowledging that the deceased died as a believer who will rise again to everlasting life, and bringing comfort to the survivors. The pastor is responsible for the religious features in the funeral and committal services. He will be guided by the general principle that Christian burial will be granted to those who were members of his congregation unless there is a compelling reason not to do so, and will not be granted to others by him unless there is a compelling reason to do so.

13

The Shepherd's Involvement
in Administration

"Decently and in order"
(1 Cor 14:40)

I. THE NEED FOR PASTORAL ADMINISTRATION

The pastor is called by a Christian congregation, and through it by the Lord, to preach the gospel and to administer the sacraments. This, stated most simply, is central in the pastor's call. Jesus made this the disciples' prime responsibility in His Great Commission, Matthew 28:18-20. Very properly the Augsburg Confession speaks of the public preaching of the gospel and the administration of the sacraments as that for which the congregation's call is necessary (AC XIV).

The congregation which the pastor serves with the means of grace, however, is a visible fellowship consisting of specific, recognizable people. It exists in this world and is subject to the conditions and circumstances that are part of a group's mundane existence. For the orderly functioning of a Christian congregation in this created world into which God has placed it some kind of organization with an administrative head is necessary.

There is no biblical mandate stating that the pastor must provide administrative leadership in a congregation. In practice,

304

however, it generally turns out that way. For one thing, it is not always possible to make the clear-cut distinction which is indicated when it is said that the pastor should concern himself with spiritual matters and that others can take care of the church's business and externals. Then, too, the pastor often is the only full-time person involved in the congregation's work and carries the broadest responsibilities. His term of office has no specific limitations. All of this leads to the practical result that he will inevitably need to concern himself with congregational administration. When he fails to do this, an administrative vacuum will almost surely result.

Development in Congregational Organization

In the first New Testament congregation at Jerusalem it seemed only natural for the apostles, chosen and trained by the Lord, to assume a leadership role. This extended into all areas so that they even administered the congregation's gifts that were to provide for the widows and the poor. But as the congregation grew, the task soon became too extensive for the apostles to carry out by themselves. They suggested a plan to the congregation whereby others could be chosen for the administration and distribution of gifts to the widows. The apostles recognized that they must not permit this "serving at tables," as they called it, to come between them and their prime work, that of preaching the gospel.

In the early life of a congregation, the pastor may personally need to take care of much of the administration of the congregation. The life of the congregation and its administration often depend quite directly on the pastor. The entire organization and its functioning may be centered in the pastoral office. As a congregation grows, the pastor can and should divest himself of time consuming administrative duties. He continues to provide leadership, not in the sense of doing all things, but by developing the leadership qualities and potential God has given the members of the congregation and by establishing an organization in which various duties are delegated to a number of people. This can be done even in the smallest of mission congregations. Also the pastor who has native leadership abilities should strive to develop a congregational organization that can function during a vacancy and will not suffer through a change of pastors. Such an organization will demand less of the pastor's time and energy. These he should reserve as much as possible for the teaching and preaching of the gospel, which his call requires of him.

The Church as an Organization

The congregation as an organized body has some characteristics that make it unique, others in which it corresponds to any corporate body functioning in God's created world. The congregation is a confessional fellowship of God's confessing people. In it are gathered such who are priests and kings before God through faith. It is rightfully called a church, for it recognizes the Lord Jesus as its Head. It acknowledges His Word, the Holy Scriptures, as normative in all matters of faith and life. It knows that the Lord Jesus dwells in its midst, that He sends His Spirit to guide and direct it. It functions not only under the general providence of God, as does every organization in the world; it enjoys the special care of its Head, who in grace uses such a gathering of Christians to accomplish His saving purpose.

At the same time it is true that the congregation, like every organization, is made up of people. These people while living in the world are still imperfect. A congregation too is subject to this world's limitations of time and space. It requires earthly goods and property to carry on its business, the Lord's business. If men are to function together as a group, the individual must give up some of his personal freedom for the good of the group as a whole. In the church, too, all things must be done "decently and in order" (1 Cor 14:40), lest the free exercise of one individual's rights results in injury to others and to the group as a whole. St. Paul applies this to the corporate worship life of the congregation in Corinth. The same principle, however, applies to the congregation's entire life and functioning in the world.

The specific structural organization of a church and its orderly procedures are not outlined in nor imposed by Scripture. They will develop according to reason and common sense, with experience serving as a teacher. The church can even draw on the reasoned judgment and the experience of secular organizations for its instruction in this area. "The children of this world" in matters of this kind often prove to be "wiser than the children of light," for the church's first and most direct concern must always remain the eternal gospel. The church may well examine the world's acquired wisdom and experience in administration and organization and use whatever can properly be brought into the service of its gospel work. Robert's *Rules of Order*, for example, has found useful application in conducting meetings also within the church.

Summary: Although the pastor is called to preach the gospel, he cannot escape the responsibility of providing administrative leadership and performing some of its duties. The congregation consists of a group of people living in the world with a need for good order and organization as it does its work. The organization will develop as practical circumstances require. The church may apply also the world's accumulated administrative wisdom and skill to its needs.

II. BASIC PRINCIPLES

Christians unite into a congregation for a reason. The congregation, like any organization, exists for a specific purpose. Certain functions must be carried out so that the purpose of the organization finds fulfillment. Policies are agreed upon that guide the organization's functioning.

Purpose, Objectives, Goals

The purpose for which a congregation exists should have its basis in Scripture, where the Lord speaks of the church's mission. The individual Christian congregation should not have a purpose different from that given by the Lord to His church, to Christians individually and collectively. The Lord has commanded His people to gather together for mutual edification (He 10:25; 1 Cor 14), to preach the gospel for the salvation of souls (Mk 16:15; Mt 28:19), and to be His witnesses to the four corners of the earth (Ac 1:8). To this end He provides His church with the necessary gifts (Eph 4:11,12; Ac 20:28). The purpose of a Christian congregation is to put God's gifts to use in preaching the gospel so that those who hear may be strengthened and preserved in their Christian faith unto life eternal and that the message of salvation may be shared ever more widely with the congregation's community and with the entire world. This is the unique responsibility God assigned to His church and must remain a congregation's reason for existence.

307

A congregation will do well to set down a statement of purpose, possibly in its constitution, and to review this periodically so that it never loses sight of the reason for which God lets it continue in the world. Similarly, the more specific objectives of each congregational program and activity and the goals the congregation sets for itself in a given period should be examined so that they remain in harmony with and contribute toward the fulfillment of the congregation's broad, divinely assigned purpose.

Responsibility and Authority

The congregation engages in a number of activities to accomplish its purpose. Various people will have different roles in carrying out the congregational functions. Good organization calls for a careful defining of responsibilities and the outlining of authority. For example, each person involved in handling the congregation's finances (the treasurer, the financial secretary, the finance committee members) must know what his specific responsibilities are and possess authority commensurate with his assignment. The assigning of responsibility and defining of authority must cover all activities lest an organizational gap result in misunderstanding and confusion. Both the treasurer and the financial secretary, for example, need to know whose responsibility it is to deposit the church's offerings in the bank.

Policies

In its organizational life a congregation will develop policies that guide its orderly functioning. Some of these policies find their basis directly in Scripture. The policy of practicing close communion is based on 1 Corinthians 10:16-21 and 11:28. Other policies are set up in Christian liberty to enable the congregation to carry out its mission consonant with Scripture. Communion announcement is not commanded in Scripture but may help the church administer the sacrament responsibly according to the requirements of Scripture. Still other policies may simply express the congregation's will in adiaphora. The policies that control the use of the church's facilities for weddings are based on a free decision of the congregation. Never, however, may anything be permitted that violates God's Word.

308

The Constitution

The constitution of a congregation serves as an instrument for the orderly administration of its affairs. Scripture neither demands the adoption of a constitution nor does it prescribe organizational forms to the church. There is only the requirement for good order, and even this is not an end in itself but must serve the best interests of the gospel. Experience, however, demonstrates the value of a constitution that defines the purpose and confession of the congregation; that lists the qualifications for membership; that outlines the structure of the organization, listing the qualifications, duties, responsibilities, and authority of the called workers, the council, and the various officers, boards, and committees; that provides for meetings to carry on the church's business.

The constitutional document generally consists of two parts: 1) the constitution proper, and 2) the bylaws. The constitution itself is best kept brief, containing articles that pertain to basic principles that either are unalterable or will require infrequent change. Generally consideration of an amendment to the constitution proper is required at two congregational meetings, with adequate previous publicity and a two-thirds majority necessary for adoption. The bylaws contain the details of congregational organization and functioning. These should be subject to change with greater ease than the constitution itself.

When a congregation is first organized, there is no need for a constitution that is intended to serve for the indefinite future. Simple "model" constitutions are available that serve the needs of a beginning congregation very well. As a congregation grows and its organization becomes more complex, a constitution tailored to its particular needs can replace the simpler "model." The Wisconsin Ev. Lutheran Synod requires synodical approval of the constitution prior to a congregation's reception into membership, as well as the approval of a major revision or complete replacement on the part of congregations already holding membership.

Whatever in the constitution is based on Scripture should not be subject to repeal or alteration. A constitution generally lists those articles which fall into this category. However, the congregation must avoid going beyond Scripture in such a listing of articles. Scripture, for example, does not require confirmation for communicant membership nor does it establish a specific voting age. To make such matters unalterable is to bind consciences beyond Scripture and can create problems in the future.

The provisions of the constitution should be kept current and should be followed with care. If the bylaws no longer outline the details of the congregation's current organization and practices, they become a dead letter and no longer serve in the interest of good order. The pastor must be on guard, however, against a legalistic use of the constitution so that its provisions and policies become a kind of canon law for the church. For example, simply to point to the congregation's constitution as the reason why a member may not belong to the Masonic Order is legalism. The application of policies outlined in the constitution dare not replace gospel motivation and instruction from God's Word.

State laws provide for the incorporation of religious and charitable institutions. At the time of its organization a congregation will do well immediately to seek incorporation. This enables the congregation to function as a legal entity so that it can own property, sign legal contracts, and become liable as a corporation rather than having each member individually be liable. Since state laws pertaining to incorporation vary, a congregation is well advised to seek legal counsel when incorporating.

Summary: The congregation as an organization exists for a purpose. This, according to Scripture, is that the gospel of eternal salvation in Christ may be preached in the congregation and its community and throughout the world. The objectives of all programs and the goals the congregation sets for itself must aim toward fulfilling the congregation's purpose. The congregation will assign responsibilities and set up policies so that its work may proceed in an orderly manner. The constitution is set up as an instrument for the orderly administration of the congregation.

III. CHURCH MEMBERSHIP

Membership in the church is the fruit of the gospel. By means of the message of God's forgiving grace in Christ the Holy Spirit works faith in our Savior's atoning blood. Through this faith the individual becomes a member of Christ's church, "for you are all sons of God through faith in Christ Jesus" (Ga 3:26-NASB). This spiritual membership in Christ's church is of supreme importance since only those who are members of Christ's body share in the treasures of heaven.

The individual who has this faith will confess it. Whoever believes must speak (Ps 116:10-14; 2 Cor 4:13; Ro 10:10). In this way, through their confession, Christians find one another, and a gathering, or congregation, of believers comes into being. Impelled by living faith, they will promote the gospel's proclamation in their midst. Whoever comes to such a gathering of confessing Christians with a confession that agrees with theirs should receive fraternal recognition and be accorded spiritual rights in their midst. Externals like nationality, race, age, sex, financial or social status should not divide those whom God unites in His church through faith and whose unity has become evident from confessions that are in full agreement.

Circumstances will determine how extensive a confession must be sought. In an ecumenically minded world more than a vague confession to the Christian faith is called for, and Lutheran congregations must look for a confession that corresponds to the Lutheran Confessions even if a knowledge of all confessional writings and their detailed contents is not required. Then, too, if a person's life proves his confession to be insincere and false, the church may not ignore such evidence. Cf 2 Corinthians 6:14-17; 1 Corinthians 5:9-13; 10:21.

It is generally the pastor's responsibility to establish the eligibility of those who wish to be received into the fellowship of the congregation. His theological and pastoral training and the call that confers on him the public administration of the means of grace make him a logical choice for this responsibility. The entire congregation could, of course, participate, but such a practice is so cumbersome that it is seldom, if ever, followed. On the other hand, there may be circumstances in which the church council or the board of elders could share this responsibility with the pastor. In any case, it must be carried out in a responsible manner that shows concern for the spiritual welfare of all involved.

It is generally understood that the pastor may receive those whom he finds qualified into communion with the congregation without any formal action on the congregation's part. This applies to those who are applying for membership in the congregation as well as to those who for valid reasons wish to be served by the pastor only temporarily. Children receiving baptism within a

311

congregation become members of Christ's church and of the respective congregation through this sacrament.

Congregational Membership

Scripture does not provide for a particular external form of congregational membership nor direct us to the manner in which such membership should be established. What is of first importance is the bond of unity that is recognized among confessing Christians. What type of external relationship in an organized congregation is then established is a matter of Christian liberty. The injunction to good order should, however, be applied. Hence the congregation's constitution will express itself on membership and how it is established in an orderly manner.

Usually the application for membership is to be made through the pastor. This may be done orally or in writing. A congregation may provide a convenient "application for membership" form that asks for the pertinent information. (See Appendix.)

The pastor must establish the qualifications of the applicant. Those who come from a sister congregation (one in confessional fellowship) should receive a letter of transfer from their previous congregation. Such a transfer is evidence of the person's confessional agreement with the receiving congregation, establishes that no moral hindrance prevents his reception, and recommends him to the spiritual care of the receiving sister church. A transfer generally is adequate to establish a person's qualifications for membership.

In the case of such who come from Lutheran congregations not in fellowship with the receiving church, the pastor will need to establish that they hold to Scripture as the inspired, inerrant Word of God and to the Lutheran symbols as a true exposition of Scripture. Of these symbols they should have studied Luther's Small Catechism. The pastor will want to be certain that the applicant is not attempting to evade proper discipline and is not a member of an antichristian association, e.g., a lodge. The applicant must understand that his joining the present congregation will preclude any further practice of fellowship with his former church. There should be evidence that the applicant has either been released from his former congregation or has resigned. Except in cases where the Lutheran orthodoxy and Christian knowledge of the applicant are unmistakably evident the pastor will recommend attendance at his Bible information class (cf chapter on

Education, p 125f). This will not only assure the church of the applicant's eligibility, but also make the applicant's decision to join this particular congregation more meaningful. The above applies also to confirmed Lutherans whose membership in a Lutheran congregation had lapsed. Their reception on the basis of a confession of faith will best be effected after attending a Bible information class.

Whoever has not been a member of any Lutheran church (non-Lutherans, non-Christians, or such who have no formal religion of any kind) becomes eligible for membership through the confession of faith (at the time of baptism or confirmation) to which it is hoped the Bible information class will lead him. The pastor will need to determine whether such a person was baptized and whether his baptism was a valid one. If the answer is negative or doubtful, the applicant will be baptized upon completion of the necessary instruction for membership. In such cases the form used will cover confessional agreement and the desire for communicant status so that the rite of confirmation becomes superfluous.

Upon finding an applicant qualified for membership, the pastor may announce his application to the congregation and present it to the church council for recommendation to the voters' assembly for final action. Or a congregation may assign to the church council the actual reception into membership with subsequent ratification by the voters' assembly. The *Lutheran Agenda* provides a form for receiving new members in the public worship service of the congregation. This may be used on the Sunday after the meeting in which the formal resolution was passed and serves to stress the spiritual implications of church membership and the Christian fellowship that is its most significant element.

The membership of a congregation is customarily listed under three categories. These find their origin not merely in an arbitrary decision of the congregation but result from the application of certain scriptural principles to the life of the church. Every baptized person associated with the congregation, from the newly baptized infant to the aged shut-in, is counted in its total membership (souls). Those in the congregation's membership who possess the spiritual maturity and understanding called for by Scripture for the reception of Holy Communion are counted as communicant members. A portion of the latter constitutes the voting membership.

Voting Rights

The church as a Christian fellowship has certain functions to perform. It calls pastors and teachers. It elects those who are to perform the work necessary for its life as a congregation. It carries out church discipline. It purchases property and does whatever is called for by property ownership. All of these activities call for making decisions. Certain people must make them, and as soon as a group is involved, this happens through the process of voting.

As a legal corporation the congregation has certain people who legally are recognized as its members and possess the legal right to make decisions for the corporate body. In practice, the same group of voters will act for the church as a Christian fellowship as well as for the congregation as a legal corporation.

The right to make decisions by voting is a leadership role. It is a means of ruling the body. It is an exercise of authority. For this reason certain scriptural principles must find application in deciding the question of voting rights.

Scripture calls for obedience on the part of children to their parents and to their elders (cf 1 Pe 5:5; Col 3:20). Children are not to exercise authority over their elders nor to rule over them. This, therefore, excludes children from active participation in the voting process. Scripture, however, nowhere prescribes the exact age at which a child should be considered an adult and accorded adult rights. It is most natural for a congregation to follow the customs of the culture in which it finds itself unless these clearly violate God's Word. In the past the voting age was generally placed at 21, following the laws of the state. When these laws changed the age of legal adulthood to 18, many congregations found this acceptable also in the church. If, however, this age were reduced much further, the church might ask whether requirements of the Fourth Commandment are not being evaded.

According to 1 Corinthians 14:34,35 and 1 Timothy 2:12-14 women are not to speak in the church but to subject themselves; they are not to teach nor to exercise authority over a man. It should be noted that Paul does not base this on a custom of the day but on what the law says, that is, God's Word in the book of the law, and on the order of creation, Adam having been created first, and Eve as a helper for him. Paul is concerned not with preserving a custom of his day, but with maintaining the male-fe-

314

male relationship God established in creation. This is not to be subverted in the church. In these texts Scripture, it is true, does not specifically refer to voting rights, yet the speaking and teaching that go with the discussion leading up to the vote and the authority that is exercised in the voting process show the validity of its application to voting in mixed assemblies. That a woman may teach in the church when the question of exercising authority over the man is not involved should be self-evident (as in teaching children in the Sunday school and the Christian day school). That she may vote in ladies' groups also goes without saying. It would likewise be a legalistic application of these passages to prohibit a woman from protesting against what she in conscience considers an unscriptural action of the congregation, since this involves the truth of God's Word.

On the other hand, to allow women the right to vote on all matters in the church except those directly involving the means of grace (like calling a pastor or excommunicating an impenitent member) is an arbitrary distinction not found in Scripture. The principle God wants upheld has a broader application than simply to decisions that involve the means of grace.

Scripture thus supports the limitation of voting rights to the adult male members, without defining the exact age of adulthood. Since the congregation is also a legal corporation, a specific manner of gaining voting rights is necessary, even though Scripture is silent on this point. This will generally require acceptance as a voting member by a congregational resolution and signing of the congregation's constitution. The pastor and male teachers through their calls become voting members of the congregation. The pastor will need to show good judgment in the extent to which he practices this right, especially if it appears that his vote might become the deciding one. His right to speak will be more influential in preventing a decision that violates Scripture than his lone vote, and the right of protest always remains.

Termination of Membership

Besides death, there are several ways in which a person's membership in a congregation is terminated. Whoever wishes to join another congregation that is in confessional fellowship may make such a change of membership through a *transfer*. Application for a transfer should normally be made to the pastor of the congregation from which a transfer is desired. The request should prefer-

315

ably come from the member desiring it rather than from the pastor of the congregation which the member wishes to join. A transfer does what the term says — it transfers the membership from one congregation to another specific congregation. The letter of transfer should be sent to the pastor of the receiving congregation and possibly a copy sent to the member as a matter of information. A letter of transfer is issued only to a congregation with whom the transferring congregation knows itself to be in doctrinal unity.[1] A transfer also implies that the person whose membership is being transferred has been a member in good standing in the congregation which he is leaving.

A *release*, in contrast to a transfer, is a simple statement that a member at his request has been released from membership in a congregation. It is not a recommendation to another congregation. This may be used when a transfer cannot be issued because a recommendation to the congregation someone wishes to join cannot be made. Although earnest efforts will be made to dissuade a person from joining a heterodox church, a congregation cannot force anyone to remain in its membership against his wishes. A release breaks the fellowship bond without denying the possible presence of saving faith. A release differs little from the acknowledgment of a resignation from membership.

If a member's doctrinal views change and he persists in them in spite of admonition, this may call for suspension of fellowship. This, too, releases a person from membership but with the initiative for it generally taken by the congregation. This action assumes that the erroneous views are not such as make the presence of Christian faith impossible.

Excommunication is called for when through the application of Matthew 18:15-17 it becomes evident that the person under discipline has through impenitence lost the saving faith. This action not only expels from the congregational organization, but declares the impenitent person to be no longer a member of the church, the body of Christ, and so on the way to damnation. In this way this action differs from a release or severance of fellowship.

---

1. If a pastor of the Wisconsin Synod does not know what congregation to recommend to a parishioner moving into an area where Wisconsin Synod congregations are sparse, he should send the name and address to WELS Soul Conservation, 10729 Worden, Detroit, Michigan 48224.

There are times when it becomes necessary simply to *remove* someone from the congregation's membership roster. If a congregation over a longer period of time is unable to establish contact with a member who has moved, it may assume that this person no longer wants to be considered a member or may have joined another church. He may then be dropped from membership. Such a procedure should, however, not replace the admonition and discipline that the congregation owes delinquent members who are accessible.

Summary: Membership in a congregation presupposes unity of faith. The pastor is responsible for establishing an individual's eligibility for membership. A transfer from a sister congregation constitutes eligibility. The pastor will need to determine whether those who are to be received by profession of faith are in confessional unity with the congregation and have had adequate instruction in the Word of God. More often than not a Bible information course is advisable. Whoever has previously received no instruction in Lutheran doctrine becomes eligible for membership through his confession of faith made on the basis of the instruction received in a Bible information class. The congregation will receive all who are in confessional agreement. The membership is generally grouped into three categories, souls, communicants, and voters, based on the application of certain Scriptural principles to the life of the church. Termination of membership may occur, apart from death, by transfer, release (including suspension of fellowship), excommunication, or removal. The manner of termination will be determined by the circumstances of the case.

IV. THE ORGANIZATIONAL STRUCTURE

What form the congregational organization will take is a matter of Christian liberty. Scripture does not provide a list of required officers. All of this will develop according to need (cf Ac 6:1ff) and will not be identical in all congregations. Everything that is necessary for the furtherance of the congregation's gospel ministry should be included but no more. The constitution will outline the structure of the congregation and list the responsibilities of the various officers, boards, and committees.

Voters' Assembly

The largest administrative group in a congregation is the voters' assembly. Complete and final authority is vested in this most inclusive meeting of the congregation's voters. Thus it will make all important decisions, formulate policies, hear reports, and hold elections. Other groups and officers have only those responsibilities and privileges which the voters' assembly assigns to them. The size of the congregation may determine the extent to which the voters delegate responsibility, especially to the church council. Larger congregations may ask the council to assume a more comprehensive role than smaller churches, where the congregational meeting may be able to concern itself with a greater proportion of its more limited amount of business. It is to be hoped that a maximum of four or five meetings per year may suffice to conduct the congregation's regular business lest too frequent meetings result in decreased attendance.

Church Council

Generally the church council plays a key role in the congregation's organization. Many of the details of congregational business may be delegated to it. It may make certain decisions for the congregation, at least tentatively, between meetings of the voters' assembly. The various boards and committees usually report first to the council and thus through it to the congregation. The council may be asked to make certain appointments, especially to positions that do not lend themselves well to election by the entire congregation. It is a sound principle of church administration to have the council discuss in a preliminary way the business that is to come before a congregational meeting and to make recommendations. Because of its broad responsibilities the council must receive corresponding authority. It may have to consider some of the matters discussed as confidential.

The council should have in its membership the chief officers of the congregation, e.g., the president, secretary, treasurer, and financial secretary. It should include representation from the various boards and possibly the more important standing committees, e.g., those concerned with stewardship and evangelism. The constitution may designate either the pastor or the congregation's president as chairman. The secretary of the congregation is expected to serve also the council in this capacity. In most congregations regular monthly meetings will be adequate, with special meetings called only if business arises that cannot wait for the regular meeting.

318

Three Boards

The congregation's functions and responsibilities may be conveniently divided among three important boards, the board of elders, the board of trustees, and the board of education. The members of these boards, or at least their chairmen, should belong to the church council.

The board of elders has the special assignment to aid the pastor in the spiritual affairs of the church. The elders will have the general responsibility for good order in the worship service. They may assist the pastor in visiting the delinquent members and in cases of discipline.

The board of trustees is responsible for the congregation's finances and its property. The trustees concern themselves with the maintenance of the congregation's property and supervise the janitorial work. The treasurer may function under their direction. Generally they are designated as the legal representatives of the incorporated congregation.

The board of education concerns itself with all the educational agencies of the congregation. In a congregation with a Christian day school this agency will undoubtedly require a great part of the board's attention. However, the other educational agencies should also be its concern. It may choose the Sunday school superintendent and help secure Sunday school teachers. It may assist in planning and promoting the vacation Bible school and Bible classes. The board may periodically evaluate the congregation's total educational efforts and seek to improve and promote them in every possible way.

Committees

Besides the above three boards there may be quite a variety of committees, most of which may serve under the direction of one of these boards. Those most frequently found are the following: evangelism, stewardship, finance, budget, auditing, nominating, ushering, property and grounds, and salary review committees. The congregation should not forget that it needs delegates for representation at conferences and conventions. The needs and circumstances of each congregation will have to determine what boards and committees should be a part of its organization. The

319

Lord's business calls for His people's best efforts. This includes also an efficiently functioning organization.

In the selection of qualified persons for the various offices and committees, the congregation will keep in mind the words of Scripture in 1 Timothy 3:8-13 and 5:22. While there is no direct command for following the procedure used in the selection of the deacons in Acts 6, it can serve as a worthy example. First the qualifications required for the office were cataloged; then the people possessing these qualifications were listed; from these the congregation selected those who were to serve.

A smaller group like a nominating committee lends itself best to selecting those who have the qualifications for a particular position. It will be the pastor's responsibility to keep the scripturally required qualifications before the nominating committee and the congregation. In addition, he may be the one person in the congregation who is familiar with the entire membership so that his role in the nominating committee is an important one. Sometimes it may be felt that new and less active members may be drawn into the life of the church more fully by placing them into an office or on a committee. Nevertheless, for the more responsible positions, Paul's words, "Lay hands suddenly on no man" and "Let these first be proved," should find application. It should be understood by all members of the nominating committee that what is said in its meetings remains confidential.

It is important that each officer and member of a board or committee know exactly what his responsibilities are and to whom he is accountable. It should not be assumed that those elected or appointed will know what their duties are without instruction. But before the congregation can instruct the individual, it must determine exactly what it expects of him. Carefully written job descriptions are helpful in determining whether all of the congregation's necessary functions have been properly provided for and will help to instruct each person concerning his responsibility.

Meetings

It is important that all meetings, whether regular or special, of both the congregation and the church council be called according to the provisions of the constitution. The validity of a meeting and its decisions, if irregularly called, could be questioned by any member of the congregation. What constitutes a quorum will be

320

determined by the constitution. For the voters' assembly the percentage required should not be set too high lest failure to have a quorum present become a frequent problem. Most often a quorum consists of those members present at a properly announced meeting. In the case of the church council, it would hardly be wise to transact business with less than half of the council present. A higher percentage is surely preferable.

The pastor will encourage wide participation in the voters' meetings. Such encouragement will, however, avoid legalistic coercion of any kind. One cannot insist that everyone's sanctification must find expression in this particular way even though it is recognized that the business of the voters' meeting is important. Those, however, who have been elected to the council and the various offices and have accepted the positions should recognize the importance of faithfulness in this special trust committed to them. Their attendance at meetings should be considered a self-evident part of holding office.

The pastor's particular concern will be that nothing is done at any meeting which does violence to the Word of God or that conflicts with the spirit of the gospel. He will open the meetings with prayer, preferably spoken *ex corde*. A prayer, a hymn stanza, and/or the benediction will close the meeting in a manner befitting Christians.

The pastor will also promote good order at all meetings. This begins by starting the meetings promptly at the time announced. Delay in beginning a meeting is a discourtesy to those who have arrived on time and encourages those who are late to continue their bad practice. A printed agenda, distributed to all present, may promote good order and help avoid disorganized discussion and tedious, drawn-out meetings. Let the pastor discipline himself lest he fail to speak to the point and lest he speak too long and too often. Although the pastor frequently serves as chairman of the church council, he should avoid serving in this capacity at the voters' meeting.

Church Records

Part of good organization are well kept records. The secretary of the congregation is responsible for the minutes of all voters' and council meetings. These should be carefully written, adopted, and preserved so that they are a permanent record for future reference to decisions made at the meetings. The financial secretary, perhaps with the assistance of a finance committee, receives and records the contributions of all members; the treasurer keeps an account of all receipts and of all disbursements he makes in behalf of the congregation. Their record books should be audited at least annually.

The pastor is responsible for the statistical records of the congregation. These must be kept with care so that they are current and accurate. In smaller congregations the pastor may make the entries into the records himself. This should be done as soon as the pastoral act that needs to be recorded has been performed. To delay until there is an accumulation of entries makes the task tedious and may result in incomplete records. Application forms for the various pastoral acts will help assure that all necessary information is secured so that the records will be complete. A larger congregation may provide secretarial assistance to the pastor so that not too much of the pastor's time is consumed with work that can well be done by a secretary. Well kept records will enable the pastor to provide the Synod with a statistical report promptly when it is requested.

Some records should be of a permanent nature and are therefore best recorded in a bound book. This includes the records of baptisms, confirmations, weddings, funerals, possibly of the installation of pastors and teachers, of the congregation's officers and council members. Part of the permanent record should be a chronology of important events in the congregation.

The working records of the congregation must be flexible so that they can readily be kept up to date. These include the list of the congregation's membership, its souls, communicants, and voters, as well as a record of communion attendance. Either a card or looseleaf file allows for entries and removals while keeping the list alphabetical.[2] The importance of keeping an accurate record is evident when the pastor prepares his annual report and when there is a change of pastors.

A pastor may wish to keep a personal chronological record of his ministry. While the permanent and working records of the congregation remain its property, the pastor may find it de-

2. the Rossin Church Records include a convenient looseleaf record for communion attendance. These forms are available at The Shepherd Co., Hopkins, Minn. 55343.

sirable, or at least interesting, to have a record of his ministry that he can take with him, should he move to another parish.

Public Image of the Church

The congregation as an organization presents an image to people, both to those within the congregation and to those without. Good organization will concern itself also with the church's image. This must remain a truthful one. The church must be willing to bear whatever reproach faithfulness to Christ and His Word brings upon it. But let it not add to this reproach through faults of its own. If pastors "must have a good reputation with those outside the church" (1 Tm 3:7-NASB), the same applies to the congregations they serve. Dusty pews and soiled walls, a poorly printed bulletin with spelling and grammar mistakes will hardly impress the visitor at divine worship. There is no virtue in having the church property look rundown and unkept, as though the church meant little to its members. Bulletin boards and church signs that would fit into a ghost town project a poor image. Let both the pastor and congregation guard their reputation so that the gospel may not suffer through their neglect.

Summary: The voters' assembly is the largest administrative group of the congregation and possesses final authority in all congregational affairs. It may assign to the church council a rather comprehensive role so that the council, which includes the congregation's officers, may attend to many of the details of congregational business. The congregation's functions and business are generally divided among a board of elders, a board of trustees, and a board of education. Besides those concerned with evangelism and stewardship, a number of committees may complete the congregation's organization. For effective operation the congregation must inform each official and board or committee member what his specific duties are, to whom he is responsible, and what authority is granted him. Meetings should be called and conducted according to the constitutional requirements. The pastor in particular is responsible that the Word of God suffers no violence in any way at the various meetings. Good order and organization call for well kept records. A poor public image of the church must not add to the reproach of the gospel.

V. PASTORAL LEADERSHIP

Definition

Leadership has been defined as "the work a person does to enable people to work most effectively together."[3] If a congregation is to fulfill its God-given purpose, the edification of Christ's church through the gospel, then the effective working together of its members is vital. This must be a working together that is not merely an end in itself, but a working together aimed at the purpose, objectives, and goals the congregation recognizes as its own. Pastoral leadership is to help attain such purposeful working together.

Some men possess natural leadership abilities. The nature and strength of their personalities attracts people and invites cooperation. In a congregation's early life such leadership may serve it well. However, if the pastor's leadership remains dependent on his personality, the congregation may remain dependent on the one man and never grow into maturity in its functioning as an organization. What is more, not all pastors possess such natural leadership abilities. Pastoral leadership must depend not merely on the pastor's natural ability to lead. He must consciously seek to develop those qualities that will enable him to provide leadership. He will need to learn and to perform those functions that help a group of people in a congregation to work together most effectively toward their common purpose.

Qualifications

There is no need to repeat the various qualifications for the ministry as outlined in Scripture (cf chapter 1, "The Shepherd"). That these all have a part in making the pastor a good leader of God's people goes without saying. We shall, however, here take note of some qualifications that have a rather direct bearing on the pastor's leadership role and can affect the type of pastoral leadership he may be able to provide.

A *spirit of service* on the part of the pastor will inspire others to serve. This does not mean that the pastor serves by simply doing everything that needs to be done in a congregation, but that he knows and shows that he is there to serve the congregation, even

3. Louis A. Allen, *The Management Profession* (New York: McGraw-Hill, 1964), p 6.

324

beyond the requirements specifically spelled out in the call. He is there to serve the congregation and not the congregation to serve him. This will make the pastor a true leader rather than a dictator. The latter says: Do as I say. The leader with a spirit of service invites: Serve as I serve.

The pastor's *love for people* will promote good leadership. He will look upon and respect the members as priests of God. This will prevent his speaking down to people from a lofty pastoral pedestal, a practice that would hardly result in a willing, joyful working together of pastor and congregation.

The pastor's own *well-disciplined* life will promote good organization and purposeful activity within the congregation. If the pastor in his own life drifts along aimlessly, the congregation that looks to him for leadership is in danger of doing the same. The pastor who recognizes priorities in his life and practices self-discipline in following them inspires confidence and can hope to develop a purposeful spirit in the congregation he serves.

An *open objectivity* will prevent the pastor's being overly critical of what others propose and overly proud of his own ideas. The pastor needs to be able to judge and evaluate, openly, objectively, not becoming sensitive and even angry if a congregation does not look to him for every good idea and for a solution to every practical problem. He is a true leader when he can get the members to work together toward finding the best way to attain their goals.

A *spirit of urgency but not impatience* on his part will lead a congregation to recognize that the Lord's work requires haste. "The night cometh when no man can work" (Jn 9:4). At the same time this spirit of urgency must not let the pastor become impatient with those who tend toward caution and require a longer time to arrive at a decision. He must lead them to see the urgency of the Lord's work and not impatiently force them into unwilling submission.

Functions

Detailed attention has been given to the pastor's leadership role in the congregation's organizations. Some other leadership functions as they apply to the pastor have been mentioned in passing or given only brief consideration. Several should be considered more fully.

1. Planning

Important for any organization is the function of planning. The church, as it looks to the future, needs to plan. Each week a service must be planned. Special festivals must be planned during the course of the year. The congregation must plan its educational program, its mission activity, its finances. It may even look farther into the future and plan a building program.

Planning tries to affect the future. There is always the hope that what is planned will happen. Scripture commends wise planning. It is foolish to begin building a tower without careful planning, also of the finances required to complete it (Lk 14:28). But in planning, the church will always remember the Lord's warning: "Ye know not what shall be on the morrow" (Jas 4:14). The church must not forget to say: "If the Lord will, we shall live, and do this, or that" (Jas 4:15). Whether spoken or not, a Christian's planning will be done with the thought ever present, "If the Lord will."

Planning involves a number of activities. Louis A. Allen in *The Management Profession* lists seven activities as part of planning: forecasting, establishing objectives, programming, scheduling, budgeting, establishing procedures, developing policies.[4] We shall examine each briefly, noting their application to the church's planning function.

Forecasting is an attempt on the part of the manager "to anticipate the conditions, problems and opportunities that will probably confront him at future periods of time."[5] A congregation, for example, that is planning a new school building will try to anticipate its enrollment at given times in the future. Projections are made, estimating the population growth in the area, the increase in membership in the congregation, the enrollment in the school. One can hardly conceive of planning which does not include some form of forecasting.

Establishing objectives is the work of "determining the end results to be accomplished."[6] A congregation may have the objective or goal of paying its building debt within two years. The evangelism committee may have the objective of finding and entering with the gospel every unchurched home within a certain

4. See note 3.
5. Allen, p 69.
6. *Ibid.*

number of blocks around the church during the next year. In its educational functions the church sets up objectives which are to be accomplished. All this results in purposeful planning and working. The importance of stating a congregation's purpose, objectives, and goals was discussed earlier in this chapter.

Programming concerns itself with establishing the specific activities that will be followed in order to reach the objectives. The evangelism committee may decide on the canvass of a designated area. The stewardship committee may decide on an every member visit. The pastor may choose a particular series of texts to follow in his sermons. In 1 Corinthians 16:2 St. Paul outlined a program for gathering the offerings for the saints in Jerusalem.

Scheduling consists of establishing "the time sequence of action steps to be followed in reaching objectives."[7] The evangelism canvass is to be so timed that prospects can be channeled into the pastor's Bible information class at the right time. In planning a vacation Bible school the recruiting of personnel, the ordering of materials, the training of teachers, the publicity must be so scheduled that the steps are taken in proper sequence with adequate time for each to be carried out. Paul too set up a schedule for gathering the offering at Corinth, calling for its completion by the time he would arrive so that the Corinthians might then take the next step of choosing those who should bring the offering to Jerusalem. Scheduling looks not only at what will be done on the next week and the following Sunday. Setting up a church calendar for an entire year can help avoid annoying conflicts. Long range programs will require long range scheduling.

Budgeting involves the allocation of resources that are necessary to accomplish objectives. It seeks to prevent thoughtless and useless spending, lest an activity must be abandoned for lack of funds. Note again Jesus' parable in Luke 14:28-30 of the builder who had to abandon his tower for lack of proper financing. The church will, however, need to realize that an element of faith is involved in its budgeting process since its resources consist of voluntary offerings, brought as a fruit of faith. The congregation's budget committee is involved in this phase of the planning process.[8]

---

7. *Ibid.*
8. Cf "Building the Budget" in the *Stewardship Workbook* (Milwaukee: Wis. Ev. Lutheran Synod Stewardship Office, 1971), pp 15-23.

Establishing procedures, according to Allen, "is the work a manager performs to develop and apply standardized methods of performing specified work,"[9] and *developing policies* is defined as the work of interpreting "standing decisions that apply to repetitive questions and problems of significance to the enterprise as a whole."[10] A congregation may establish a procedure for the counting and depositing of the money contributed. It may develop a policy concerning the use of church property. Care must be practiced lest procedures and policies which are in themselves adiaphora become so fixed that they attain a hallowed status by virtue of tradition. Periodic and systematic review of procedures and policies is therefore highly desirable.

That these activities are to a greater or lesser degree part of congregational planning is evident, whether a congregation realizes this or not. To carry out these activities quite consciously in its planning may result in better planning. In this the pastor can provide leadership. This does not mean that the pastor is to do all the planning, but that he leads the congregation to carry out all activities that are part of good planning.

2. Decision Making

For plans to result in action, decisions need to be made. A plan remains a plan until the decision is made to follow it. In a congregation the making of some decisions is assigned to the pastor, the council, or to officers, boards, and committees. Many decisions, especially the more important, will be made by the voters' assembly.

For effective working together, it is important that as many of the members as possible know what the decision is and join in supporting it. Hence *communicating* and *motivating* are important activities associated with the making of decisions. Those responsible for planning need to communicate to the voters' assembly the necessary information for making a decision and motivate them to agree to the decision as adopted. Or it may be that those who have been responsible for making a decision need to inform the entire membership of it and provide motivation for wholehearted, active support of the decision. For example, the

9. Allen, p 69.
10. *Ibid.*

budget committee must communicate to the voters' assembly and congregation the rationale for a 10 per cent increase in the mission budget and provide motivation for such action. A favorable decision by the voters' assembly would require further communication and motivation aimed at the entire membership to be successful.

Communicating is important because it leads to understanding. The members are led to understand what is involved in a decision and why it was made. Bulletins, a regular newsletter, reports, special information meetings or home visits are some of the means that can be used to communicate proposals for decision and to gain support for those that have been made. Good information and understanding can hope to develop wide support for worthy programs.

Motivating will inspire, encourage, and impel people to make and support decisions. That only such motivation should be used as is in harmony with God's Word is self-evident. Christian motivation must find its roots in the gospel.

Experience shows that leadership on the part of the pastor in making decisions and in the communicating and motivating which they require is essential. This does not mean that he must do this alone or in a way that puts him into the limelight. In fact, it is better if he does so without ostentation to avoid any impression that the projects and decisions are primarily his and the possibility that they are carried out by the people as a favor to the pastor. Too much then depends on the popularity of one man.

3. Implementation

A resolution remains a resolution until it is implemented. Someone must carry out the action called for by the decision of the congregation. If the responsibilities of the various officers, boards, and committees are clearly defined, it should generally be evident who is to implement a particular resolution. The trustees can expect to implement the resolution to purchase a new lawn mower, while the elders will recognize their responsibility for the resolution that calls for organizing a group of men to greet people as they come to church. Should there be any question about implementation, the congregation or church council should assign the responsibility when the resolution is passed.

The pastor's leadership role does not mean that he will personally become involved in the implementation of most if not all resolutions. Only those that pertain to his pastoral work will be his direct responsibility. The pastor can expect to implement a resolution to have a guest preacher for an anniversary service. Resolutions that would involve him in the kind of work the apostles called "serving at tables" are better not made his direct responsibility. The congregation has members with a variety of gifts. These can serve in positions which entail responsibility for carrying out the congregation's decisions. Pastoral leadership will be involved in tapping this reservoir of talent and putting it to good use in the life and work of the congregation. The pastor will be alert to discover the abilities and gifts that are possessed by the congregation's members. He will encourage wise selection of responsible officers in accordance with their varied gifts (cf again the work of the nominating committee). Responsible, meaningful lay involvement in the congregational organization will result in personnel that will implement decisions in accordance with the wishes of the congregation.

4. Self-examination

A congregation must never forget that it has been called to do the Lord's business. That demands its best efforts. But a congregation is made up of people, fallible sinners, gloriously redeemed, but still fallible. A congregation will never be satisfied that it is doing the Lord's work so well that it could not be done better. The need for improvement and ways of improving may become evident as a result of self-examination.

At the conclusion of a year the boards and committees may pause to examine how well they have carried out their assigned tasks. Preparing a report for the council and congregation may provide occasion for such a self-evaluation. They can ask themselves questions such as these: What were our assigned responsibilities? What were our objectives and goals? How well did we accomplish these? What remains undone? Are there better ways of reaching our objectives than those we used? They may ask more specific questions. The elders, for example, may ask: How was the church and communion attendance? Have we concerned ourselves adequately with the delinquent members? What can be done to bring the admonition of Scripture to them more effectively? The evangelism committee may ask: Into how many unchurched homes has our congregation brought the gospel? Have we followed up all leads? How mission-minded is our congregation? How well does it support synodical mission work? Where can we improve? Similarly each board and committee can ask itself questions about its work, examining past performance, looking for areas of improvement in the future.

As the pastor and congregation thus examine themselves, they will, looking to the cross, pray, "Lord, in mercy forgive our past failures." But trusting in God's promises, they will add, "Give us wisdom and strength for future service and bless all that is done in the interest of the gospel."

Summary: The pastor will provide leadership toward bringing about an effective working together on the part of the congregation's members. To that end, the pastor should cultivate a spirit of service, love for people, self-discipline, open objectivity, and a spirit of urgency that does not, however, lead to impatience. Leadership involves certain functions. Important among them are planning, making decisions, implementing them, and self-examination. At all times the pastor and congregation must remember that the Lord's business calls for their best efforts.

For Additional Reading

Allen, Louis A. *The Management Profession*. New York: McGraw-Hill, 1964.

This volume describes the work of a professional manager of a business corporation. The pastor too is involved in management functions and can profit from the author's insights even if everything is not directly applicable to the pastor's circumstances.

Leach, William H. *Handbook of Church Management*. Englewood Cliffs, N.J.: Prentice Hall, 1958.

All phases of church administration are covered in this handbook of over 500 pages.

Merkens, Guido A. *Organized for Action*. St. Louis: Concordia, 1959.

What is presented in this volume has been tested by the author during "rich years of practical experience." A suggested "Officers Manual" is especially helpful for outlining the responsibilities of officers, boards, and committees. The chapters on "Records" and "Keeping the Membership Informed" provide a variety of suggestions.

Schaller, Lyle E. *Parish Planning*. Nashville: Abingdon, 1971.

The author, a church planner and consultant, discusses among other topics, the church budget, the importance of self-evaluation and accountability, and the implementation process.

Walz, Edgar. *Church Business Methods*. St. Louis: Concordia, 1970.

Contains many helpful suggestions about congregational organization, church records, financial matters, and building maintenance. A chapter on "Legal Aspects of Church Business" can alert pastor and congregation to aspects of church business in which legal advice should be sought. Included is a chapter on "Public Relations Aspects of Church Business."

14

The Shepherd
and Organizations

*"For brethren to dwell
together in unity"*
(Ps 133:1)

The congregation, its members, and the pastor will become involved with various types of organizations. Some are limited to the congregation, others have wider connections with members from other congregations of the Synod, still others are not church-related but do seek to enlist members from among the church's ranks. The pastor's responsibility will vary according to the type of organization involved.

I. ORGANIZATIONS WITHIN THE CHURCH

Various types of organizations may be found within a congregation. Most common are women's guilds, men's clubs, youth organizations, and church choirs. There may be a couples' club, a parent-teacher society, and an altar guild. Although many types of organizations are found within congregations, the pastor need not consider it his responsibility to organize every type within his particular congregation so that one is available to every age level and for every purpose. Organizations should develop because of a need for them that is felt by both the people and the pastor.

Some church organizations have ties beyond the congregational bounds. Youth groups may seek contact with those of other congregations within a circuit or conference. A women's mission guild may be a part of a synodical mission society.[1] A local Lutheran Pioneers train[2] has connections with the national organization.

The pastor will recognize that the organizational life of the church is an adiaphoron as long as it does not violate good order or involve itself with anything contrary to Scripture.

Role in the Congregation

Organizations serve an auxiliary role in the congregation. They do not exist to replace the congregation in any way. Attendance at organizational functions should not be made a matter of conscience. Primary is attendance at divine services where the Word is preached and the sacraments are dispensed. To insist that a family is more Christian when all its members attend all and sundry organizations of the church may in fact prove disruptive of family life. Nevertheless, an organization may provide opportunity for further spiritual growth and the practice of one's Christian faith together with fellow Christians. It can assist the congregation in organizing programs of service helpful to the church.

Any organization within a congregation should be brought into existence through a congregational resolution, is responsible to the congregation, and can be dissolved by the congregation. This is true also of organizations with ties beyond the congregation. They, too, must remain under the supervision of the congregation. The pastor most often is the link between the congregation and its organizations. Periodic reports to the congregation from each organization can preserve the sense of accountability both within the organization and the congregation as such.

---

1. The women of the Wisconsin Ev. Lutheran Synod are organized in a national organization, the "Lutheran Women's Missionary Society." The address at which information about this society is available is found in the *Wisconsin Evangelical Lutheran Synod Yearbook* under "Church Related Organizations."
2. See the *Wisconsin Evangelical Lutheran Synod Yearbook* under "Church Related Organizations" for the address of the central office of the Lutheran Pioneers.

Objectives

An important objective of the church's organizations is growth in Christian knowledge. Although the various organizations are not considered a direct part of the congregation's educational program, they can serve an important educational function. At most meetings time can be allotted to the discussion of a topic of interest. The type of organization, its specific functions, the age level of its members and their particular concerns, problems facing the church and its members as pilgrims in the world, will suggest topics that can profitably be discussed in the light of Scripture. The members may be asked for topic suggestions. The presentation should not be permitted to become monotonously long and is best kept informal. It is better to speak freely from notes than to read the presentation. Time for questions and discussion is important. The pastor will find it helpful to plan the program and topics of the various organizations for a year at a time. In this way he can work ahead and need not search before each meeting for a suitable topic. In some organizations guest lecturers are in place. Growth in Christian knowledge must remain an important objective of the church's organizations.

Christian Fellowship

Christians will be drawn to one another by their common faith in Christ. Having experienced the riches of God's love through the redemption purchased with Jesus' blood, they will recognize the truth of what John writes: "If God so loved us, we ought also to love one another" (1 Jn 4.11). John points out that we cannot claim to love the unseen God if we do not love our fellow Christians whom we see about us in the world. "This commandment have we from him, That he who loveth God love his brother also" (1 Jn 4:21).

The congregation's organizations can provide opportunity for Christians to be with one another and experience Christian fellowship. Through the church and particularly through contacts within its organizations Christians may form friendships that carry over into their social life in general. The organizations through their activities may provide opportunity also for the entire congregation's membership to assemble for Christian fellowship.

Care must, however, be exercised lest the Christian fellowship enjoyed in an organization degenerate into cliques and factions

335

within the congregation. Fellowship within a particular organization should not be viewed as establishing an elite group, thus fostering a pharisaical spirit.

Christian Service

The third objective of the congregation's organizations is to provide opportunity for Christian service. The pastor can direct this service into proper channels by suggestions that will avoid commercializing motives and serve a useful purpose. To provide for the church's sick and shut-ins, to assist in its divine services, to care for its property and implement its programs, Christian service of various types is called for and can be rendered according to ability. Organizations can undertake projects that benefit the church at large, that assist its missionaries, that show concern for the needy in the world. The heart in which Christ dwells by faith looks for opportunities to serve the Lord Jesus by reaching out to the need of even the least of His brothers (cf Mt 25:34-40).

These three objectives will not be present in all organizations in the same way. The altar guild will have service as its major objective while the couples' club may provide especially for Christian fellowship. Some may give more opportunity for growth in Christian knowledge than others, although this objective always deserves special emphasis. That an organization must be eliminated if all three objectives are not met cannot be said. However, the pastor will hold these objectives before each organization lest all three are lost and the organization no longer has reason to bear the name of the church.

The extent to which an organization needs formal structuring to keep its purpose and objectives in effect will vary with the type of organization and the congregation's traditions and locality. A society of the congregation, whether formally structured or not, should not be allowed to become a mere club for the community with no church-oriented objectives. Persons who are not members of the congregation ought not be permitted to become members of any of its organizations, though they may attend as guests.

The Pastor's Role

The broad scope of the pastor's call includes involvement with the congregation's organizations. The pastor will demonstrate his interest by active participation, in most cases by personal attendance. While a children's group like the Lutheran Pioneers requires active lay counselors with the pastor's participation less in evidence, the pastor should not absent himself from the ladies' guild or the young people's society lest his ministry give the impression of haphazard interest and planning. He will welcome the opportunity for contact with members which organizations give him and the rapport such contact can develop.

The pastor has the particular responsibility of providing for inspiration and growth in Christian knowledge through the opening devotions and the discussion topics. Neglect in this area can lead to an organization's deterioration and failure in meeting all of its objectives.

The leadership that is expected of the pastor expresses itself best in the organizations by providing guidance without ostentation. The members can assume the direct leadership as much as possible, the pastor serving as guide and counselor. In this way the organizations are useful also in developing a solid core of competent lay leadership that can serve the congregation well. Bad practices and faulty objectives (for example, that of raising money for the church) can be avoided or overcome by guidance and instruction, and by constructive suggestions in line with the objectives previously outlined.

Although the organizations require the pastor's interest, participation, and guidance, they must not be allowed to presume too much on the pastor's time. They must not rob him of the time needed for thorough sermon preparation. The Sunday service, where the means of grace are dispensed to the entire congregation, dare not become subordinate to the organizations in its demand on the pastor's time. At the same time, the sick, the troubled, the delinquent should not be neglected in favor of attendance during the social part of an organizational meeting. Our Savior's parable of the shepherd leaving the flock to go after the one lost sheep shows the importance of the pastor's work also with individuals. When there are conflicts, the pastor will have to determine what has priority on his time. It will not necessarily be the organizations.

The pastor's responsibility toward the congregation's organizations is not shared by his wife. Some organizations may look to her for leadership because she is the pastor's wife, as though his call from the congregation extends in some respects also to her. But she is the pastor's wife, not a called worker of the church. Her close relationship to the pastor will, in fact, most often make it desirable for her not to serve as president or chairman of organizations whose meetings she chooses to attend. Let her be an example of a faithful wife, a good mother, and a consecrated church member, and who as such becomes involved in organizations.

Summary: Various types of organizations can serve an auxiliary purpose in the life of a Christian congregation. They should remain under the control of the congregation that has called them into being. To provide opportunity for growth in Christian knowledge, for Christian fellowship, and for Christian service are three objectives that can make such organizations serve a useful purpose. The pastor will attend meetings, provide for devotions and inspire spiritual growth through discussion topics, and give guidance and direction to the organizations without taking over their direct leadership. A congregation must guard against letting the organizations preempt that part of the pastor's time which should be allotted to other necessary pastoral work.

II. ORGANIZATIONS OUTSIDE THE CONGREGATION

The twentieth century society abounds in organizational life. Almost every type of endeavor, every area of life, every social, cultural, religious, economic, political, educational, professional concern results in organizations that bring people of like interests together. The members of a Christian congregation, as well as the pastor, will be confronted with numerous decisions about membership in organizations that are part of the society in which the church and the individual Christian find themselves. The pastor must be in a position to counsel with a member as to the possibility or advisability of being a member in one or the other of such organizations. It is not the purpose here to catalog the many organizations outside the congregation that may appeal to the Christian for membership and to express an opinion on each of them. The purpose is rather to examine the scriptural principles that need application in determining the Christian's possible involvement.

Two Types of Organizations

For purposes of evaluation, organizations can be grouped into two categories. The one consists of such organizations that have antichristian or unscriptural principles, policies, or programs as

338

an intrinsic part of the organization. The very existence of the organization depends on principles that are hostile to Christianity. The Masonic order, for example, cannot exist without the antichristian features that become evident in its rituals, prayers, and symbolism. Salvation by character is part and parcel of Masonic thought and teaching. Any society for the promotion of "a woman's right to abortion" exists for a purpose that is intrinsically contrary to Scripture. The Christian dare not compromise his faith by becoming identified with such organizations.

The other category consists of such organizations which in themselves have no inherent principles and purposes that make membership impossible. They may, however, at times have incidental adjuncts, like promiscuous prayers or doubtful activities, which are not an essential part of the organization. Frequently organizations may inject religious elements that are to give the organization respectability or the appearance of piety. Political conventions, for example, call in a pastor, priest, or rabbi to open their meetings with prayer even though religion is in no way a part of the organization's purpose. The Congress of the United States does not exist for religious purposes, and the opening prayers at its sessions are only incidental and not an intrinsic part of its existence. Many organizations are in this category, and membership in them cannot categorically be ruled out even when undesirable features attach themselves in an incidental way. The Christian may be able to divorce himself from the undesirable or unscriptural adjunct while remaining a member of the organization. His influence may, in fact, help avoid or eliminate such objectionable nonessential additions.

The above distinction and its application will become clearer by examining several groups of organizations in both categories which most often confront the Christian in the world.

Lodges

The constitution of a Lutheran congregation will have a statement in the article on Church Membership that reads something like this: " . . . a member of His Church will . . . refuse to hold membership in any organization whose teachings and practices conflict with the Word of God (lodges, etc.). John 5:23; John 8:31, 32; 2 Corinthians 6:14-18."[3] Lodges are specifically mentioned as

3. *Constitution and Bylaws* (Milwaukee: Northwestern, 1968), p 7.

organizations that have objectionable religious elements which make membership in them incompatible with Christianity. There are certain typical objectionable elements that have found their way into lodges or similar organizations to a greater or lesser degree.

A false view of Scripture. The religious concepts and teachings of these organizations are not based on Scripture as the only revealed Word of God. Scripture is viewed as a source of religious truth, but only as one among many. In Freemasonry,[4] for example, the Bible is used "as a symbol of the will of God, however it may be expressed."[5] In fact, "whatever to any people expresses that will may be used as a substitute for the Bible in a Masonic Lodge."[6] Hence one of the Landmarks of the Masonic Order reads as follows:

> It is a Landmark, that a "Book of the Law" shall constitute an indispensable part of the furniture of every Lodge. I say advisedly, a book of the Law, because it is not absolutely required that everywhere the Old and New Testaments shall be used. The "Book of the Law" is that volume which, by the religion of the country, is believed to contain the revealed will of the Grand Architect of the Universe.[7]

This means that, in fact, reason and nature are the source of religious truth, and this truth is something that is common to all men and all religions. "Its (Freemasonry's) religion is that general one of nature and primitive revelation — handed down to us from some ancient Patriarchal Priesthood — in which all men may agree and in which no man can differ."[8] This rules out Scripture as the special, necessary revelation of God, as the inspired, infallible Word of God which it claims to be. The fact that organizations with this principle will be satisfied to have the Bible present as a symbol of God's will and as a source of religious truth must not prevent the Christian from recognizing its true naturalistic basis. The mere presence of Scripture does not assure its proper

---

4. The Order of Ancient, Free, and Accepted Masons is the oldest and largest of the lodges and can serve as an example of the kind of religious elements that may be found at least in part in other lodges also.
5. Albert Gallatin Mackey, *Encyclopedia of Freemasonry* (Chicago: 1946), I, 133.
6. *Ibid.*
7. *Acimnos Ceihpr* (Oshkosh: W. W. Daggett Publishing Co., 1922), p 174.
8. Mackey, *Encyclopedia*, II, 847f.

use. For the Christian, Scripture is in a category all by itself as the revealed will of God, divinely inspired and infallible, and must be the sole basis for religious faith and life. Cf 2 Timothy 3:16,17; 1 Corinthians 2:12,13; 2 Peter 1:20,21; John 17:17; Psalm 119:105; Luke 16:29; 1 Peter 4:11.

A false view of God. Masonry makes belief in a god a requisite for membership. Organizations that base their religious views on nature and reason will speak of God in vague, general terms. They require recognition of a god, but do not define Him in the specific manner in which He reveals Himself in Scripture. God is called the "Grand Architect of the Universe," the "Divine Artist," the "Supreme Grand Master," the "Nameless One of a hundred names," etc. Anything, however, that goes beyond such a general concept of God may not be introduced into Masonry. "The religion, then, of Masonry is pure theism on which its different members engraft their own peculiar opinions; but they are not permitted to introduce them into the lodge, or to connect their truth or falsehood with the truth of Masonry."[9] That the one true God has revealed Himself as triune and that Jesus, of necessity, must be recognized as the second person of this Trinity, true God from eternity, is according to Masonry a peculiarly Christian opinion concerning whose truth or error the lodge does not want to concern itself. The concept of god held by the Muslim or the Jew, the Brahman and the Buddhist, is equally acceptable to Masonry. According to the Bible, however, any view of God that does not specifically acknowledge the Trinity revealed in Scripture and Jesus as true God is false and thus idolatry. What do you think of Christ? Whose Son is He? These questions must be asked of lodges and similar organizations, for it is in their view of Christ that their denial of the true God most often becomes evident. Cf Matthew 28:19; John 17:3; John 5:23; 1 John 2:23; 2 John 9; Matthew 4:10.

A false view of the way of salvation. Naturalistic, rationalistic religions with their false view of God and their rejection of Jesus will inevitably teach work-righteousness. Whatever they say about man's hope for a happy hereafter will be a form of salvation by character. That this is the very heart of Freemasonry is evident from its symbolical interpretation of the various tools the operative mason uses in building. The speculative Mason uses

9. Mackey, *Lexicon*, p 404.

these in building his "Temple" of character. He wears a lambskin apron so that by it "the Mason is reminded of that purity of life and rectitude of conduct which is so essentially necessary to his gaining admission into the Celestial Lodge above, where the Supreme Architect of the Universe forever presides."[10] Thus all tools, the square, the plumb, the level, etc., are interpreted in moralistic terms. The "pass" that assures admission to the Celestial Lodge above is "a pure and blameless life."[11] If an organization expresses this work-righteousness less clearly in its general rites and rituals, it can be expected to express it more explicitly in the funeral ritual, especially in the prayers. Any organization that has work-righteousness as an intrinsic part of its teaching is inimical to Christianity. The Christian may have no part in it because his hope for salvation rests alone in the vicarious atonement of Christ through which he by grace through faith has the full remission of sin. Cf Ephesians 2:8,9; Romans 3:23,24; 1 John 1:8,9; John 14:6; Acts 4:12.

False prayers. The prayers in organizations with naturalistic, rationalistic religious views will address themselves to a god in general, will eliminate any reference to Christ. They are unchristian prayers and idolatrous and have no promise of fulfillment. Cf 1 John 2:23; John 5:23; John 15:16; 14:13; 16:23.

An ungodly fellowship. A lodge establishes a brotherhood. It brings its members into a fraternal fellowship. We are concerned here with organizations whose brotherhood has religious elements, as is so evident in Freemasonry. They share secrets, recognize one another by their handshake, unite in rituals and prayers, and show special consideration to one another in all of life's contacts. It is a brotherhood in which men are united on the basis of general religious views that can be held in common by all religions. That such a fellowship is ungodly and sinful is the clear testimony of Scripture. Cf 2 Corinthians 6:14-18; Romans 16:17, 18.

Many of these organizations have other intrinsic features that are objectionable. It may be their secrecy. It may be their oath. They may set up their own moral standards and in fact allow immoral actions. Since not all organizations have all of the same objectionable elements, each organization must be examined and

10. Mackey, *Encyclopedia*, I, 95f.
11. *Acimnos Ceihpr*, pp 197f.

the implications of membership determined. The five points discussed above are so basic that any examination needs to watch for these in particular.

The Boy Scouts of America

Among organizations for children and adolescents which have intrinsic elements contrary to Scripture, besides those associated with lodges, the Boy Scouts of America is the most prominent. Although it insists that all religious teaching should be left to the church, its purpose, aim, and program inherently conflict with biblical truth. The purpose of the organization is character training. Its aim, according to the Scout Oath, is that the Scout may do his duty to God and his country; help other people at all times; and keep himself physically strong, mentally awake, and morally straight. Its program has to do not merely with teaching certain skills, especially such as involve camping and the outdoors, but centers in the Scout Law. It must be noted that the Scout Oath (also called the Promise) and the Scout Law are necessary parts of Scouting. Without them no Scout troop may exist, even if it is sponsored by a Christian congregation. They are considered essential to the spirit of Scouting.

This calls for a careful examination of the role of the Scout Oath and Law in the character training of Scouting. While the aim of doing one's duty to God and country are shared by Christianity, the manner of attaining them differs completely. An examination of the Scout Law in the light of Scripture shows that it subverts the function of God's law, Christian sanctification, and the way of salvation.[12] To promise "on my honor" to do one's duty to God hardly accords with the Scriptural confession that "I can do all things through Christ who strengthens me" (Php 4:13). The spirit of Scouting builds self-righteousness and is hostile to Christianity. Its type of character training conflicts with Christian character training, based on Holy Scripture.[13] These objectionable elements of Scouting are not mere adjuncts that may attach themselves to a particular troop but are essential to its existence.

12. Cf Jerald J. Plitzuwcit, "The Scout Law in the Light of Scripture," a series of three articles in *The Northwestern Lutheran*, LVII (1970), 60f, 90f, 127.

13. Cf Carl Lawrenz, "Natural Knowledge of God, Civic Righteousness, and Their Application to the Boy Scout Question," *Wisconsin Lutheran Quarterly*, LXIX (April 1972), 67-79.

It is an organization with which the church and its members may not become identified.[14]

Service Organizations

Professional and business men may find themselves attracted to membership in the Rotary, Kiwanis, or Lions clubs. These are not secret fraternal societies or lodges. They are service clubs, having the goal of improving business and professional ethics and of working for social betterment and the general welfare of the community. While membership cannot be considered impossible because of the inherent nature of the organizations, it will be necessary to warn against religious elements and doubtful programs with which the Christian will not want to become associated. Examples of such are unionistic prayers and sponsoring of a Boy Scout troop. The church member in such an organization should consider it his responsibility to keep the organization from adding such nonessential elements that conflict with his religious principles.

The pastor may be invited to join one or the other of these clubs. Remembering that membership makes him responsible for all that the organization does, the pastor will decline the invitation. All his talents, his time and resources, have been called into the service of the gospel; time devoted to these organizations could raise the question of wise stewardship. His association with an organization for social betterment could give a wrong emphasis to his ministry and be misunderstood by people. His presence could encourage religious practices that should not become part of the organization or its meetings. Any seeming advantages through the contacts made in such organizations are outweighed by the reasons advanced against membership.

Veterans' Organizations

Veterans' organizations, among which the American Legion and the Veterans of Foreign Wars are most prominent, cannot be classed as lodges. Although they provide for the office of a chaplain and certain rituals and prayers, these religious features are not mandatory nor necessary for the existence of the organization. They often are omitted at the local post. The burial rite is

14. Cf Armin W. Schuetze, "Can We Make Use of the Boy Scout Organization," in *Guidance From God's Word* (Milwaukee: Northwestern, 1967), pp 116-119.

available upon request. Members of the congregation affiliated with these organizations will need to recognize that they must resist the use of such optional religious practices. In the case of the funeral of a veteran, his military service may be acknowledged by the presence of a flag and possibly a military honor guard. These may be provided locally through the veterans' organization.

Although there may be no religious elements that prohibit membership, the pastor may see the need to warn against the general spirit and some of the activities of these organizations. The members will always have to ask themselves whether they as Christians feel completely at home in such organizations. The answer will differ according to the nature of the local post.

Labor Unions

Labor unions do not have a religious purpose. This is generally true also of railway brotherhoods or farm organizations. Although some of these provide for rituals and prayers, these religious elements are generally optional, not part of the essence of the organization. If his job forces him to be a member of a particular union, the church member will avoid participating in religious practices and use his influence to eliminate them.

A warning is in place against the materialistic spirit that can easily attach itself to these organizations. It should be self-evident that no Christian will condone the use of violence and destruction of property. He must remember both the positive and the negative elements of the Seventh Commandment.

Fraternities — Sororities

Young people attending a college or university may be confronted with the decision to join a fraternity or sorority. Membership in these organizations is sought or encouraged for social reasons and has no direct religious implications. However, the Christian may need to ask whether the program, activities, and reputation of the organization are such that he can conscientiously identify himself with them. The above naturally does not apply to honorary or professional societies as, for example, Phi Beta Kappa.

Pastoral Practice

It is not enough to have a "lodge clause" in the congregation's constitution; the pastor must show the congregation the full signi-

345

ficance and application of it. This involves a general instruction of the congregation concerning the various types of organizations, the implications of membership, and the church's objections either to membership in them or to certain possible adjuncts that must be opposed. This instruction should be a part of the confirmation instruction course both for children and for adults. The pastor must, however, be certain that the necessary basis in Bible doctrine has been laid for an understanding of the objectionable elements in the organization, for example, in a lodge or in Scouting. Such instruction can continue in Bible classes and in the church's organizations. This instruction may concern itself with classes of organizations without going into depth on each of them in particular. If, however, a specific organization is prominent in a community, a more detailed analysis of its objectionable features is called for.

The use of the Sunday sermon for such instruction is questionable. Unless the sermon lays the necessary biblical basis and can enter into the objections to a particular organization in sufficient detail so that the reasons for the objections are very clear, it is advisable to reserve such instruction for a forum where questions can be asked and discussion can take place. Merely to mention the name of an objectionable organization in a sermon without further explanation will inform members only that the church opposes it and may confront mission prospects with questions for which they are not sufficiently prepared. The result may be that they turn away from the church without further discussion.

When a member joins an antichristian lodge or organization, the pastor will take this up personally with that individual. In preparation, the pastor must acquaint himself as well as he can with that specific organization.[15] He must guard against drawing sweeping conclusions that he cannot verify with clear evidence. In cases where a member appreciates the pastor's concern, it may be possible to study the organization jointly on the basis of materials the member has received. In any case, it is more helpful to be able to study the organization on the basis of its own writings and rituals than merely on the basis of articles and pamphlets written about them. The latter can, however, be useful when they do quote from the literature of the objectionable organization and examine it in the light of Scripture.

15. See the bibliography for materials that can be used for such a study.

In his study the pastor must find the answers to certain questions about the organization. What kind of organization is this? Does it have religious elements that are part of its essential character or is it basically social, political, professional, etc.? It must be noted that some organizations that began as lodges with objectionable rituals dropped these and continued only as social organizations or life insurance companies, retaining a kind of fraternal status for tax purposes. What are implications of membership? A membership that binds the individual to a religious ritual must be viewed differently from one in which religious elements are purely incidental and optional. Sometimes various kinds of membership are possible, not all of them equally objectionable. In such cases the further question arises: Will such distinctions be fully understood by the entire congregation, or could a permissible type of membership still cause offense?

In dealing with the member, the pastor's responsibility is first of all that of a teacher. He must instruct the member regarding the objections to the organization and the biblical reasons for them. In this he will be patient, firm, and evangelical.

Patient

To be patient means not to confront a member simply with an ultimatum. It means allowing adequate time for the needed instruction to be given and to take effect. How long patience should be extended will depend to a great extent on the reaction of the member. One can bear much longer with a person who has honest difficulties understanding certain points than with one who obviously has a closed mind and desires no instruction. At what point congregational discipline is called for will vary from individual to individual. Patience is a virtue, but not when it becomes procrastination.

Firm

Patience does not eliminate firmness. While one can patiently instruct, the instruction must remain firm in its application of the Word of God. If something is contrary to God's Word, the pastor may not ignore this fact in his practice. For a pastor and a congregation to delay taking a firm stand in the hope that the problem can be resolved at a later time is unscriptural practice. To build a mission congregation on a lax lodge and Scouting practice in the expectation that the practice can become a firm one as the congregation grows is laying the foundation for future trouble. Where a certain practice is called for by Holy Scripture, the pastor has no choice but to be firm, even if he will show patience in carrying out the necessary instruction.

Evangelical

An evangelical practice also does not conflict with firmness. To be evangelical does not mean to be lax. It means not being legalistic. To demand that a member give up the Masonic lodge, for example, because the congregation's constitution requires this is legalism. Evangelical practice finds its motivation in the gospel and its guidance in Holy Scripture. To apply this with firmness is to be evangelical. To operate simply with laws and rules is legalism. The pastor must be evangelical.

Should a child that remains a member of the Scouting organization be confirmed and become a communicant member of the church? To continue voluntarily in an association prohibited by Scripture and at the same time to profess full acceptance of Scripture is a contradiction. One cannot ask a child to make such a confession until the contradiction is eliminated. If, however, his membership in the Scouts is beyond his control, demanded by his parents or guardians, the child cannot be held responsible. It is to be hoped that the parents may be brought to permit the child to make his own decision in such cases.

When a person who is already a member of the congregation joins an antichristian organization, instruction, admonition, and discipline will proceed while he retains his membership. It should be understood that he will refrain from communion while he is being dealt with. Persistent refusal to follow the admonition and heed the discipline ultimately leads to a termination of his membership in the congregation. If those who are seeking to join the congregation are found to be associated with an antichristian organization, their membership in it must be terminated prior to their reception into the fellowship of the church.

Summary: Two types of organizations outside the congregation require the church's attention. The one type has objectionable re-

348

ligious elements as an intrinsic part of the organization, making affiliation on the part of church members impossible. The other type may have objectionable adjuncts that are not an essential part of the organization. While membership in such organizations cannot be forbidden, the members must be warned against participation in the organization's objectionable elements and encouraged to work for the elimination of those that are optional. Antichristian lodges, like the Freemasons, have a false view of Scripture, God, and the way of salvation and involve their members in false prayers and an ungodly fellowship. Service and veterans' organizations as well as labor unions generally have no intrinsic religious elements, whatever rituals and prayers they provide being optional. In dealing with members who have joined antichristian organizations the pastor will by patient, firm and evangelical instruction and admonition seek to lead them to renounce their sinful affiliation lest their persistent refusal lead to termination of their congregational membership and even eternal damnation. In the case of those seeking membership in the congregation, all antichristian affiliations must be terminated before reception into the congregation may take place.

For Additional Reading

Acimnos Ceihpr. Ushkosh. W. W. Daggett Publishing Co., 1922.

A Masonic handbook, containing the ritual in code. With a little practice one can learn to read the code of the ritual. The volume also contains a listing of the Masonic Landmarks, which are not in code.

Coil, Elijah Alfred. *The Liberal Churches and the Fraternal Orders.* Boston: American Unitarian Association, 1916.

A Unitarian minister shows that it is inconsistent to be a Freemason and a Trinitarian Christian at the same time. A Freemason should consistently also be a Unitarian.

Fritz, John H. C. "The Ladies' Society," chapter 24 in *Pastoral Theology*. St. Louis: Concordia, 1945. pp 326-328.

Graebner, Theodore. *A Handbook of Organizations*. St. Louis: Concordia, 1948.

> A volume that is still useful although in some cases it will be necessary to supplement the information from more recent materials. The discussion on the Boy Scouts of America is useful only for information on the reasoning that led to the 1944 resolutions on Scouting by the Lutheran Church-Missouri Synod. The conclusions are unacceptable.

Graumann, William. *The Christian Degrees of Masonry and the Bible*. St. Louis: Concordia, 1962.

> The two so-called "Christian" degrees in the Scottish and York rites that go beyond the three basic degrees of the Blue Lodge are examined and exposed as no departure from nor improvement on the errors of the Blue Lodge.

Kowalke, E. E. "The Church and Its Youth," in the *Theologische Quartalschrift (Wisconsin Lutheran Quarterly)*, XXXIV (Oct., 1937), 246-263.

> This synodical essay is still timely in its sane approach to the church's ministry to its youth. Its value lies particularly in the theological basis that provides a proper scriptural perspective for work among the youth as well as in all of the congregation's organizations.

Krueger, Ottomar. "Societies in the Congregation," chapter XXII in *The Pastor at Work*. St. Louis: Concordia, 1960. pp 374-383.

> A general discussion of societies, showing their possible dangers and how to make them useful in the church.

Mackey, Albert G. *Encyclopedia of Freemasonry*. Revised and enlarged by Robert I. Clegg. 3 vols. Chicago: Masonic History Co., 1946.

> An authoritative source of information for all questions about Freemasonry. Will readily yield quotations showing the "salvation by character" nature of Freemasonry.

Maier, Walter A., Jr. *Should I Join a Fraternal Society?* St. Louis: Concordia, 1961.

> Useful for distribution. The pamphlet examines especially the Masonic order.

Masonry in the Light of the Bible. St. Louis: Concordia, 1954.

A pamphlet, in its tenth printing in 1969, that lists what "Scripture teaches" and what "Masonry says" in two columns on the same page. The numerous quotations from Masonic literature on six topics make the pamphlet very useful.

Pike, Albert. *Morals and Dogma of the Ancient and Accepted Scottish Rite of Freemasonry.* Richmond, Va.: L. H. Jenkins, Inc., 1871.

This work was prepared and published by authority of the Supreme Council of the Thirty-third Degree for the Southern Jurisdiction of the U.S. by its Grand Commander, Albert Pike. Its copyright was renewed in 1906, and it has been republished since.

Preuss, Arthur. *Dictionary of Secret and other Societies.* St. Louis: Herder, 1924.

A Catholic work on fraternal societies that together with Stevens' Cyclopedia is frequently quoted as an authoritative source.

Stevens, Albert C. *Cyclopedia of Fraternities.* New York: E. B. Tread and Co., 1907.

A work frequently cited in critical studies of fraternal societies.

Whalen, William J. *Christianity and American Freemasonry.* Milwaukee: Bruce, 1958.

This volume by a Roman Catholic author contains a chapter on "Protestant Criticism of Masonry." Included is also reference to the Lutheran and WELS rejection of Masonry.

Whalen, William J. *Handbook of Secret Organizations.* Milwaukee: Bruce, 1966.

Although this handbook was written by a Roman Catholic, it provides much information on the various organizations that can serve to supplement and update the Graebner Handbook.

Zuck, G. Irving and Roy B. Zuck. *Youth and the Church.* Chicago: Moody Press, 1968.

This volume of over 400 pages consists of 28 chapters written by various authors. It contains a wealth of practical material to give the pastor ideas for his youth program. The theology of the various authors is one that begins with the acceptance of Scripture as the inspired Word of God.

Zuck, Roy B. and Gene A. Getz. *Adult Education in the Church.* Chicago: Moody Press, 1970.

A number of chapters contain practical suggestions that may be adopted or adapted in various church organizations. Since its background is Reformed, discretion is in place even though the general theological approach is evangelical, viewing Scripture as authoritative. The chapter on "Instructional Methodology for Adults" provides an explanation of many different methods that may be useful in carrying out an educational program in connection with organizations.

15

The Shepherd's Place
in the Synodical Flock

*"The apostles and elders,
with the whole church"*
(Ac 15:22)

I. THE SYNOD

Its Essential Nature

A synod, like a congregation, is essentially a gathering of Christians. Those who through the gospel have been brought to faith in the Lord Jesus will seek the fellowship of those who are of like faith and mind. The Lord wants this, for He bids Christians not to forsake gathering together with fellow Christians (He 10:25). This command of the Lord finds its primary and most complete application and fulfillment when Christians locally in a congregation gather to hear God's Word, to find edification in the gospel, to carry out the responsibilities that are incumbent on a Christian. This command finds further application when Christians are gathered into larger groupings like synods, united by their common confession to Christ and the joint work of proclaiming His saving message.

By their confession to the marks of the church, the gospel in Word and sacrament, such groups, whether large or small, whether locally limited like a congregation or reaching out nation-wide like a synod, are called churches because in them the *una sancta* is present. Thus in its essential nature the synod is a body of Christians which is recognized as a church by its interest in and confession to the gospel.

This essential nature of the synod needs to be distinguished from the synod as a corporate body, even as these two must be distinguished in the case of a local congregation. The organizational form a synod receives is determined by its members in Christian liberty. The Lord has imposed no specific forms on His New Testament church. A synod's corporate, organizational structure, even as that of a local congregation, will be set up to enable it best to fulfill its purpose in the world.

Its Purpose and Assignment

Because it is a gathering of Christians, the WELS has stated that its continuing purpose "is to serve all people in God's world with the Gospel of Jesus Christ on the basis of the Holy Scriptures."[1] This ultimately must be the purpose of any group that claims to be a church. Exactly how this purpose is realized in practice will be determined by various considerations. A synod will need to recognize that God's injunction for good order will not permit it to compete with a congregation in what it is doing. Christian love should prevent a synod, although the larger body, from imposing its will dictatorially on a congregation. The fact that a synod is larger than a congregation does not mean that a synod's work must be more comprehensive or that it inherently possesses greater power. A synod will generally be called on to do that work of the church which cannot be done by one congregation alone or that can be done better by a larger body. The Christians, gathered first of all in congregations, will determine in what areas that is the case.

The tasks most often assigned to a synod are the following: 1) to confess and preserve the truth and thus also to supervise doctrine and practice among the congregations; 2) to carry on mission work both at home and throughout the world; 3) to provide an educational system so that the church may be supplied with a well-trained ministry; 4) to produce and publish sound Christian literature, books, etc., for use in church, school, and home; 5) to assist congregations in calling pastors and teachers; 6) to provide

1. *Reports and Memorials for the Fortieth Biennial Convention* (Milwaukee: Wisconsin Ev. Luth. Synod, 1969), p 125.

opportunity for works of charity toward fellow Christians and toward all the needy. In all of these tasks the role of a synod is to enable Christians in one congregation to render helpful service to Christians in many other congregations and to engage in joint work with them. Thus the WELS has stated its objectives as follows:

1. To share the Gospel of Jesus Christ with all people.
2. To uphold the Truth of God as fully revealed in the inspired, inerrant, infallible Holy Scriptures and set forth in the Lutheran Confessions.
3. To provide a preaching and teaching ministry qualified to proclaim the Word of God faithfully, effectively, universally in accord with the Lutheran Confessions.
4. To assist in counseling and equipping all members of the Synod for ever greater service to the Lord, to each other, and to the world.
5. To assist all members of the Synod in being active in deeds of love toward our fellow men in need.
6. To foster confessional unity of faith among Christians throughout the world.[2]

Confessional Implications

Because of a synod's essential nature as an assembly of Christians whose purpose is worldwide testimony to the gospel, membership in a synod is a confessional act. The individual or congregation that holds membership in a synod thereby expresses agreement with its doctrine and practice. Those who are affiliated with an erring synod share its errors (2 Jn 11) and must accept responsibility for them. Romans 16:17 shows that such a fellowship is not one that is God-pleasing.

Formal Membership

Since the organizational form of a synod is not determined by Scripture, formal membership will vary according to the wishes and good judgment of each church body. The WELS has found it expedient to set up its synodical organization in such a way that individual congregations, pastors, and male teachers make up its formal membership. Thus the individual Christian in a congregation is a member of the Synod through his congregation, whereas the pastors and male teachers join as members directly. The

2. *Ibid.,* p 125.

voting delegates at a synodical convention thus consist of laymen from congregations, of pastors, and of male teachers.

This type of organization provides for a pastor-congregation-synod relationship which establishes a direct link between each congregation and the Synod and between each pastor, or male teacher, and the Synod. Thus the congregation is joined to the Synod, not through its pastor, but directly as a member, and the pastor personally is a member of the Synod and not merely through his congregation. On the other hand, the pastor and congregation have a direct relationship to one another through the congregation's call. Thus there is a kind of triangular relationship that can be illustrated as follows:

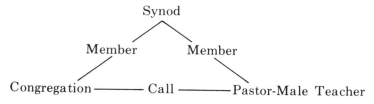

This kind of relationship has distinct advantages for all concerned. Both the pastor and the congregation have a direct connection with and access to the larger fellowship of Christians which the Synod provides. At the same time, the Synod must recognize that the congregation's call has established a close, direct link between the congregation and its pastor. It is especially when problems arise that the relationship as it has been set up among the three can be mutually helpful and enable Christian brothers to come to one another's aid. A few examples can illustrate this.

Should the Synod find that a pastor persists in false doctrine, it can terminate his membership in the Synod. It cannot, however, dismiss him from the congregation's call. The Synod can, however, inform the congregation directly of what has happened so that the congregation can ultimately make its own decision, either to dismiss its pastor for what it too has recognized to be false doctrine, or to leave the synodical fellowship which in its opinion has wrongfully expelled its pastor.

A pastor who experiences difficulty in convincing a congregation of the correctness of his doctrine and practice can call on his fellow Christians in the Synod for help. A congregation, seeing that its fellow Christians in the Synod agree with the pastor, hopefully will accept his position as correct.

A congregation that finds its pastor unfaithful can turn to the Synod for advice and guidance in regard to what may properly be done in such circumstances. Since a congregation does not frequently experience such a problem, it may feel very helpless when faced with it and will appreciate the help of its fellow Christians, available through the Synod.

In this way this kind of pastor-congregation-synod relationship, when used properly, can provide opportunities for brotherly help and encouragement in problems that the church militant still experiences.

Summary: Essentially a synod, like a congregation, is a group of Christians, recognized as a church by its confession to the gospel and its concern for the gospel's proclamation. A synod may engage in such work as the Christians in its congregations assign to it. Its larger size does not give it special authority over a congregation nor should it compete with a congregation in what it does. Christian love and good order will control the relationship of a congregation and synod toward one another. The corporate, organizational form of a synod, like that of a congregation, is set up in Christian liberty so that the working together of congregation, pastor, and synod will serve the best interests of the gospel and its worldwide proclamation.

II. BENEFITS AND OBLIGATIONS OF SYNODICAL MEMBERSHIP

Benefits for the Pastor

His synodical membership provides ready opportunity for the pastor to remain in *close contact with fellow pastors* of like confession. Such association can give the necessary incentive for continued theological study. It can encourage and strengthen the pastor in bearing the burdens of the ministry. The pastor can look to synodical brethren for help when doubts plague him, for correction should he stray from sound doctrine, for reproof if sin should overtake him.

As a member of the synod a pastor's *opportunity for service* in the Lord's kingdom is extended beyond the limits of one congregation. The Lord grants a variety of gifts to His servants and to the church. (Cf 1 Cor 12 and Eph 4:1-16). Through a synod these gifts may be put to wider use for the edification of Christ's body, the church.

The pastor may *call on synodical brothers for help* if differences between him and his congregation persist. Synodical officials are available for counsel so that under God harmony may be restored.

By receiving him as a pastor member, a synod gives *public acknowledgment of the pastor's fitness* for the ministry and of the soundness of his doctrine and practice. Thus his synodical membership is in effect the pastor's credentials to his congregation and to some extent to the world.

The Pastor's Obligations

The pastor should expect to *serve and help his brothers* in a synod even as he expects their helpful service. Only when pastors are willing to encourage, strengthen, admonish, correct, and reprove one another with the Word of God will a synod remain truly united and spiritually strong. Without becoming officious, each pastor is to be his synodical brother's keeper, but in a spirit of humble helpfulness void of pride and self-righteousness. At the same time, he should be willing to accept brotherly admonition either when it is given informally or by someone who has an official responsibility.

The pastor should feel obliged to *attend conferences* regularly and participate actively. He should welcome the opportunity for receiving Holy Communion with his brother pastors, for studying God's Word, and for discussing the work of the church. Active participation includes accepting the assignment of a conference paper.

According to the WELS constitution all pastors are to *attend* district *conventions*. One of every 10 pastors is chosen as a delegate also to the biennial convention of the Synod. Only pressing reasons should prevent the pastor's attendance. In this way he keeps himself informed and participates in making decisions. He can prepare himself for conventions by reading the published reports and memorials. By subsequently reading the printed proceedings, he will know what action was taken. Reading the Synod's periodicals will help keep him informed the year round.

The pastor has the obligation to *keep the members of his congregation informed* on what they are doing through their Synod. A congregation's interest in and support of synodical work will depend largely on how effectively the pastor encourages its members. Careless criticism of the Synod on the part of a pastor will do more harm than he thinks. Nor should the pastor set himself up as a judge of a congregation's potential for mission support and place a ceiling on it. Encouraging generous giving for synodical work will not hinder support of local work; generally the opposite is the case: there will also be more generous giving for the support of work at home. The pastor may also through his neglect, or in other ways, become a barrier that prevents a close relationship between a congregation and the Synod. He should rather be a bridge that forms a link between the two. Although it is not through the pastor that the congregation holds membership in the Synod, he does have this in-between position when it comes to information and encouragement.

If a district or the Synod asks a pastor to *assume an office*, he will serve the church at large with faithful zeal. In carrying out his official tasks, he will remember that the added responsibility and authority of his office do not make him a lord over God's people. He remains a servant of God and of his fellow Christians and in that spirit will carry out the duties of his office. Although there may be times when parish duties curtail his availability for serving the church at large, he must realize that only as he and others take on these added labors will the work of the Synod progress. If he is elected to an office that requires considerable time, like that of district president or mission board chairman, he may find it advisable to consult with his congregation and receive its approval.

In general, if the pastor remembers that his relationship to the Synod is not merely that of membership in an organization but is a fellowship of Christians united by faith in Jesus Christ, he will *avoid doing anything that may be disruptive of synodical unity*, that places a strain on the fellowship, that could lead to strife and division. Paul's words to the congregation at Corinth (1 Cor 1) apply equally to the fellowship enjoyed on a broader scale in a synod.

A Congregation's Benefits

A congregation's membership in a synod brings it into a *close fellowship bond with many other Christians and congregations* that share its faith. It is a genuine encouragement for a congregation to know that it does not stand alone in its confession to the truth. It is a joy for a member, when traveling or moving, to find a sister congregation where the same gospel is taught and confessed. The same joy is experienced when members of sister congregations come together at conventions, conferences, or other services or meetings involving a limited or a wider area.

Through its synod a congregation can *participate in kingdom work beyond its local area.* A congregation is to help proclaim the gospel in all the world. It is to train men and women to supply the church's need for pastors, teachers, and missionaries. A congregation should welcome the opportunities the synod provides to broaden its areas of service.

Through its membership a congregation gains a *voice in planning and deciding on a synod's work.* While this influence may seem minimal to each member and even to an individual congregation in relation to the many Christians and congregations that make up a synod, the congregation does have the benefit of sending representation to conventions and the right to prepare memorials to its synod, whereby its wishes can be expressed. Through its representatives the congregation votes on resolutions and in elections. Membership makes the congregation and its members a part of a synod. When a synod makes decisions, it therefore is not some distant organization making decisions for the congregation. In referring to its synod, a congregation ought to learn to say "we" and not "they."

A congregation has *direct access to synodical help and counsel.* It can receive help, for example, in planning its evangelism or stewardship programs. Help and counsel are needed especially during a vacancy. It can secure temporary help as needed and assistance in calling a pastor or teacher. A congregation may seek counsel in a difficult case of discipline or if problems arise in connection with a called worker.

A congregation can look to its synod as a *source of qualified pastors and teachers.* Thus the synod's help in filling a vacancy goes beyond mere counsel.

A congregation can look to its fellow Christians in the synod for the *needed warning and admonition* when it is in danger of succumbing to false doctrine or of following practices not in harmony with Scripture. A congregation that is concerned about the truth should view such warnings and admonitions not as interference in its private affairs, but as a demonstration of genuine concern on the part of fellow believers. A congregation and pastor with no ties to a larger fellowship can more readily be tossed about by winds of deviating doctrine and practice than one that finds support in its fellowship with Christians beyond the congregation.

A Congregation's Obligations

A congregation should consider it not only a privilege, but also an obligation to *send delegates to conferences and conventions,* and to make its facilities available for such meetings. The pastor or male teacher is not representing the congregation. According to the WELS constitution every member congregation may send a lay representative to delegate conferences and to district conventions. Generally one out of every 10 congregations elects a layman to serve as delegate to the Synod's biennial convention.

A congregation is called on to *provide laymen for boards and committees.* Such lay participation is important to retain the concept of the universal priesthood as a working reality in the church.

In matters not decided by Scripture a congregation will *accept the majority decision of its synod.* For each congregation to decide individually which program it chooses to support and which to eliminate would put an end to effective cooperation among the member congregations. It is self-evident that a congregation should not, however, blindly follow decisions that involve matters of conscience and confession to the truth. The congregation which believes that its synod has erred from Scripture has the responsibility of brotherly admonition toward its brothers in the synod.

Without the congregation's *prayers and financial support* a synod could not carry out its work. The congregation should view this support no differently than that given for local purposes. The congregation, as a part of the synod, is not supporting someone else's work, but its own missions and schools, etc. Actually in all its giving it is supporting the Lord's work. Such support should not be casual or a giving of what is left after the congregation's needs are fully met. Synodical support deserves consecrated, ongoing effort that recognizes the high privilege and responsibility of participating in the church's worldwide mission.

Congregations have the further obligation of supporting their synod's schools by *encouraging young people to prepare for the*

361

preaching and teaching ministry. This encouragement can take the form of making scholarships available locally or synodwide.

In carrying out its program and doing its work, a congregation will *show consideration for its sister congregations in the synod.* A congregation may, for example, permit its pastor temporarily to serve a vacant congregation. It may open its school on a favorable financial basis to the children of a new mission. It will avoid practices that could become an irritation to other congregations.

Its membership in a synod should move a congregation to *permit its pastor to devote time to synodical work.* How much time this can be without doing injury to the congregation's work may have to be determined, especially when a synodical position is involved that calls for many hours of the pastor's time. In some situations it may be necessary to provide for pastoral assistance. The WELS has been willing to assume the cost of such assistance, at least in part.

The congregation should *keep itself informed regarding the synod and its work.* It can do this by using the various informational materials provided by its synod. Its members should receive and read the synodical periodicals which contain both inspirational and informative articles.

Summary: Membership in a synod has definite benefits for both pastor and congregation. At the same time it brings with it certain obligations for each if a synod is to fulfill its purpose in the Lord's kingdom.

For Additional Reading

The Constitution and Bylaws of the Wisconsin Ev. Lutheran Synod. Available at the Synod office, 3512 W. North Ave., Milwaukee, Wis. 53208.

Meyer, J. P. "Synod and Congregation" in *Wis. Luth. Quarterly* (Oct. 1964) LXI, 233-265.

16

The Future Shepherd
and His Supervisor

"As a son with the father"
(Ph 2:22)

I. THE VICAR

A. His Call

The Lord has not defined or limited the form which the public ministry is to have. He is concerned about the service which it renders. Therefore many forms are mentioned (1 Cor 12:8-10, 28-30; Eph 4:11), and terms like elder, bishop, overseer are used without distinction. "The Gospel creates its own forms" as circumstances and special needs require. Therefore, although Scripture does not use the term "vicar," the vicar's office is a proper form of the New Testament ministry.

This form of the New Testament ministry is limited. It is limited in time. Experience has led the WELS to set the period from September 1 to August 31 as the normal time of service for a vicar.

A more important factor is that the ministry of the vicar is limited in responsibility. The very language of the vicar call indicates this. "We agree to consider your service among us as part of your theological training under the general supervision of the supervising pastor." The full scope of the functions of a pastor's office is not conferred upon the vicar. He is required to "assist with preaching, visiting the sick and unchurched, administrative work, and other ministerial duties, as directed by the supervising pastor." He is not the assistant pastor of a congregation, but an assistant to the pastor; not under the congregation to be directed by it, but under the pastor to be directed by him. He shares no responsibility with the pastor for making decisions. This responsibility rests solely with the pastor. The vicar is not on his own to promote new ventures, no matter how desirable they may be or seem to be. After all, he will not be there to follow through because his call is limited in time. It is a different matter if the pastor asks him for his opinion or encourages him to promote some new venture, but the vicar is not to take the initiative.

B. Duties

The prospective vicar will want to know in a general way the nature of the work which he will be expected to do. We shall first see what is said about it both in the "Application for Pastoral Vicar" and in the call form which he will receive at the time when he is assigned. (See Appendix.)

While the details of a vicar's activities may vary somewhat from place to place, in general they will include much of what follows:

Preaching. Since the vicar will be functioning as a student and not as a graduate, he will be expected to prepare his sermons in consultation with his supervising pastor.

Teaching. This may include a children's confirmation class, classes for adults, Bible class, Sunday school, Sunday school teachers' meetings, vacation Bible school, or the Christian day school. The vicar will conform to the directives of his supervising pastor. On his part, careful preparation and concern for evangelical discipline are required.

Administration of the sacraments. Since the sacraments as part of the ministry of the keys have been entrusted to each believer and thus to the church, which is all believers, in principle every believer has the right to administer the sacraments. Since, however, believers do not exist in isolation but normally in some form of outward fellowship with other believers, the use of their inherent rights is governed by considerations of love and order. When

364

the believers who form a congregation have called a pastor to administer the sacraments in their name, it would be a violation of love and order for the members to perform baptisms except in an emergency or to have a communion service on their own. Ordinarily, however, congregations do not rigidly restrict the administration of the means of grace to their pastor. They have the tacit understanding that if circumstances require, he will invite guest pastors or theological students to preach, to assist in the distribution of the Lord's Supper, or in his absence, to conduct the entire communion service or to perform a baptism. Where this situation prevails, there will be no question about the vicar's right to administer the sacraments. If, however, a congregation has qualms about having a vicar consecrate the elements, administer private communion, or baptize, the vicar will not ride roughshod over their scruples, but bear with their weakness until such a time when patient instruction will have led the congregation expressly to authorize the vicar to administer the sacraments when the situation warrants. Legal requirements in most states exclude him from the right to perform marriages.

Calls. These will include calls on the sick and shut-ins, mission calls, and general pastoral calls, but not calls involving serious disciplinary cases. The supervising pastor will assign the calls which the vicar is to make except when emergencies arise during the pastor's absence.

Administration. The vicar may expect to be invited to attend some or all of the meetings of the voters' assembly, the church council, the board of elders, the board of education, the board of trustees, the evangelism committee, the stewardship committee, or special committees. His purpose will be to observe and learn, and perhaps at times to conduct the devotions. It is not his prerogative to suggest policy.

Organizations. A large congregation may have a multitude of organizations: a cradle roll committee, children's groups, youth groups, altar guild, ladies' groups, men's groups, mixed adult groups, a golden agers' club. The vicar may be asked to attend in order to observe, to conduct devotions, or to present topi

Intercongregational organizations. In areas where there r concentration of sister congregations there may be various c ganizations which have been formed to carry on work which is o common concern: high schools, charities, and others. Furthermore, the congregation which the vicar serves is part of the synodical family and as such will be represented at various meetings: circuit, delegate conference, pastoral conference, district convention, and periodically, Synod convention. The vicar will be expected to attend these meetings with his supervising pastor to observe and to learn.

Secretarial help. While most larger congregations have a church secretary who takes care of much of the routine work, the vicar will be expected to become acquainted with it and, if need be, take care of such matters as the bulletin, the monthly letter, church records (baptisms, confirmations, marriages, funerals, communion attendance, statistical reports), and official correspondence (transfers, releases).

C. Problems

Work Load

Frankness requires admitting that problems may arise in the pastor-vicar relationship. There is a diversity of gifts both in supervising pastors and in vicars. Some pastors may be demanding, others more considerate, others perhaps too lenient. On the other hand, what is not too heavy a load of work for one vicar may tax another beyond his capacity. Hence there may be a measure of justification for the complaint on the part of some who have vicared that too much has been expected of them. A vicar ought not, however, to be hasty in coming to the conclusion that too much is being required of him. He ought first to make a determined effort to carry out all of his assignments, for there is such a thing as getting one's second wind in the work of the ministry just as there is in athletics. If there seems to be just cause for complaint, the first step which the vicar ought to take is to admit to his supervising pastor that more is being expected of him than he can do. If there is no relief the vicar will bear in mind that faithfulness is doing what he is able to do (*ultra posse nemo obligatur*) and making the most of a trying situation. It would be proper for him to report his experiences to the Seminary dean. If such complaints concerning a given pastor are made also by his subsequent vicars, the information would be relayed to the man's district president, through whom requests for vicars are channeled. The Seminary is concerned about fair treatment for the vicars, for they are still part of its student body. But vicars ought to beware of feeling sorry for themselves if they find their work taxing. Their future work as pastors will be that too. It is that work for which they are not only being trained, but also conditioned (cf "work," 1 Tm 3:1; "labor," 1 Tm 4:10).

Conflict of Personalities

Another problem that could arise is a conflict of personalities between the supervising pastor and the vicar. Then it behooves the vicar to yield. The "gentle" of 1 Timothy 3:3 implies a willingness to yield. And 1 Peter 5:5 says: "Ye younger, submit yourselves unto the elder."

Diversity of Gifts

Because "there are diversities of gifts" (1 Cor 12:4), it could be that a supervising pastor is not as gifted as his vicar. His English may be faulty or his homiletics leave much to be desired. But that fact does not give the vicar a right to look down upon his supervising pastor. It is written: "Who maketh thee to differ from another? and what hast thou that thou didst not receive? now if thou didst receive it, why dost thou glory, as if thou hadst not received it?" (1 Cor 4:7.) The vicar's attitude toward his supervising pastor is also to be governed by the admonition: "Esteem them very highly in love for their work's sake" (1 Th 5:13). Such a supervising pastor may all the more need help from his vicar, and the vicar can still learn from him if he will only try. In cases like this the vicar would do well to remember that his initial adverse evaluation of his supervising pastor's qualifications is contradicted by the fact that the Lord has granted the pastor a number of years of practical experience and blessed his ministry to the extent that his people have sought to lighten the burden of his work by providing him with undergraduate assistance.

Laxity

The most trying situation arises in a case where the vicar discovers laxity in practice on the part of his supervising pastor. He needs to distinguish carefully between standards which he has set for himself and principles which are laid down in God's Word. In the latter case submitting to the supervision of the pastor does not include acting contrary to one's conscience. "We ought to obey

God rather than men" (Ac 5:29). Admonition of the pastor becomes a Christian duty, but in the spirit of 1 Timothy 5:1: "Rebuke not an elder, but entreat him as a father." To go further by taking public issue with the pastor or seeking to institute disciplinary action or agitating privately against the pastor is not part of the vicar's responsibility, if for no other reason than because his call is limited in time. If admonition proves to be fruitless, and intolerable anguish of conscience results for the vicar, it may be necessary for him to ask his district president to relieve him of his assignment. "Neither be partaker of other men's sins" (1 Tm 5:22). Cases in which such an extreme step is taken ought, however, to be the rare exception. Since there is a terminal point to the vicar's service, a better solution would be to consider the need of the people and serve them faithfully until the terminal point is reached. At times we have to suffer what we cannot condone. Here, too, however, it is proper for the vicar upon his return to the Seminary to acquaint the dean with his experiences. If a case history develops in the case of any pastor or congregation, the district president will be informed by the Seminary. We want learning during the vicar year to be done under normal, not abnormal, conditions.

What is a vicar to do if the members of a congregation complain to him about the pastor? He will need to remember that even to be willing to listen to such complaints or accusations involves him in a violation of the Eighth Commandment. Such members will need to be reminded of their duty in the light of the Eighth Commandment and of Matthew 18. Their proper course is not to come to the vicar, but to go to the pastor and if need be to the congregation, the visiting elder, and the district president. Malicious gossips must be shut off firmly. Troubled souls are to be comforted by speaking well of the pastor and stressing his good points, and to be reassured in their own faith by the use of the Word of God.

D. Suggestions, Cautions, Motivation

Congregational Membership

It is advisable for a vicar to transfer his membership to the congregation in the midst of which he will be serving for the year of his vicarship. If he is married, this applies also to his wife and family. To say the least, it would be confusing to a congregation for the vicar himself not to be a member of the body in the midst of which he is endeavoring to foster loyalty and full participation in its work, and to whose numbers he is seeking to add. Nor would he be setting a good example in the grace of Christian giving. Neither would he be setting a good example for the congregation from which he came if for an entire year he were to be an inactive member.

The Married Vicar

While the role of a pastor's wife has been discussed in the chapter on the pastor and what is written there applies *mutatis mutandis* also to the vicar's wife, a few specific reminders may be in order. The vicar who marries shortly before he begins his vicar service needs to bear in mind that once he has begun his ministry his honeymoon, during which he could center his attention upon his bride, is over. Now his work must receive priority, and that involves putting in long hours often extending well into the evening. He will have to acquaint his wife with these facts. As for his wife, spending a year with her vicar husband will provide her with an excellent opportunity to learn what life will be like for her when her husband becomes a pastor. To that end it would be well for her to participate in as many of the activities of the congregation as are open to her and in general to display a wholehearted interest in her husband's work and in the well being of the congregation.

Pastoral Dignity

After years of dormitory life and various types of secular employment where he may have developed an easy-going familiarity with his associates, the vicar will have to realize that his position as vicar calls for somewhat different standards. Not that he is to become pompous, arrogant, or aloof. Rather, he will endeavor to be friendly toward all with whom he comes into contact. But he will need to cultivate with that friendliness a reserve which, while allowing people to respond to his friendliness, will keep them from presuming upon it. People may appreciate a buddy whom they can kid on the golf course, but at their sickbed they want a pastor or vicar whom they can respect as a spokesman for their Lord.

Confidences

The vicar in the performance of his duties will learn things about the members or hear things from them which are confidential in nature. He will therefore be careful lest in an unguarded moment he reveal such confidential matters. He will need to be careful even about what he tells his wife. Once members get the impression that the vicar cannot be trusted to keep a secret, his future usefulness will have been seriously impaired. There may be some matters which a vicar may not divulge to others but which he will reveal to his supervising pastor since his is the on-going responsibility for the spiritual welfare of his members. Such a pastoral sharing of information would not be considered a breach of confidence. The same principle would apply if the supervising pastor as a part of training his vicar for his future work in the parish ministry were to discuss a problem case with him and tell him how he is dealing with it. The supervising pastor will be willing to undertake this phase of a vicar's training only if he is sure that the vicar will respect confidential information.

Attitudes

There are two attitudes against which vicars ought to be on their guard. The one is that of the man who prior to his vicarship has done some church work, thinks that he was eminently successful, and was inflated in his self-esteem by compliments. As a result he views his supervising pastor's methods with disdain and is sure that he could do a much better job if given the opportunity. He fails to appreciate the evangelical attitude, the patience, and the wisdom and experience with which his supervising pastor conducts his ministry, and misses out on learning what he might have learned if he had been more humble and observant.

The other attitude is that of the vicar who is so humble that he is overwhelmed when he sees how unfavorably his gifts and abilities compare with those of his supervising pastor. He fails to realize that the Lord entrusted the supervising pastor with his large congregation because He had equipped him for the amount of work which is required. He also fails to consider that there are areas of service which can well be filled by men with lesser gifts. The outcome could be that instead of being stimulated in his desire for the bishop's office such a vicar might because of his false modesty and humility succumb to the temptation not to enter the ministry at all.

Consideration for Successor

Once a vicar has completed his year of service, his situation is like that of a pastor who has left his congregation to accept a call elsewhere. He is not to keep himself before his former congregation by means of frequent visits or by corresponding with a segment of its membership and thus give the impression of meddling. He will rather want those whom he had served to focus their attention upon his successor.

Avoiding Wrong Conclusions

A final word of caution to the returning vicar is that he must be careful not to let his experience as a vicar spoil him. People tend to be rather tolerant of mistakes and instances of poor judgment on the part of a vicar, excusing them as evidences of immaturity on the part of one who is still a student. They are not that tolerant when a graduate comes to them as their pastor. Again, a vicar serving in a larger congregation may have seen how because of its size there was a proliferation in its organizational structure. When after graduation he comes to his first charge, which generally will be much smaller, he may imagine that he ought to introduce all of this organizational detail too, only to encounter reluctance and opposition. The wiser course is to operate with the existing structure until better acquaintance with the situation indicates whether more organization is needed. Again, as vicar a man may have served in a large congregation where he could preach to many people, where the facilities were impressive, where things were well organized, and where the office equipment was of the best. He dare not expect to find a comparable situation in the area of service into which he receives his first permanent call. He dare not allow himself to become unhappy because he will have only comparatively few people to serve, or because the church is humble, organization is at a minimum, and office equipment is meager. The ministry is always a privilege and may be carried on wherever the Lord places a man and with whatever means He places at his disposal.

Motivation

From what has been said concerning the vicar it ought to be evident that the Seminary student who has the proper motivation ought to look forward eagerly to his year of vicar service. During it he will have the privilege of serving in the public ministry (Eph

3:8); he will have the opportunity of providing assistance to a busy pastor (Eph 2:10); he will have the privilege of becoming acquainted with the many facets of the parish ministry and of learning to participate in them and while doing so, because of his status as a student, be shown a measure of understanding and tolerance which he may not expect to experience in his later career. For him it is a one-time opportunity. His underlying motivation will be love for his Savior and thankfulness for being entrusted by Him with a share in the care of a portion of His flock.

Summary: A vicar receives a limited call into the public ministry. He works under the direction of his supervising pastor as part of his Seminary training. He is to become acquainted with and active in all normal phases of the parish ministry. He will need to be circumspect in his private and family life, and in his relations with his supervising pastor and the people whom he serves in order that all who are involved, and especially the vicar himself, might receive under God the maximum benefit which can come from being entrusted with the opportunity of serving the Lord and His church as a vicar.

II. THE SUPERVISING PASTOR

While with few exceptions every Seminary student will serve as a vicar, the number of students who will be serving as supervising pastors during the course of their ministry is much smaller. But for their benefit, especially when they will be working with a vicar for the first time, the following is included in this book.

A. His Privilege and Responsibility

To have a vicar is a privilege and a responsibility. The reason why congregations decide to call a vicar is to provide their pastor with needed assistance in his work in the person of an undergraduate Seminary student. As the orientation of the vicar and his training for the performance of his specific duties progress, the pastor in normal cases will find that at the end of several months the amount of assistance that he receives more than compensates for the time which he has had to devote to the initial and subsequent training of his vicar.

Under our synodical policy concerning the vicar program more is involved than the providing of undergraduate assistance. The year of vicar service is considered part of the four-year course at our Seminary. It is considered a year of in-service training, an internship. Thus the pastor becomes involved in the work of the Seminary and is properly called the supervising pastor. The vicar is not an assistant pastor who as a graduate has completed his Seminary course and is now called by a congregation to share in the performance of the pastoral work in its midst. The vicar is a student who is still in training, and the solemn responsibility of providing that training devolves upon the supervising pastor. The vicar is not on his own, but is to be guided and instructed. The supervising pastor will assign the vicar's work, hold him responsible for carrying out his assignments punctually, and encourage, rebuke, admonish as the circumstances may require. All of this he will do in the spirit of Christian love with the understanding that he is to look for progress, not perfection. In the area of homiletics, for example, the supervising pastor is to discuss with his vicar the outline and the written copy of his sermon and, after it has been preached, his delivery.

Since the supervising pastor is involved in the work of the Seminary, he is also in a position to assist the Seminary. He does this by means of the report which he submits to the Seminary after the vicar has completed his year of service. Having had an opportunity to observe what was accomplished at the Seminary in the two years preceding the year of vicar service, the supervising pastor is in a position to evaluate the strengths and possible weaknesses in the Seminary program and to supply constructive criticism. In his evaluation of the student he may call attention to particular areas upon which emphasis ought to be laid in the final year of the student's training before he is recommended to the church as a candidate for the public ministry.

B. His Relations with the Vicar

Installation

Because the vicar's call is a call into the public ministry, albeit in a limited form, it is desirable that he be installed into his office in a public service. In this installation the vicar will be impressed with the duties which he is to perform, and the congregation will hear his promise to endeavor to perform them faithfully. The congregation, in turn, will be reminded of its obligations toward the vicar. A suggested form for the installation of a vicar has been included in the Appendix.

Orientation

Since the vicar is to work under the supervision of the pastor, it is essential that there be an orientation session before the vicar begins his work. While certain areas may be made the vicar's special responsibility, for example, the work with young people, it is expected that he will be involved in all normal phases of parish work. The orientation session will provide him with a general overview of this work and the extent of his participation in it, without, however, swamping him with details. These can be supplied in subsequent consultations. It will also be well to acquaint the vicar with the congregation in a general way, its history, its special projects, perhaps its special problems. If a printed roster of the congregation is available for the vicar to carry with him, it will be an aid to him in familiarizing himself with the names of the people whom he is serving. The vicar may need to be oriented in the community in which he is to serve, especially as far as the location of hospitals, nursing homes, and other institutions is concerned in which he will be ministering to people. It may be well to introduce him to responsible personnel. While the vicar will have been acquainted with the theory of making pastoral calls while at the Seminary, he may not have had any practice. In such cases he will appreciate it if his supervising pastor at the outset takes him along to observe while the pastor makes a sampling of the various types of calls which his vicar will be expected to make. Some supervising pastors have found it practicable to have the terms of the departing and the new vicar overlap for a short period so that the departing vicar may show the new man around and even introduce him to the shut-ins whom he will be serving.

Since the vicar in many facets of his work will be doing something which is comparatively new to him, it is to be expected that as he undertakes his first assignments he will spend a considerable amount of time in planning and preparation. For that reason it may be wise not to give him too many assignments at first, but to add them one by one after he has had an opportunity to familiarize himself with each in turn. This will involve rather frequent consultations at first.

Consultations

Periodic consultations with the vicar after the initial period will be necessary if the supervising pastor is to carry out his responsibility of assisting in the training of the vicar-student. The individuality of the supervising pastor will no doubt determine whether these consultations are scheduled regularly or as favorable opportunities arise. The vicar will report on his progress in carrying out his assignments, on unusual experiences, and on problems which he may have encountered. His assignments for the succeeding period may be reviewed, revised, or augmented. As he directs his vicar, the supervising pastor will try to assist him to improve the quality of his work. But he will need to guard against attempting to shape the vicar in his own mold. There is a golden mean between direction and allowing the development of individuality and originality.

Attitude Toward Vicar

In his contacts with his vicar the supervising pastor, motivated by his love for his Savior, will endeavor to display in a special measure those virtues which Scripture mentions as an outflowing of brotherly love. Here too, he will endeavor to set a good example for his people. He will be understanding and kind, but also firm if need be. He himself will find a good example in the manner in which the Lord Jesus treated His disciples, an example which St. Paul emulated in his treatment of his understudy Timothy. He may quite naturally come to call his vicar by his first name without encouraging reciprocity in this respect. Informal social contacts may develop spontaneously. The main matter is that the supervising pastor win the confidence of his vicar so that the vicar will feel free to consult him or unburden himself to him whenever he feels the need to do so.

C. Problems

In the section about the vicar it was considered necessary to refer to abnormal situations where a vicar might have problems with his supervising pastor. There have also been cases where the situation has been reversed.

Crystallizing the Desire for the Ministry

One problem which does not reflect unfavorably upon either the vicar or the pastor is that which the supervising pastor faces when his vicar has not yet come to the firm conviction that he wants to serve in the parish ministry. The Seminary does endeavor to win to firm conviction those students who may still be wrestling with the question whether they should become pastors. But where conviction has not crystallized it will encourage such students to enter upon a year of vicar service in the hope that the practical experience which it offers might help them to overcome their wavering. The supervising pastor is usually informed of the student's problem via the proper channels.

What shall the supervising pastor do? To employ high pressure methods or even threats to compel the vicar to complete his Seminary training and become a condidate for the holy ministry is not evangelical. Nor will they produce the desire for the bishop's office (1 Tm 3:1) which must come from within. Rather, the supervising pastor will encourage his vicar to perform his assignments faithfully in the hope that as he experiences the privilege of proclaiming the good news of salvation and observes the comforting power of the Word as he brings it to the sick and shut-ins and distressed he will be more and more moved to want to spend the rest of his life, if the Lord wills, in continuing to do the work which he has been permitted to do for the short span of his vicar year.

The example and attitude of the supervising pastor will also have their impact. If he is constantly complaining about his burdens and his troubles, or if his wife does it for him, his vicar will hardly be inspired to desire to become a pastor. But if the supervising pastor shows by his entire attitude that he considers it a privilege and a joy to be permitted to serve in the ministry and if he has learned to keep his troubles in perspective like Paul, who said, "I endure all things for the elect's sake, that they may also obtain the salvation which is in Christ Jesus with eternal glory" (2 Tm 2:10) — in such cases the vicar may well be won over to desire the same privilege which has been granted to his supervising pastor. Beyond that the supervising pastor has no responsibility for results and need not chide himself for having failed if his vicar after all decides to serve the Lord in some calling other than the public ministry.

The Incompetent Vicar

A more serious problem arises when a vicar appears to be incompetent or becomes guilty of giving offense. At the outset it might be said that in such a case we need to deal with the same measure of long-suffering with which others once dealt with us when we were still immature. People do not expect a finished product in the student who comes to serve in their midst as vicar, nor should the supervising pastor. Unless it becomes absolutely necessary, the vicar ought not to be rebuked publicly for his ill-advised words or actions lest he lose stature and his future usefulness be undermined. A friendly word of correction spoken to him privately by his supervising pastor will be more effective. The periodic consultations between supervising pastor and vicar afford ongoing opportunity for calling attention to areas where the vicar ought to strive for improvement, as well as for commendation and encouragement.

If there is continuing evidence of incompetence or ineptitude, the supervising pastor may be helped by consulting the Seminary dean, or having his vicar do so, or by a three-way consultation. The background of previous contact with the vicar-student on the part of the dean may provide a clue for the solution of the problem.

If an intolerable situation persists, it is advisable that the supervising pastor consult his district president, through whom the vicar was assigned. The church council and the voters' assembly ought to become involved only if the welfare of the church seems to make necessary the termination of the vicar's assignment. While no one would want to foist an incompetent candidate upon the church, every effort will be made to salvage a man who manifests an ability to learn from his mistakes.

D. The Report to the Seminary

When the vicar has completed his year of service, his supervising pastor is expected to report on his work on blanks which are provided by the Seminary. (See Appendix.) It is not advisable, because of the confidential nature of the report to the Seminary, to permit the vicar to read it. It is after all a report to the Seminary, and not to the vicar. The supervising pastor may, however, want to review the year with the vicar, and the vicar may be eager for such a review. The vicar will be helped to realize on which subjects he will have to place particular emphasis in his final year of seminary training and, perhaps, in what areas he ought especially to strive to grow in sanctification. On the other hand, he will be encouraged when he is told where he has shown discernible progress during the course of the year.

As indicated above, the report of the supervising pastor to the Seminary is confidential. While the professors may use it to alert them to matters on which they will want to place special emphasis in their work with a given student, they will never justify such emphasis to the student by referring to the report. If the report calls attention to a problem which calls for stern admonition, direct reference will not be made to the information given in the report unless the consent of the supervising pastor has previously been obtained.

In order that maximum use might be made of the reports on the vicars, it is essential that they be submitted before the beginning of the school year.

E. Evaluation

The Seminary appreciates the benefits of the vicar year and the cooperation of the growing number of supervising pastors which makes it possible. It has, for example, gained a fuller perspective on its course offerings. The returning vicars with their increased maturity and dedication and interest have made for a favorable teaching situation in the Senior year. By their maturity, assurance, and initiative, the returning vicars give proof of the fact that they have been blessed by their vicar year. The fact that congregations repeat their requests for vicars shows that the benefits of the vicar year have been reciprocal — not only do the Seminary and the vicars benefit, but the congregations and supervising pastors as well, since they receive needed assistance in the work which the Savior has entrusted to His church.

Summary: While the supervising pastor receives assistance in his work from his vicar, the pastor in turn is being entrusted with a part in the training of the student and is assisting the Seminary in its work. The training of the vicar involves both orientation and continuing consultation. The reports which are submitted to the Seminary at the end of the vicar's term of service are essential for the maximum effectiveness of the vicar program.

Appendix A

Application Form for the Sacrament
of Holy Baptism

(To be filled out by the parents or guardians)

1. Full Name of Child: _____

2. Date of Birth: _____

3. Place of Birth: _____

4. Father's Name: _____

5. Maiden Name of Mother: _____

6. Address of Parents: _____

7. Desired Date of Baptism: _____

8. Name and Church of Sponsor or Witness: _____

_____

9. Address of Sponsor or Witness: _____

10. Name and Church of Sponsor or Witness: _____

_____

11. Address of Sponsor or Witness: _____

Signature of Parents: _____

_____

Appendix B

Marriage Arrangements

Name of Groom _____ Date of Birth _____

    Address _____

    Father _____ Mother _____

Name of Bride _____ Date of Birth _____

    Address _____

    Father _____ Mother _____

New Address (after Marriage) _____

Best Man _____

Maid of Honor _____

Groomsmen _____

Bridesmaids _____

Witnesses _____

Ushers _____

Organist _____

    Hymns _____ Text _____

Soloist _____

    Selections _____

Date of Wedding _____ Time _____

Date of Rehearsal _____ Time _____

Single or Double Ring _____

Has either party been married before? _____

If so, how was the marriage terminated? _____

Dates for Meeting with Pastor _____

Appendix C

Funeral Arrangements

I. The Service

    A. Date and Time _____

    B. Place _____

    C. Text _____

    D. Hymns _____

    E. Special Music and Musician _____

II. The Burial

    A. Place _____

    B. Funeral Director _____

III. Obituary

    A. Full Name _____

    B. Date and Place of Birth _____

    C. Father _____

    D. Mother _____

    E. Baptism: Date, Place, and Pastor _____

    F. Confirmation: Date, Place, and Pastor _____

    G. Marriage: Date, Place, and Pastor _____

    H. Spouse _____

    I. Place of Residence _____

    J. Employment _____

    K. Cause of Death _____

    M. Survivors _____

        1. Parents _____

        2. Spouse _____

        3. Sons _____

        4. Daughters _____

        5. Brothers _____

        6. Sisters _____

        7. Grandchildren _____

        8. Others _____

    N. Other Information _____

Appendix D

Application for Membership

_____   _____   _____
Last Name   Given Names   Address and Phone

_____   _____   _____
Birthdate   Father's Name   Mother's Maiden Name

_____   _____   _____
Date of Baptism   Where?   By Whom?

_____   _____   _____
Date of Confirmation   Where?   By Whom?

_____   _____   _____
Date of Marriage   To Whom?   By Whom?

_____   _____
Place of Marriage   Former Church Connection

_____   _____
Date of Leaving Last Church   Vocations, Skills, Hobbies, Interests

Do you belong to a lodge, secret order, or veteran's organization? _____
If so, which of the above? _____

Please list names of children and their birthdates: _____

_____

_____   _____
Date of Application   Signature

Appendix E

Application for Pastoral Vicar

Application For Pastoral Vicar

TO THE ASSIGNMENT COMMITTEE, WISCONSIN EVANGELICAL LUTHERAN SYNOD:

Dear Brethren:

We, _____

Congregation or Board

of _____

(City   and   State)

do hereby formally petition you to assign to us a student of theology to serve as a vicar.
We wish the student to serve as

☐ a regular pastoral-assistant vicar in our congregation_____

☐ a pastoral-vacancy vicar at _____

      of _____

☐ _____

_____

In addition to routine duties, we would require as special assignments:

_____

_____

We submit the attached vicar call blank, including our agreement to the usual terms set down by the Wisconsin Lutheran Seminary, the Conference of Presidents, and the Assignment Committee.

Our specific reasons for requesting a vicar are:

In the name of _____

(Name of Congregation or Board — City, State)

_____ _____

(Supervising Pastor)   (Chairman)

Approved by _____

_____ District President

Vicar assigned: _____ of _____

(To be filled in by District President after assignment)

PURPOSE AND POLICIES OF OUR VICARSHIP PROGRAM

I. To give assistance in the work of our congregations and institutions:

1. Under the supervision of the pastor, the vicar is to give assistance in youth work, Sunday school, confirmation classes, etc. Work which is not directly related to the administration of the Means of Grace (secretarial and custodial tasks, social functions, errands, and the like) should be kept to a minimum.

2. Requests for vicar assistance are to be made through the District President to the Assignment Committee. In the case of World Mission Boards and the Boards of Control of our Worker-Training institutions, the requests are to be made directly to the Assignment Committee.

3. Both an Application Form and a Vicar Call Blank should be filed with the District President prior to the week of the Assignment Committee meeting in May.

4. A definite vicar stipend is established by the Conference of Presidents. Since the vicar program is a part of the Synod's ministerial training curriculum and thus under its control, this stipend code is to be adhered to by all congregations and boards. The present vicar stipend code is a) $_____ per month without housing or board, or b) $_____ per month plus parsonage and utilities, or c) $_____ per month plus room and board, in addition to hospitalization insurance, adequate car expense, and travel allowance for one trip from his home and return.

   (1968 code: The present vicar stipend code is a) $305.00 per month without housing or board, or b) $255.00 per month plus parsonage and utilities, or c) $205.00 per month plus room and board, in addition to hospitalization insurance, adequate car expense, and travel allowance for one trip from his home and return.)

II. To give the students practical experience in church work. The following suggestions are offered by the Wisconsin Lutheran Seminary regarding a regular pastoral-assistant vicar's duties in order to accomplish the training purpose of the vicarship program:

1. General: That as much as possible, both through participation and observation, the vicar become acquainted with every phase of the parish ministry.

2. Preaching: An average of once a month, depending on the vicar's ability and circumstances in the congregation. Less often for a teaching vicar.

3. House calls: A sampling of various types of sick calls is desirable, but certainly not a major share of this work. — Calls on unchurched prospects and guests according to the discretion of the supervising pastor. The vicar is not to be used in serious disciplinary cases!

4. Start of vicar's term: It is strongly urged that the vicar be called to start his work with the beginning of September. Two reasons for this suggestion: It allows the Middlers to plan ahead for one summer of employment, even though assignment is made toward the end of May. — It permits the vicar to become acquainted with his work before he is asked to serve the congregation during the pastor's customary summer vacation.

III. To aid the Seminary in its training program:

1. A report of the vicar's service, his growth, his abilities, and the general conduct of his work is asked of the supervising pastor. This report is to be submitted to the President of the Wisconsin Lutheran Seminary at the close of the vicar's term of service before the beginning of the vicar's final Seminary year.

2. If any problems arise relating to the attitude and application of the vicar, the supervising pastor should discuss these with the President of the Seminary as soon as possible. If problems arise involving matters of conscience in regard to doctrine and practice within the congregation, the supervising pastor has the obligation to resolve these concerns, if necessary with the Visiting Elder of the Conference.

Appendix F

Vicar Call

In Nomine Jesu

_____

(Name of Congregation or Board)   (City   and   State)

hereby extends a call through the Assignment Committee of the Wisconsin Evangelical Lutheran Synod to you,

_____

to serve us as a pastoral vicar for a term beginning _____ and ending _____.

We agree to consider your service among us as part of your theological training under the general supervision of the Wisconsin Lutheran Seminary, Mequon, Wisconsin, and also under the direct supervision of

_____

(Name of Supervising Pastor)

We agree to provide you with the opportunity for training in all phases of pastoral work which are commensurate with your abilities and experience according to the objectives and policies of our Synod's theological training program. To this end we will require that you assist with preaching, visiting the sick and unchurched, administrative work, and other ministerial duties, as directed by the supervising pastor. In addition we list the following special assignments:

_____

_____

_____

We require that you conduct yourself at all times as becomes a minister of Christ so that by your Christian life you may be an example to all men.

We pledge to accord you the honor, love and cooperation due one standing in the work of the Lord. We will ever be mindful that you work among us primarily to learn as you serve and, accordingly, we will pray the Holy Spirit to bless you in your work. We pledge ourselves to provide for your maintenance according to the code salary and the travel and car allowances established by the Conference of Presidents and thus for the present we will pay you $_____ per month; plus car expense of $_____, and travel allowance for one trip from your home and return.

In the name of

_____ of _____

(Name of Congregation or Board)   (City   and   State)

_____   _____

(Chairman)   (Supervising Pastor)

_____   _____

(Secretary)   (Supervising Pastor's Address)

Appendix G

Suggested form for the Installation of Vicars

Dear Brethren in Christ:

Mr. _____ , here present, has been appointed by our Wisconsin Ev. Lutheran Synod Committee on the Assignment of Calls as Vicar to our congregation.

As such, Mr. _____ , you are to assist the pastor in the preaching of God's Word and in the administration of the sacraments in our midst.

As such you are also to assist the pastor in serving our sick and shut-ins with the means of grace and in comforting them in their affliction.

As such you are to assist the pastor in teaching our children the Word of God and in serving our youth with your counsel and advice and in fostering (or, furthering) their growth in the knowledge of Jesus Christ.

As such, under the direction of the pastor, you are to aid in the general welfare of our congregation and set us all a good example by your pattern of good works and Christian life.

In order that this congregation may know that you are willing to assume these duties and obligations, I now ask you: Mr. _____ , are you willing to serve as our Vicar as here indicated according to the ability which God has given you? If so, then answer: YES, WITH THE HELP OF GOD.

Upon this your solemn promise, may the Lord grant you wisdom from on high to serve us as is pleasing in His sight. May He bless you and us as you learn and labor in His Word in our midst.

Let us pray: Lord Jesus Christ, who art the Chief Shepherd and the only Head of the Church, we pray that Thou wouldst train and keep this Thy servant in Thy Holy Word and in the sound doctrine set forth therein; that Thou wouldst strengthen him in the faithful performance of his duties in this congregation and bless his labors in Thy service, that Thy holy name may be glorified and Thy kingdom come, who livest and reignest with the Father and the Holy Ghost, ever one God, world without end.   Amen.

Appendix H

Report on Vicar Service

Vicar .... Period of Service: From .... to ....

Location ....
                (Name and Place of Congregation Served)

PREACHING

Number of Sermons prepared .... Language ....

Delivery ....

General remarks ....

....

TEACHING
(Indicate grade level and whether teaching was regular or occasional)

Christian Day School ....

Sunday School ....

Vacation Bible School ....

Confirmation Instruction ....

Bible Class ....

Other Agencies ....

Comments on this area of work ....

....

....

PASTORAL CARE

(Indicate both type and scope of work as well as
specific aptitudes or weaknesses)

Sick and shut-in calls ....

Mission calls ....

Pastoral calls on members ....

Activity in organizations ....

....

General remarks ....

CLERICAL WORK

(Indicate the type of work and the approximate amount of time devoted to it)

....

....

OTHER ASSIGNMENTS

Nature ....

Comments ....

GENERAL CHARACTERIZATION

Organization of own work schedule ....

Initiative ....

Cooperativeness ....

Dependability ....

Devotion to the ministry ....

Ability to meet people..

Evangelical leadership..

For what type of work do you consider him best adapted?

Rural .... City .... Institutional ....

Established parish .... Mission station ....

ADDITIONAL GENERAL REMARKS

MONTHLY STIPEND

    (a) $ .... (without housing or board)

                         or

    (b) $ .... (plus parsonage and utilities)

                         or

    (c) $ .... (plus room and board)

Monthly car allowance $ ....

Total remuneration for the year $ ....*

*Because vicar service is considered part of the students' training, their remuneration is considered a stipend and not a salary, and is not subject to income tax.

                     ....
                     Supervising Pastor

                     ....
                     Name of Church

                     ....

Date ....
                     Address